Contents

D0503383

Preface

LET ME *try to tell why I have chosen* Rumor and Reflection *for the title of my diary.*

The greater part of it was written while I was in hiding from the rage of the gangs who, in the enjoyment of Nazi approval and support, could throw off the restraints of the more bourgeois elements of the Fascist regime, and return to the reckless violence with which it had started out. I read Italian and German dailies and listened to radio news from France and England, but direct contacts with the living world were limited to my hosts and fellow guests, or to a changing number of acquaintances of my hosts who found it convenient to disappear for short periods from Fascist-Nazi eyes.

After more than sixty years in which I have been reading intellectualized, geometrized, dehumanized, or tendentious history I have come to question whether we get through it a more intelligible panorama of a given period in the past than by reading bards like Herodotus and Livy on Persian and Punic wars, or Carlyle and Michelet with their somewhat more trustworthy account of causes and consequences, of motive and realization in the French Revolution. Even these do not give me the warm feeling of intimacy with the past that I get from diaries and letters. When I read Greville or the correspondence contained in the lives of public

*men, say of the Lord Clarendon of a hundred years ago, I feel the
same sensation as being in it, of touching history in the making, as
when looking through a batch of morning papers.*

*Yet of what do the papers consist? Of rumors that may turn out
to be events, of gossip about yesterday, of guesses about tomorrow, of attempts to shape the past into a model for the future and
to steer tomorrow as today (but perhaps not when tomorrow has
become today) in the direction that we wish it to go.*

*Nobody denies that this or that occurrence took place in the
past: say the change-over from an orderly world state like the
pagan Roman Empire to the all but anarchical, monastic one of
Western and Central Europe in our seventh and eighth centuries.
Discussions as to how, why, whether for worse or for better that
make up the bulk of history books are not in the nature of events
but of what people think and tattle about them. For my part I see
little difference, except in quality, between pompous, self-admir-
ing historians like Gibbon, and romancers writing about the same
period like Felix Dahn or Amédée Thierry. Or, coming nearer to
our day, I wonder whether the majority of Frenchmen do not get
a better acquaintance with their sixteenth and seventeenth centuries reading Dumas when boys than they acquire later from
Chartist historians. Dumas gossips in evocative, glowing fashion
about the past and the others add up statistics and philosophize
about them in a way that is just as much a mere interpretation.
And all interpretations or conclusions, based as they are in the
realms of history on data so inadequate, so questionable, can only
be in the nature of what we happen to feel and think about them
—of gossip, in short. Indeed, William James used to say: Come,
let us gossip about the universe! Six decades have passed and marvelous discoveries have been made, yet I question whether he
would be less inclined to feel that it was all gossip.*

*Maybe even the principal actors do not know from day to day
just what is happening. Man, say a Hitler, proposes but a complex
of forces beyond his control, beyond his ken even, disposes. He
too can only guess.*

What matters is not events but what we think about them. Any number are now occurring that in a few years may change the quality of living. Yet they do not affect us until we begin to hear rumors, and gossip, and chatter about them.

To conclude: I seldom took the rumors that reached me for more than suspensions for inquiry. As revelations of states of mind they were positive, for they told me what a representative section of Tuscan, and perhaps all Italian upper-class society, had been trained to feel, and what they fancied they were thinking about each day's events.

Their state of mind, their reactions should not be ignored if we would understand how, in the long run, Italians are likely to take trial and error in the field of politics.

So much for rumor. I need not explain what I mean by reflection. According to mood and humor and leisure I put down what the gossip of the day, what conversation, what the books and papers I was reading, what my musings and daydreamings stimulated me to write. Not all then put down appears here. Omitted are subjects that unfortunately have grown more controversial with time, and liable to rouse exasperated feeling rather than calm reflection.

I have changed nothing in the text and added nothing to make me appear wiser after the event. Only repetitions and short passages that might hurt friends and names not worth publicizing have been omitted.

I am indebted to Raymond Mortimer for his help in preparing the manuscript for the printer. Also to Hugh Trevor Roper, who in reading over the proofsheets has made a number of valuable corrections.

B. B.

I TATTI, SETTIGNANO
May 4, 1952

1941

January 1st — New Year's Day

No RESOLUTIONS at my age, unless to be as little of a nuisance as possible to others first, and then to myself, for the rest of my days.

How deeply patent conventions like the days of the week, the numbers attached to dates, the holidays, feast days and fast days, have sunk into our minds and furrowed channels of habit! Here I am, a rational being, convinced that within the universe, as we know it, there is no force outside ourselves that we can appeal to with prayer or compel with magic, no *conceivable* intelligence aware of our existence, ready to marshal the stars in their courses to serve our individual, momentary needs. Nevertheless I am unable to forget that a year, a month, begins on a Friday, or that a birthday falls on a thirteenth. Moreover, I dislike to see the new moon on a Friday or on a thirteenth, and I avoid initiating anything or undertaking a journey on the same unlucky day or date. How absurd for a person with my education, my reading, my life-long efforts to think clearly and to think things out, to remain affected by such primitive superstitions.

So it is, but when I come up against people with no feeling for the numinous, no awe before the universe, no ever-present sense of the precariousness of human life, as happens with my Mary and many other Americans of English descent, I feel almost as remote

3

from them as I do from the prescientific mind of the Mediterranean lower classes, be they Spanish, French, Italian, Greek, Turkish, Arab, or Berber, Christian, Jewish, or Mohammedan. I wonder
at times whether art of any kind, poetry, painting, music, sculpture, and architecture, can flower and ripen on a humus entirely
free from the state of mind that lies open to superstition.

At my age, dates and seasons get nearer and nearer to each
other. Soon they will be like the spokes of a wheel going so fast
that they merge. Scarcely does it seem worth while any more to
take count of the differences between summer and winter. Each
passes so swiftly. Yet provision must be made against the cold,
which I fear more and more: I have already reached the limits of
clothing that in hard winter days will keep me warm out of doors.
Thus far I have discovered but one place where I could be comfortable in the worst winter months. It is not Egypt, which is nowhere warm enough without heating in the evening. And heating
is all but unprocurable. Only at Wadi Halfa by the second cata-
ract of the Nile have I discovered a temperature and air that are
bland enough to suit me. The present man-quake makes transporting oneself impossible, and when it is over, shall we be able soon
to go so far, or to find creature comforts if we get there?

The past year has been one to rouse indignation because of the
most deliberate attempt to destroy the humanized society that for
many centuries we had been trying to create. Besides, there were
for me private worries. Mary's health, whether physical or mental,
was far from satisfactory. I foresaw trouble in transporting her,
should we have to leave and take refuge in America—in America,
where private attendance is so difficult to procure. Yet friends
were urging me to go, because foes were suspecting and accusing
me of carrying on propaganda and even spying. We were avoided
by all but the fewest. An atmosphere increasingly hostile thick-
ened around us.

Little good to be said for the old year. So humble have we got,
so modest in our expectations, that all I venture to hope for in this
new year is that it shall not be worse than the last; and that a year
hence we may still be here, all of us, that I may still be enjoying

my library, my walks, my few faithful friends, my meditations, my daydreams.

January 3d

WHAT SHALL we be like when this war is over? I expect Italy to change least and England most. Not only will so many English cities and towns have to be rebuilt almost entirely (and in what style!), but it will be an England where no longer the gentry but the laboring classes will govern. Will these last be seething with resentment and hatred of *les riches* and *les aristos,* as they do in France, in which case the future will be black indeed; or will they have been permeated by ideals and sentiments that their upper crust preached and tried to practice, as for instance fair play, tolerance of opposition, reasoned humanitarianism? Will they, in short, not only entertain the wish to govern for the nation as a whole but be ready to recognize that their good cannot be bought at the expense of others? Will they think of their fellow English-men first, to be sure, but of the rest of mankind as well, as partners in a great estate, everybody's care and everybody's reward? If they can take up the burden of the previous governing class, which, despite its too human shortcomings, meant well by the others, then there will be hope of recovery with the best elements coming to the top, and forming a good as well as great society, a model to the rest of the world.

There is the possibility that the English will come out of the war fearing that safety is to be had only by keeping themselves as well prepared for defense as their resources and genius will al-low. There is a chance that they may take to militarism as a perma-nent condition of society. In that case, despite themselves, they would lose little by little what has been their dominant quality, and end as another European Continental power, a middle term between Germany and France.

And we Americans—we shall scarcely remain on the defensive only if we too get militarized with huge standing armies and great navies. With like weapons in our hands, we could not resist seeking outlets for our energies in attempting—with the best intentions, of course—to boss the world, to impose our standard of life, and our own adolescent ideals, behind which would hide our own abuses, greeds, and cannibalisms. It would not be a pleasant prospect.

A pleasant prospect would be a constellation of English-speaking peoples with England and America revolving around each other like a double sun, and the dominions and colonies like planets of varying magnitudes.

January 5th

CALLED YESTERDAY on acquaintances living on the slopes between via Bolognese and Montughi. The approach, which, during my first years in Florence, went from the city gates through farmland studded with ancient cottages, is now over boulevards lined with morose buildings, ending in a vast hospital city. This hides away Cosimo de'Medici's villa with the *loggia* where he and his friends discussed Plato as they looked over the chimneyless, hangarless, uncrowded expanse of field and meadow stretching towards Prato, Pistoia, and the Apennine. The house we visited enjoys a view over the town, with its soaring yet massive cupola, to the hills beyond. From the terrace rippled the curve of the horizon. As a level skyline is rare in Tuscany, it was pleasant to contemplate.

Indoors the house is full of winding staircases, recesses, and cozy corners. Everywhere odds and ends of pictures, engravings, artistic knickknacks which I delighted in.

We had scarcely got back to the front door when Mary, with her *œil dénigrant,* began to make grunts of relief leading up to severe disapproval of that way of furnishing and living. I on the contrary am easily pleased with the unusual. It affords a variant to my own stereotyped surroundings, and offers me other modes of thinking and feeling. These newnesses overpower me, and while submitted to them I am as uncritical as a registering instrument.

For good or for evil, my first meeting with people is of the same nature. Either there is no coming together at all, no hooking of atoms and nothing happens, or I take to the new presence without reserve. The result is at times disastrous. The critical faculties which vanished while the novelty of the contact lasted, no matter whether it was inanimate or animate, begin to peer through, to hiss with serpents' tongues and, likely enough, end by persuading me that my enthusiasm or sober appreciation was misplaced or excessive. I then sidle away from the new acquaintance, no matter what resentment it stirs up.

It is not newness alone that fascinates me out of all critical sense, but rather an admiring wonder at ways of living that I could not have planned and executed. What lay not beyond my ken, but had failed to occur to me and to inspire me to action, seems at first too exciting, too absorbing, too wonderful. In the same way an idea, one that I assimilate instantly but which I had not thought of, so delights me that I feel no trace of self-contempt for not having had it myself.

To return for an instant to the new, or recent, acquaintance, his physical presence so bewitches my judgment that I cannot get myself to believe that he is deliberately lying or trying to get the better of me. That, rather than softness or weakness, is the reason why I find it so against the grain to refuse a request or deny an interlocutor a favor. That too explains why I am so poor at negotiation. If the other party puts his case plausibly I tend to run ahead of his effort to persuade me, and to assure him that he must be in the right, and that I have nothing to oppose.

January 8th

I CANNOT UNDERSTAND why I feel so embarrassed when being thanked. When thanks are at all profuse I get flustered, begin to wriggle and twist so that to cut things short I get rude. The other day I gave my hairdresser a New Year's tip. Handing it to him, I dismissed him abruptly to avoid his thanks, and forgot to wish him a happy New Year. I wonder whether he, a pure Florentine, was aware of my awkward shyness, or whether he took it as an ungracious act to be passed over in a *pazzo inglese*—a mad foreigner.

I am in a way as irritated by praise, even of the most tactful kind, especially when verbal and to my face. But even in print, in reviews of my books and still more when the praise is of myself, as distinct from my books. As for flattery, it gives me an imperative call to run away without looking back. By which I do not claim to be insensible to treatment worthy of my merits, provided it is disinterested, and with no afterthought of material advantage.

Long ago the sense of myself—to the extent that it is at all definite—was stabilized; nor is it subject to much inflation and deflation. No laudation or vituperation will affect it. I am far too well aware of my shortcomings, far more than others can be, but at the same time I know that, in the moral sphere, I am incapable of most meannesses and perfidies; and I can guess to what degree, in the realm of mind, I am able to cope with certain problems requiring thought, and feeling for antecedent probabilities.

January 9th

HENRI BERGSON is dead. Pity he lived long enough to die at this particular hour, when France has fallen lower than at any other moment in her history. For this time she has suffered defeat not only at the hands of the stranger. She has gone through such unhappy days many times in the course of the centuries. Celts, Romans, every species of Teuton, the Saracen, the Norseman, the Briton, the Spaniard, and again and again the Borussian have trampled over her soil and massacred its inhabitants. Yet never before has she been so utterly humiliated and betrayed as now; and by a gang of her own meanest, cheapest, falsest elements. Not even by the cannibals who came to the fore during the Dreyfus affair, foaming with fury because they feared for their authority in the army, in diplomacy, in society. Not even by them, but by lowborn snobs, cads, and gangsters who by flattering, aiding, and abetting the stupidest of heraldic classes expect to be accepted by them, and to share with them the thrones and powers of the land.

To die like this, he who lived through the Dreyfus civil war, and came out believing that France was made safe for humanity and enlightenment; to die while the France he loved so much was abjectly prostrated at the feet of the mechanized, nonhuman foe; to leave at the moment of deepest darkness before one reassuring ray of light could cheer him with its promise—that indeed is sad. Perhaps we shall never know how he felt. Who was there to record his last words?

January 14–24

CARLO DIED this morning between four and five and thus brought to an end a friendship of fifty years. It is now January 14, 1941, and the last time I saw him was in May, 1940. I passed the rest of that month and the first days of June in Rome. When I got back here war against France and England had been declared, and as we were notoriously friendly to both these powers, a ban of excommunication had secretly been protocoled against us by the elders not of Israel but of the Florentine "high life." I had not expected Carlo to submit. He did. He preferred their society to ours. Worse still, he took no means—it would have been easy enough—to let me know by word or sign that he was sorry, but could not afford to be cut by all the nice people. I should have understood, regretted, condoned. Worst of all he, who had been so friendly to France and England because of every material and social and society interest, began to talk, and even to write letters abroad, expressing his full sympathy with the program and hopes of the "Axis powers."

I confess I felt bitter, for the only people who can hurt us are those we have loved and trusted. Others can do us material harm, malign and calumniate us. I feel no resentment, no indignation. My moral sense is not insulted.

Yet what other conduct could I have expected of Carlo Placci! He was so completely socialized that death itself might have seemed preferable to being boycotted by the people in whose midst he was living. In the Cannibal Islands he would have been

a cannibal, and would have talked as glibly in the defense of cannibalism as our Southern clergy before the Civil War spoke of
their peculiar institution, God-ordained slavery. During the Paris
of the Dreyfus affair, Carlo out-Heroded the worst Herods of anti-
Dreyfusism with the furious defense of their cause. True, there
was an attenuating circumstance. He was head over heels in love
with Mme Jean de Montebello, one of the chief prophetesses,
if not the Deborah, of that cause. The "Great War" found him in
Munich, frequenting the elegant salons of the capital of good beer
and bad art. He was expecting his government, a member of the
Triplice, to join in with Germany, and, on the anthropological
principle of "my country right or wrong" and always ministerial in
foreign relations, this notorious Francophile, accompanied to the
station by "all" Munich, waved his hat as the train was starting
and shouted, "À bientôt à Paris." But earlier still, while the Libyan
campaign was on, we did not see him while it lasted. That happened when he was suffering from a nervous breakdown, and on
that score it was easy to forgive him.

This time I smarted, and smarted so much that I swore I'd never
see him again if we survived this war. Then I began to hear how
unhappy he was over things in general and over our broken
friendship. More recently he wrote a touching letter to my wife,
and I spoke of him to Elisabetta de Piccolellis in a way that, if
reported to him, would please him.

I forgot to add that we were together in Paris during the so-
called Peace Conference. The Fiume affair came up, and although
he hated it himself he went about among acquaintances to say
that, born a Russian subject, son of a noted nihilist, I was brought
up as an enemy of bourgeois society, was a formidable Bolshevik
propagandist and secret agent. That was why I opposed Italy's
most just, most sacred, most invincible claims to a bit of her own
territory, without which poor Italy could exist only miserably, exposed to every danger of aggression and invasion.

❖   ❖   ❖

When I first went out in Florence—it was in the spring of 1889
—wherever I went I heard of Carlo Placci, but did not come

across him. My curiosity was excited as is everybody's about a name grown familiar but as yet without sufficient substance behind it. Unexpectedly a year or two later I encountered him at Vernon Lee's. It was evening. The light was dim. I got no clear impression of his features, but they seemed pleasant, and extremely friendly. The voice was mellow, beautifully pitched, with a seductive timbre.

To my surprised gratification, he looked me up the very next afternoon in my eyrie some hundred and thirty steps up in Lungarno Acciaiuoli, and we had a long talk, I cannot recall about what. Nor can I recollect how soon acquaintance flowered into friendship and friendship into intimacy. He pulled me into his circle, not only inviting me to his house, then presided over by his mother assisted by a sister, and by a Miss Gibson, an old Englishwoman who had been their governess, but he made a point of introducing me to all his friends, whether Florentine, Italian, or foreign, who enjoyed his hospitality. My gregarious propensities would have succeeded surely in finding satisfaction of some sort and, for all I know, more profitable perhaps and even more suitable; but as a matter of fact I owe most of my social and nearly all of my society contacts to Carlo. He was generosity itself in passing me from friend to friend, and never could I discover in him the least desire to monopolize or keep me away from others. Nor did he expect gratitude or compensation as if he had sacrificed certain claims on the people he brought together. I have had acquaintances who could not forget after decades that they had introduced me to a person who became a vital factor in my life. These acquaintances are like a character in a French comedy who ejaculates: *"Je vous ai prêté cinq francs, je ne l'oublierai jamais!"*

Carlo was unlike that, yet there were drawbacks to his way of bringing people together. He prepared the ground by extravagant praise of the newcomer. That suffices to prejudice against the latter. In which connection I cannot refrain from telling what happened to me one day in Thebes, in the American House at Der-el-Bahari. It was presided over by a member of our smart classes who had taken to digging and was at the same time a fine Egyptologist. We had not met before and as we sat down to lunch, he, tired after a long forenoon's work in the choking dust and scorching winter sun, scarcely mumbled a how-do-you-do, and looked as if he would rather bite than talk. I tried to engage him in conversation but he only growled back. Finally I asked: "What is the matter? Why do you look so sullen and why won't you be civil?" "I'll tell you," he burst out. "That damned Joe Breck so rammed you down my throat that I got to hate the name of Berenson."

Carlo was not only apt to stir reaction against his estimate of the friend he proposed introducing, but roused resentment, more often than not, by something in his tone implying that you were altogether inferior to the person he was going to present.

*   *   *

A similar tone, far more aggressive, he frequently, in truth nearly always, took when the conversation was about politics in general, but in particular of international affairs, when addressing himself to us outsiders, who had not his access to Foreign Office men of all countries nor his acquaintance with their secrets. As a matter of fact the utmost he could substantiate was knowing this evening what the newspaper would print early next morning. Perhaps there were exceptions. I suspect that at times ministers and even ambassadors used him as a lie-carrier.

Be it so or not, with increasing years, like the tart in the story of Maupassant *qui n'aimait que dans les Affaires Étrangères,* Carlo got more and more to divide his acquaintances into diplomats all glorious, and outsiders who could but weep and gnash their teeth for being excluded. He persuaded himself, I believe, that he was one of the chosen, and his most sacred privilege, the one that meant most to him, was a diplomatic passport he had from his government. The innocent vanity of a rich and idle man! Did not his mother, the blue-eyed Castillo-Aztec Mexican lady, widow of a banker from Faenza, did she not speak of this son as *il ministro degli affari inutili,* minister of affairs that do not count? He would not take it that way, but expected us to receive his pronouncements and prophecies in dead earnest.

Time and time again he would begin with an offensive-defensive "Of course you will not believe, but take it from me." At other times, when he was most aggressive, it occurred to one to suspect that he was provoking us so as to draw us out and thereby come to some bit of gossip that his interlocutor might have picked up, once in a blue moon, from some transient diplomat. Later he confessed that he liked to "put fleas into people's ears" to see what would happen.

Needless to add that his political views were based on neither economics nor sociology nor history but were a matter of the *œil-de-bœuf* and the alcove, as in Saint-Simon. And like that prince of memoir-writers he had his *entrées* everywhere, and was of course much more traveled. Wherever he went, kings and queens, dukes and duchesses rejoiced to see him. In Brussels, as he once drove off in a royal carriage to dine at the palace, the hotel people asked his faithful Giuseppe: "Who is your master, anyhow?" In a drawling Sicilian voice came the answer: *"Il mio padrone non è nessuno, ma tiene delle buone relazioni."* (My master is nobody, but has important acquaintances.)

*   *   *

He had because he retained his early reputation of being genial, amusing, entertaining, even a jollier. As a guest he was perfect, and people used to say that he spoiled the trade of being a guest, *qu'il gâtait le métier de visiter.* He could condescend to parlor tricks, to imitations of types and even of individuals, but these were never unkind. He could be comical on the piano. He could organize theatricals and take the principal part in them. He could carry on games with children of all ages and keep them panting with pleasure.

Perhaps he felt that he was paying enough with his wit and humor and brightening, and need not return hospitality. His mother kept open house and few foreigners or strangers passing through Florence failed to appear at her board. When this delightful Mexican, whom some of us fondly called Vitzli-Putzli, died, Carlo was already well on in the fifties. Hitherto he had found no occasion for forming habits of spending on bread and butter and butcher's meat and the other realities of daily life.

Without such habits formed before the threshold of old age, people are awkward about spending, and easily get the reputation of being close, and at times deserve it, because of their miserliness.

A case in point was Boston's precinema star, Mrs. Jack Gardner. While Jack was alive, *he* did all the paying out not only abroad but at home. Isabella spent only on clothes, pearls, diamonds, and, later, on almost as expensive old masters. When her husband died, and bills of the baker and butcher and electrician were brought to her, she got into a panic from which she never quite recovered. She who in Europe had traveled like royalty, with compartments reserved for her in railways and luxurious suites in hotels, now went second-class, and, frequenting the same hotels as before, would take the cheapest rooms and order the least expensive dishes. Remaining wealthy, but having had no training in the workaday use of money, she lived like a "Latin" *rentière* in constant fear of losing it. She all but ceased acquiring works of art on the ground that she was poor, and this at a time when those nearest to her used to beg me to induce her to buy, assuring me that she could amply afford it.

Another case in point is a friend of ours who, like Placci, inherited late in life. He had been kept on short commons by a very close parent. He was generous to the point of folly almost when it was a question of giving large sums for charity, or art. When it was a question of paying out a shilling or two he could not bring himself to do it. More than once he invited me to a meal and I had to pay the scot. If one took a cab with him he fumbled and the friend paid.

Well, Carlo had not learned to spend on ordinary things, although I am sure he too was large in his charities. He received less and less in the home where his mother had entertained, be it remembered, not for herself but for him. When abroad, say at Saint-Moritz when all were living at hotels, he never sat down to a meal of his own, and although he could have afforded as much as anyone to feed and drench a dozen people at a time, he never did. I discovered one fine day that it was not naïve thoughtlessness as I had supposed, but was calculated. He told me with a

grin of satisfaction that he would wait till the fag end of the season and invite the last survivors to a tea at Hanselmann's.

So reluctant was he to empty his pockets that, years after everybody who could afford it had a motorcar, he went without. He
would come to our house every few days and always telephone
to inquire whether our car might not happen to be in town and
bring him up. This got to mean sending for him. As he could afford
it better than many others, I finally lost patience and made him
get a vehicle of his own. When he got it he treated it as gingerly
as if it were a young wife in her first pregnancy. There was always a sufficient reason why it was not in condition to climb up
the hills to take us out for a walk, and why it would be preferable
to use my car for that purpose.

✳   ✳   ✳

I said he came every few days to lunch or dine. When to the
first, it was followed by a walk, during which *en tête-à-tête* he
could be, and nearly always was, as reasonable as he was apt to be
aggressively provoking in company. Boasting constantly of his
tact and society experience, he could be, and quite deliberately
so, the bull in the china shop or worse. No master of jujitsu knew
one's weak spots better; no one could get one on the raw as he did;
and always in company and at my own table. I cannot recall such
behavior on his part when we were alone together, he and I.

Singular how company goes to people's heads like bad drink. It
made Placci jeer and sneer and cavil and quibble and boast, because he could not sustain a cool discussion of current events in
the presence of witnesses. It turned D'Annunzio into a performing
ape. He, who was such delicious company when you had him to
yourself, talking with the greatest naturalness and self-forgetful-
ness, talking always impersonally of literature, of poetry, of books,
and with keenest zest for words, rare and sonorous words which
he would caress as a jeweler caresses precious stones; this same
D'Annunzio was not the same when another man was present, and
if it was a woman, and a society woman at that, he lost interest in
everything except in the impression he was making. Deplorable as
this seemed to me, let me add by the way that women did not feel

it. On the contrary, I have seen some of the most delicate, charming, and intelligent of women subdued, enticed, bewitched, and
confessing that they could not resist him.

To return to Placci, his mother and sister, when they saw us
getting intimate with him, warned us that he would behave to us
as he did to them, that with intimates he could be quarrelsome,
tiresome, and even offensive. And he was. Yet when driven to
exasperation and on the point of refusing to see him again, I
would as it were take a "last ride," and return feeling that I could
not split with a character who could draw one out so caressingly,
hanging on one's lips, anxious to let no word pass unappreciated,
putting in his own in a way that would elicit one's best.

Never shall I forget a walk we took nearly forty years ago over
the Sibilla range on the descent to Ascoli. The day had been quarrelsome, and Carlo had called out the worst in me. Perhaps it was
the fault of the sirocco lowering over the stewing pan that is the
plain of Norcia. By the time the car had brought us to the top it
had turned fresh. The road was barely completed and as yet so
little used that it was grass-grown. We got out and walked. We
talked of ultimate things, of beginnings and ends, of whence and
whither, of why and how. He was then already reconciled to the
Church, a practicing Catholic, and in company odiously dogmatiz-
ing, making a point of gargling the a's as, in imitation of English
coreligionist converts, he pronounced the word "Ca-a-a-tholic."
His arguments could be so silly that on one occasion I cried out:
"Carlo, I respect your beliefs, I do not quarrel with them, but I
cannot swallow your second-rate arguments." "There are no
others," was his reply.

To his conversion, and to his agreeing to reasons that he himself knew to be feeble, I shall return presently. Meanwhile, let me
go back to the evening stroll down the slopes of the Sibilla. We
"gossiped about the universe," we thrilled with cosmic emotion;
we discussed revealed religions and their relation to mysticism;
we deplored the inevitable necessity of institutions, churches, and
governments; we touched upon the burning questions of the day
and never disagreed, not even in opinion.

Carlo could be like that when he wished, and often he was when we were alone together, as I have said again and again. What made him so different in company was not merely the insistence on having the last word or the irresistible impulse to show off, but the fact, so foreign to Anglo-Saxons, that, like most Latins, Placci made a clear division between his private and his public self. No bridge, not even the Mazdian or Mohammedan, sharp as a knife's edge leading from earth to heaven, traversed the abyss. What an Italian thinks remains his own treasure hidden away in a safe, to the unlocking of which he alone guards the elaborate secret.

I remember a jolly Irishman one met everywhere, when I first went out in Florence. His father came as a jockey in the court of the Grand Duke, did so well, and rendered such services beyond those devoted to the peaceful and polished society of horses, that he was made a baron. His son, my friend, used to say: "You can easily get an Italian to say what he feels. He revels in it. But no power on earth will drag a word out of him as to what he thinks."

Intimate as we were, Carlo did not often give one a peep into the depth of his private thinking; yet enough, however, to make me suspect that to the end he was incapable of a wholehearted conviction about anything whatever. At bottom he was an integral unbeliever for whom existed neither deity, nor principle, nor quality, nor value—a nihilist, in short. And I also suspect that to the end he was haunted by a tormenting doubt, *Le pari de Pascal*— "What if there were a hell?"—that had no little influence on his conduct.

*   *   *

When I first knew him he was like most advanced young Italians in the early eighteen nineties, like most young writers of those hopeful days, a declared atheist, a positivist, a fervent socialist, and all else that then was up-to-datest. That none of those professions was more than skin-deep was manifested by the rapidity and the completeness with which he turned away without even saying "good-by-to-all-that," and by the ardor and even fanaticism—the fanaticism of a person who cannot get himself to believe in anything—that he displayed in burning what he had been adoring.

The change-over was so sudden that we did not perceive it or as much as suspect it. We had just moved down from Fiesole to San Gervasio, he had been spending the day with us in the late spring, and we kept him company to the tram which was to take him back to Florence. I cannot recall what brought up the subject of divorce, but he startled us by pronouncing himself against it.

Now the English-speaking reader, if Protestant, will not find it easy to believe to what a degree, early in this century, the question of divorce and remarriage became the storm-center around which "ignorant armies" of practicing and not-practicing Catholics "clashed by night." A divorced woman encountered nothing but resentment and disavowal, and if she remarried she was boycotted. It went so far that Paul Bourget wrote a novel to manifest his admiration for wives who murdered their husbands rather than to live in mortal sin as a divorcée who had married again. My wife, a red-hot feminist for whom divorce was identified with the emancipation from the oppression, exploitation, and exasperation of women by the odious but zoologically indispensable males, my wife pricked up her ears and asked what he meant and whether by chance he had returned to the Church. He answered with fervor that he had. We discovered soon that this conversion, always prayed for, as he knew, by his genuinely and deeply religious mother, had been brought about by the same Mme de Montebello who later made an anti-Dreyfusard of him. He turned as violently, as vehemently, as aggressively reactionary as he had been "leftist" only a few weeks before. He even boasted of being a *forcaiolo*—that is, to say, one who would make liberal, even extravagant, use of the gallows, and he favored every cause backed by force, fraud, and violence. I recall a quarrel over the conduct of his government, which gave its approval to Austria when, backed by Germany, Aehrenthal annexed Bosnia and Herzegovina and refused to receive it, as Grey proposed, from the Concert of Europe, thus making the first breach in those ramparts of legality which for nearly a century had kept Europe safe from a major and general war.

I am trying to write about Placci and not about Mme Jean de Montebello. I should have no little to tell if she were my theme. A word or two I cannot resist putting down.

She regarded herself as an Egeria of international relations, and it was said at the time—a time when China was still Cathay, with its almost moveless cycles—that a caller, on being ushered in, found her looking preoccupied and distressed. Asking what was the matter, he got the answer: *"C'est la Chine qui m'inquiète."* Her interest in foreign affairs had been fanned and shaped, it was said, by a M. de Chaudordy who had represented France at the court of Pius IX. I do not remember whether still at the Quirinal or already at the Vatican. I had the honor, and I must add the pleasure, of meeting him at Mme de Montebello's, where I greatly enjoyed his conversation. I recall an amusing anecdote in connection with his Roman mission.

The Pope wished to reward him for his services and bestowed on him the title of count; but the bureau that made out the diploma for this grant demanded as its perquisite a sum that seemed exorbitant to Chaudordy. He refused to pay it. When this reached the ears of His Holiness, he said: "Yes, I have made him a count but I have not decided of what. Very well. He shall be Count of Monteporcone" (of Pig's Hill). It should be added that the word *porco* is never used by Italians except as an insult—far worse than our "swine."

To return to Placci, this swift and sure turnover from the extreme of leftism to the opposite extreme was made easy in his own eyes by a book just published that I had in all innocence lent him: William James's *The Will to Believe*. It gave him the pragmatic justification for choosing the principles which his whim of the moment and his tropism led him to prefer. Like the Scot who when politely told that he was eating asparagus from the wrong end retorted "I prefer-r-r it," Placci would bang the lid on every discussion by rejoicing in iniquity, despising reason, and rejoicing in the right James had extended to him, to believe what he *willed*.

I dare say Carlo reserved his aggressiveness, his *Rechthaberei*, the need for having the last word, for his more intimate friends.

Once in a while I overheard him with ambassadors—his gods—
and was amused to discover how soft-spoken he was with them.
At the same time, let me add, I was struck with admiration for the
tactfully flattering way in which he drew them out.

I have often heard him accused of being a snob, by which the
accuser meant presumably that he treated people according to
their position in society, whether owing to rank, office, or fame.
He did enjoy approaching people of whatever kind of eminence.
I must add, however, it was more for individual distinction than
for claims of group, class, or heredity. He delighted in what used
to be called "high society" for its brilliance, its quicker pulse, its
life-enhancing elegance. He was not displeased that, in all capitals,
he received several invitations for each meal. By the time I knew
him, society everywhere opened its doors wide to him on every
occasion, and he did not need to work for admission. I cannot say
that I have encountered anyone with gregarious habits and social
qualities who would have acted otherwise and, like a desert her-
mit, refused the appeal of good company.

If to be a snob means above all to throw over one's own standards, one's own values, one's own beliefs, for those of the barbarians, no matter how gorgeous, then Placci surely was not a
snob. On the contrary. For instance, when he first met me, sought
me out, and introduced me to his friends and, I might almost say,
forced me upon them, including the most exalted, I was unknown,
from nowhere, with no guarantees, and introduced to him by a
lady who was still under the impression, because I had lent her
a book on the subject, that I was specializing in pre-Mohammedan
Arab poetry. Likewise with Salvemini, who came to Florence fresh
from one of those villages of Apulia which count fifty or sixty or
seventy thousand peasants huddled together because it had not
been safe to remain out for fear of the Barbaresques, those same
pirates who infested the Mediterranean until little more than a
hundred years ago, when the American navy followed by the
English and French put an end to their man-hunts. This unkempt lad, with his huge square head, broad shoulders, and provincial accent, was destined to become the idol of all that was

most cultured in Florentine society, as well as of his pupils in the university, and to become one of the historians of the day and prophet and defender of every good cause. It was Placci who discovered him on arrival and passed him on to the rest of us. So it was with the martyred Amendola, but also with Papini, Soffici, Prezzolini, and other, equally rubber-necked exploiters of the moment. Not only young writers but musicians, painters, sculptors—he would catch them on their first flight and bring them home for us to sample. They did not always turn out the geniuses he expected them to be, yet often enough to make it worth while. Nor did he, unlike others in similar positions, the Napoleonid Count Primoli, for instance, demand from them any return, or regard them as clients who owed allegiance and gratitude for his patronage.

I have mentioned musicians, and it was with them that in earlier years his relations were the most active; for he was himself a highly trained connoisseur of everything musical, a tolerable pianist, and, as many singers and fiddlers used to tell me, an ideal accompanist. The sympathy, the almost uncanny way he could, when he wanted to, get under the skin of others made him feel the tact and the tempo of the performers exactly as they themselves did. There used to be a great deal of music in his house. His teacher, Bonamici, played four-handed with him once a week, and Bonamici had studied with Liszt and with Bülow. No musician stopped over in Florence, even the most celebrated, without being seen and most likely heard at Placci's. With them he seemed at his most genial, most appreciative, at his best. He was generosity itself in praising the talents of others.

I have already spoken of how welcome Placci was in Paris, in London, in Munich and Vienna as well as in Rome. Hans von Bülow dubbed him the "cosmopolisson," and he remained proud of the nickname long after he had rejected cosmopolitanism, to belch anathemas at all who were not furious nationalists, and patridiots, as I beg pardon for punningly calling those who would be cannibals for their own dung heap.

Carlo used to travel with us. The first long journey I can recall

our taking together was in 1899 to Budapest for the millennial
celebration of the Crown of St. Stephen, I believe. There we
encountered people from the world over, and colleagues of every
branch of study, who had gathered for an art congress. We
punned, we chaffed, we poked fun, we drank or rather sipped
sticky, sickishly oversweet but famous Tokayer; we even discussed,
but one thing we did not do, we did not attend the meetings—not
once.

From Budapest we took train to Fiume, then still as unaware
of being Italian as Italians were unaware of its existence. By boat
we wandered in the company of a much-traveled M.P., Philip
Stanhope, a great admirer of Austrian rule in Bosnia-Herzegovina,
to Spalato, and from Spalato we crossed over to Ancona in a
cabin not only first-class but numbered A-1. Ancona was at the
periphery of a region I had made my own years earlier in connection with a monograph I was preparing on the Venetian Lorenzo
Lotto. Crivelli too, whom I then enjoyed inordinately, left many
paintings there. Carlo was happy to be shown the best of everything, enjoyed the works of art he was seeing "under authority,"
and delighted with the prospect of talking about them. At last we
got to Perugia, a day in early October. We had been sight-seeing
and Carlo was in raptures. Toward the end of the day we were
taking tea—not literally, for tea was not being served in Italy
outside the few hotels frequented by the English. He no doubt
had ordered chocolate, and the richest, creamiest cakes in the
place, and sopped up the one with other, enjoying it all the more
as he knew that it annoyed me. Having consumed a dozen of these
cakes, he rose from the table, shook hands merrily, and told us he
had enough of our company, had all the Berenson he could stand,
and was taking the train to Florence.

Neither he nor I owned a car for quite a while after motoring
came in; but his French nephew, Lucien Henraux, did. For several
years this sensitive, this quick and gifted youth—destined, alas!
to a premature end—came, spring and autumn, to take us to
various parts of Italy, Piedmont, the Friuli, the Abruzzi, Calabria,
Sicily. I used to make out the itinerary of the journey, but it often

was thwarted by Carlo's sudden recollection that we should be passing the dwelling of an acquaintance and must stop to lunch or tea, no matter how boring he might be or how little use he could have for us. Or he would become aware that it was a Sunday, a holiday, and that he must attend mass. A low mass, no! It must be a high mass because that would give him the satisfaction of procuring the greatest inconvenience to the greatest number— a pleasure inbred in Latins by all their governments no matter whether black or white, red or blue. Carlo did love to tease and sometimes he went on till it turned from a rather malicious joke to a more and more exasperating nuisance. He would insist on the sudden halting of the overcrowded open car at the crossroads of a Calabrian village, a stinging sun pricking like a swarm of angry bees, with our own dust choking us, and stop to question and cross-question the crowd, in an imitation of their own dialect, about the roads, their direction and condition, and about anything else that could prolong what to the rest of us was real distress. The more exhausted he got, the worse grew his teasing, the more sneeringly aggressive; and more than once it ended in a row which came close to breaking up the party.

When we reached our destination after a long day of sitting three abreast in the smallish, far from luxurious vehicle, exhausted by sight-seeing, by the open air, by the driving, badly fed at that, he would insist, rain or shine, on dragging himself along through crowded streets and cobbled alleys before joining us for the evening meal. In calm moments, he would apologize winningly for his naughtiness, and I would answer that his, like an infant's naughtiness, was the result of exhaustion and that he ought to avoid getting overtired. It was no use, for on the whole he enjoyed annoying and exasperating those he loved best.

A never-failing topic for teasing were my, rather than my wife's, English ways, the absurder, as while she is the purest of Anglo-Saxons I have not one drop of that precious ichor in my veins. He pretended to be annoyed by the inseparable tea-basket, by my giving thought to food, by my paying attention to no news that did not come out of the London *Times*. In short, he would call me

the "Dean of Durham." I grin, calling up the revered image of the
present wearer of that title.

I recall two experiences among many others. We had left
Benevento on a damp chilly late April morning, and taken no lunch
with us, Carlo insisting that we should find all we needed somewhere on the way. At Lacedonia, the only possible place, there
was no inn, no eating house, nothing. With difficulty we picked
up stale bread and onions. Another spring we were motoring from
Potenza to Taranto, and again Carlo would not let us take food
along. We were to stop at Miglionico to see a polyptych by Cima
da Conegliano. Where such a masterpiece had been preserved
through the centuries there was sure to be sugar and spice and all
that was good to eat. We got to Miglionico, looked at the Cima,
and long looking left us hungry. A gendarme whom we consulted
about a restaurant humped his shoulders toward an open door.
A staircase led upstairs to a large room, whitewashed. A queer
odor of phenic acid prevailed, and looking around we discovered
bunks with sick people in them. This hall was both hospital and
restaurant. I cleared out and the others followed. We foraged for
food. All we could get was a loaf of fresh-baked bread. It tasted
delicious. We were hungry. It was sunny. We had seen a fine work
of art. Above all, Carlo was drollery personified, describing our
discomfiture.

While on the subject of our early motoring days, let me add that
Placci could be as full of fun as of spleen, and often I recall our
litanies in dog Latin, *Sancta Cachuchia ora pro rotis, Sancta Cla-
vina ora pro portis* (and others unquotable): the first being inspired
by the dread of being left in the wild with no rubber tires; the
other, by the constant difficulty of entering museums and galleries
because the keeper had gone away to a neighboring town with the
keys in his pocket. To while away the time waiting for endless
roadside repairs he invented a Monsieur Dupont, an average
French bourgeois and his family, and made us talk in character.
We did it too well, with some danger of forgetting how to talk in
any other way.

He made up for everything by being delightful as a companion in churches, museums, before landscape; vibrating, stimulating, responsive, for he was, as I have said before, both sensitive and intelligent; and besides he had the required preparation. I dare repeat that he enjoyed it the more for enjoying it with me, whom he regarded as supreme arbiter of every phase of beauty that could reach one through the eyes. He felt he could rely on my guidance, and if in the course of my studies, which he followed with lively interest, we had to see artifacts that were but mediocre as works of art, he relished the satisfaction of being "in it."

A singular trait must not pass unrecorded. In the fifty years of intimacy, seeing each other so often, I never heard him talk of the subject uppermost in high society, the question of *qui est avec qui*—with what Mabel is Edward now? I cannot recall his gossiping about any particular woman. As far as I knew, sex did not seem to interest him in others or in himself. Only once did he speak of his own experience. Some thirty-five years ago we were crossing the Bernina on a sparkling late September day, and as we were crunching the hard dazzling snow he talked of the expedients he had to take in order to keep his various loves from interfering with each other. He referred to it as to "old, unhappy, far-off things and battles long ago." If he had love affairs during the half century that I knew him, I never heard of them, although I did see him flirt rather ostentatiously with this or that ripe beauty. As for Mme de Montebello, he was Dante to her Beatrice. Nor did he take interest in my affairs of the heart. I recall suffering so much from *peine d'amour* that I could not help appealing for sympathy. He pooh-poohed me, and was almost as stony as was Edith Wharton on a similar occasion.

I have been speaking of Placci so long and as yet have said nothing of his physical appearance. To foreigners he looked like Savonarola. My eye saw more resemblance to the portraits in pre-Inca, Peruvian potteries. Indeed, he had about him something Aztec, Mayan, Chiroquee—Central America, in short. He had the enormous chest of a stone-age man, not short, not thick-set, yet pillarlike. When he got out of a chair and stood up, his natural position was as frontal as an early dynasty Egyptian's, with the palms of his hands flat, turned outward, and kept close to his thighs. His face, too, was unusually frontal and after seventy looked more and more like a Mexican or Aztec mask. He kept his hair thick to the end and it never got more than iron-gray. His eyes were dark. The lower lip tended to protrude, especially when he was cross. He dressed neatly but with no elegance, and always conventionally.

Placci was not only a dilettante in music, and a tolerable pianist as already told, but a man of letters. In earlier years he wrote one or two novels which his acquaintants read: and later, till the other day, in fact, he contributed several articles a year to the *Corriere della Sera*. They were nearly always reminiscent or societyish, and did no justice to what, in favorable moments, he could say in conversation. Curiously enough, while he could tell a good story, even when not merely droll, and discuss character penetratingly, his pen remained far behind his tongue, and even his tongue could not make his ordinary doings interesting. His letters were seldom more than lists of people he had seen, and we got to dread our first meeting after a separation. He would insist on naming one person after the other he had seen, of whom so few for us had any interest.

He began to decline some ten years ago, falling asleep after meals wherever he happened to be. He still went to Paris and London and Rome for their seasons, and people remained kind and hospitable, but he had less and less to contribute. He confessed that he could not read any more, that he did not care any more for travel, and little for music. Nothing remained for him but "people, people, people," as he told me his reminiscences were to be entitled, if ever the diary he kept should be published. Less than ever could he bear to be alone. He used to boast of turning the Italian proverb "Better alone than in poor company" into "Any company rather than alone." When traveling he would look out as eagerly for the most crowded carriage as did the rest of us for the emptiest. Sad that during his last illness he would not or could not bear to see anyone.

This is what I have to say at present about dear Carlo Placci,

Placci as I saw him, put up with him, loved him, and to a limited extent knew him. I wonder what people who have not known him will get out of what I have just written. A consistent impression, no matter how little like the Platonic idea, the metaphysical portrait? In North Africa the natives attach bits of rags, wool, linen, cotton of any and every color to the scraggly bushes planted around the tombs of their marabouts or santons. Perhaps that is all I have contributed to the memory of Carlo Placci. Not even an effigy in mosaic.

January 15th

TO ACQUIRE and retain a strangle-hold on a people, a church must identify itself with the national needs and aspirations. Witness the Poles and Irish and ghetto Jews of today where the church swallows up the nation. In fact, until recently in the nearer East, church and nation were identical. Not more than a few years ago, in Yugoslavia, visiting an ancient site, I overheard my Serbian guides trying to find out of what tribe the custodian of the ruins was. Was he a Serb, was he a Croat, was he a Slovene? To each question he gave a more vehement negative. Finally he yelled: "Catholic, Catholic, I am a Catholic!"

It is conceivable that if the attacks of Moslems from south and west had coincided with the Mongol invasions from the east, Christian Europe would have been welded into one church-state of a permanent nature, and not merely into the sketch of one achieved between Gregory VII and Innocent III. Under pressure of the Moravids, Spain became the most fanatical church-state that Europe knew before Jesuitized Poland.

January 25th

DIFFERENCE OF AGE never made much difference to me at any moment of my life, nor does it now. That is to say it would not, but for the increasing age-consciousness that has crept upon us since I myself was a young person. During my visits to the U. S. A.

I began to feel more and more parked into a round where we had to keep turning with our contemporaries like Paolo and Francesca in their circle of Dante's Inferno, seldom meeting the older and never the young. Indeed, we never saw the children of our best friends at their own table, and scarcely knew them by sight.

I was not the baby monster who could not enjoy the society of other children, but in so far as I was allowed to listen, in so far as I could understand the talk of older and even old people, I preferred it. To this much I must confess: that after childhood, the further I advanced in boyhood and youth the more I sought out my elders. At Harvard I preferred the conversation of James, of Toy, of Climer, of Wendell, to that of fellow students. The former not only seemed better worth while, but were more accessible. Nothing is so cliquy and exclusive as the schoolboy or the schoolboy-minded Anglo-Saxon of all ages.

From early years, old age inspired me with sympathy and good will. Perhaps it was due to a grandmother, to whom I was attached the more as my own mother, only eighteen when I was born, was herself too much the young girl—lovely and perhaps giddy—to play the mother. She left the happy task to her own mother. My giant grandfather, who used, like St. Christopher, to carry me seated on his right shoulder, may also have contributed to my friendly attitude toward old people. What I vividly recall is a story of a little boy who was discovered by his parents carving a bowl out of a piece of wood. Asked what he was doing, he answered that when his grandfather got too unsteady to hold earthenware without breaking it, he was given a wooden bowl instead; and that he was getting one ready in good time for his own father.

I not only remember the pity and the tenderness this made me feel for the old, helpless, friendless, neglected peasants that I must have seen, but it has haunted me through life, making me feel more unhappy to think of the suffering of the aged than of younger people. Then this story made me for the first time aware, but with a poignancy I never got over, how swift, how inexorable was the passage of the years, and how soon I too, then a small boy, would be an old man. Possibly another tale read soon afterwards helped to burn it into me. It was by Jean Paul and told of a youth who dreams that he is no longer young, that he has wasted his prime and maturity, and is now old and a wreck. With difficulty he rouses himself from this nightmare, wakes to youth again, but with the will to make good use of the remainder of his days.

So I never felt that there was anything enviable in youth. I cannot recall that any of us, as youths, admired our condition to excess or had a desire to prolong it. Nor, when young ourselves, did we think of our contemporaries as looking particularly young. The older we get, the more and more childlike do the young look, and to me now all under thirty look cherubic almost, and babies.

I for one was keenly aware of being young, of being alert, eager, and zestful. I enjoyed it. Yet not for an instant would I have stopped the march of time. On the contrary, I was panting to be twenty-one, to be of age, to graduate, and then to plunge into the vague, uncharted, fascinating future.

Harvard undergraduates, when I was one, had no more cult of youth than I did; nor, living, as I have, a sheltered life on a Tuscan hillside, can I recall when and where this worship of youth began —youth as an independent, complete state of being and not, as we used to treat it, a causeway between boyhood and manhood, youth belying the old adage "Si jeunesse savait, si vieillesse pouvait," youth adding knowledge to power, wisdom to will, and dispensing not only with the experience of elders but of betters as well, and coming out the more efficient, the more creative, for doing so.

Youth, advanced youth at all events, was, for all its exuberant gaiety and wild hopes, a period of anxious indecision as to one's place in the great society, one's mating, one's settling. This was particularly the case with those of us who were favored by nature rather than by fortune. Shallow as it may seem to the German-minded divers into deep seas of ink, I venture to believe that there would be little storm and stress, few youth movements, if young men were sure of walking straight into satisfactory careers.

My first recollection of the word "youth" used in any but a temporal sense is attached to what seemed a hole-and-corner movement although it led to blood and tears, "Young Ireland."

Much later was started a German weekly named *Jugend,* which should have made me reflect, but I was no doubt prevented by the fact that the greedily devoured paper of my boyhood was the *Youth's Companion,* which certainly had nothing political, sociological, or anything beyond the interests suitable to a healthy boy. I seem to remember hearing or reading occasionally the phrase *Giovane Italia*—young Italy. If I ever encountered the word "young" as applied to a social or political movement in France, England, or America it has certainly gone out of my mind.

So when I first heard the Fascist song *"Giovinezza, giovinezza"* —sung, if I am not mistaken, on a variant of the tune of an old Bersaglieri march—I pricked up my ears and listened. How odd that youngsters should be rejoicing in something so inevitably transitory, so swiftly over and past as youth! Furthermore: real manliness, vigor, energy, creativeness, have on the one hand no such self-awareness, and on the other hand no such leisure as to make much of themselves in word rather than deed. Still less is a healthy community interested in celebrating its health, and boasting of all it means to do, and the expected rewards. That is more characteristic of used-up, of consumptive, of senile societies.

Nor when I was young was "young" synonymous with "new." When in my youth there came to Boston Wagner, Browning, Ibsen, and Tolstoi they brought wonder, they widened horizons, they were newness itself, but neither were they young nor would that have made any difference.

Is it not perhaps a symptom of decadence to take to the cult of youth, of the young? Normal youth needs no urging to be young and no drive to be enterprising, bold, and adventurous. Real youth is bursting with these qualities, with "dynamic"—to use a contemporary vocable for a concept as ancient as the Mousterians at least —and, far from requiring their encouragement, needs to be restrained. Achilles and Hector, Alexander and his marshals, Napoleon and his, did not harp on being young. The first two respected the age-old Nestor and Priam, and the latter two would have done well to listen to Perdiccas and Talleyrand.

History is being written from many different points of view, each representing another approach, inspired by another interest. Why not study the past fifty centuries in the light of the question of old and young, old versus young, of what happened when the one predominated over the other, and what when there was a perfect balance between the two? Offhand I should be disposed to believe that in the most happy moments of civilization equilibrium prevailed. When youth is at the prow, the ship of society is too likely to be steered to strange and sterile adventures like the Roman and French revolutionary wars, like the horrors we are witnessing today to the tune of *giovinezza*. On the other hand, when the aged rule exclusively they tend to celestialism, to a sort of horticultural view of society, as if man were like a flower that had to bloom, put forth its beauty, and wither, yet return unchanged again and ever again, with the seasons. This attitude entertained toward society by the Chinese, the Hindus, the rabbis, and the muftis is one into which, in revulsion from too much youth, we may drift.

February 4th

Is THERE a connection between the emerging sense of individuality and the craving for a future life? It would seem possible that down to a certain period, man felt himself to be too much part of a group, and was at the same time too absorbed in mere living, either to think of himself as distinct from his tribe or to worry about what would happen to him after death.

What was man's notion of individuality as late even as the aëneolithic period? Was it a privilege of the king only, of Cheops at Gizeh, of the ruler at Ur? And is that why they felt they must do all in their power, at the risk perchance of exhausting the material resources of the community, to prolong into an indefinite future a life that was and was not physical, was and was not immaterial?

I say "immaterial," but what could the word have meant to Cheops or a nearly contemporary king of Ur? How far could they distinguish between material and not-material? How soon did the surviving not-material begin to be more than a batlike something flitting about in a Sheol or Hades, and to take on the connotation of an existence beyond nature, altogether beyond, and not merely of one more attenuated and more helpless? It could not have been early or we ourselves by now should have got further. It would not be too safe today even to inquire what most of us meant by "spirit." We might risk discovering that for most it still meant something material but infinitely thin although endowed with superterrestrial qualities. Almost all would insist that it was related to an immortal soul. Few have got so far as to identify "spirit" with a realm of being in which we exercise those of our faculties that lead us as much beyond "nature"—mere animated sentient matter—as the fruit is beyond the soil and the seed out of which it grew. It is a realm in which we strive to attain certain qualities. Could we attain them, we should become these qualities and cease to be as individuals. We should be in Abraham's bosom, we should be dissolved in the Godhead, we should achieve Nirvana.

To go back to the question of a possible link between the sense of individuality and the craving for an afterlife, if it could be established that there was such a connection we should have a key with which to unlock many a mystery of the past, a light to illumine many a dark moment.

In Egypt if at first it was the Pharaoh only who was a conscious individual with a craving for an existence prolonged indefinitely, the grandees nearest to the ruler soon followed him. They too built their homes for eternity, and little by little they were imitated by the less important members of the state.

Perhaps it was the awareness of being individuals that led these grandees to assert themselves against the supreme power and to end as feudatories who more than once threatened the unity of the state.

Despite much desultory reading I know too little about Eleusinian, Orphic, and other Greek mysteries to do more than ask questions. For instance: Did the growth of a conscious craving for an afterlife coincide in date with the rise of tyranny in Greece?

The total individual is necessarily an autocrat, as Bismarck knew well when he confessed that if he were not employing his faculties in ruling the state he would use them as an anarchist—to be rid of it, to be free of it, one may suppose. And individuals so detached from tribalism as the Spartan Pausanias and Lysander and the wholly emancipated Themistocles, Pericles, and Alcibiades—was their integration as personalities connected with the hope of endless continuation?

In Persia, whether Achaemenian, Parthian, or Sassanian, did feudalism imply individualism as distinct from headship of a clan; and was advancing feudalism an increasing weakness accounting for the easy conquests first of Alexander and ten centuries later of the Islamic invaders? What is certain for those countries is that the belief in immortality was increasing all the time.

Owing to Stoicism in the Roman Empire combining with other-worldliness in Judea and its almost countless tentacles over the then known world, the individual of even the humblest classes was getting so emancipated from his origins, was owing so little allegiance to the community which begot him, that he was beginning to feel lonely and to seek for settled and organized companionship under the disguise frequently of a religious sodality—as was to be continued by the corporations and guilds of the Middle Ages. That these specks of human dust, in the great cities, were getting to be more and more believers in an afterlife we know, as we know that the religions of the time were appealing to them as isolated individuals with immortal souls, owing no religious duties to clan, tribe, or city, but only to God alone. The reward they prayed for, and hoped to attain, was not only the continuation of life after the grave, but one so blissful that it would amply reward them for their previous sufferings. There were thus two distinct and opposed states of mind to encourage a craving for an afterlife:

either life on earth was so irremediably dreadful that it could be endured only if there were compensations hereafter,

or life was so worth while that one wanted to live it, just as it was, for ever and ever.

The first actuated the hopeless, the depressed, the poor, and led straight to Judeo-Christianity. The second inspired the Egyptian and Iranian feudatories.

By our eighth century the belief in immortality among Jewish, Christian, or Mohammedan people had become so general that only the hardest and deepest thinkers conceived of doubting it. Probably this belief, with its terrors and hopes, not only rendered daily life more dramatic, but preserved for the common man, through succeeding centuries of oppression, repression, violence, and anarchy, a certain sense of equality. True enough, it was an equality before God only, in Whose presence everybody was himself and himself alone, responsible only for the good and evil he alone had done. In the course of the centuries, however, since thought and feeling cannot be kept in watertight compartments, equality before God, individual responsibility of man to his Maker, suggested, inspired, and finally brought about every man's equality before the law.

In our century and almost within my memory covering some sixty-five years of awareness, the belief in the afterlife has waned everywhere but chiefly among proletarianized city dwellers.

Is there a connection between the waning among these classes of the belief in an afterlife, with its rewards and punishments, and the loss of their sense of individuality, which they so readily abandon to identify themselves with the only individuals that count, the Pharaohs of our day?

February 5th

WHEN I THINK freely, as I do at times in the teeth of fear, hate, the craving for revenge, and the ambition to be found in the right; when I meditate disinterestedly, I question and wonder. I wonder whether if to beat the Germans we have to take their verbal and material weapons; to become as militarized, as mechanized, as automatized as they, with nothing to distinguish us in conduct from the Germans, I ask then whether we are wise in opposing them. Why fight if our values disappear in the struggle, if we too are to be reduced to abject totalitarianism, to be depersonalized, despiritualized, and above all deindividualized, reduced at best to rejoicing in our physiological functioning with barely more than animal awareness? In that case the cunning of the serpent might counsel us to submit while we still retained our values intact, and to submit with the firm intention of keeping these values not only uncontaminated and untarnished, as certainly can be done, seeing the Jews have done it for thousands of years in the midst of their oppressors. More than that; we could discreetly and tactfully present them—no, not present them, insinuate them rather, or better still let them be perceived as delicate but not easily named exhalations, by the more sensitive Germans.

Might not such a procedure be the least bad way of getting out of present, ever more hellish troubles?

I could laugh to think how the Germans would take it, if instead of resisting their evil we cheered their advent. They might totter as Atlas did when unexpectedly Hercules took the full weight of the earth, its whole crushing burden, off his shoulders. Pity we are not told what happened to Atlas! Had he got too accustomed to his load to feel relief?

Unfortunate it is that the experiment cannot be made and reversed without consequence to the prior conditions! Sooner or later it will be tried. In the course of time, everything will be attempted, and again and again, till humanity becomes convinced of the result as it is that two and two are four. The experiment in question is being made in Paris just now but with consequences that scarcely promise to be satisfactory to Frenchmen or even Germans. Unfortunately, they are Frenchmen with small sense of reality against Germans with no sense of humanity.

The following anecdote told by Gide in his *Journal* is rather comforting. During the First World War a German officer in occupied France was shopping when a woman came in with a baby in her arms. It seemed to have no hands but only two stumps. The officer jumped to the conclusion that they had been cut off, and rushed out of the shop crying out in despair: "Then it is true, it is true that we have cut off children's hands." As a matter of fact, the baby was born like that.

February 6th

WHAT HAPPENS to civilization under the shock of military defeat, we saw in Germany at the end of 1918 and we see in France today. We see it with this difference, however: that in both countries this same civilization has, in the interval, suffered disaster after disaster so that after another defeat the elements to fall back on will be of a much lower, coarser, more animal type. With defeat, no matter how temporary, the authority that headed and ruled a society is swept away overnight as it was in Germany in 1918. The government of that country fell out of the hands of its traditional rulers, but uncovered an administration capable of carrying on, and leaders of moral and intellectual quality, singularly free, at least to the eyes of an outsider, from partisanship, if not from a disastrous optimism about human nature at home and abroad.

If Germany is defeated now, the Lord only knows who will remain to run it! What is left over in France we see already. Wrong-headed, unpractical, fantastical romantics with their sterile and even destructive passions of blind love and staggering hate; and taking advantage of them the envious, jealous, resentful failures of healthier times, during the prevalence of which these *ratés* had small chance to come to the top. Truly in the last twenty years has been confirmed the Psalmist's utterance about his God: *"Deposuit potentes a sede et exaltavit humiles."* Yes, but humble not in contrition and feeling of unworthiness, humble in the sense only of being morally, spiritually, humanely inferior.

February 11th

THE ELDEST GRANDSON of a friend is dying if not already dead, a beautiful boy of eleven, beautiful and gifted, intelligent, dreamy, thoughtful. A couple of months ago his grandmother brought a little landscape he had just painted. It was so well observed, so

well done, that I asked her to leave it for a while in our sitting
room. Everybody who came was struck by it, and wanted to know
by whom it was.

Now he is dying or dead of leukemia, a disease for which, as
yet, no remedy has been found. My youngest sister, Rachel Perry,
died of it within the week that it declared itself. The little boy
has been kept alive by blood transfusions and other tortures to
which, I am told, he prefers death.

This same little boy looked and acted like his maternal uncle, of
whom he seemed to be the reincarnation. This uncle took part in
the First World War courageously and got through unhurt, to die
frozen in the mountains, while on a rash climb.

This same mother and grandmother is one of my oldest surviving friends and one of the dearest. She has without exception the
clearest and most vigorous mind I have encountered in a woman.
A spirit as free as air. From the late eighteen nineties, when we
became friends, I have always known her eager to face problems
and ready to treat them from every angle, except one of family
interests. I could write scores and scores of pages about her as
she presented herself to me in those days, someday perhaps!

And now at this minute the flower of her offspring, the one she
loved for himself and adored as the reincarnation of her lost son,
is perhaps already dead. We say "Man proposes and God disposes."
More fatalistic people say that no one escapes his fate.

March 18th

THINKING of amusing experiments, an entertaining one would
be to watch a European continent with the British islands not only
conquered but swept clean of their inhabitants (excepting the
southern Irish), and their place taken by Germans and their
subjects.

The most exciting expectation would be realized by the return,
in time, of similar relations between Germany and England that
now prevail. The German land has sent its children out again and
again to the conquest of England. To speak of historical times and

taking no account of previous aeons of history, there were the Belgae, the Jutes, the Angles, the Saxons. It did not take them long to forget, or to ignore, their connection with the inhabitants of the land they had left behind them. Nor would it now. One may suspect it would take less. It may be presumed that it would be the most enterprising of sea-minded and industrialized Germans who would occupy England and command and exploit the hordes of inferior immigrants coming with them. In a few decades they would feel that their interests were no longer identical with those of their cousins in the Fatherland. The last, in their turn, would be suspecting, sooner even, that they were being neglected, sacrificed. They thus would be drifting apart, the ex-Germans in England becoming more and more sea-minded, the Germans on the Continent more and more dissatisfied with these ungrateful children. Sooner or later the inhabitants of the islands, no matter how different from the previous English whom the Germans had conquered, would become a thorn in the flesh of the last-named, just as the former had been before their expulsion or extermination. The inhabitants of Germany would be roused sooner or later to want to conquer the islands, again and again. There would be but one effective remedy for German ambitions. It would be to tow England across the Atlantic and push her up against the American continent. This, by the way, is going to happen spiritually and materially and soon, but that is not at all what Germany is after. What she is after is the "geopolitical" removal of England from where this island stands in her way.

As for the French and Dutch, the Spaniards and Italians, after some decades of German rule or even hegemony—not the invisible and inaudible and merely inferred British hegemony but the obvious one which alone Germans understand—the following results may be expected.

The French may at last forget the Hundred Years' War and the Napoleonic struggles, and decide to be good neighbors of the English, who surely in the course of history have always treated them less badly than ever did the inhabitants of Germany since Ariovistus.

The Dutch may decide to bury the hatchet and forgive England for being too strong to admit again of a Tromp's sailing up the Thames, with a broom at his masthead.

The Spaniards even may mitigate their hatred of England because of the Armada, because of Gibraltar, because of the assistance given them during the Peninsular War.

As for the Italians, their fresh and fragile hatred of England will not outlive their perceiving how much better they were off under an impalpably vague hegemony—if indeed hegemony it was and not authority, attributed but scarcely purposed—than under the tremendous pressure Germany will exert. They will have learned how Germany has hemmed them in, how the same Germany has excluded them not only from their *Mare Nostrum* (in a way England never dreamt of doing in peacetime) but from all the seas, unless they, the Italians, consented to hew wood and draw water for them for a bare living wage while the Germans got the material profit, the joy accruing from successful functioning, and the glory of big achievements.

April 20th

ENEMY NUMBER ONE is the Machine in whatever form. Not only because of its ugliness as sight, sound, and smell, not only because it reduces entire counties and almost whole countries to sordidness, squalor, and disgusting rubbish heaps. My chief objection to the machine is that it exists only for an end and ignores, must ignore, the means, except in so far as the perfect functioning of the means is necessary to the end. The machine is not only a mechanism, it is a state of mind that existed thousands of years earlier than any but the crudest and simplest mechanism. It is a state of mind which for thousands of years has been aiming at an age like the present, during which the machine will go from triumph to triumph, and end by realizing its millennial endeavor to reduce the individual to a robot.

It need scarcely be remarked that a machine age as just described, or rather the machine mind, tends invariably toward not only authoritarian but totalitarian rule, practiced in dynastic Egypt more than five thousand years ago, reducing its mass of individuals to a slave-mindedness known as fellahism, from which indeed they have never recovered.

Wonder of wonders. Now comes the most efficiently totalitarian of all regimes, now come the Nazis to free the rest of Europe, perhaps the rest of the world, from the machine! They are prepared to sacrifice themselves to it, mind and body. They will now undertake all the work that can be done only by the completest submission to the machine, and they mean to go so far in self-sacrifice as to forbid and prevent other peoples from using it. No heavy industries, no trusts elsewhere. They alone are to sweat, and toil, and moil, producing everything that the most elaborate, the most complicated, the most delicate machines can produce.

The other countries will return to agriculture, to hoe culture, to horticulture, to glass-blowing, to the cottage and other charming industries that educate and amuse mind and eye, and humanize the worker. The people of these countries will be free to change about, to employ their time as the seasons and their own inclination direct. They will work and play, play and work all day long, as individuals, as freemen almost. They will be emancipated from the slavery of the machine and from turning into robots; they will be men and women again. Their towns, their countryside, their hills and valleys will be cleaned of the ugliness, the belching chimneys, the slag, the excrements piled up by the heavy industries. The Mediterranean world, with its three peninsulas and its frame of mountains, with its islands and islets, will be saved from deturpation and end by forgetting the machine age.

So the Nazis will bring about what I have been desiring and even yearning for: the return to the Italy and Greece and Spain of Winckelmann, of Goethe, of Washington Irving, of Tischbein, of the Nazarenes and the Romantics. I ought to be delighted and grateful. Why am I not? *È' il modo che m'offende.*

April 21st

GIVEN HUMAN NATURE, there is perhaps no way but violence
to bring about rapid and large-scale changes. The Nazis may be
instruments in the hand of a power making for good, no matter
how bloodily, how bestially, how recklessly, how heartlessly. They
know not what they do. They started out with the idea of de-
Judaizing, de-Bohemianizing, de-Polonizing the German people
and of bringing back into the fold all the groups that were being
lost to the Fatherland. Having achieved this, they suddenly forgot
their initial intention, and started attacking other peoples and proceeded from conquest to conquest. In a few weeks they may be
masters of the entire European Continent and before long of the
whole Eurasian land mass.

Force would unite this vast territory with its nations, tribes, and
clans in a way that centuries of persuasion have not succeeded in
bringing about. It would be unpleasant enough at first, but in the
course of some decades or even a century—a mere instant in the
course of history—the subdued peoples would begin to recover,
the Nazis to tire of totalitarianism and its methods, and Eurasia
might shake down or, at least, Europe might settle into a commonwealth of peoples, learning little by little to respect each other's
individuality, and to understand that their own might profit by
doing so.

I ought to be deeply grateful to the Nazis for another result
which they are bringing about, little though they have planned it.
They are obliging the English-speaking nations the earth over to
unite into an Anglo-Saxon constellation. It is a dream I dreamt for
decades, but it seemed destined to remain a dream for centuries if
not forever. The Nazis are bringing it about so quickly that it may
be completed before the war is over.

And what has become of the self-sufficiency, the autarchy Germany has been flirting with since the days of her economist List a
century ago; and what of the Central European economy so ar-
dently preached by Naumann during the last war? Nazism was

founded on the first, violently took up the second, and now has dropped both. For this also one cannot be too grateful. Autarchy, carried through with German thoroughness, would have brought into each country a Merovingian economy with all its narrowing, confining consequences.

April 28th

IT IS A GREAT PITY that Continental people, with the rarest exceptions, have so little acquaintance with the mind and character of England as a country, and of the English as a people; they are ready to believe anything of them. In the Middle Ages the Englishmen were credited with having tails. What Continental people will affirm about them today is nearly as absurd but not so harmless.

There is the British Intelligence Service, omnipresent, omnipotent, utterly unscrupulous, to account for any death or uprising, or disaster at all unexpected, or anything that crosses the aims of this or that Continental government. Just now I have heard of two bits of gossip regarding English policy. One is that the Egyptians are being kept under by the threat that if they are disloyal or make trouble for England, the English will turn the Nile from its course and reduce Egypt to a desert. I have tried in vain to convince my Italian friends not only that it was beyond present human power to achieve such a purpose, but that it would not occur to English people to think of such a measure. Another thing that scarcely would enter an English head is believed here by many. It is that the English arranged their entire campaign in the Near East so as to conquer Abyssinia by a certain date, which date was the anniversary of the Italian *Giorno dell'Impero,* the day when Mussolini declared the annexation of Abyssinia. I doubt whether anything remoter from the English way of feeling could be invented. Not so far from Continental ways! Witness Versailles!

May 5th

YESTERDAY a friend was here, a Roman of good family, closely related to the late Cardinal Vannutelli and thus in touch with the Vatican. He told me that soon after the death of Pope Benedict XV, his own father was dying. A priest was called in, but the father refused to see him. Thinking to comfort the son, the priest said: "Don't take it hard. Such things will happen nowadays. Why, the late Holy Father on his deathbed sent away the priests with: 'Off with you, the play is over'" (*la commedia è finita*). His Holiness surely meant *commedia* as *divina*, Divine Comedy like the title of Dante's masterpiece.

May 6th

DR. NEUMANN, the famous throat, nose, and ear specialist of Vienna, spoke one day in my hearing of Jews as "coreligionists." I quizzed him and asked him whether he believed in the Pentateuch and in the Torah, whether he followed any of the precepts, rules, and restrictions of the rabbinical code, and whether he believed in a God at all. "No, he did not." Then why did he speak of the Jews as his "coreligionists"? I pointed out to him that the term did not suit his case at all. Nor did the term "fellow sufferers," because it was too general. The only phrase that exactly labeled his case was "fellow scapegoats."

Casa al Dono, Vallombrosa. August 25th

YESTERDAY the ex-Prime Minister Orlando was here for luncheon. He is a sturdy, thick-set, and yet not ill-proportioned elderly man who, apart from the white hair which covers his head thickly, does not remotely show his age. He is in his eighty-second year and looks full ten years younger. Light and bright blue eyes, regular features, a fine mouth. He came all the way on foot from his own villa. Although but across the ravine and perhaps not a mile away as the crow flies, it is as a walk neither short nor easy. One has a long and fatiguing climb after descending to the brook which runs through the bottom of the same ravine. Orlando had been to mass at the rustic church of San Miniato in Alpe, half a mile away from here, and at eleven was strolling up to our gate with his daughter Carlotta and her husband Garabelli. They remained till 3 P.M. Orlando seldom silent for more than a minute at a time. He is an unflagging and brilliant talker. A pleasant clear voice although his Sicilian pronunciation at times veiled the shape of a phrase. Only for an instant. He enjoys talking and evidently regards it as his most peculiar gift. He believes in his powers of improvisation and oratory, and speaks of both not boastfully but descriptively as a fact there was no more need to be modest about than to be proud of. He held my attention, whatever he was saying.

Although busier as a lawyer than ever, he finds time to write about the Peace Conference of 1919. I was nothing but ears and eyes when he told us this and my attentive looks encouraged him to go on. Quickly he came to President Wilson.

All the evils that have happened since are due to Wilson's hostility to Italy. He refused to send troops to Italy. He would not listen to reason the moment it was a question of Italy's claims to Yugoslav territory. He liked Orlando personally and hated to make him unhappy. He insisted on giving Italy more of the South Tyrol than she ever claimed, and the claim itself had been encouraged (if I do not misquote Orlando) by Wilson. When the differences got acute the latter went so far as to propose Constantinople to the Italians.

Orlando went on to say that on almost every other point Wilson grew more and more supple and ready to compromise and yield. Only on the question of Yugoslavia he remained adamant.

By elimination of every other conceivable reason, Orlando came to the conclusion that the Yugoslavs had some kind of stranglehold on Wilson. Of what nature he did not know, but of its effectiveness he was certain.

Is it not possible that Wilson and the American people behind

him were horrified at the idea that Italy should aggrandize herself
at the expense of the small nation to save which from Austrian
greed the war had been started?

But this hypothesis is one not easily entertained by any Continental European, unless perhaps by a Scandinavian, seeing that
he considers it right, virile, heroic to fall upon a neighbor and do
what he likes with him and his. So much do Continental Europeans still consider this right as universally axiomatic that to them
any word against it is written down, with contempt and indignation, as gross and insulting hypocrisy.

While Continental Europeans continue to hold these views it
is all but hopeless to expect good will and peace in the world.
Sooner or later one or the other will fall on his neighbor. The average European does not seem to feel free until he succeeds in enslaving and oppressing others.

November 3d

ITALIAN NATIONALISTS envy our riches, call us "plutocrats,"
and incite their fellow subjects to insult us with cries of *"detentori
di dollari, detentori di sterline."* My retort is that they are heliocrats. Our riches may easily fail us, may vanish into thin air, as so
often happens in moments of financial crisis, or be taken from us
by dishonest agents, by tax collectors, etc., etc. No power on earth
can deprive Italians of their heliocracy, the riches stored up in the
sun for their disposal, as for no other white people. They nevertheless are among the most discontented mortals known to me, always complaining of their poverty, their indigence, of the unfair
distribution of the world's goods, of their having no coal, no iron,
no precious metals, no cotton, etc., etc. When you point to the sun
that enables them to live at half the outlay that it costs us Northerners, and to their own proverb which speaks of the sun as half a
meal and the sun as father of the poor, they answer that you can't
sell any of it or hand it on to your heirs.

That is true enough and leads one to the reflection that when
you own a thing in common, and cannot cash it or exchange your

share in it for something else you desire at the moment, your ownership is dust and ashes.

If ownership in the sun is so little appreciated by the individuals who share its indivisible, inalienable wealth as to leave them dissatisfied, rebellious, and ready to run amok against people who have riches they can do what they like with, does it not make one ask what would happen under Communism, where all wealth would be indivisible and inalienable? The individual would have to be painfully and thoroughly reconditioned before he could be happy without the right to own something he could do what he liked with. I doubt whether human nature could stand such a restriction on one of its chief demands on life, the enjoyment of power as exercised in making and spending money.

The conduct of the Italian heliocrats makes me wonder whether we Northerners, detainers of sterling and dollars, could not retort and say: "You do not appreciate your benefits. You see no good in all that the sun is shedding upon you. Though you toil not, neither do you spin. You long for Essen, for Glasgow, for oil fields and diamond mines, and for the hell their presence produces. Very well, you shall have them. Long enough have you enjoyed the blessings of the sun, so long that you have ceased to regard them as benefits or to be as much as aware of them. It is time you gave place to the miners and operatives of Wales and Pennsylvania, of Baku and Batum, of the burning sands of Iraq and the grim deserts of Iran. To them shall you go, and at once. Let others come who will appreciate, more than you do, what it is to live in an earthly paradise like Italy."

November 6th

As I was driving up the road yesterday afternoon, in a light mist which gave a somewhat unreal aspect to the landscape, I suddenly beheld striding before me tall, fair, well-shaped men in sporting jackets and short breeches, a costume easily neolithic. For part of a second I was transported to the Scottish Highlands, and wondered whether I had not Fingal and other Ossianic heroes before me. Then I recalled that there were superior British officers being held as prisoners in the castle I had just passed. Sure enough, little fellows in greenish gray coats with guns in their hands ran along before, behind, and at the sides of these Northern giants. So the Normans must have looked who, though a handful, conquered Apulia, Calabria, and Sicily, establishing an empire that lasted long enough to decide West Mediterranean history for centuries.

December 17th

IN MECCA there congregate every species, type, and color of human being. What unites and identifies them all as of the true faith is their genuflections, prostrations, and ejaculations—not words and prayers and sentences that can easily be learned, whereas the first are difficult to acquire after early and unconscious childhood.

Thus the state of mind of a convert to Catholicism can never be the same as that of a born Catholic. The convert will always overformulate, overintellectualize, overdogmatize, because as a grownup the appeals for his conversion have necessarily been mental rather than emotional, excepting, of course, in rare cases, of which St. Paul is the type. This must be so particularly where Jewish converts are concerned. They cannot entertain the same instinctive attitude, have the same automatic reactions, as one who was suckled on Christian myths and values with his mother's milk, or in his pre-self-conscious years.

This applies almost as much to naturalization as to conversion, now that the only effective religion is nationality. Unless one has taken its fetishes, its aspirations, its ambitions, its indignations, its hates in the pre-self-conscious years before one could criticize them, one will never be as a native. One will either be coldly utilitarian or try to identify oneself with the mind and heart of the nation. As, however, the effort is inevitably deliberate and not instinctive and spontaneous, it is bound to be more explicit, more reasoned, and, by that very fact, more dogmatic, more aggressive, than the native's feeling for his own country.

Sure enough! Among the most rabid Italian nationalists, or

wide-sweeping annexationists, among Italian patriots whose patriotism consists more in hating other people than loving one's own,
are the offspring of English and worse still of American mothers.
They have invariably been "patridiotic," as I call it, that is to say
grossly nationalistic for the land of their fathers, as if they felt the
need of justifying themselves for having had an Anglo-Saxon
mother, from whom, in pre-self-conscious years, they could not
imbibe the national folk prejudices of their fathers.

How about the Jews who are natives of the lands they live in,
and have been living in long before the ancestors of the greater
number of its present inhabitants settled there? Yes, physically
they may be descended from forebears who have been there
longer than those of their fellow subjects, but spiritually they have
not, till recently, partaken of the political and religious life of the
rest of the community. They are therefore, in their native lands,
like recently naturalized aliens, and the more so as those of them
that still cling to the synagogue cannot feel in every respect like
the overwhelming majority brought up as Christians.

Jews too, then, whether as converts to Catholicism or to nationalism, tend to exaggerate manifestations of their faith-patriotism.
It is notorious that converted Jews are apt to turn bitterly and rag-
ingly anti-Semite; and by "converted" I refer this time not to religion alone but to standards of living, feeling, and thinking.

I am not concerned just now with the converts from Judaism to
Christianity, although even today some of the most passionate and
effective defenders of Thomism and Neo-Catholicism are born
Jews. It is in the political field where I am shocked by the super-
patriotism of German, Italian, and French Jews.

The fact first identified by Heine, namely, that a Jew to be taken
for silver must be of gold, militates against his being as much a
matter-of-course citizen as his other fellow beings in the same
land. He has to force his qualities to bring them into evidence, to
court approval.

The same applies to sons of Anglo-Saxon mothers in foreign
lands, and, of course, to all members of a permanent minority anywhere.

December 18th

NEO-CATHOLICS in particular, but all apologists for and defenders of their Church or the foreign policy of their nation, talk up to a point rationally and talk my language—I mean a language we have in common. Suddenly they go off at a tangent and behave like the asylum guard who was showing an inspector around a madhouse. This guard explained every case quietly and feelingly until they came to one patient who made him cry out: "This is the craziest individual in the asylum. He believes he is God and will not see that it is I who am God!" I do not mean that they believe they are God; but their plunge into an irrational, a magic universe is as unexpected.

December 20th

WAR is a barbarous affair, but it is necessary for so long as we remain the barbarians that we are, violently impatient, unable to use our reason, and thus to learn what we are and what our adversaries are worth, instead of letting wishful thinking flatter us into overestimates of our own might. War is necessary because it is desirable that after a too burdensome accumulation of hubristic self-confidence we should come to a trial of strength. When this is done seriously and with unquestionable results, we take the ensuing situation as something to build on, and for a time we look facts in the face and use them for repairing our old or for designing a new House of Life.

Here let me put in a parenthesis and say that the last war—the one of 1914–1918—failed to bring about a settlement, because though way down it was a struggle between France and Germany, the French would not have got the better of their enemies but for the aid of the English, the Russians and the Americans. The French could not fool themselves into believing either that, without this aid, they would have been victorious or that they would get the Germans to agree that they had been beaten by the

French alone. France feared her foe, though conquered, more than ever before, and her consequent conduct served only to inflame the vindictiveness and conceit of the Germans. Hence the present war—hence chiefly, if not only.

The part of me that is a relatively dispassionate student of history and politics is as pleased with the Japanese attack on the U. S. A. as a chemist may be who is eager to see how two elements will behave whose reciprocal reactions are not fully known.

Americans who, above all others, have been preaching for generations contempt for talk and the value of action, have found such apt pupils in the so recently petted Japanese that these have caught them not napping but talking, and have acted while the Americans kept discussing. Comical it is that, knowing that the Americans were still in a conversational mood, they sent a special negotiator to make them fancy that they, the Japanese, also were disposed to go on talking.

They, the Japs, had meanwhile made the most precise and detailed preparations, and while appeasing talk was going on in Washington, Tokyo bombarded, ignited, exploded, smashed, invaded from the air, by sea, on land every American as well as every British position within reach.

The initial advantage of the Japanese is most spectacular and a marvelous pick-me-up for their allies as well as for their own populations. Yet—is it a *frischer, froher Krieg* like the Franco-German War of 1870, or is it simply Malays running amok? And by the way, we must not forget that it is the Malay strain in the Jap that makes a fighter of him.

It is hard to believe—hard for me, at least—that the Japanese will not be stopped. Assume that they will not, and that the British will be driven out of all their possessions this side of Burma, and we Americans compelled to withdraw to the Sandwich Islands or even to our own mainland.

Would the Japanese be wise enough to wait and digest the Anglo-Saxon as well as Dutch possessions that they had taken? Would a conqueror know, for once in history, where and when to stop? Would they not attack Burma and threaten India, Australia,

New Zealand? Would they know how to persuade the conquered peoples that, under the circumstances, they, the Japanese, were the least possible evil? If not, could they afford to occupy these wide-flung vast territories, and hold them down with air and naval and land forces? If they turned out to have the skill and the strength to maintain themselves, and to reconcile an adequate number of the vanquished, they might play in Asia the part played by the Normans in Europe in the eleventh and twelfth centuries. Even if, owing to their being relatively so few, they ended by being absorbed by their subjects, they might modify these as advantageously as the Saxons were manifested by their more adventurous kinsmen from across the Channel.

Could and would the Anglo-Saxon peoples sit down under this "New Order"? If they did, then it is well over with their "superiority," which so puzzled French students of politics not long ago.

They are expansive peoples. Their family is centrifugal and not, like other families, centripetal. There is no cry of *Ma mère* and *mia mamma* and whatever the Japanese equivalent, to keep them unweaned and to pull them back to mother's bosom. They leave home with the will to stay away.

Then they are explorers, pioneers, inventors, openers out of new territories, and know how to make something out of them, recklessly, rashly, hastily perhaps but doing endlessly more than anybody else has done in the last few hundred years. They are not cuckoos waiting for well-built nests to occupy. Thus the Japanese have been in possession of Korea for nearly fifty years and of Manchuria for nearly twenty. To neither have they come as colonists, like the British in America, in Africa, in Australasia, but only like the same British in India, with the significant difference, however, that in India the British have invested not only brains but capital, have not merely exploited but benefited in a thousand ways.

It may be doubted that the English-speaking people would sit down to being excluded from the Far East, even if the Japs proceeded no further in Asia and Oceania. A Japanese victory now could scarcely be more than an armistice to last only till their adversaries got ready to attack them. Fear of attack would keep the

Japs in a state of continuous tension, unable to turn their minds to productive matters. The determination to oust them would tend to militarize the Anglo-Saxons. I am not sure that a militarized United States, with all its contiguous material resources and power, would behave as England has done. It might turn into a conquering, annexing, world-domineering empire, and might behave no better than its predecessors in the past. Europe might live to regret the invisible, inaudible hegemony of the sea-minded English, with their readiness to live and let live, and to share with whoever was disposed to work with them.

There remains another possible result of a Japanese victory or, even, defeat. It is that the Chinese fighting desperately against the Japs, if the struggle lasts long enough, may learn not only to be good soldiers but accurate and punctual organizers as well as loyal administrators, and find themselves in a position to start on a career of military adventure whether against the Japanese or to begin with under them. If they did, who could withstand them? From Han to Yuan the Chinese drives westward not only took them far towards the Caspian but initiated movements which, like tidal waves, reached Europe and threatened to overwhelm it.

These considerations are not practical politics, I know; yet much that is murderous and destructive could be avoided if they were not altogether absent from the minds of practical politicians.

December 23d

I SPOKE two or three days ago of the Japanese having been the pets of the American public. Their popularity was founded first on the fact that they were rediscovered, so to speak, by our Commodore Perry. Then came Mitford's *Tales of Old Japan* and the avalanche of netsukes, swordguards, lacquers, ceramics, silks, screens, colored prints, kakemonos, makemonos, and other *objets d'art*. They told us of an idyllic people, living exquisitely artistic lives, brave, no doubt, and ready to defend themselves, with a delicate sense of honor, but far from aggressive. Followed Lafcadio Hearn, with volume after volume of momentarily captivating prose-poetry about the Japanese soul, the Japanese heart, the Japanese mind. Even when they attacked the Russians without warning we were delighted and fancied that these Japs defended our own ideals.

Now that they have attacked us in the same way, the legendary Japan of Hearn has faded and we ask ourselves how we could have been so silly as to be taken in.

Before going further I want to say that Hearn lived to write *Japan, an Appreciation,* which gave a very different picture, a far less attractive, a more stern, an even forbidding picture of this people. Few read this valuable book. His revulsion of feeling was bound to come, seeing he was no fool, nor hireling propagandist. It was perhaps expedited by what happened to him directly he had become a Japanese subject, a step to which his enthusiastic sympathy led him. He was at the time professor of English at Tokyo. The minister of public instruction came to thank him, the American, the famous author, the glorifier of Japan, for having done that country the great honor of becoming its subject. As he was leaving he observed casually and with a twirl of his fan: "You are, of course, aware, Professor Hearn, that as a Japanese subject you now will receive but half the salary you enjoyed as a foreigner."

How is it that we were taken in by the Japanese and did not realize that "they"—in so far as one can apply that pronoun to an entire people—that they had much more in common with the Malay running amok, or the Siberian tiger preparing to spring, than with folk whom we assume to be charming because they are so daintily, delicately artistic!

I am reminded of a visit we had many years ago, during the height of enthusiasm for Japan. It was of a highborn lady of that land who was at the head of a school for girls of the noblest houses. We talked of education and she complained of her difficulties. We thought they were financial or perhaps administrative. Not at all. She went on to say that we could not imagine what cruel, ferocious, untamable savages these young things were, and how hard it was to lick them into shape. It required an iron discipline, and nothing less could keep law and order among a people like hers with instincts still so wild, so unruly, so bloodthirsty.

The error results from our almost ineradicable belief that the art of a people is the transcript of its workaday actuality, whether in family or public life.

That is seldom the case, and when it is it tends to be a caricature nearer, no doubt, to what is called reality but yet not reality. "Realistic" art seldom escapes caricature and is no more representative than classical, idealistic, idyllic art. Justly we discard the deliberate malformations and monstrosities, often pornographic, that Japanese no less than Greek art abounds in. We regard such things as grossly exceptional and do not let them touch our illusion about the art in general.

Art is not based on actuality but on the wishes, dreams, and aspirations of a people. Even the art of today has no other source. In the same way that we have had enough of reason, of free order, of elastic as well as plastic government because we get bored with our civilization despite its advantages and amenities, so we get satiated with all, and more than all, we can take in of what has hitherto meant art, and crave instead for the confused, the enigmatical, the ugly, the absurd, the puzzling.

No doubt whatever that the Japanese, like the Greeks, like the Chinese, like Europeans ever since the twelfth century, have represented in their art what they hoped life would someday yield, but not what it gave them already. Greek actuality was, except for a small number, much less livable, not to speak of its being so much less secure, than it is now. Hence the longing for a mode of existence, an order, a clarity, a distinction, a charm, a loveliness that actuality seldom if ever could realize and art alone could offer for contemplation at least.

December 24th

JAPANESE LIFE in even its highest moments could not have been exactly as pictured in Murasaki's *Tale of Genji*. Life there was lived "above the clouds," was given over to passing the days, and nights, and hours in various artistic occupations, and in delicate refined human relations, as well as in sweet love-making with its bitter lees. The men of the Olympus were the emperor and his court. They governed, they administrated, they commanded, they must have had no end of tasks, of scarcely soluble problems, of boring duties. Scarcely a word of all this. It offers no more complete, no more faithful picture of life as lived in Japan toward the year 1000 than Dante's *Vita Nuova* does of Florentine life toward 1300.

There is perhaps no more elaborately refined verse than Turkish. Yet the cruelty and perversity of the Turks had no limits. Nero died exclaiming, "What an artist perishes with me!" Caligula was a happy "interior decorator" and perhaps a good one.

1942

January 1st

I BEGIN the New Year of 1942 as a civilian prisoner, in this Italy where I have resided for fifty-four years, in this Florence where I have lived, first, at 24 Lungarno Acciaiuoli, then at Villa Kraus, Fiesole, then at Camerata, and since 1900 in this house of our own, I Tatti. Of all the improbabilities that could have been suggested when I first trod its earth in September, 1888, none would have seemed more fantastic than that in my lifetime Italy would be at war with the United States. Nor would it have sounded less absurd during the "Great War," or the years following, when America was the idolized model of the Italian public.

Yet here we are and here I am. We have not blundered into remaining here. We have done so after due consideration and despite orders from Washington, prayers of friends at home, and the warnings, the urgent advice of people devoted to us here.

Many of the reasons for staying I will not go into, as they are of more or less material nature; the chiefest being that, given Mary's physical condition, the journey home, under recent circumstances, would have been difficult, and more difficult still taking up life over there at our age.

The spiritual reasons are more interesting. They are three:

In the first place, I felt so identified with the people, I mean the so deeply humanized majority of Italians, that I could not face deserting them in a moment like this, little as anybody would have felt that I was deserting them, and much as many would have been pleased at having got rid of such a nuisance as these regarded me.

Then came the consideration, deepest down in me, that if I returned home or went even to Switzerland, it would be hard, if not impossible, to avoid serving in some capacity against this Italy which I love so much, against this people who will have to pay the piper no matter who called the tune.

This last, I now feel, was the determining factor in the decision to stay on and risk it.

The third consideration is one of curiosity. I want to round off my acquaintance with the Italian people as a whole, by seeing how we shall be treated. I have cherished the hope, amounting almost to a conviction, that given the conventions of war, we shall be treated as humanely as possible.

I should be disappointed if we were not, and delighted if we were—both disappointment and delight being of an even more aesthetical than practical nature. Despite all blemishes inherent in human nature, my idea of the Italian people is a picture that I have been painting, as it were, for more than half a century; and I am eager to see how it will be perfected, *en beauté* or otherwise.

Friends in Rome are alarmed, fear that the government, though having the best intentions, may be compelled by "public opinion" to take measures against me. These friends urge me to lie low and let people forget me. To see nobody, so that talk about me will die down.

Will it? Most of it is pure invention, and what is to prevent its continuing? Thus the other day a Florentine gentleman asked Maestro Gui whether he had not heard that the British war prisoners confined above me in the castle of Vincigliata were frequently having tea with me at I Tatti.

Measures against me might mean being ordered to leave my paradise of a house, and to be exiled to some village where one would perish of cold.

Whence this bitter hostility against me on the part of persons

I do not so much as know by sight, except one or possibly two?
The leading and most active of these enemies is the already mentioned Florentine. I have never exchanged ten consecutive words
with him, and I do not remember meeting him even casually more
than twice or possibly thrice. Why this war against me? I cannot
recall ever getting in his way, or having anything to do with him
except once in an official manner. It was like this. While he was
in office as *Podestà,* commissioner as we should say (not mayor)
of Florence, the town wanted to widen the street running through
Ponte a Mensola. This could be done only with my land. I was
asked to sell what they needed, I refused to sell, but I let them
have it as a gift. He is a patriot (which of course means an impe-
rialist and annexationist), he is devoted to the Fascist regime and a
stout believer in the "Protocol of the Elders of Israel." Does he
take me for one? But there is a heat and persistence in the hostile
group which he leads that smells of personal hatred stoking the
fire of political differences.

I can guess what this hatred is based on, but it would take the
gifts and style of a Saint-Simon and his remote successor Proust to
go into it in a convincing way. The central fact seems to be that
he and his clan cannot bear that any of their society, let alone
their own sort, should frequent us. Their chief charge against me
is that I am debauching the snow-white lambs of his fold and that
instead of being inculcated with the teachings of Hitler and Rosenberg they may imbibe the "Judeo-demo-plutocratic" milk of
humaneness.

"He is crazy on the subject of anti-Semitism but so sincere," say
his friends, as if being "sincere" justified his conduct. In that case
any cannibal conduct is justified.

I cannot follow the convention that "sincerity" is an excuse and
even justification.

To begin with, what does the average man or woman mean by
the word "sincerity" and the word "sincere"? They mean, probably, that it implies saying what one thinks and believes. Why
should that be approved or even admired!

Few have the right to claim "sincerity" as I would define it. It should mean that when a proposition is presented to a person with a mind trained in critical investigation, he should do his utmost to examine it in order to reach an unprejudiced, logical conclusion. How many, in a given number of individuals, have the right to claim the capacity for "sincerity" as just defined? As it is, a premium is set for those who are too stupid, too ignorant to know or to understand what is involved. The less competent they are to have an opinion, the more likely they are to hold it "sincerely."

It is these "sincere" folk who constitute one of the great dangers to a progressively human society. Evil is a species of microbe that can be carried only by the tolerably healthy, in this case tolerably decent, respectable, well-placed people. Left to their own devices, evildoers soon come to the end of their tether. As out-and-out criminals—I mean vulgar gangsters, bank robbers, embezzlers, speculators, bribable officials—they have a short run. Even in our commonwealths, so far from perfect, they do relatively little harm. Serious evil attitudinizes, as Good, before the "sincere," who cannot pierce the thin imposture, and are so taken in by it that they are ready to defend it till it comes down on them like the hammer on the head of the ox in the slaughterhouse.

No, give me rather the "insincere" people who know to the bottom what they are about. We can approach them as a matter of business, drive a bargain with them, and make it worth their while to serve us with their talents and their experience.

January 3d

My "ENEMIES" seem to insist that, if I am suffered to remain in my own house and home, it must be as an "untouchable," as a tabooed person not to be approached. They cannot fear the contagion of my other-mindedness, for one of the many accusations brought against me is that I see only people of my "subversive" way of thinking. They must therefore be hoping to inflict punishment by depriving me of company.

How often have my "enemies," here, there, and everywhere, plotted to do this or that and done it successfully enough from their point of view, only to deprive me as a rule of something that no doubt would have distressed them but not me. This time I am isolated. Nobody comes near me. The fact is that for a while, at any rate, I do not know for how long, I am glad to be left alone. Even recently I have been seeing too many people for either pleasure or health.

One goes on seeing people, all but a few of whom one can dispense with. They afford so little stimulus, or life-enhancement of any kind. They come for an outing, for a better meal than they may get usually, and with the hope of picking up something to repeat, or to boast of. I do not grumble and am tolerably cordial, enough to mask my indifference. They have wearied me and I am glad to be without them. In ordinary circumstances it is so hard to find a polite way of getting rid of bores. Even outboring them won't do, as they come for the prestige of being received.

How conventional one can go on being about company! It is not unlike making oneself believe that one is glad to hear from So-and-so. Deep down very few letters that I receive touch me or even interest me. And yet I go on believing that I miss them, and get alarmed when they are delayed too long. In the case of real intimates that is true, but the glimpse of their writing on an envelope suffices. I know they are alive and learn where they were on a given date. The content matters little except in the rarest cases.

In Herodotus I read this morning a passage that bears on my situation (VII, 10, translated by A. D. Godley in Loeb Classics). Artabanus says to his nephew Xerxes: "Calumny is a very gross business, there are two in it that do, and one that suffers wrong. He that utters the calumny wrongs another, accusing an absent man, and the other does a wrong likewise in that he is overpersuaded before he has learnt the whole truth; and he that is absent, and hears not what is said of him, suffers wrong in the matter being maligned by the one, and condemned by the other."

It has occurred to me again and again on returning to London or Paris or New York after an absence of perhaps three, four, or five years, to hear for the first time of accusations brought against me that meanwhile had had ample time to spread, seeing there was no reason why they should not be believed. Nobody is more exposed than one whose name is known to people who can attach nothing to it, having no acquaintance with the man bearing the name, or with any friends of his. It is in human nature to want to hear something besides the name; and something of a disparaging nature is more savory and therefore more likely to be remembered than anything favorable.

Even here in Florence where I reside, I am absent as far as all but a few are concerned. I hardly ever go out, not even to my best friends'. Having lived here for a half century, at least, and having for the last forty years enjoyed a certain position, I am known by name to many. Naturally, they are glad to pick up anything about me. What they pick up is not likely to be good or true. Against a person who will not solicit the much-sought-for privileges of a society, there is a certain resentment that makes its members inclined to believe anything against him. Then there are one's resident countrymen (and countrywomen) who dislike one for keeping aloof, and resent not being invited and welcomed.

*　　*　　*

My hairdresser this morning told me that when he was a little boy he lived at La Lastra on the Via Bolognese. Every day Prince Demidoff drove from his villa into Florence and, as he passed in his coach and four through the hamlets on the roadside, would throw out shining copper coins to the children. The elder brother was working where the Prince's agent every day brought a bag of coppers to be cleaned with acids, and furbished up to look as if fresh from the mint. By the way, my barber went to work himself when he was eight years old, walking into town early and returning late, a chunk of bread for his midday meal, and a copper for onions and figs. "Ah, but how happy we were then, wanting so little and getting it."

*　　*　　*

Read in Ruskin's letters to Norton, the end of December, 1858, about his conversion to life, away from evangelicalism. He had been to a dreary gray Waldensian conventicle at Turin and then went to the picture gallery and fell in love with a Paolo Veronese. He fell in love with it, began to question whether the connection between art and puritan Christianity was as close as he used to believe, and regretted his previous publications.

He wrote December 28th: "I want to macadamize some new roads to heaven with broken fools' heads."

January 5th

"THERE ARE TALENTS made for scientific, formulated truth, reached methodically by analysis and synthesis. There are others for whom this truth is too abstract, too bald, besides being unswerving as well as devitalized—talents in short whom truth can reach only when it is presented through life. Emotionally, Amiel belonged to the second; by his mental schooling and habits, to the first category. His wavering personal feelings, mounting from the fathomless depths of his nature, were too strong to allow him to attain the 'objectivity' of the philosophical thinker or the scientific investigator. Yet he longed for the objectivity to be able to exchange the irrational that was his private affair for the rational entertained universally. But this again did not satisfy him: the universal is the nought; the sentient subject only is alive.

"Against this contradiction, both his creative powers and his intellect broke down. In an age when criticism and creation were unusually opposed, because critical scientific reasoning, which should only accompany, check, and collect, claimed to govern creation; in such an age one has to be overwhelmingly one-sided to remain in the realm of genuine creativeness. Amiel, however, was nothing if not many-sided, centripetal, protean. He hovered, his life long, between the two contrasted activities, between science and art, between analysis and presentation." (Heinrich Homberger, *Selbstgespräche*, pp. 134–135, written in 1866.)

Excellent as the above is as a description of Amiel's mental constitution, it fails to realize that he nevertheless was creative. He succeeded in analyzing and recording a character and situation alike, on terms so accessible to less gifted individuals of his own kind that it helps them to understand their own souls as they never would have otherwise. That surely is one of the principal functions of literature as an art.

I am as split-up a nature as Amiel. I am perhaps as cultured, perhaps even as intellectual, but I have nothing of his art. Wherefore I have scarcely attempted and certainly have not succeeded in writing about myself in a way that could manifest to even the most kindred spirits visions of themselves that lay hidden too well to be perceived more than dimly, if at all.

January 6th

FINISHED *Waverley*, which I had never read before. I enjoyed it because I unconsciously swing over from an aesthetic to a scholarly interest. The first half, and much of the rest, is ethnology, manners, customs, history in the raw and not art at all. The rest is delightful enough as narrative but not as character. The pedantic laird is too much of a caricature, the hero, as heroes usually do, remains shadowy. Rose does not exist; Flora is too much of a piece. The figures that stand out are the Chevalier as a charming sketch, and Fergus, although the latter is good only in parts, which somehow do not make a whole.

How account for the sudden and great popularity of *Waverley*? I am too uninformed as to what preceded it. Was it the newness of the subject matter for which perhaps *Ossian* had prepared the public? Was it a reaction against the novel of mystery and horror on the one hand, and on the other against the novel of commonplace ordinary society?

In the hero of *Waverley*—in Edward, I mean—there is more than a little that is autobiographical—not infrequent in a first novel.

January 9th

READ IN LAST NUMBER of *Forschungen und Fortschritte* two articles. A very long one on origin of Shakespeare's name, rebutting various attempts made by English scholars to trace it back to the Norman conquerors. Strange how snobbish scholars and men of letters can be, and how seldom they miss a chance of oozing, and spraying, if not loudly expressing, contempt for themselves as a class, attributing merit to their own members when it can be proved to their, the scholars', satisfaction that they, the great among themselves, Shakespeare in this case, were of gentle birth!

The other article was about another ice age being due in about five thousand years. Will science in the interval find ways of obviating its consequences? Even now Finland and northernmost Scandinavia manage to carry on a highly civilized existence. The greater part of Central, let alone Western, Europe may not be worse off under an ice age than those regions are now. Progress in heating and lighting may have rendered possible all sorts of comforting alleviations, may have got so far as to prevent the glacier's advancing to cake with ice the neighboring land. *Tutto può darsi!*

So this prediction, although of so cosmic a nature, has not upset me.

Twice have I been upset, in the sense that my universe tottered. Once in Cambridge, Massachusetts, when walking down Brattle Street to dine with Miss Grace, the noble and highly cultured sister of Professor C. E. Norton, a friend convinced me that they had succeeded in disintegrating the atom. I felt dizzy with nothing to cling to for support, now that my ultimate, as I then and there realized, the atom, had been shattered. The other time was when the Austrian and German imperial houses collapsed, dragging all princes, potentates, and powers down with them. The fall of Tsardom did not affect me as a cosmic catastrophe, for as a grownup I never had much faith in its stability. But Austria and still more Germany!

The fact is that, as a youth and young man, I was so convinced of the stability of the universe I was bred into, and accepted as a matter of course, that no dissatisfaction of mine, no crying need of change, no projected reforms, could remotely touch it. I suspect most young people are still in the same state of mind, and their slings and arrows are hurled so joyously at society because they do not dream of shaking it.

❊ ❊ ❊

Much talk of disarmament after this war. No artillery, no submarines, no aircraft to be allowed the vanquished. Very good and relatively easy to achieve; but how useless if hearts and minds are not disarmed! The best beginning for that kind of disarmament would be: to allow no schoolbooks concerned with the teaching of any kind of history, not only political but cultural history as well, that had not been approved by the disarming powers. Later, whatever international body will be set up to control our destinies should see to it that history is taught nowhere the way it has been taught in recent decades, everywhere, with the exception of England. There a serious effort was made in the last thirty years to inculcate it decently.

❊ ❊ ❊

Soon after the Russians occupied Galicia in the autumn of 1939, Dorothy Palffy reported that their equipment both in arms and in clothes was of the poorest. For instance, officers even had no waistcoats and some no underclothes under their tunics, many nothing under their overcoats. They seemed amazed at the uniforms and accouterments of their German colleagues, and even of the Polish prisoners they made. Their curiosity was as boundless as it was indiscreet.

All this left the impression on Polish gentry and German officers that the Russian army was in a state of utter unreadiness to encounter another army. The Finnish war seemed to confirm this conclusion, for, during the greater part of that campaign, the Russians cut such a poor figure that when, finally, they got the better of the Finns, most of us believed it was due to the help in arms, and even in officers, that the Germans gave them.

Is it possible that the Russians deliberately misled the Germans into the belief that they would not be able to resist an aggression?

January 11th

JUST A MONTH AGO war was declared between the country and people I most love on earth and the people to whom I owe whole-souled allegiance.

Reading Herodotus now with no philological, I mean grammatical, cares of any kind, reading him as so much literature and history, I am amazed to find him not only so fascinating but so contemporary in the workings of his mind. How much of him, with change of name regarding persons and places, could be recent history. Take, for instance, the expedition of the first Cyrus into Scythia, and then of Xerxes into Greece. How much the first resembles Napoleon in Russia as described by Ségur, Caulaincourt, Tarlé, and others!

What films, and what ballets, could be extracted from the marshaling and reviewing and marching of his forces by Xerxes, each nation with its own dress, its own accouterments, its own arms. And the ships with the Sidonians at the head, the swiftest with ablest captains. All commanded by brothers, cousins, and other relations of the king's. In fact, the Persian Empire seems to have been run as a family affair and, as in all closely knit families, a great deal by women. Of Atossa, the wife of Darius, the heroine of Aeschylus' *Persae*, Herodotus says that so great were her authority and influence that they would have sufficed to secure her favorite son Xerxes the throne, even if he had no right to it. We know from Xenophon how Parysatis plotted to make her favorite, the younger Cyrus, king. Herodotus recounts without comment that "when Xerxes's wife Amastris attained to old age, she buried fourteen sons of notable Persians as a thank-offering, on her own behalf, to the fabled gods of the nether world." All Herodotus says by way of comment is, "to bury alive is a Persian custom."

Where did this custom originate? The earliest instances are Mesopotamian, going back to the fourth millennium B.C. Did it spread thence all over the world as things will, given time, or did it spring spontaneously from the human mind at a certain stage of development?

All that I read in Herodotus about Persia makes the Bible story of Esther so plausible that its author must have had access to the same sources that the Greek drew from, or indeed was a reader of his history. The influence of women must have increased rather than diminished, if we may judge by their role in the late Sassanian romance of *Vis and Ramin.*

The writer of the story of Esther must have been a Hellenized Jew. It is one of the best-constructed stories in literature, and unlike what we know of prior Hebrew narrative, so syncopated, so ejaculatory, so disjointed. The same is true of the exquisite idyl of Ruth and the tale of Tobit, probably as late and as Hellenized.

January 19th

A. C., MY FRIEND and lawyer, came yesterday to ask what I wanted him to do in dealing with a publisher who intends to undertake a translation into Italian first, and then into French, of my *Florentine Drawings.*

Afterwards he began to say it was all over with Europe; that if the Allies won, England would less than ever count as a European power; that she would drift away toward America, toward her dominions, and leave the Continent to its own more and more negligible devices.

That England is not a European power, that England not only fails to understand Europe but succeeds too well in misunderstanding it, its material no less than its spiritual interests, appetites, and aspirations, and therefore can never be other than mischievous, is a thesis not new to me. It was made in Germany not for this occasion, yet lately, in fact since the introduction of the Nazi New Order; and the cyclonic, typhonic winds of propaganda that like a new Aeolus it sends out have taken hold of many minds in the Latin world.

Far from being no part of Europe and opposed to its interests, England in the last century led it to the effective conquest of the earth, taking the lion's share, if you will, as befits the pioneer, the discoverer, the inventor, but letting every other people that could follow have what advantage it could take. This was particularly true of Germany and, so far as I can remember, remained true until the Germans kicked England into awareness of their own hostile intentions.

The fabulous inflation of the nineteenth century, due to the exploitation of the entire earth carried on by Europe with England at its head, could not go on forever. Europe in the future can no more hold the center of the stage in world affairs than Italy in European ones.

It is not here that I would, if I could, put down the reasons for this impossibility. They are too many and chiefly in the nature of things. Thus, it would seem that no colony is truly successful until it begins to clamor for autonomy, if not complete independence. England's policy or, if you like, something less deliberate, more like a drift, almost a tropism, makes in the long run, not too long a run, for the training of her colonies and conquests in self-government, in self-help, and in building up their home industries.

Non-European people, the Japanese most conspicuously, have learned the mechanics of the Anglo-Saxons so well that they could attempt to undersell them and the other Europeans, in their homes and elsewhere.

The hegemony enjoyed by geographical Europe is going or gone, and would go even if the wars of the last forty years had not given such golden opportunities to the Japanese to build up their power, both industrial and military. The nation to feel it most will necessarily be the one that has most to lose, the English. In the present historical horizon, they cannot retain the advantages they had for a century and a half before 1914, any more than Italy could retain, in recent times, the position she had in later antiquity as the center and exploiter of the Europe of those centuries. If England's adversaries on the Continent rejoice in her impending decline, they must be filled with hatred and blinding rage, for England's decline means their fall.

So much for geographical Europe, and geographical England.

There is, however, another Europe and another England. I shall go on thinking and speaking of them as Europe in short. This Europe is not identified with the proboscis of Asia known by that name since Herodotus at least, but is the name I would give to all countries where Europeans live in compact, coherent, self-governing masses; where they carry on materially and spiritually as nations of Europe would under similar geographical, climatic, and economic conditions. Just as down to our sixth century Greek, Southern Italy, Sicily, and even Marseilles, even Emporia and remoter settlements both to west and to east, were Hellas; so, for me, America north and south, whether English-, Spanish-, or Portuguese-speaking, has for a long time counted as European. That even the U. S. A. was not aware of this and would not hear of it, if told, made no difference to me. Since 1917 at latest, the U. S. A. has been as much a European power as England. Only too much like England, in being slow to recognize the solidarity of her political interests with those of geographical Europe.

In this greater Europe which now comprises the whole western Continent, Australia, New Zealand, much of South Africa, coastal Turkey, Syria, Palestine, Egypt to a certain extent, and to a like extent Italian and French North Africa—in this Europe, for many a year to come, the English-speaking, English-thinking, English-feeling people will count for at least as much as they have in the last two centuries. This result would scarcely be affected by an issue of the present war unfavorable to the Motherland.

The Latin, the Central European, and others who would rejoice at the downfall of geographical England would not rejoice for long. They would soon discover that its place had been taken by an England over the seas which, given present and future communications, would not be in a strategical sense farther away, and politically far less disposed to mildness, to living and letting live, and to fair play.

I may have already referred, since I began this journal, to the unfortunate fact that few intellectuals or even professionals on the Continent speak English, and that not many read it, while still fewer English-speaking people can converse in a Continental language. The result is that living contact between English-speakers, whether British or American, is kept up by diplomats, whose object is not to understand but to negotiate and cultivate the society of frivolous, smart creatures whose sole thought is of amusement —amusement not only as an end but as a means. Of these, the disgruntled on both sides, suffering from offended vanity or material disappointment, do much more to envenom than those of good will do to understand each other. It remains a distressing fact that among the people who count in France and in Italy more read and even speak German than English. The one Continental country where acquaintance with Anglo-Saxon language and institutions was most widely spread is Germany. Unfortunately, the propaganda carried on, more and more intensely, against England in the last fifty years has succeeded in nullifying its benefits and bringing about the present situation.

January 23d

HAVE FINISHED Johannes Volkelt's *Aesthetik des Tragischen.* The preface to the first edition is dated October, 1896. Whether his *System der Aesthetik* appeared earlier I do not know, but suspect it did. I was unaware of him and his work until a couple of months ago, when I found a reference somewhere to this book on tragedy. In October, 1896, I was completing or had already completed my *Central Italian Painters,* in which, along with the previous essay on the *Florentine Painters,* I stated my theory of art-enjoyment as fully as I ever have. Had I read Volkelt's *Aesthetik,* assuming, as I do, that it had already been published, I should have had to acknowledge that he had anticipated me. His approach, judging by this one book, seems psychological and empirical, based on the concrete and specific, and not merely spun out of his inner consciousness. I wonder whether he has anticipated me as well about "tactile values"!

Should I have read him when I was in my late twenties? Perhaps not. I did not read Lipps, of whose writings I heard. I went so far as to buy one or more of the earliest but did not read beyond a few pages. I disliked his vocabulary and his way of developing his theory of *Einfühlung* or "telling the clock by algebra," as if putting oneself in the place of the art object needed elaborate demonstration. I might have avoided Volkelt out of fear that he would rob me of my job, making me feel there was nothing left for me to say.

Now I have read him out of pure curiosity to see what can be said on the subject of tragedy. He cannot influence me any more. My mind is like the omnibus with the sign "full up" hung out. No more passengers can enter. So why do I read?

I read in the first place to feed a ravenous curiosity, a curiosity perhaps not unlike the thirst of Münchhausen's horse, insatiable because its rear half had been shot away, and there was nothing to retain what poured through the mouth. Then I read for sheer entertainment: verse, prose, narrative of all kinds, whether fiction pure, or the story which facts cannot disprove that we call history, besides travel, memoirs, correspondence, etc., etc. Finally I read books that, as I peruse them, stimulate my own thinking, interrupted by much woolgathering, musing, and sheer idling.

Volkelt comes among the last-named. Although I enjoyed myself over him, I should be put to it to say what it was all about, excepting in the most general way and far from what a *précis* should be.

The same holds true of almost every book that deals with abstract thought or criticism. I cannot read much of that sort. The little I do seldom holds my attention. When it does and interests me, as Volkelt certainly has, it leaves, after a little, no more than the vague recollection that I enjoyed it. Thus I could not for the life of me say what were the contents of Gundolf's colossal work on Shakespeare, though I read it from cover to cover. I enjoyed dreaming over it in connection with Shakespeare and the drama.

I am led on to say that old people, like myself, feel less and less tempted to publish as their age increases. It is not due to declining faculties, diminished capacity for concentration, or senile dawdling so much as to the paralyzing conviction that others have said what one might still say, and if not, that younger people will do it soon and do it better. Better if for no other reason than that they will do it with no questionings about its being worth while, about their being able to do it better than anybody else, about their claims to the world's attention.

January 30th

ALL DAY YESTERDAY it snowed. Little by little the featherlike flakes blanketed the landscape with soft down, that wrapped the tree branches and their twigs as if with a woman's hand. It was just not full moon when I looked out at midnight. The snow had stopped falling, the sky was crystal clear and of gemlike purity. The stars sparkled and one of them, beaming opaline, amethystine almost, I should have liked to hail. The moonlight fell upon the persimmon trees and changed their branches into white coral, the rounded tops of the cut laurels cast deep oval shadows.

What an interpretation, or better still translation, is afforded by this disappearance from the landscape of every color but black and white! The same and yet how unexpected, how much in shapes and ribbings is revealed, and how it effaces the ever-present feeling of being in Italy! I speak as an American who, though he has spent more than fifty years here, recalls New England winters, walking to school through tunnels cut in the snow, sledging and sleighing, and taking snow seriously as a material to be mastered for use and for pleasure; not as Italians, for whom it is a mere nuisance soon out of the way.

This snowfall is a windfall, for there has been little rain for close on to a year. Returning in early October, I found the lawns here looking like powdered tobacco. Since then, there were just enough showers to encourage the planting of wheat. The cold came on more biting than usual and threatened to destroy the hoped-for crops. The lack of water power has led to alarming restrictions in the use of electricity. From this desperate situation, the snowfall will save us. Considering how the countryside has been deforested and increasingly so in the last two years with pitiless tree-cutting for fuel, rain would have run off the hillsides, doing little good. The snow will seep in and irrigate.

To the small credit side of war should be placed "summertime" through the winter. It means that when at 8 A.M. I look out of the window, it being seven by solar time, the sun is still out of sight. It has barely begun to dawn. Then the sky begins to flush faintly in the east, in the way I used to love to see it pictured when I was a small boy. Most mornings, before sunrise, there is a still, restful blue-grayness over the landscape that is solemn and soothing.

Later. Walked or rather tramped in the Laghetto wood, my feet sinking into the virgin snow still soft on the paths. Many of these were turned into arbors by overladen branches of the younger trees, so weighed down by their burden that when I shook it off, they could not spring back at once. A pine tree was broken at the stem and lay sprawling on the ice of the pool. The sky was clear, the dome of the cathedral shone with snow decking its ribs. The shadows cast were blue, and lavender, and purple. A cypress produced a cone of shadow as defined, and constant, as if it were a rug of blue velvet spread out over the snow.

February 1st

JUST RETURNED from a morning stroll in the garden. It snowed the livelong day yesterday, in soft, fluffy flakes. In the night it froze. So walking was not easy. There was a light crust which crackled crisply as my rubber boots sank ankle-deep into the snow, which snow lay virgin, white, unsullied. Not a human being in sight, not a sound except the soft thud of a falling flake or the piping of the returning thrush. The distant hills pale blue.

Last night I looked out about eleven. The moon, already a day past its full, had risen an hour or more previously. It was strong enough to light up the entire sky in a way that made it look as if it were a mother-of-pearl shell. Yet the same moon was low enough to strike the cypresses and stone pines sideways, so that these threw long shadows over the inner garden and the snow-covered roof of the orangery. Not a light visible, not a sound, but far from estranging as "real" nature would be (the high mountains, for instance), it was cozy, friendly, silent, because everybody had gone to rest, leaving the world to moonlight and to me.

Two days ago, walking up the road, we met a squad of soldiers, some very good-looking. A few minutes later a slim officer came striding down, half singing, half whistling the chorus to "John Brown's Body." I could not help stopping and asking whether he (an Italian serving a totalitarian, authoritarian state) was aware that he was singing a battle song of the American Secession War, chanted by soldiers who supposed they were fighting for universal freedom, for individual liberty and all that is opposed to totalitarian authoritarianism. The young officer took my question in good part, and said he did know it was American and introduced himself. Nicky told me he had the charge of the British prisoners at Vincigliata, the castle just above us. I asked him whether it was not marvelous to have so much snow and sunshine together, and remarked that nothing could spoil the beauty of the world, not even the war. He sighed: "If only it ends soon."

Since our first glimpse of the British war prisoners we have met them again and again. It seems such a stupid convention, such an annoying farce not to be able to speak to them, to lend them books. My "enemies" lost no time in spreading the report that I had found a way of getting these carefully guarded prisoners to come to tea with me, presumably despite the watchful authorities—such was my diabolical power.

February 3d

A RUSSIAN VICTORY that ended in the complete occupation of Germany might be the only way to convince the Germans that their interests lay with France and England, and at the same time might persuade the French and English that they were as much concerned as the Central Europeans to keep Russia from dominating the whole of the Continent, including Western Europe. If the Germans could and would be brought to feel that they must not again attempt to trample the rest of the world under their heel, and had better join France, England, and America in the defense of the West against the East, this war would not have been fought in vain.

When I say "East" I have in mind civilizations where the horde, the tribe (as in Japan), the mass (as in China) prevails, and individuality exists only negatively, not positively; by what the single person fails to do, not by what he could do if he were encouraged. Ever since my first long visit to Germany in 1888 I have been given to saying, half playfully, that Asia begins at the Rhine.

Nazism is an attempt on the part of Germany to Asiatize itself completely, destroying and eradicating everything in itself that spells Europe, which Europe is equivalent to Mediterranean. It began with the easiest to accomplish, the wholesale massacre of the Jews, always the spearhead of Mediterranean civilization. Not so easy to get rid of is the Mediterranean's greatest and most indestructible achievement, Christianity, whether considered as culture or as institution. If Nazism wins it will not rest until it eradicates its every root and retains, like the Japanese, the mechanical side only of our common civilization.

The Russians may be as gifted a people as any in European history, which history they have, however, as yet barely approached. Their masses are little more than what I call, by a word of my invention, "androplasm"; that is to say, raw material awaiting individualization. For that reason it has been relatively easy for Stalin to treat the Russian people like so much dead matter, tearing them away not from their fields alone (fields in the sense of a patch of ground) but from their native land: Kirghizes from their horses, Buriats from their reindeer, other nomads from their sheep and cattle, and throwing them into furnaces to be melted into every kind of day laborer, whether as kolkhoz worker, miner, gold-washer, or factory hand. For the present, the Russian, having got rid of his Europeanized classes, is further from individuality than ever, and his doctrinal influence, bad enough as it is already, will be immeasurably surpassed if military conquest reinforces it. For which reason Europe, the Mediterranean-Atlantic world and its offspring everywhere, not only in all the Americas but even in Australia, must in the present historical horizon regard Russia and not Germany as the most serious menace. For the German soul has been too deeply affected by the Mediterranean vaccine to let itself be overwhelmed by the ochlocratic upheaval that is now threatening it.

February 5th

"AS THE STARS are the ornament of the heavens when the air is clear, and as the flowers adorn the meadows in the spring, so do lively sallies and appropriate anecdotes constitute the charm of polite conversation."

This seriocomic aphorism, which I recall learning at Oxford in January, 1888, applies signally to Herodotus, whom I have just finished reading. It is, by the way, the third time I have read him from beginning to end in the original, apart from the second book that I read in Egypt, and the pages on the rest of North Africa in a later book. Shall I ever find the time to do so again!

I know no other historian who has such a keen sense of the characters and humors that go to shape events. He never lugs in an anecdote. It comes of itself as a witness to substantiate what he wants to recount, and it seldom fails to be amusing, or significant, or both. Character and humor adorn events, but these are determined by inexorable forces which it is not only absurd but wrong to oppose. Mycerinus succeeds a series of wickedly oppressive rulers, and does his best to repair the evil they have done. Yet all goes wrong with him, and at last he consults the oracles. They answer that he is punished for putting himself against destiny. So before the Battle of Plataea, at the banquet offered by the Thebans to the Persians, one of these, unable to keep himself in any longer, bursts into tears, saying that he knows his countrymen will lose the war and perish miserably; that he has not failed, not only he but many of his friends, to warn the commander-in-chief Mardonius, but all to no purpose, for destiny has decreed their destruction.

The Jews of that time seem to have been free from this belief. Among the Greeks it was so deep, and so strong, that according to Herodotus every state, every ruling family was constantly consulting oracles and putting them in cold storage for future use, and that the Pisistratidae had a wondrous collection of them. From this state of mind spring the various Sibylline books, including of course those sold to Rome. Yet it is hard for us to understand the immense authority of Delphi as the foreteller and interpreter of destiny. As reported by the Greeks themselves, it would seem to have been a sinister humbug. No doubt, people were so eager to believe that they lost critical sense, like those of us today who frequent fortunetellers.

The feeling that one must not, one should not, interfere with destiny still persists in Aegean lands. In his nimble, airy account of a journey through Asia Minor, just after the last war, Carl Burckhardt meets with a Nathan the Wise. It is at Tarsus I believe, and in the course of being taken to all the sights, that he comes across a young woman of the best Russian society fallen to the lowest steps of degradation. His heart leaps to help her, and the sage chides him for not letting things happen, for not letting "determined things to destiny hold unbewailed their way."

But it is not about Herodotus that I mean to write just now, rather about the striking parallel between the present war and the war with Persia that he narrated. The war news, the war comments, the war gossip we nowadays get from both sides make us indulgent to any error of fact he may have committed. We wonder that he did not fall oftener out of reckoning, considering the violence of prejudice, and the proneness to lap up information agreeable to this violence; given as well the far greater difficulty he must have had in getting at the sources. Moreover, he was seldom deliberately unfair, and perhaps never so to the enemy in chief, the Persian. This Persian, let me add, he depicted as cruel at times, and arbitrary, but always as a gentleman, and not a too overbearing one.

As for the parallels with the present war, we begin with the fact that Herodotus does not tire of reiterating how the Persians regarded the whole of Asia as belonging of right to them, and being subject to their "order."

We turn to the Greeks. They sent envoys to Syracuse to ask Gelon to join them. They plead that although Xerxes pretends to be warring against Athens alone, his real purpose is to subjugate Hellenes wherever he can find them. "Think not," they say at the end, "that if the Persians defeat us in battle, and subdue us, they will leave you unassailed, but look well to yourself ere that day come. Aid us and you champion your own cause; a well-laid plan commonly leads to a happy issue" (VII, 157).

How often has not England said this in the last thirty years to Belgium, to Holland, but above all to the Sicily of the Anglo-Saxon world, the U. S. A.!

Close parallel between Xerxes and Hitler in their efforts to win over, the former the Athenians and the latter England in particular and Anglo-Saxons in general. "Medizers" no less frequent in England than in America and in the Dominions. The Greeks could have found their equivalent in South Africa, with its Hertzog, and in Eire, with its De Valera. Likewise their neutrals, the most respectable being the Thessalians, who honestly declared that unless they were sure of help they must submit to Xerxes. "Fifth columns" were not lacking, and the Persians had Delphi and the greatest Greek singer of all time, Pindar, on their side.

Parallel again were the discussions between allies then and now, even to Spartan "weekending" at leisure, for ten whole days, engaged in celebrating the feast of Hyacinthia, while the Athenian envoys were "peppering" to know whether they would or would not be supported. At home they were meanwhile receiving the most flattering proposals from the Persians if only they would "collaborate." A parallel, and a contrast with Vichy.

Herodotus recounts that after Thermopylae, Xerxes hastily

buried nineteen out of the twenty thousand Persians that had
fallen, and invited all and sundry to come and see that he had lost
only one thousand, whereas the Greek dead were ever so many
more. He had no more success in blinding onlookers to the facts
than the Germans who led American correspondents around Berlin to see with their own eyes how little damage British aircraft
had done.

The equivalent of the mined roads were not lacking. The Pho-
caeans met invading horsemen by "digging a great pit where the
cavalry had to pass and filled it with jars. The horses fell into them
and broke their legs."

After Mycale the Lacedaemonians proposed removing all
Greeks from Ionia and settling them in those Greek cities that
would be evacuated because they had taken the Persian side. The
Nazis have been doing such transfers to any and every extent.

February 6th

HAVE WRITTEN of the interest in the character and humor of the
individual displayed by Herodotus, with his anecdotes about the
various persons he has occasion to mention, their wit, their foibles,
their wisdom.

Where else in the whole world's literature at so early a date as
the middle of the fifth century B.C. does one find record of such
an interest! If it is already so lively and so ever-present it must
have been widespread in conversation before Herodotus wrote.
So, as they invented everything else, save perhaps mechanics and
mathematics, the Greeks invented gossip and the significant anecdote. Biographies, autobiographies, memoirs, recollections are
possible without anecdotes and gossip, like Vico's autobiography,
for instance, but how lifeless, dull, and dry they are—like things
cooked without butter, oil, or other generous fats. One has to be as
great as Thucydides to write history without them. The Greeks
seem to have reveled in them; and as the easiest and most fetching
stories are naughty and malicious, the better known a name, the

more disparaging the anecdotes gathered around it. Yet how much
we owe to what has come down to us of this gossip!

February 10th

READ THE OTHER DAY that they are preparing to celebrate the
fourth centenary of the Council of Trent—that Council which
definitely turned the Church Catholic into a sect, the greatest
numerically, the most coherent and highly organized, the most
powerful, the most awe-inspiring of sects—thus denying her high
claims to be the entire body of Christ and reducing her to the
status of a fragment. One could speculate as to what the fragment
consists of, and how much of the body it represents.

Just now my speculation takes another turn, more consonant
with my profession.

It is whether the immense increase of priestly authority and
power enacted by the Council had any effect on the interior arrangement of church buildings.

I never made express study of the subject, but I seem to recall
that as time went on, the choir, the part assigned to the clergy,
crept more and more from the apse towards the façade, leaving
relatively as little room for the congregation as in a college chapel
—that, for instance, of New College, Oxford. In this chapel as in
all monastic establishments the available space was intended first
and foremost for the monks or friars. I seem to recall, however, in
sixteenth-century and in later Spanish churches the exorbitant
disproportion between the space allotted on the one hand to the
clergy and, on the other, to the laity; and I ask again how much
this was due to the increasing claims of the clergy.

Two distinct attitudes toward the use of churches are implied
in the division of space between clergy and laity. One attitude,
held increasingly under the tendency of the Catholic Church to
monasticize itself, was to regard its chief function as a sanctuary
for continuous prayer and praise to God. Belief, if not dogma,
feared Him as being so wrathful against mankind that if adoration

and supplication were interrupted for one second He would wipe it off the face of the earth. The other was to regard the foremost purpose of congregating in churches as instruction, as catechizing, as preaching. The first took little or no account of the laity and tolerated, rather than solicited, its presence. The second, on the contrary, existed chiefly for the laity; as indeed is the case with all communities genuinely Protestant, as well as with Catholic churches, like most Jesuit ones, where the laity counted almost as much.

Fifty years ago I wrote a "Plea for Renaissance Churches," a short paper in which I pleaded that these had a much finer feeling for space than had those in the Gothic style. How just my plea was I did not realize at the time, for I too was impressed by the grand naves and transepts of medieval cathedrals. Space, however, could not have been much in the minds of the builders, and not at all in the heads of the public. In those edifices where we now are tempted to believe there was feeling for splendid space the rood lofts, the rood screens, the *jubés*, and all sorts of other contraptions cut up the space in such a way that you never got a full view from west to east except along the roof. Where the contrary now is the case, where the lungs can dilate in a space that is harmoniously uplifting, it is due to quite recent, to nineteenth-century, taste, which removed impediments to continuous vision and swept away the chantries, sepulchral chapels, confessionals, etc., etc., which still clutter up churches in Spain. Yet I must confess that these Spanish churches, with their rich paraphernalia, the visual equivalent of the incense and candle smoke filling the air, feel as if lived in night and day; whereas churches like Saint-Ouen at Rouen are as unhomelike as a dwelling that has been empty for a long time.

February 11th

THE QUESTION of suffrage is a serious one. Universal suffrage, as now practiced, leads easily to plebiscitism and that quickly to *Führertum* and all that it brings in its train. Yet to abolish universal suffrage, and leave the proletariat unrepresented in the discussion of public affairs, cannot be advocated by people like ourselves who want every class in the community to get what it legitimately and sanely can out of life.

How would it be, then, if something like the following were proposed? Every person above twenty-one, male and female, to have one vote. Property, public service, professional merit, intelligent and active interest in politics, to increase the number of votes the individual is to have. Instead of bestowing Legions of Honor, orders, decorations, and titles the citizen shall have granted to him, with the increase of his merits, an increasing number of votes.

Naturally, this idea would encounter objections, as for instance: that there would be no way of preventing greedy swopping of illegitimate favors in order to procure the promotions. Against human nature one cannot legislate. One can only try to educate it, and that is a slow process with only a distant hope of success.

February 13th

MY BEGINNINGS as a writer encountered no little opposition. Not so much on account of my ideas. The crime was that I used the first person singular instead of the plural, or the various awkward circumlocutions, each serving only to draw attention to the fact that you were trying to avoid saying "I."

What is wrong with "I"? Used as I have innocently used it, it is nothing but a grammatical fiction without which discourse becomes exceedingly difficult, nay, true discourse impossible.

Deliberately avoiding it implies a self-consciousness about your own personal ego that is far from what happens when I write "I." "We" has through such long and constant use got to be almost as natural as "I," but substitutes like "it may be said," "it may be allowed," "it has been thought," or, worse than all the other subterfuges, the four words "the idea is that" seem to me increasingly absurd, and the last cynical and impudent.

Shyness about the use of "I," common in England and America

as late as fifty years ago, may be connected with the convention
of polite society in previous generations, that assertion of individual opinion should be avoided and that private tastes, private notions, private ideas were to be eschewed.

In one of Jane Austen's novels she says, speaking of her hero,
that he was too well-bred, too much a gentleman to have, in matters of art, tastes that were not of his class. When, as a youngster
fifty-five years ago, I was taken to picture galleries by ladies old
enough to be my grandmothers, never did any of them pull me by
the sleeve toward a painting and say, "I like it." No, they would
say: "Now we shall look at that Madonna. It is *considered* to be
very fine."

In these old ladies there may have lingered a certain humility.
There surely is little left in the young of today or perhaps of yesterday who say "the idea is" when they mean "I think" or "I believe" or "I fancy."

February 15th

AN INTERESTING STUDY of anthologies might be made from the
point of view of changing taste.

Thus Palgrave's anthology, on which I lived so many years, did
not contain Andrew Marvell's "Coy Mistress." It was first revealed
to me, although I may have read it years earlier without feeling it,
it first was brought home to me in the *Oxford Book of Verse* of
1919. In a little while everybody was quoting it, and one encountered it here, there, and everywhere in periodicals.

Likewise in a selection of a hundred best French poems published by Gowans and Grey, I first met La Fontaine's "Volupté."
Since then I have murmured it frequently, and I doubt whether
many anthologies of French verse have appeared in the last fifteen
or twenty years that do not contain it.

The anthologies I had as a boy in Boston were still eighteenth-
century in taste. Wordsworth, Shelley, Keats were barely coming
forward, although Byron was represented with his "Isles of

Greece" and Hebrew melodies. Tennyson and Browning were as
yet unknown.

What do these changes in taste reveal of changes in the mind?

March 13th

JUST AFTER the First World War I made my way in Naples to
Donna Anna Regina, and after some difficulty and delay was admitted to the church. I found it filled with workmen who evidently
had turned it into a meeting place. I was horrified to see ladders
placed against the frescoes, and other signs of utter indifference
to the Cavallinesque paintings that we, students and lovers of art,
prized highly. When I drew their attention to the damage they
were doing, they rather insolently answered that it did not matter if they disappeared. They could replace them with creations
of their own.

Their huffy tone was largely bluff, but their state of mind was
that of the medieval scribe who scraped clean a perhaps irreplaceable Greek text to use the parchment for a work he could appreciate, some dreary theological affair, at best a Church Father.

Neither the socialistic workman nor the medieval scribe was an
intentional vandal. The latter understood no Greek, so it had no
value or interest for him. The former feels no art that is not of his
own day, and has no use for frescoes painted in a language as
strange to him as Greek was to the scribe. For art, visual art, is as
much a language as any other, and like language has to be acquired unconsciously in infancy, or consciously later on.

When does decline of a ruling nation or of a ruling class within
a nation set in? Perhaps when it begins to parry challenges with
palliatives and worse still with the pretense of ignoring them.

That is what England did from 1920 till 1939, first toward
France, then toward Italy, and finally toward Germany.

Ruling class and ruling nation are happily not identical. When
the challenge turned into an attack, as it did in May, 1940, the
English people leaped to the defense, dragging the reluctant part

of the ruling class with it so quickly that this class may have fancied that it was taking the initiative. In a sense it did, in the sense only that in England the difference between ruling class and people is less than elsewhere, excepting perhaps in the U. S. A.

A ruling class begins to decline when it ceases to be enterprising and acquisitive, and begins to play for safety, for securing its privilege, power, and wealth and while sitting tight on its moneybags opposes innovation.

It distressed me to become aware that, with few exceptions, the ruling class in America was taking that turn: first with its cult of Coolidge, and then with its hatred of the present Roosevelt. It manifested its sympathies with every effort to secure "loranorder" by whatever agency, unless this struck directly at capital. Its idol was a banker who advocated a loan to Mussolini, admitting that with its help the latter would enslave the Italian people for a good ten years. But what of it, if Fascism would save the world from Bolshevism!

The authority of our ruling class, whose wealth was more often the consequence of the country's rising prosperity and of the "unearned increment" than of its own enterprise, will scarcely survive this war. Despite its suicidal faults, I shall regret it. It attained a relative mellowness, excellent, not merely showy, standards of life, sensitiveness to cultural, not merely intellectualistic, interests. Besides, this class was already producing individuals who were in themselves works of art.

March 16th

IT IS IMPOSSIBLE to punish the misrulers of a nation. In the first place, by the time you are in a position to punish them, their power is gone; and shorn of that power they cease to be worth the trouble. Punishment, to the extent that it is possible to inflict it, falls on the people of all classes, not only the relatively few who aided and abetted misrule, but the overwhelming majority who could not help putting up with it. Such punishment, if it is done on statesmanly grounds, not out of sheer vindictiveness, cannot be serious. To be serious, Italy as a punishing power would have to destroy England and leave the Europe of which Italy forms part—I often fear an unconscious part—to the unchallenged control of Germany. If it is Germany that wanted to punish England, she might find herself, even though she dominated all Europe west of the Vistula, in no position to face a combination of Eurasia ruled by a Russo-Japanese alliance, always a possibility. On the other hand, if England wanted to punish France for her conduct since Laval's treachery coming on top of all other French follies since 1920, she, England I mean, would only strengthen Germany. This is so obvious that an Italian journalist during the Laval betrayal had the effrontery to encourage the French government, saying whatever it did, could, or would do, England out of self-interest could not afford to drop her. Likewise, if England tries to punish Italy, it could end only in giving France an undesirable preponderance in the Mediterranean, etc., etc.

Seeing, then, that there is no way of punishing a nation for the crimes of its rulers against other nations, it should be the imperative duty of its neighbors, near and far, to prevent it from falling into the hands of mischievous men even if, to prevent it, recourse must be had to force.

Before power passes into the hands of those usurpers (whose traits it is easy enough to recognize) the nation destined to be their victim has not yet been stupefied enough physically and mentally to give the assistance their misrulers would need to maintain themselves. If these dared to try their luck it would go back on them. True, it may be no easy task to get rid of them and their supporters, but no difficulty encountered is to be compared to what neighboring states will have to put up with if they wait until they are attacked. They surely will be; for certain types of rule, totalitarianism and autarchy, for instance, serve no purpose but war, and war which must be made piping hot when ready.

It is difficult to believe that statesmanlike persons sincerely entertained a policy of pretending that what went on within another state was no other government's concern, or took in earnest the slogan of the last ten years and more, that "ideologies" must not invade international affairs. Useless to discuss the cowardice—for I take it to be that rather than sheer folly—of such a policy. One can only point to the results. On what grounds are England and America fighting now, if not to defend their ideologies against the diametrically opposed "Axis" ones!

March 24th

IT LOOKS as if Turkey would not be allowed to remain neutral much longer. For the present, she can do little for the Allies except to keep a strict neutrality; at most, a benevolent neutrality. For the Axis, Turkey can help to decide in their favor by joining against Russia and invading the Caucasus. Turkey would be wiser than other powers if she resisted the bribe that the Axis may be offering, the bribe of the Dodecanese and other Aegean islands (which naturally England could not offer), and perhaps as well the further bribe of Syria, Palestine, and Iraq—in short, the restoration of the Ottoman Empire as before the last war. Will Turkey resist?

April 30th

TOO BUSY PRUNING, filling out, correcting my *Art Theory and Art History* to have had the leisure of mind to write here.

Last night the *Christian Science Monitor's* radio speaker talked of China, how big it was, and how ready to form part of our American civilization, and what a power for stabilization on a humanitarian plane it will be when the war is won and China is thoroughly mechanized.

I suppose it is necessary propaganda to rouse fraternal enthusiasm in favor of a numerous nation whom, not long ago, we excluded from America, and not more than three years ago refused loans of sums as petty as fifty million dollars, to be expended on armament for defense. All sorts of mean, sordidly pacifistic and cowardly reasons intervened, covered by the cry that we must not goad Japan into making war on us.

I recall vividly how we throbbed in united sympathy for Japan forty years ago when Japan attacked Russia at Port Arthur just as she attacked us a few months ago at Pearl Harbor. We had ample reason for wishing to diminish the power of the Tsardom and its menace to our civilization. Japanese prints, Japanese netsukes and ceramics prepared the way for Lafcadio's keepsake pictures of Japan, penned with a luscious language that captivated. What has been the progress of Japan since? What reason have we to believe that a victorious, united, mechanized, commercialized, and of course militarized China will act any better? On the contrary, her immense population, her more central position may be more of a menace. It seems a law of history—if indeed history has laws— that once aroused to a feeling of nationhood, a people cannot stop till it goes the whole way of nationalism and annexationism. A people in that condition will not settle down till it has had the sat- isfaction of enslaving and oppressing others; or else fail so mis- erably, as the Greeks did in 1919, that they sink into impotent dissatisfaction with themselves as well as others. So I should expect the Chinese to regain the territories recently taken by Japan, and Indo-China and Korea as well, and then to set up a Mongol soli- darity which would include Siam, Burma, Nepal, and much else, as the lust for conquest increased with its satisfaction.

May 2d

HEARD JUST NOW of Delfino Cinelli's death. Death, like the sun and the rain, acts on the just and on the unjust. I knew nobody who less deserved to die, whose disappearance can bring so little profit to anyone, whose loss will be mourned so unanimously by all who knew him.

Not alone because he was one of the most delicate and genuine verbal artists of recent years, communicating the full perfume of the Tuscan countryside and its folk as I have never felt in another writer; not only because he had a fine sense of letters. As well, and as much, because of his deep and generous humanity and coura- geous attitude toward events, and his understanding of what was behind them.

His business took him often to America and he learnt to appreciate and to love us. So he was one of the few Italians with whom, as with Carla Garabelli Orlando, I could discuss things and persons American as if he were one himself. His looks used to puzzle me. Slender, tallish, with pronounced features, blue-gray eyes, and a shock of darkish chestnut hair over a full, slightly beetling brow, at first he suggested the Russian. I was not satisfied with this classification and one day I perceived how much he looked like the "Dying Gladiator." So that was what he was, a Celt whose idioplasm, disappearing for centuries, returned to life with him, its characteristics tempered by Italic elements into the completely rational, frank, and fearless being whom we loved and cherished.

May 6th

THE HIEROGLYPHS in the innermost chamber of Zoser's pyramid are perfect as sculpture in low relief. So are the masterpieces of the earliest Egyptian dynasties, whether in the round or in relief. Wonderful also are the works of figure arts, mostly in the round, dug up in Mesopotamia and dating from its earliest periods and dynasties. A head like the one discovered at Warka a few years ago, although of the Jemseh-Nasr period, some 3000 B.C., would, if found in Greece or Aegean lands, be placed in the fifth century and ranked with the masterpieces of that century.

Verbal utterances nearly coeval with these early creations of Egypt and Babylonia are scarcely to be graced with the name of literature even in the most generous and indulgent sense of the word. One may question whether these antique lands in the course of their entire history ever produced literary works comparable to their plastic arts.

This leads me to wonder whether poetry as we understand it is not a later product than the visual and, more specifically, the figure arts. It is true that we have no specimens of Minoan or even Mycenæan *Dichtung*, poetry, whether in prose or verse. Someday they may be discovered and deciphered, but I am willing to affirm that they will not be of the value interest of the figure arts produced by the same civilizations. Although I do not share the boundless admiration for their wasp-waisted, cakewalking, bull-fighting heroes, or their young women easily mistaken for creatures out of *Vogue*, their representations of animals are of the highest order, and their action has a spring, a lightness, a gaiety that makes one feel eager and happy.

Then comes the *Iliad*, centuries after the occultation of the Mycenæan world by a darkness that swept down from North Central Europe, as it did many centuries later when it produced our Dark Ages. It took nearly as long to recover from, but in technical tradition as in subject matter Homer may have been the singer of a past whose memory was preserved and nostalgically transfigured in Aeolia by descendants of Mycenæans there sheltered from the worst brutalities of the Nordic invaders on the Greek mainland. In that case, the *Iliad* too would date much later than the visual representations to which we owe acquaintance with the Mycenæan world.

I suspect that early mankind, when feeling its oats, danced and shouted, chanted perhaps, and that castanets, tom-toms, and even some crude wind instruments may have been among its early artifacts.

Its shouts when exuberant, its grunts, its howls when satisfied or angry, ultimately were organized into units of sound, and these units in the course of numberless ages were split up into bits, each bit carrying a distinct meaning. This meaning was stamped upon it as the value was stamped at first roughly upon the earliest coins into the casting of which chunks of gold and silver and bronze and electrum were broken up and then with more and more defined images, until they attained the beauty of Syracusan and other Greek coins of the fifth century and later. Indeed, one may be led on to say that units of sound reached their perfection as words, at the same time that mere bullion attained its greatest beauty as coinage.

Which brings me back to the question whether words, in our sense of the term, were not latecomers in poetry, although they may have existed in some utilitarian connection long before. Without the aid of appropriate gesture words till late did not attain precision and currency enough to serve for something so prismatic as poetry, not to speak of the exigencies of prose.

May 8th

I CAN RECALL what, as a little boy not over seven, I felt about parents, teachers, and other grownups. I must pay attention to what they said and obey their orders. Why? Not for fear of punishment chiefly, although that, no doubt, played its part. No: it was that I felt these elders were betters and spoke with knowledge. Most of all, they enjoyed "authority," and I knew that "authority" was not force alone, the power to do what they liked with me, but something numinous which filled me with awe, with a sense of its moral right to utter commands that I had to obey. I might and would rebel, yet knew that I ought not, that it was naughty to do so. It made me unhappy and compelled me to seek reconciliation.

Need I add that this numinous authority, with which I endowed my elders, ended by embracing government and all its agents? Moreover, their authority was a moral authority that could not act except in a moral way. Nor was it there merely to secure and guarantee life and property; it had to serve besides as a model for conduct, a model we had but to follow in order to enjoy what was good for us here and hereafter.

I left America too soon to have heard in my sheltered and unpolitical school and college days of the venality and brutality of the executants of the law. Nor did much happen abroad to open my eyes till toward my thirtieth year, when I began to take an interest in international affairs. Even then I did not wake entirely, and it took yet a while before I began to realize that, internationally at least, governments, excepting possibly the English and American, did not believe in moral conduct toward each other, and scarcely claimed to be guided by anything but their advantage, and the power to secure it.

It was a discovery that would have turned me into an anarchist if I had made it as a youth. Happily, it occurred when I was capable of reflection; and although I had not yet consciously reached the conclusion that government was a necessary evil without which we could not get on in our present civilization, I was prepared to act on it and accept the inevitable.

I go on asking, however, how one can expect morality, decency, and humanity from individuals who corporatively have none, who corporatively expect to be praised for being regardless of the rest of the world, and glorying in any cannibalism that may seem materially advantageous—at the moment.

May 9

THE COLORED picture postcard, following on the heels of the one in black and white, as that had succeeded to the plain photograph, is putting an end, if indeed it has not already done so, to an elegant accomplishment of young and mature gentlewomen that was still common in my earlier days. An exact contemporary of mine, Mme de C. B., can turn over the pages of albums into which are gathered the vignettes and "Prout-bits" she water-colored long ago, in Egypt and other antique lands. It must give her raptures of transfigured memory that no view of the same place not done by her own hands would give, least of all the mechanical ones now current. Quality apart, the thing done with one's own hands has a power to call back the past, and just how a given place or scene felt, as no ready-made reproduction can offer.

Now it is the turn of the amateur pianists and songsters to vanish. How shall they compete with the ever-improvable radio that brings us the music we want, performed by the best artists? Teaching the piano and singing may be carried on, but the end is not far.

We shall then have a completer and more decisively final divorce between artists and enjoyers of art, between painters, sculptors, and amateurs—in short, between producers and consumers.

May 22d

AT THE FUNERAL of Novalis, his father was deeply touched by a hymn that was sung. He asked for its author and was told, "But it is by your dead son." Father and son had fallen out over what the former, strictly and narrowly evangelical, regarded as religion. He was moved to contrition when the hymn revealed how truly religious his son had been all along. Without the identical trappings of myth and dogma he had failed to recognize this quality in his child.

May 24th

WHILE READING Huizinga, it occurs to one to ask who first thought of the questions one puts regarding this or that period of history in a given region, as in this case the civilization of France and Flanders at the end of the Middle Ages, or of an individual, as Taine did in the case of La Fontaine. When we deal with an entire civilization and not a single person, I with my limited reading can trace the kind of question no further back than to Jakob Burckhardt. I suspect that he owed something to the Schlegels and more to Herder; but for us who come after him, it is to him we owe the problems to be solved when we attempt to inquire into a past civilization.

How to set about to discover what are the problems touching such a chaotic affair as an epoch of the past requires great antecedent knowledge feeding imagination, and a creative gift without which one has no idea how to find one's way through such a jungle. In that sense Jakob Burckhardt was a real pioneer. After him it is easy for any instructed person to apply the same questions, to pose the same problems, to set up the same categories for any period of the past and with relatively modest gifts reach satisfactory results. It is easy for these mediocrities to ignore their debts, and to be accepted as great scholars and interpreters.

"Who fished the murex up?"
"What porridge had John Keats?"

June 8th

WHEN I WAS YOUNG, aristocracy and *le monde*—society—fasci-
nated me. To begin with, like most not born to it, I was attracted
by its seeming access to a larger, more intense, as well as freer life.
Its manners, its customs, its habitations, its relations to others
seemed more beautiful intrinsically than ours. Then, when I realized how few members of this class were the better for these advantages, how sordid, how greedy, how predatory, how vulgar-
minded, how heartless, how rude the majority of its individuals
could be, I still entertained the hope that there were enough of the
better sort to keep up its *cadres,* in the sense that an army defeated and decimated but keeping up its formations can expect in
time to fill them up properly.

Royalties made me feel shy because I did not know how to get
on with them. Obviously, they expect other treatment than is
meted out to mere mortals in whose veins flows no drop of the
ichor of the gods Odin and Thor. I am reminded of what a diplomat told me in Rome. Whenever an officially important foreign
personage was coming to Rome, information was asked as to the
amount of enthusiasm with which he was to be received.

Aristocracies may continue to exist and the great society to afford them as the humblest cottages can afford to cultivate flowers
in their patch of garden, and poor city folk a geranium in a pot on
the window sill. So long as aristocracies continue to give satisfaction either through the nobility of their *mœurs* or the beauty of
their ways and aspects, we can profit by the aesthetic pleasure
they give us, as well as by the example that they furnish to us
plebeians.

When they degenerate to mere smartness, and rot into parasites
of the *nouveaux riches,* whether these are rich in money or rich in
power, then they are at best a nuisance, and at less than best a

pernicious model for the rest of us. The sooner they are eliminated the better. It is to be feared, moreover, that even the worthier sections of the aristocracies in all countries have sunk to the state of mind that possesses people who live on inherited incomes, which they cannot creatively increase, but only diminish through stupidity, bad luck, or taxation. They sit tight on their moneybags with little thought for the community as a whole, except to the extent that it serves their needs and greeds. Their more enterprising men go into business of an adventurous and hazardous kind with the hope of getting rich quick. The others wait for the marriage broker to bring them an heiress to increase their income and discolor the blueness of their blood.

June 25th

THE GERMANS again are threatening Egypt. If the experiment could be reversed, it would interest me to see how the Egyptians would enjoy German rule for several years, for long enough to have a good taste of it and see how they liked it. The Nazis might play into the hands of the effendis, letting them at the start oppress and squeeze the fellahin as they did before English rule limited their privileges.

In India likewise the baboos and their like might prefer Japanese totalitarianism to British rule.

Eastern, and semi-Eastern, and Near Eastern people seem to find difficulties in distinguishing between a government that cares not how much harm it does to attain its ends, and one that tries to reduce to a minimum the odious but necessary evils that accompany politics and administration.

England does the latter consciously, but as it cannot get rid of all evil-doing, hard as it tries, every Oriental or semi-Oriental from Gibraltar to Japan points a finger and boohoos at its hypocrisy, cant, and fraud. You would think they could not conceive a middle term between a cannibal and Gandhi.

One or the other, a cannibal or a Gandhi, if a Gandhi could rule, they might understand and be reconciled to.

A Gandhi being out of the question, it is by no means certain that these peoples would not settle down to Nazi rule with resignation as to an act of God, in submissive and reposeful irresponsibility, and be much happier than under the English, who allow them to clamor for more and more advantages.

England necessarily is least English in her connection with India. Scarcely an international action one may disapprove that England does not commit because of India. Keeping Cyprus from the Greeks, Egypt from the Arabs, Palestine from the Jews—all this is to provide for the safety of India and of the route to India.

I should be happy to let the Hindus stew in their own or in authoritarian juice and free England from the ungrateful task of protecting and ruling. An English-speaking union strong enough to defend itself against attack—that for the present would be my international ideal.

July 2d

"THEY" HAVE CUT our telephone, without even letting us know. What harm could we do through the telephone? It is carefully watched. If one attempted to communicate anything seditious, let alone of military interest, the spy at the station could report at once. It would serve counterespionage to let the few decrepit, tottering "alien enemies" like ourselves use and abuse the telephone, on the chance that they might betray something of interest to the authorities. But no: in wartime an alien enemy must not be allowed to use a telephone. Discussion strictly forbidden.

July 3d

HOW I USED TO LAUGH forty years ago at Salomon Reinach's when I saw that almost all the Academicians and members of the Institute I met there wore elastic-sided boots. I had no idea then as I have too clearly now that this saved those elderly people the trouble of bending to lace their footgear.

* * *

When the Germans first attempted to invade Egypt from Libya, I was assured by even such a military authority as Prince Rupprecht of Bavaria that they would reach Alexandria in five or six days. Other Germans could not find adequate terms to praise Rommel as perhaps the finest mind in their army: all had been arranged like clockwork, and timed for the defeat of the British and the conquest of Egypt. Beaten, Rommel became a rash, headstrong adventurer who, without orders and without consulting his superiors, had let himself into a gamble foredoomed to failure. Again, he is a hero, he is field marshal. What will be his reward if he reaches Cairo? On the other hand, what will Germans say if, like Sennacherib, he mysteriously retires?

August 27th

I HAPPENED to go to the window at about an hour before sunrise. The full moon was still some degrees above the western horizon. To the east the sky was beginning to flush with the dawn. The moon had a dimmed luster as of old gold and was bedded in its own rays, making a halo like a great wheel, and touched with faint rainbow color. Under it, the hillside rising to Poggio Gherardo looked grayish green and the olive trees did not come out singly or in clusters, but as rolls of felt folded back on the ground. The sky had a strange, almost uncanny air, both gay and solemn.

I looked and gazed and breathed deep and recognized that in seventy years and more that I have looked at landscape consciously I had never seen the like effect. While contemplating the scene I did not think of any poet, whether Homer or Wordsworth or Goethe, who might interpret what I felt but could not put into words. For some minutes I was the world seen by my eyes and felt by my senses, the landscape, the freshness of the air, the smells coming up from the garden, the caress of the breeze.

December 28th

IGOR SAID yesterday that it was the English of course who had had Darlan assassinated. I was shocked and told him I should have to revise my idea of England if I thought her capable of such an act. To the Continental mind, nothing seems more likely. Darlan's disappearance serves England's policy and besides, under the circumstances, is a blessing for the Allied cause. So why not? That, I suppose, is the kind of *Realpolitik* that you cannot eradicate from the Continental mind. They are always ready to accuse the "British Intelligence Service" of any and every crime that, in their misinformed opinion, might serve British policy. Indeed, so insistent is this belief that at times I am tempted myself to wonder whether there is anything in it.

1943

January 1st

FOR THE LAST three years I have been reading one of the most
respected dailies in Germany, the *Deutsche Allgemeine Zeitung*.
According to this authority, Germany has in these years committed no act of aggression, never fought except in self-defense or, at
most, to anticipate ascertained attack; never done more than repel
hostile forces; never suffered defeat, never retreated except to occupy better strategic positions, never massacred, never acted
cruelly to Jews or Poles or Czechs; never behaved in any but exemplary fashion in all occupied countries, except of course where
it had to defend its so humane police against *Heimtückische*, dis-
loyally sinister plots and conspiracies. How different the behavior
of the British in India, of the British and Russians in Persia, of the
British and French in Syria, and now of the Americans in North
Africa: brutality, bloodshed, sadic ferocity, and everywhere Jews
let loose to wreak their hatred of the human race on the so exquisitely civilized Arabs.

Nor is the radio of the Germans more truthful than their newspapers.

So the great, the overwhelming majority of the German public
will come out of this war indignant at the way other people will
speak of them, hate them, and behave towards them. As after the
last war, they will think they are being wronged, and again their

state of mind will become a bouillon in which all sorts of revenge-ful microbes will flourish, ending in another mass revolt against wicked and inhuman treatment.

German young people must be taught all that. They and their like must be taught that what they do to others they must suffer in turn and that they have no right to howl and foam with indig-nation when not half or even quarter is paid back to them of what they have inflicted on others. They must be taught that just being German does not make them superior to the rest of mankind; they must learn that taken all around and considering the whole course of known history, it is doubtful whether one people can lay claim to superiority over another. They must learn that there are no chosen peoples.

January 2d

CURIOUS how faithful the Nazis are to the Israelitish pattern. Not only are they the chosen people; not only have they the exclusive right to trample upon all others and to dispossess them of their territories in good Hexateuch fashion. They must not intermarry, Nazi with Jew or Pole and ultimately with any person whose blood cannot be scientifically proved to be Teutonic. Finally, like ghetto Jews of the later centuries, who were not allowed to read anything in a language not Hebrew, or about matters not reli-gious, the Nazis must not read anything written by a Jew and, to make sure that they shall not, all writings by Jews must be burned. So much for the present, and presumably this applies only to the books of the last couple of centuries. Yet I doubt not that if they prevail, the Nazis will end by excluding all printed matter not written by uncontaminated Teutons. Thus a day may come when a German will encounter the same difficulties in starting to learn another tongue that Maimon in his eighteenth-century Polish ghetto experienced.

From Ezra down, this Jewish exclusiveness was due less and less to a feeling of superiority, certainly not in the ways of this world, but rather to a fear of contamination. Rabbinical Judaism is first and foremost an organization for keeping a small minority, scattered among the nations, from dissolving and disappearing. It was thus based on fear and on a reasoned fear. Why should the Germans of today have such a fear? In the Germany of before the Nazis' conquests, the Jews were not one per cent of the population. The only way of accounting for this fear is that the Jews were believed to make up for quantity by quality, that is to say that one Jew was able to affect the German nation more than one hundred non-Jews. In the course of three thousand years, this despised handful of so-called Semites has never had such a compliment paid to it.

To the Nazi, whether he is conscious of it or not, the Jew is the begetter of Christianity, and for this he can never forgive him. This religion begotten by Judaism, fostered by Hellenism, and imposed upon the Germans by Rome, has according to the Nazi doctrine gone far to corrupt, emasculate, and soften—in our speech, to humanize—the wild ardor and berserker ferocity of the primitive Teuton. This religion, the most recent phase of Mediterranean culture, must be washed away, in blood, if necessary, from the Nordic peoples; and, to make sure that it does not return, they must wipe out after the Jews the Italians, followed by Greeks and finally the Spaniards. Then Wotanism will be sure of ruling the earth.

Meanwhile Italians and Spaniards are allied to the present incarnation of Wotan, as if Ulysses had come to terms with Polyphemus on the promise that he would be devoured last.

January 3d

PAUL ELMER MORE pleads in his *Christ the Word* for the Redemption, the Incarnation, Purpose in the Universe, Revelation. Pity that God gave us minds incapable of receiving a revelation and hearts too feeble to accept and hold it without doubt and fear! As for Purpose, one may ask whose? Every purpose proposed or suggested smells of the blood of a human being—is so anthro-pomorphic that I can only smile at the touching infantility of the idea.

January 4th

IT WILL BE INTERESTING to learn, when the war is over, what discoveries have been made under pressure of privations. One seems already clear, although not exactly a new discovery. It is air transport, not only of passengers but of goods. Should the sub-marines continue to raven for another couple of years, air trans-port may be so perfected and so generalized that the ship will cease to be a carrier, except for bulk of the least perishable kind, demanding the least outlay for freight. In that case, before an-other war overwhelms us, the submarine will also have disap-peared.

In war all is fair. So we may not speak of the cruelty of the sub-marine. Despite individual heroism, the submarine is not a chiv-alrous arm. *Ce n'est pas de la bonne guerre.* Its use is a confession of weakness. It serves the Nazis in this war because their ships have been as good as swept from the seas. Nor could they profit by it, as they do, if they did not control the coasts of the Continent from the Baltic to Biscay; and I daresay they have stations in the Cantabrian *rivas* and the Spanish coast all the way to Finisterre as well as support and supplies of Venezuelan profiteers and sym-pathizers.

January 7th

I ALMOST NEVER read the highly advertised and fervidly praised book of the hour. So I looked at no Steinbeck while I could have got him in English. Now that I have waked up to him, I can find him in Italian translations only. Luckily, these are excellent.

Pian della Tortilla—Tortilla Flats, in English—is scarcely a picaresque novel or story. It is too innocent, too infantile, although naughty enough. Rather than of *Lazarillo* or *Gil Blas,* it reminds one of *Huckleberry Finn* or *Tom Sawyer.*

What a distance America has traveled since the last two were written about small boys of pure British descent! How little, even in his mature much later books, Mark Twain betrays familiarity and understanding of Latin peoples and their religion! Steinbeck on the contrary is amazingly intelligent about popular Catholicism and the state of mind of foreigners so utterly unlike Anglo-Saxons as are these *paesanos* he is exhibiting. He does not describe them, he stages them, and makes them play. The worst that could be said, although with small justice, is that they would tend to turn into marionettes.

Are they a community of degenerates like our "mean whites" of the South, or those of New England described in Edith Wharton's *Summer*? Scarcely. They rather are a survival, or throwback, to the period of human development before hunting (and still less agriculture) had begun to be pursued and the straggling groups of bipeds lived by gathering what they could pick up for food. They have scarcely any sense of property, decency, or decorum although not free from the kind of snobbishness which we find already among horses, cattle, and even sheep. Few signs of sexual morality, no scruples, no loyalties. The only one who possesses the last-named virtue is wanting in even the animal intelligence which guides his companions. Their demands on life limited to food, drink, and sex. They have no difficulty in satisfying their erotic needs, and food they pick up somehow with little trouble. The only serious problem is how to get drink. What brains they have is devoted to overcoming that difficulty. Much of the fun in the book is connected with the devices they use for that purpose.

January 11th

BEGAN TO READ for the fourth time Greville's *Memoirs*, now in a more complete edition than any previous one. It starts with the return of Napoleon from Elba. Rumors were rare and contradictory. Nobody knew how the army would act, nor how the people would react. There was the wildest guessing before it was definitely known that the so-recent monster, ogre, and brigand, now

His Majesty the Emperor, had returned to his palace of the Louvre.

More and more I enjoy reading history in the making, as we get it from diaries and the press of the day. As for the press, it has for the last fifty years and more become so voluminous, so unscrupulous, so corrupt, represents so many divergent and even warring interests, or indeed is so severely controlled in favor of one national interest, that the future student of our own epoch will not be able to cope with it. The past, down to even Waterloo, does not suffer from a like abundance, and we welcome any information we can gather.

The contradictory rumors and fluctuating opinions that constitute the coming event as we see it approaching give it an uncertain shape and an indefinite content: it is finally formed by unpredictable so-called accidents—accidents in fact as well as in appearance.

The last consideration and similar trains of thought have led me far from the doctrine, lapped up in my youth, about the inevitability of events and the Moloch still devouring us today, "historical inevitability." I believe less and less in these more than doubtful and certainly dangerous dogmas, which tend to make us accept whatever happens as irresistible and foolhardy to oppose.

❖   ❖   ❖

Have just read in Kierkegaard's *Riens Philosophiques*, an interesting discussion as to whether the people who knew Jesus in the flesh enjoyed any advantage over us who know Him only by hearsay. He concludes that unless they had faith they had no advantage, and I agree with him. Miracles happen to those who believe in them. Otherwise why does not the Virgin Mary appear to Lamaists, Mohammedans, or Hindus who have never heard of her?

❖   ❖   ❖

During the last war before entering it himself President Wilson used to proclaim that he would not allow it to end either with victors or vanquished, with profiteering, with booty, with land-grabbing, with reparations.

What he could not achieve, although he went into the war to do so, this war will bring about by the sheer force of events.

No victors or vanquished. We shall all be far too ruined to insist much on the slight advantages that may be seized by the "victors." Excepting perhaps in the Pacific islands. There will be no annexations because the Anglo-Saxons are not hungering for more territory than they already rule over. It is not likely that Russia will want to extend her frontiers westward beyond what was allotted to her by Germany in August, 1939, if indeed she will want to retain all that rather than to return to her frontiers of 1914. As for Germany, the utmost she can hope for is a compromise peace that will oblige her no more than to give up everything she did not have before 1938, excepting possibly Austria.

There will be no talk of indemnities and reparations because nobody will be in condition to pay them either in money or even in kind. What will the nominal vanquished have to give to the nominal victors? Of goods, none; of money, the mere idea of it is absurd; of labor, to make good destruction or damage the nation that takes it will have to feed it and care for its being kept in condition to yield satisfactory results, for the country obliged to give it will not be able to do anything for them. And besides, what of native labor that in consequence would be out of work!

I recall what Bismarck said after 1871: that if he beat France again soon, it was Germany that would pay her an indemnity. It took a genius like Bismarck to see that it was to the interest of the victor to help restore the vanquished.

That lesson the Anglo-Saxons have learnt, at least in theory. Will they have the sense to carry it through? Will they be in a position to do so with even the best will in the world?

Then why this war? No rational explanation possible. One is tempted to fancy that extrahuman wills are at work to prevent mankind from humanizing itself too rapidly. If there are to be "victors" in this war it will not be the nations engaged in it actively as belligerents, or passively as neutrals, but the proletarian classes in each of the belligerent countries. There the upper classes will all but disappear, and the survivors lose most of their incomes and, with their wealth, their authority. The fourth estate will triumph at last, and thereby put back the clock of essential human progress for many a generation.

Another victor will be the state within each nation. It will consist of a formidable bureaucracy which will impose first its own standards, and then its own convenience masked as efficiency, and finally its own advantage.

There will be little room for the individuals when this war is over. For every unavoidable reason, restriction will follow restriction, and the individual will find that freedom from persecution because of race, religion, or opinions will not carry him far, or procure him much beyond the barest mass-produced comforts and satisfactions. As super on the stage of life, as member of a chorus, in highly favorable conditions as impresario or orchestra conductor, he may manage to enjoy himself. Woe betide him if he is unable or unwilling to keep step with the crowd.

January 15th

AS A SPECIMEN of what Fascists could believe, the following account of talk overheard in the train between Florence and Milan a few days ago may be of interest.

The principal speaker was a nobleman whom we shall call the Duke of Green Mansions. He had spent a number of years in New York, received as only dukes are, and had then transferred himself to Berlin, where he lived as a privileged person. His countrymen naturally regard him as a great authority on America as well as on Germany. The other two, a well-known count and a financier.

Duke, delighted with sinking of sixteen American oil tankers.

Count hopes this blow will favor operations in Tunisia. No time must be lost in freeing North Africa from the Allies.

Duke: "On the contrary. Let them stay there. Hitler not only expected their invasion, not only did nothing to prevent it, but indirectly drew them into a trap. Our victory can follow only after the destruction of the enemy's tonnage. In northern seas our progress was too slow. It is therefore providential for us that the African front has come about and is being so generously and continuously refurnished by Anglo-American shipping in waters where it is an easier target for our attacks. We now sink about eight million of their tonnage while they can rebuild only three million. They are now losing five million tons a year, that is to say one fourth of their total, which is twenty million.

"So then while the armies of the Axis are making an end forever of the Russian peril our navies are giving the deathblow to the British Empire."

Financier: "I have just come from Tunisia, where I was with our aviation, and it is clear that there the situation of the Allies is hopeless. Russia cannot resist much longer. If it is the armies that are to win the war, the Axis victory is already assured. How can England and America go on having illusions?"

Duke: "They go on with their illusions because they rely on other forces and give no great importance to the military situation. England has never fought with armies but always used disloyal and indirect methods. Today everything is in the hands of international Jewry, which controls the gold reserves of the earth and employs as its agents men of the highest order."

Count: "But is international Jewry a concrete fact and does it really head an organization?"

Duke: "How can you question it? It is the one real enemy that we must fight without quarter. It is all the more dangerous as it is so hard to lay hold of. It has armed Russia, it has guided every step of Roosevelt, has intrigued with every small nation, compelling Hitler to intervene with violence to prevent greater peril. Take one instance: After the Munich conference, Jews plotted with Beneš to establish air bases in Czechoslovakia, and this obliged Hitler to go back on his word—in appearance only. Similar conspiracies forced us, little prepared as we were, into the Greek adventure, which, as it happened, turned out providentially, for it showed up the treachery of the Serbs and allowed us to master Yugoslavia in good time."

Count: "Who is at the head of this organization? Where are its headquarters?"

Duke: "They have no headquarters because they operate the world over through an elaborate net of financiers and politicians. When I say the whole world, I do not exclude the vast region under Axis control. But their chiefs are known and someday it will seem beyond belief that these problems were treated with so little understanding and seriousness. The real chief is Baruch, the adviser of Roosevelt, whom he blackmails into obedience. Close to him stand three others as heads of this stupendous organization (which to a certain extent has absorbed the freemasons). One of these chiefs is Rabbi Wiseman [sic] of New York, but for us the most dangerous is Bernard Berenson, who lives undisturbed in his villa at Settignano."

Count: "I have heard about Berenson and know that he counts as an enemy of Italy, but what harm can he do now, isolated as he is? Is he not cut off from the others?"

Duke: "That is where you are mistaken. Berenson is the most effective of them all and for that reason has decided to remain here. He had the idea as brilliant as it is simple: to use the Vatican. He has encountered no difficulty in getting what he wanted because the Vatican, to exercise its activities in the Catholic world, needs a lot of money. It lived a good deal on American Catholicism. Nowadays this contribution has been reduced to a third, while at the same time its expenses have almost doubled. Who could make up the difference? International Jewry alone, which rushed to the rescue, and by that means got hold of the most powerful propaganda organ in the world. Thus the Church is nowadays an unconscious instrument of Jewry and freemasonry. Of this the last allocution of the Pope furnished dazzling proof. In the very center of both the Nazi and the Fascist parties there lurk most dangerous individuals whom the Church uses for its own ends with the excuse of imaginary religious persecutions and infringement of individual liberty. Only one Italian has understood this danger, Preziosi. It is comforting to see how this man's merits have been recognized and rewarded with the appointment of Minister of State. It leads me to hope that this Judeo-Vatican peril will be met in earnest, and that serious measures will be taken to fight these enemies of ours whose arms are more potent and more deadly than the mechanical ones with which they have armed the Russian soldiers."

The financier tries to explain the apparent successes of the Russians: "The German front is not continuous. The forces are grouped in armies, islets of armed posts at strategic and vital points. In the winter months when the rivers multiply their possibilities of access, the Russians break through the various groups and push forward for hundreds of kilometers. But they do not extend their conquests, so that their effort is profitless—on the contrary, it helps the Axis because it weakens their resistance at vital spots and uses up their reserves of men and material. Their successes therefore are but the death throe of a body in its last agony."

The Count assures them that the food situation on the Continent has improved considerably and that in eighteen months Europe will have resolved the food problem by the exploitation of the Ukraine. Already there is more grain than necessary, more cereals, more fats; in short, the Axis has already reached autarchy, complete self-feeding.

January 20th

IN THE NOVEMBER *Critica* Benedetto Croce asks whether we may call ourselves Christians and decides that we must. We must, he writes, because the Church has been so marvelous despite all that can be said against it.

His apology, which is a eulogy, will offend violent radicals and scarcely satisfy Churchmen. If the last are genuine believers and a bit thoughtful, they will not be disposed to accept Croce's defense of the Church on its merits, on what it has done for humanity. With them it can be no question of "damn merit." The Church does not exist for man, but for the glory of God.

Are we Christians? What else can we be, we Europeans who for eighteen hundred years have imbibed the teaching of Christianity! Unless we have shut ourselves up in spirit-tight ghettoes, like the Jews between 1000 and 1800 A.D., we have not drawn a breath during eighteen hundred years that was not affected by its enfolding us, by its possessing us, by being the very condition of our existence.

Today everybody who has been brought up as a European, no matter in what country of the earth, is the product of that culture, that civilization which under the name of Christianity absorbed nearly all worth preserving that was left over of the Judeo-Hellenic-Roman world, and acting both as a nucleus and as a leaven, has shaped mankind, for good and for evil, into what we are now. It has not done for our hearts what it started out to do, what on the whole it always meant to do, what human nature would not let it do. It has had more success in shaping our minds, and to this day, despite rebellions and revolutions, few of us are entirely emancipated from its categories and very many still cuddle into its cosmos, as into a placenta.

Christianity is still sovereign in the modes of our verbal expression. We cannot utter a dozen words without some turn, some touch, some reference which goes back to Christian myth, Christian liturgy, or Christian doctrine. It does not matter whether we are believing, let alone practicing, Christians. It holds true of Soviet Slavs and Nazi Teutons despite their bitter hatred of Christianity, and of European Jews whether they have left the synagogue or still cling to it. For the present and who knows for how many further centuries to come we can no more get away from Christianity than from the earth's gravity, can no more exist without it than without the air we breathe.

January 25th

C. E. Norton in a letter says he never touched English soil without feeling that he had come home. I can't say quite that, for Norton implies almost as if even on coming from America, England felt more like home. But arriving from the Continent, particularly in my earlier years, I felt as if I was coming to a country where things and people were almost as at home, I mean Boston, and New England.

I never felt as a foreigner in England, and great was my shock when, happening to be there when the last war broke out, the police treated me as one and subjected me to restrictions.

It was a pity and a mistake. Americans should be made to feel at home in England and no difficulty should be put into the way of their getting there, nor should they be subjected on arrival to the same treatment as out-and-out foreigners. During the last war coming and going travelers were parked off into three divisions, British subjects, Americans, and foreigners. After the war Americans and foreigners were treated alike and I could not help resenting it; particularly when landing at Harwich to be interrogated by overworked inspectors with curtness if not rudeness.

January 29th

A FEW DAYS AGO we celebrated Funtyki's sixth birthday in the absence of his father, Igor Markevitch, and his mother, Kyra Nijinskaia. We presented him with his heart's desire, a magnificent helmet, a gun with a folding bayonet, a sword in its scabbard, and a belt. All this he had on him, when he came to luncheon, and a bow and an arrow as well. With some difficulty I persuaded him to take the helmet off his head and to put it as a centerpiece on the table. He was so excited that he could not eat, and scarcely listened when we drank to his health. Even in bed he would not be separated from his panoply and insisted on having it in his grasp. You would think intoxication and illusion could go no further.

A couple of afternoons later, arrayed in his martial magnificence, his nurse took him for walk on the road. A squad of soldiers were passing and seeing him shouted: "You are one of us and you must come with us! Come along now, right away!" Funtyki hid behind his nurse, crying he would not go with soldiers, that he was a *persona onesta*.

What did he mean by the words *"persona onesta"*? I asked him the next day and he answered that it was the same as respectable, in other words, the late Roman, the medieval and Renaissance Italian as well as French *honnête,* as it was used as late as a hundred years ago.

Funtyki was thoroughly frightened, put off his soldierly trappings, and has not reverted to them, confining himself to the bow and arrow. He was so afraid the military would come after him that he begged the servants if they did to deny his presence.

What does all this mean, if not that he is perfectly well aware that he was playing soldier, but not the least illuded into imagining or even believing that he was one? At his age I should have abandoned everything to join the troops I used to see drilling and parading. Thus even with six-year-olds, temperament and disposition differ.

February 10th

DID THE CULT of the Madonna not so much as Virgin but as Theotokos, as Mother of God, go hand in hand with the increase of sacerdotal celibacy? If it did, one would be tempted to inquire whether it was not a return to the worship of the Magna Mater. This worship was perhaps not quite dead at the time of the Council of Ephesus, and the majority of the bishops who proclaimed the Theotokos were from the lands where the Magna Mater had been worshiped for millennia. Her priests were celibate, but celibate in deed, not merely in doctrine, for they were castrated.

February 20th

There are people who deplore the breakup of the unity of the Christian world. What is it they regret, I mean what kind of unity? Is it unity as such? If that is it, why do they not lament over the passing of a far more comprehensive, far more extensive unity with a uniformity far more complete, ever so much more pervasive—the union, namely, of the ancient world under Rome as it was, say, under Trajan? Or is it the unity of dogma of faith, of ritual? But there never was a unity in these matters comparable to what medievalizers would have us believe.

To begin with, there was the division between the Latin world and the rest of Christendom. Even in the Latin world, except for short periods, there was no actual unity except in one respect. This, the only unity which imposed itself during the Merovingian and Carolingian periods, and which the Catholic Church down to our own day insists upon and fights for, is the use of Latin wherever practicable, wherever possible. As for the rest of Christendom, each language group ended sooner or later by going its own way, although the reason given, the excuse made was always of dogma, ritual, or both.

To return to our—to the Latin world—as a matter of fact the Catholic Church never before enjoyed such complete, such far-reaching, deeply penetrating uniformity as increasingly it has since the Council of Trent and the triumph of the Jesuits. Since that Council the Church has needed unity and uniformity more and ever more to fight open and organized opposition and seems to have attained it. It keeps it because, out of growing indifference, opposition is slackening, I mean opposition from within. It would seem that Catholics, like non-Catholics, have one and only one real religion nowadays, the religion of exasperated nationalism.

If uniformity is what certain people hanker for then surely we have it now as never before, whether in extent or in intensity. Everywhere on the face of the earth there is the same lust for its prizes, the same trust in government as the power best able to provide them, the same disregard for all human beings outside our own country, the same freedom from all superstitions, prejudices, considerations that would militate against appetites and ambitions. We employ the same vocabularies, and we use them to vituperate others and to flatter ourselves with the same cynical disregard to the suddenness of the change-over.

As for material and cultural civilization, when have they been remotely so uniform? Go to Manchester or Mandalay, Calcutta or Cape Town, Berlin or Boston, Baltimore or Buenos Aires, the same cinemas, the same radios, the same self-belauding speeches, the same manners and customs, the same newspapers, the same dances and drinks. If a universal language could be imposed, differences would vanish, and a smooth, slack, soft uniformity would adorn the surface of life over nine tenths of what is now dry land.

July 27th

EVENING BEFORE LAST after dining at the *villino* with Igor and de Simony we got back in time to hear the German radio transmission for Austria from London. After a while the usual propaganda-tinged war news was followed by the announcement that the King of Italy had accepted the resignation of Mussolini, had appointed Badoglio to succeed him, but that the war would continue. My movement was of joy at the first words, slight disappointment over the second phrase, and distress over the last.

Yesterday morning the barber appeared and told me what rejoicing there was in Florence, how people embraced in the streets without knowing each other, and how the feeble attempts at rebellion on the part of the Fascists had been foiled. He himself was drunk with happiness. In the course of the day I learned that the departure of Mussolini had been received everywhere with acclamations as relief from an incubus, and that the gayest flags were hung out of the windows in token of gladness.

Toward eleven yesterday forenoon Carla Garabelli, the daughter of the former Prime Minister V. E. Orlando, appeared and stayed till after luncheon. She began with indignation over the way the proclamation of the King was being received in America as she learnt from the radio at 6 A.M. Clearly the Allies would not understand what royalty meant to Italians, how it alone could hold them together, how upon it alone could be built a new Italy. She had suspected something must be up because her father, although he had no professional duties calling him to Rome, went there thrice in a few days. He is there now.

Later in the day the radio proclaimed the state of siege, including curfew, and decreed that all front doors in towns must remain open and lit through the entire night. The *case del Fascio* had been shut up everywhere and Fascist inscriptions are already being painted and hammered out on walls and house fronts.

In short, the revolution, like all revolutions, including the French and Soviet, begins with roses, roses all the way and rarely a spray of rue. I fervently hope that it may proceed as bloodlessly and quietly and in as orderly a way as it has begun.

If it does—and I expect it to—one may ask now, as I always asked, if a similar act by the King and the army would not have had the same result at any time during the last twenty years. Amendola assured me in 1924 that if the King on the occasion of the march on Rome had proclaimed the state of siege and had opposed a few battalions to the marchers, we should have had no Fascism. In more recent years Badoglio is rumored to have promised the King that he could put an end to Fascism with a regiment. Why was it not done? Was it the King alone who would not have it? They were certain that any attempt to get rid of the Fascists by force would lead to civil war and toward disaster. Patience! Let Fascism age, decay, and die a natural death.

In the evening, Igor joined us and we listened to English and American radio news. They proclaimed their intention to go on fighting the Fascist King of Italy and the Fascist Badoglio. This morning Alda comes from town and is indignant that they have not already announced the abolition of racial enactments, and the decrees about listening to Allied radio, etc., etc.

They do not realize that the first call on the new government is to secure order and prevent rebellion on the part of the more headstrong Fascists, relying on passive resistance from the others as well as the retributive popular justice against more obnoxious members of the outgoing regime. Not only Igor and Alda but the Allies should understand this, give the new government credit for knowing what they are about, and have patience.

I myself am now thinking that it may have been wise not to be silent at the first announcement, but to pretend that the war would go on. It surely cannot stop on the Italian side until they see what happens in Sicily, what German forces remain in Italy, and what chances there are of getting rid of them at small outlay of Italian life and property. A few days may decide.

Meanwhile, all sorts of rumors reach me from the "servants' hall"; that Badoglio was in full understanding with the Allies, who would stop bombing Italy; that Hitler committed suicide yesterday; that Mussolini and Ciano have both been arrested to save them from violence, and that Scorza has been killed. More authentic and interesting reports are sent by Carla to the effect that the ministers now coming into power are trained for their several jobs, and that the former chief-of-police Senise, much liked and trusted by non-Fascists, has returned to his post.

July 29th

DAY BEFORE YESTERDAY H. was here. He is a young German art historian and has been working with the German armistice commission at Turin. It seems to be composed of retired colonels and generals. H., although anti-Nazi, is *treu und fromm* in his feelings toward the army, and absorbs their opinions with reverence. Well, he said that the withdrawal of Italy from the war would be an alleviation for Germany, for Italy has never been more than a dead weight. On the other hand, they would not tolerate North Italy being turned into territory from which Allied aircraft and eventually armies could attack Germany. If, therefore, North Italy was not neutralized they, the Germans, would defend it tooth and nail, no matter what the destruction entailed upon monuments and what miseries inflicted on the population.

The same evening we heard transmitted to Austria more of Churchill's speech. So far as I could make out, it betrayed no little comprehension of the difficulties attending the emerging non-Fascist government, counseled patience with the Italian people, and warned against the danger of turning them into intractable soreheads.

What I gathered of Roosevelt's last utterance sounded less statesmanlike. The present Italian government has its hands full keeping outs and ins from massacring each other, and has no time to think of punishing offenders. It is a pity Roosevelt started with that as his first greeting to the new Italy.

It is a pity also, if this new regime wishes to gain the sympathy of the Anglo-Saxon world, that it does not hasten to abrogate the racial enactments, and does not free political prisoners, whether in jails or concentration camps. It is a pity too that, if I may judge by the glimpse I had just now of the Florence *Nazione*, it allows the press to talk nonsense about American internal conditions, and to publish the fantastic claims of Germans and Japs regarding their air and sea victories over the Allies.

July 30th

NOT A STRANGER only like myself but most of my Italian friends have been impressed by the way the peasants, the artisans and small tradespeople have kept their heads over imperialism, annexationism, and nationalism. The answer occurred to me yesterday in the following way.

The woman who valets me is a remarkably intelligent as well as levelheaded person of canonical age. Being from upper Valdarno, she speaks agreeable Tuscan and her handwriting is excellent. I supposed therefore that she had had considerable schooling. I happened to quote some lines of Dante that suited what we were discussing, and I noticed that she did not take them in at once, and looked vague at the mention of the poet. I asked whether she had not learned about him at school. No, she had left after learning to read and write.

Then it flashed on my mind that she had not been influenced by the catchwords of the elementary history books, not poisoned by the rhetoric of writers, that she remained innocent of the high-falutin, bulging, pompous periods that Italians acquire at school and college, and feed on for the rest of their lives.

Books might be written about the influence of rhetoric in all shapes over thought and feeling, and worse still over action. Perhaps nothing separates and unites nations so much as their different rhetorics. Ours (Anglo-Saxon) remains Biblical still, but the Italians, French, Spaniards, and Rumanians are common sufferers from the same rhetoric. This common rhetoric goes so far as to make them believe that, although they have so little else in common, they are of the same "Latin" race, whereas they are merely victims of the same Latin rhetoric.

October 23d

ALMOST THREE MONTHS have slipped by without a word of mine in these pages. There are various reasons. I have a limited amount of energy, and hold a limited quantity of ink. Both were being used up on a book I am writing. At the same time, the confusion of the situation, the endless rumors that reached me, each contradicting the other, the continuous vapor or, if you like, smoke of my own reflections, were at once discouraging to the effort of putting them in black and white and far too numerous to be written down, unless I took all day for it.

An hour or two after the *feux de joie* and the delirium of the servants, who while we were dining out of doors announced the armistice, the confidential chauffeur of Carla appeared with orders to carry me off at once. It was far too sudden, and Nicky would not hear of my leaving so precipitously. The decision turned out happily, for the place I was to be taken to would not have suited the requirements of my age-weak flesh. Carla feared that the Germans, taking possession, would allow the local Fascists to return to power and wreak their will upon well-known anti-Fascists. Besides, there was danger that the Germans on their side would treat me not only as an American but as enemy number one, the enemy for whom and with whom there were no possible pacts, namely, a Jew.

So a couple of days later, the Marchese Filippo Serlupi, Minister to the Holy See of the Republic of San Marino and enjoying the privilege due to an active diplomat, came and brought me and Nicky here, where I am now writing.

It is a villa built on the site of the house where nearly five hundred years ago lived the Platonist Marsilio Ficino. It stands high over the palace of Careggi built by Cosimo de'Medici on the brow of the Monte Vecchio, which towers over it and shelters it completely from the cruel north wind that we suffer from at I Tatti. In consequence, the house and the grounds, wood and tilth, enjoy all the sunshine there is, and a climate like the more sheltered parts of the French Riviera. The trees, olive, oak, ilex, pine, cypress, and mimosa, take the most shapely and even romantic aspects. Everywhere they cluster as in a Titian, and one is tempted to wonder whether they are planted after his model, or whether he found them thus in favored places in the Veneto, and painted them from nature. Then there is a sweep of sky that I miss from my own house. I enjoy watching the soft sunlit vapors curling up after sunrise and turning into gentle clouds. I grow ecstatic over the sunsets which I see here, not reflected only but in full splendor. They are sublime, they are gorgeous, they are romantic, they are passionate, they are tender, they are menacing, they are reassuring, they are apocalyptic; everything except indifferent.

The grounds as they climb the hillside are spaced with grassy terraces which are almost as soft and springy as English lawns. The peasants seem to like their work, greet one pleasantly, and are ready for a chat. They are well-informed and full of sense. One family has its own radio and listens intelligently. Its head is an old man of eighty-six who tells me every day, as I come across him in the fields, that he still enjoys life and would feel perfectly well but for a flat foot. It is singular, by the way, and greatly to the credit of the Tuscan peasants with whom I come in contact, how little they are disposed to complain, and how ready to express satisfaction with their lot and its incidents.

Above the house, the well-wooded hill rises sharply to a flat top crowned by a towered farmhouse. It was the goal of our walks when we lived on the Lungarno in Florence, and used to come out on foot to climb up from the stream and walk down again by the Via Bolognese. I speak of more than fifty years ago, when there were no houses beyond the Mugnone except ancient villas. Now, alas! a huge suburb has grown up, filling the valley all the way to

Sesto with the tenements of the poor, with factories around huge cylinders as hideous as gasometers and with belching chimneys. Besides, the bottom of the hill is crowded with the buildings of the hospital city which wreck the nearer part of the view—although no doubt the site is well chosen for its climate.

I recall bringing William James here—I mean to the towered farm. He hated walking between high walls because they shut out the view. I protested that one enjoyed it all the more for not having it constantly before one. He would not listen. It was churlish to deprive one of the view. It made him mad.

I am not writing memoirs of my past, or about the friends and acquaintances of the present, and must not let myself be tempted to speak in detail of the great psychologist's stay in Florence, or of my hosts and fellow guests in this and a neighboring villa, more or less like myself in hiding, *alla macchia,* as it is called. *Macchia* is the Italian for bush. *Darsi alla macchia* means to take to the woods when one is wanted by the police. Just now, however, as so many are in hiding, *macchia* means a variety of things. For civilians, not being in their own homes when the police come for them. As many of these officials are far from zealous in the interest of the republican Fascists, they are glad not to find the subject they had orders to arrest, and do not take much trouble to discover him. Of course, when the authorities really want a person they can get him, as happened some days ago with all and sundry who had connections with royalty, particularly as ladies and gentlemen in waiting. Some who could not be found in their houses have been ferreted out easily and jailed.

It is hard to imagine what advantage the Italian Quisling regime—for that is what Fascism is now reduced to—hopes to get out of putting against it court people and their friends, the greater part of aristocratic society in the country. If it is done to win over the lower orders it is a mistake, for these orders in Italy, excepting some rabid Communists and half-educated intellectuals, have no feelings of resentment and still less of hatred against the upper classes. This action can therefore be no more than a *sfogo*—an outburst—rather a sign of helplessness than of power. The persons arrested may suffer discomfort or even worse for some weeks. They will come out realizing, at last, what was behind the regime that the majority of them approved, supported, or tolerated. Among them, as a matter of fact, are ardent propagandists who did no little to spread the Fascist gospel both in England and in America.

Thus many who fear what the Fascist rump may do in their brief last moment of sunshine are *alla macchia* in fairly comfortable quarters, hiding neither from Germans alone nor from Fascists alone, but from Fascists taking advantage of the German occupation to do their worst. As this worst can happen only under the German occupation, it is they, the Germans, who are held responsible, and it does not tend to increase the number of those who favor them.

Indeed, nothing surprises me more than the universal hatred of the Germans that is revealed by recent events. It is manifested in every class, except perhaps the highest, most of all in the peasantry, the artisans, and the "lower orders" generally. It is based on fear, for it is believed that Germans without exception are capable of every cruelty, every atrocity, every robbery, every theft, and not merely while doing their duty collectively as commanded but as private individuals.

So it is accepted as beyond question that before leaving Naples they fired the university library and deliberately poured petrol over the books, to make sure that nothing remained unburned. Every kind of vehicle is fair booty, but they are particularly keen on smart and powerful cars. They do not steal them—oh, no, indeed. They leave a receipt, and payment in some sort of marks is to be effected after the war. They carry away everything made of wool, mattresses included, and all other apparel and footgear. They make no bones about emptying wardrobes, and show a preference for silk pajamas, underwear, and ties. These appeal to the officer class of all grades.

The real *macchia* is naturally the woods and hills and any more inaccessible nook or haunt. These are said to be full of soldiers and officers who will not fight under this regime. Also police and

carabinieri who, out of patriotism or, perchance, prudence, prefer
to keep away. Numbers, too, of youngsters liable to service, or
fearing forced transport to Germany. Also war prisoners, English
chiefly.

The Germans and Fascists together do their utmost to capture
or disperse these bands, but so far with no great success. The peasants are almost to a man on the side of the refugees and prisoners,
including the British. They feed them and shelter them and help
them to get away. Even shepherds driving their flocks to the Ma-
remma from our own hills will dress British soldiers with their
own clothes and take them along. Persons of the upper classes, too,
are said to be contributing a great deal with money and organization to feed, clothe, and house "these brigands and Communists."
It is reported that they are receiving arms, and that they crawl,
creep, and drift towards the Allied forces whom they hope to join.

Although I have been in a *macchia de luxe* for six weeks, I have
not written a word either in these pages or on the three books I
have on the stocks. After more than two years without leaving my
grounds, except for visits to the dentist, I felt the change on coming here as if I had gone to a distant and softer land. I relaxed in a
way that spoke of overwork and tension. I more than relaxed: I
collapsed, not nervously, but physically. I was too tired to touch
a book connected with my work. My hosts did not force me to
strenuous conversation. So I spent the days strolling gently on
these charming slopes, chatting, reading, and being read to.

Little by little an itch for something more strenuous began to
trouble me. First it was for more serious reading. Then for research. At last I am writing, having got the better of difficulties
that I found absurdly disconcerting.

I am reminded of what a Belgian friend told me early in the
last war. He had been sent over to England to see how his humbler refugee countrymen were faring. He discovered that they
were ill-fed and disgruntled. Were they not provided with sufficient foodstuffs and was fuel wanting? Neither, but the women
could not cook because they did not have their own pots and pans.
So it has been here with me. I am so spoiled in my own home, with

just the right desk, the perfect light, the drawers and pigeonholes for paper and slips, for pen and pencil, that here where everything of the kind is missing, I have been put off from making the effort I always have to make before starting to write.

And after all, what have I to say? Rumors only—gossip that reaches me—and my own reflections based on a certain acquaintance with international affairs, history, German and French and Italian character and politics. All was confusion and contradiction. I heard nothing convincing, even when assured that the information came straight from the horse's mouth. It generally turned out that it was handed on by somebody who had had it from somebody else who, perhaps, had it firsthand. It was like hearing of ghosts who appeared to somebody one's interlocutor had seen, but never to that gossip himself.

In one way all these rumors, alarming, frightening, or comforting, and inspired by wishful thinking, were profitable. They confirmed the conviction I had been reaching that we can never know why things happened, seldom how, and rarely as much as what—not, at least, till they are over, and an event has turned out conclusive, a *fait accompli*. Until that moment, not even the principal actors, neither a Hitler, nor a Stalin, nor a Churchill, nor a Roosevelt, knows exactly what is going on. Put in this way, it is, of course, an obvious commonplace.

Therefore history should not be too busy about the Why, as is too often the case with German-minded books, nor too strenuous about the How, but insist on finding out the exact What.

So far as one now can tell, the Gran Consiglio met and was followed by the dismissal of Mussolini. After six weeks or so the Badoglio government announced the armistice and the threat to all and sundry who should oppose it. This, of course, was equivalent to a declaration of war against Germany.

I suspected that something was being prepared to upset Mussolini. It was rumored that Orlando and Cini and presumably Grandi were in touch with Badoglio. I cannot yet understand what induced some seventeen members of the Gran Consiglio to vote against the Duce, thereby jeopardizing their own position, perhaps their lives. It would raise one's estimate of these men, and make one think better of politicians, if one could believe they were actuated by no other motive than the public weal.

Different and contradictory versions are current as to just what happened at the Gran Consiglio. It seems that, expecting trouble, Mussolini brought with him the incriminating documents he had gathered against his colleagues. When, in his wrath at their opposition, he was about to begin to read them, he was asked why he did not reveal them before.

Conflicting stories, too, about the way Mussolini behaved on his arrest: some saying that he wept, and others that he was stony. Some reported that he was confined in a fort where the heat was suffocating, and that the Pope intervened to procure him better treatment. According to others he was carried out to sea, but never allowed to land.

Followed every kind of rumor about the fate of Ciano, of his "Augusta" Edda, of Grandi and others; and to this day I have heard nothing convincing about their whereabouts.

Just what was going on during the six weeks between the dismissal of the ex-omnipotent Duce and the armistice I have not been able to gather.

Could the King-Emperor and his new Prime Minister really believe that they still might carry on the war on the side of the Nazis? If not, did they not realize that for them as for every Italian the problem was how to get rid of the Germans without turning Italy into a battlefield? Were they trying to induce their allies to leave the country, bag and baggage, so that the Anglo-Saxons might occupy and use it as a springboard for the invasion of the *Vaterland*, or at least to use Italian airdromes for attacking it from the air? It remains a mystery that the King and Badoglio did not wait till the Allies could have landed in force to go against the Germans, at the moment that these heard of Mussolini's dismissal, and of the simultaneous declaration of the armistice. Taken by surprise, the Germans might have had to withdraw in haste, if not from the entire peninsula at least to the valley of the Po. I suspect that the King, to save the dynasty, and perhaps the empire as well, had some scheme of his own. Whatever it was, it did not work; and finally when the armistice did come, the way it was brought about exposed Italy not only to accusations of treachery but to ridicule as well.

The German pretense that they were taken unawares by the armistice is absurd in view of the fact that they had made all their preparations to occupy all of Italy that was not yet in Allied hands. Although they were anxious to set up a Quisling or Vichy regime to help them out in local administration, and with them to share the blame of unpleasantnesses, and although they hastened to liberate Mussolini, with whom and his republician Fascists they pretend to be allies and not conquerors, they nevertheless act exactly as in Norway and France. They are the masters and the local authorities dare not take a step without orders from the Kommandantur, except when the Blackshirts want to do something against private persons unfriendly or disaffected. In rounding up recalcitrant Italian troops or deserters, the Blackshirts do the spying and, guided by them, the Germans, when they feel like it, do the shooting and killing.

This must surely open, if need still were, the eyes of the population to the weakness of the pretended Fascist republicans, and the small account the Germans make of them. It is, by the way, rather mysterious that the Duce, who used to love to strut and utter oracular, crisp declarations and commands has spoken but once or twice since his liberation and then in a husky voice, uttering banal phrases so as to leave one doubting whether it was he at all.

It is believed by many that he and Graziani are both dead, the latter assassinated by the Germans, and the Duce dying under an operation necessitated by a mortal wound inflicted while they were rescuing him. From two "perfectly certain sources" this has been communicated to me. As for Graziani, the Nazis suspected him of being in league with Badoglio to do what he could for Italy during the German occupation.

As they do not "intend" to hold Rome against the Allies, it is said that they, the same Germans, mean to carry the Pope away with them. When they announced this decision, His Holiness is said to have answered that they would take away no Pope but only Cardinal Pacelli; that his abdication was ready and that the moment he was seized, the election to the Papacy of Archbishop Spellman of New York would be made public. A conclave is supposed to have been already held, and the smoke of the burned voting slips has been seen by the Romans.

A further version is that the Germans have let the Pope know that, not being able to answer for his safety, they would carry him, his court and chancellery to the principate of Liechtenstein, of which he was to be temporal sovereign during his exile from the Vatican.

The Germans here, as in other countries, seem to be carrying away all of those who might resist them, or who could serve their several countries when liberated. Persons like Vittorio Cini have been transported to Germany for safekeeping. It is even rumored that they have already shot him. All the Italian troops who have refused to co-operate with them have been packed off in cattle vans to Germany. People speak of a press gang snatching individuals in the streets and cafés to be sent to the same land as laborers.

Whatever the conduct of the Nazis may be, that of the Fascists is worse. They miss no trick to make themselves not only hated but despised. They behave foolishly in things great and small. They might have announced that they would have no dealings with the present King, and many would be with them; but to declare a republic is to alienate the possessive and upper classes still attached to monarchy, whether out of sentiment, interest, or the belief that monarchy is a guarantee for property and privilege. At the same time, this declaration automatically transfers to the King all who wanted to get rid of him because of his agreement with Mussolini for twenty-one years.

So much for big mistakes. As for smaller ones, they are innumerable, consisting chiefly of doing the dirty work for the Germans, as well as performing every kind of pettily vindictive act. Of this nature have been the numerous arrests of high-placed people. Indeed, I am told that the Kommandantur has forbidden further arrests without their express permission. The Fascist prefecture is said to be furious and to be talking of the German Consul as a monster, as a public enemy who must be got out of the way.

It would seem that out of disgust with the behavior of the Blackshirts, the Germans are getting almost popular. They are here to win the war or, at least, to defend their country. The others behave like the mean gangsters and rancorous proletarians that the overwhelming majority of them have always been.

Meanwhile, the snail's pace at which the Allies are advancing up the Peninsula is distressing. As yet it inspires good-natured criticism, but it may turn sour and bitter if it does not soon improve. The Allied radio speaks apologetically of the difficulties of the terrain. That means that they had not given it sufficient study—a sorry confession and all but incredible. The Germans are mining every furlong of the roads they are leaving. Should not that have been foreseen?

Did they expect a walkover, and that the Nazis would not defend the territory that was serving them, the continental part as shield, and the peninsular one as spear, to prevent or delay the invasion of their own country?

Why did the Anglo-Saxons not invade Yugoslavia, where they would have had the full support not only of the extremely warlike and apparently well-organized and armed natives but of entire Italian armies as well? It looks almost as if they followed the apparently easiest, the obvious way. Having taken Sicily, it must have seemed a matter of course to cross over to the mainland and march north.

I speak as an outsider. There may be cogent reasons unknown to me for the campaign in Italy. But I am equally at sea about the rest of the affair. There must be fully three million soldiers in Great Britain, armed, equipped and ready for battle. Why, then, is no landing on a grand scale attempted over the Channel? A successful invasion of France and Belgium would surely lead to the heart of Germany much quicker than through Italy or even the Balkans. Am I entirely wrong? Are the difficulties there still unsurmountable?

I am tempted to believe, at times, that the Anglo-Saxons want to shed their own blood as little as possible, while both Germany and Russia are letting themselves bleed white.

Something of that sort has been urged in defense of French military tactics since the last war—at all costs to spare French lives. No doubt it is now being preached by Lavallists: that after all France will come out of this war with small loss of life and far less sacrifice of wealth than if she had taken a full share in hostilities.

October 29th

AUGUST 5TH LAST the director of the German Institute in Florence, Friedrich Kriegbaum, having expressed a desire to see me, came to lunch. Such was the state of mind of all of us that I did not have to guess what he was coming for. It was to procure my influence in favor of saving the German Institute of Art History from confiscation or even dispersal by the Allies. He was in touch with the German authorities, military as well as civil, an intimate friend of the German Consul (of whom more later), and it was clear that none of them expected to remain here many days. In fact, a few weeks later all German residents were being advised, urged, and even forced to leave, and did leave.

Why did the Allies fail to appear? They were expected to land anywhere and everywhere, near Rome, at Grosseto, at Piombino, at Leghorn. Even a day or two after the armistice the prefecture here let it be known that a force had been landed at Leghorn, was already at Pistoia, and in a few hours would be here.

Instead, it was the Germans who had moved inland to occupy Florence and adjacent places.

What palsied the movement of the Allies, I, and the majority of dwellers in this paradise, ask again and again, and discuss without ceasing. Was it the shifty and shilly-shallying Italian King-Emperor, was it the diplomats with their Byzantine finessing, or was it the English tendency to refuse to fight until the enemy had every advantage?

Yet I wish Italy would be accepted as a full ally. It would strengthen the authority of the King and his cabinet, which, despite every fault, is the least bad rallying point just now. Italians would be readier to do their utmost against the Germans and even to fight alongside of the Allies if they were assured they would not have to pay materially or morally for a war which, as Hitler himself as good as declared, was wanted only by Mussolini. It would encourage Hungary and Rumania, perhaps even the Bulgars, to follow.

What is the alternative? Granted that the ruling classes and the people, too, were held responsible for having made war against the Allies. What ways have these of punishing them? None of them would take as a gift a foot of Italian territory; and it is to be hoped they will not allow their half-barbarous Slovene, Croat, and Serb adherents to annex any district that is not overwhelmingly Slav. Imposing reparations, indemnities—whence can they be drawn in a country so bankrupt financially and so incapable, as it will be for a long time to come, of producing exportable goods or capital in adequate quantities?

International affairs will be placed on a better footing when it is understood that there is no way of punishing a people for the crimes of its rulers. You might conceivably kill them off, seventy-five million Germans, forty-five million Italians, etc., etc. What would you do with the void thus created? Have you enough men and means to replace the energies, mental and moral, that you have destroyed? Not likely. You simply would have got rid of so much genius and talent that would stimulate your own, and injured your trade to the extent that you would have slain your potential customers.

There is no way of punishing a people that does not boomerang back on yourself.

Wherefore the moment a people begins to show signs of preparing to run amok, stop it even by force of arms. See what it has cost England, whose government is chiefly responsible for having encouraged Mussolini and saying: "Good doggie, nice doggie, only growls a little bit, will never hurt anybody," until both he and Hitler were ready to spring, with the results that we now are enjoying.

There is no more suicidal doctrine than what has prevailed in my lifetime—the notion that no one has a right to interfere with the internal affairs of another country. It is, by the way, a doctrine followed only towards countries of considerable strength. In my own memory there was constant interference in Turkey, in Bulgaria, in Yugoslavia, and by Americans almost anywhere and everywhere to the south of us, in the Western Hemisphere. Immediate intervention may be annoying, may even be expensive. Yet think of the consequences of letting trouble pile up till you can stand it no longer, and you have to fight—as we are fighting now. How small would have been the cost in lives and property and every kind of cultural value if Mussolini had been nipped in the bud, long before he played the part of the ape that opened the cage for the tiger Hitler.

As it is impossible to punish peoples without injury to ourselves, it would seem that the policy of the Allies should be to reconcile them, beginning with those most likely to yield to immediate kindness. Thus between the dismissal of Mussolini and the armistice I should have tried the following experiment: While bombarding war industries I should have showered from the sky millions of tons of chocolate, coffee, sugar, rice, cigarettes, etc., etc. I am almost certain that the result would have proved so favorable to our cause that the tragicomic return of Mussolini and the ghoulish reappearance of Fascism would have found no trace of the favor that it is still to a certain extent enjoying.

I am told, however, that yesterday, October 28th, to celebrate the 21st anniversary of the march on Rome there were scarcely two hundred Blackshirts in the procession, and most of them ragamuffins. The raging prefect is said to have had the air alarm blown, so that the public should not see how few and of what kind the republican Fascists of Florence were. Indeed, to procure adherents to the militia they have gone so far as to take the lads out of the reformatories, and to arm them with guns and pistols. These parade in open cars singing Fascist songs, and insult and provoke the passers-by. It will be recalled that when the Soviets began to massacre the upper classes, they were accused of employing boys of sixteen or seventeen, because at that age these are supposed to have no human feelings and no capacity for pity.

This is far from being the only practice of the Fascists at all times, and most of all now, that is exactly parallel to Bolshevism. Thus, great estates were taken over for the benefit of the so-called proletariat—the which often enough, in ways as strange as for the Heathen Chinee in Bret Harte's ballad, ended in aggrandizing the already vast possessions of prominent suddenly enriched "hierarchs" of the regime. A few days ago an estate near Ravenna was taken over and another near Siena, that of the Chigi-Zondadaris. Then there is raging a crusade against individuals, like Cini and Volpi. Of course they enriched themselves as perhaps would not have been so easy in England, or even in America, in the last twenty years; but there is no reason to think that they did more than take that advantage of a situation which any financier and promoter would have taken quite legally, under the same conditions.

This conduct of the Fascists is what they have been practicing ever since they came into their own twenty years ago. Yet this is what England, leading the procession, followed, as always in European matters, by the U. S. A., aided and abetted because Mussolini was a shield and buckler against Bolshevism. And the Fascist rump still has the impudence to proclaim that it is fighting Bolshevism.

A distressing trait of human nature comes to the top in times like these. We were told by a German officer that his fellow victims of Nazism were horrified, when they occupied Paris, by the number of charges brought against each other by people in fair standing. They accused one another of anything that might induce Germans to act. So it is here now, and it seems that the Germans are disgusted.

October 30th

BEFORE THE OCCUPATION by the Nazis I felt sure Florence would not be bombarded. I was less confident afterwards but hoped it would not occur. I was not a little surprised when, on September 25th, out walking towards noon, we saw Allied aircraft forming in triangles and throwing down bombs over the town. It is my belief that the aviators were returning from a serious expedition and, without previous thought of doing so, happened to see a train passing along the edge of the town and thought it would be fun to pot it.

The result was a sad one. It destroyed the lives and the houses of innocent people. Among them was Kriegbaum, whom I have already mentioned. He was calling on the Viennese connoisseur Planiscig when a bomb fell and killed him. He was one of the most thoroughly humanized and cultured individuals of my acquaintance, gentle and tender, incapable of evil, and was doing nothing but good. He was one in a thousand, and if Germany had seventy-five thousand like him she would be worth saving and cherishing. Unfortunately, it seems impossible to bring them together, unite them in common action. Man seems to find it so easy to organize for evil, and so difficult to unite and remain united for good!

To return to Kriegbaum: not long ago he went through two terrific air raids in Germany. They shattered his nerves, and, for fear of bombs, he dreaded returning to his own country. His dread was well founded; but he could not escape his destiny.

When he came to see me on August 5th it was, as I have already told, to ask protection for his Institute. Two or three days before his death it was our turn to ask his. He was not only willing but eager and said that he and the Consul frequently put their heads together as to how they could save I Tatti from depredation. It seems that a member of Göring's gang approached him some eighteen months previously to inquire about a villa belonging to an American which they had been told was full of valuable pictures and books. He put them off by assuring them that at I Tatti there were no paintings except of Catholic subjects, and no books of more than local interest.

Immediately on the German occupation we got hints, not only from the art superintendent but from a friendly German, that we had better put books and pictures in safety. No time was lost in doing what one could, in the expectation that the enemy might be upon us at once. Happily, there were so many pictures of smaller value in the house that they could cover the walls and thus prevent any suspicion that important works of art had been removed. With the books it was, and remains, more difficult. Nearly half have been removed, the more irreplaceable ones. Yet some twenty thousand remain, and I should be sorry if any of them fell into rough hands, with small profit probably to German students, and considerable loss to myself. The serious loss would be not the money so much as the labor it would be to replace them.

Until recently I remained skeptical about the predatoriness of the Germans in this war. I was ready enough to concede that they would snatch the vehicles, woolens, leather, anything more or less necessary for carrying on. But that, as reported, they would in an allied country like Italy, whose government they were recognizing as an equal, carry away works of art, libraries, and every kind of valuable that, being under sequestration, was temporarily Italian national property, seemed too improbable. Let me add that thus far there has been no attempt on the part of the occupying Germans to touch my property.

Privates, particularly if from Austria or other territory annexed by the Reich since 1938, are said to be deserting in numbers. They sell their arms and whatever they have been able to raffle and take to the *macchia*. Their money will in time be spent, the weather will turn cold and wet, and the humanity of the *contadino* or villager will become exhausted. Then these deserters may become a public danger. It is not only now, and as deserters, that Nazi troops are said to be free and easy with war material in their keeping. More than a year ago I heard of their selling benzine, rubber tires, etc., etc., at Leghorn and all along the coast.

It seems that the German Consul goes on believing that he will not remain here long. He wishes he could. He would like to, so as to see whether the Allied troops would behave better than his. Evidently he does not expect them to. Troops must average pretty much the same everywhere in our world. There will be so many roughs, so many brutes, so many gangsters, so many petty thieves, so many sadists. Discipline relaxes as war goes on.

The same Consul is said to feel so insecure in his tenure here that he is anxious to put the library of the German Institute in safety. He seems certain that when the Allies arrive they will seize it as booty. It shows what he knows the Germans would do in similar cases where they felt they were entirely free to do so—as perhaps they are not quite here.

For me, it is hard to believe that the English or Americans would do such a thing as seize the cultural instruments of the vanquished—the instruments by which they may be humanized. Yet one wins wars only by employing the arms that, at first, one was horrified to see the enemy using.

It seems that the Nazis have ordered the library of the German Institute to be packed and sent to Germany. As in that land of learning and libraries the books and even the photographs would be of relatively little use, the order can come only from authorities so disgusted with Italy that they never mean to return. The Consul, on the other hand, realizes the importance of Italian art as a civilizing instrument; and, as it can be properly studied here only, he is eager to have the Institute continued.

I gather that we have barely escaped having as one of our rulers under this regime Dumini, the assassin of Matteotti. I recall traveling about in the autumn after this murder, and finding in Umbrian and Latian villages, painted in red on the walls, "Viva Dumini." This vulgar slayer was to be exalted as a national hero, a benefactor, a friend of the people. It did not work; and after a while he was *totgeschwiegen*—complete silence with regard to him. Many years later we were motoring from Cyrene to Derna and as we were approaching the last-named place the chauffeur pointed out a fine villa and told us it belonged to Dumini. Last spring it was rumored that he had been made prisoner by the English. Yet here he is, a living remembrance of what is and has been under and behind the Fascist regime.

While penning these last few paragraphs a letter written in English reached me. It is from a woman in Florence, one quarter American in blood, but far more than that in spirit, although Italian for the rest and born and bred in Italy. It contains passages confirming or supplementing what I have noted down, and I cannot resist the temptation to insert them here:

"One sees strutting about Blackshirts with faces of convicts, but behind their arrogant mien lurks a good deal of wholesome fear. They make me think of Neapolitans under the last Bourbons who were drilled to look *feroce, cchiù feroce* [fierce, more fierce]. They seem to be quite oldish men with gray hair or young *beceroni* [town riffraff] under twenty. I have now spent two nights here in the Via dei Bardi. The Germans have handed over the guarding of the Ponte Vecchio to the Blackshirts. The first night I was startled out of my sleep by wild shooting, which was kept up half the night; and this morning the house shook from hand grenades being hurled into the Arno. These people are so terrified of being pounced upon in the dark that they bolster up their courage by warlike display.

"I have been almost a month in a faraway *fattoria*—estate of my daughter's. It is out of the way in the upper Chianti, a most beautiful region with fine woods of huge chestnut trees, brooks all over, steep stony paths that climb right up to the ridge, from which one dominates all the Valdarno, way up to Arezzo. It was the moment of the *vendemmia*—grape-gathering—and as like Benozzo Gozzoli as one could wish. Whole hills and valleys covered with vines, bowed down by huge purple branches of grapes. The peasants winding in and out among them, picking and carrying the overflowing crates on their backs up to the *fattoria*, to cellars lined with huge barrels. The heady smell, the swarthy faces, the big paunches of the vats in a dim half-light, were picturesque and gave one a feeling of the plenty and riches of the soil that was comforting to behold."

I interrupt and ask for the thousandth time what a paradise like this, where I spend the sunny hours of the day writing out of doors, where life for people of the same condition is so much easier than anywhere else in the white man's world, where, but for one per cent of one per cent, the population is the most peaceable and peace-loving, having long ago passed the age of militarism— I ask what it can have to do with such an inhuman, that is, so mechanized, sapper-and-miners', engine drivers', artillerists', and airmen's war. Even under occupation I look over this lovely town, this landscape, and wonder.

Returning to my friend's letter, she writes further: "I walked a lot and sat about under trees or on warm sun-baked stones to read and dream away the hours. Then news began to come up of raids in the middle of the night, of plunder and of the proprietors of villas taken away under arrest. Needless to say that almost everyone hides, and helps the poor young men who refuse to serve the Germans and their satellites. It makes things pretty dangerous. We did our share as best we could. So we were advised to leave, for in the country one is trapped in the middle of the night, although we had organized means of escape with romantic ladders, and slept with our clothes on. At Bagno a Ripoli in a house near by, a young couple, she having just had a baby, were spirited away in the night by the police. As soon as they had left, two enormous trucks with Fascists on board arrived and looted the whole house. The same plundering is going on in town. A couple of nights ago young Fascists were emptying a house in Via Masaccio, and the regular police had to use hand grenades because the young gangsters were armed and threatened to shoot. These got away with all they could carry."

November 4th

FROM ALL that we hear regarding the conduct of the Fascists during their *Cent Jours,* one sees what kind of foundation the party had in the country, even though at the start the upper crust may have been inspired by a certain *idealità,* which word, however, is the Italian for a passing disregard of self-interest and fear.

Between the dismissal of Mussolini and the declaration of the armistice, there were constant demands for the abrogation of the "racial laws." They could not be touched because they were an *essential part of the "Steel Compact."* They were quietly dropped.

With the Nazi occupation, Jews naturally feared the worst and took to the *macchia*. As many as ten or twelve are hiding in a villa near Siena. One great landed proprietor, brother and cousin of officers high in army and navy, has been flitting from hole to hole, and at last has decided to take shelter in the small apartment of a friend in the heart of Florence on the Arno. It was said that the Fascist prefect, the moment he was installed, warned Jews to leave their homes and to go into hiding. It is not easy to believe this, seeing that most reports make him out a blackguard. But, happily, human nature is centrifugal!

To the credit account of the Fascist government in the last years, it must be said that, while fierce laws were kept on the statute books, and new ones were being framed, the administration did everything it could to prevent their execution. This made zealots furious but they seldom prevailed. In France, Italian consular authorities went out of their way to help Jews hounded by the "collaborators" and on the least pretext offered them protection and easy entrance to Italy.

Some time ago it was rumored that the Germans in Rome ordered the Jews of that town to bring them fifty pounds' weight of gold, failing which they would be transported to Poland, presumably to be gassed. As the well-to-do Israelites had fled, only the poor remained, and they could raise ten pounds at most. The Vatican offered twenty and the Roman aristocracy as much again. It is hard to believe such a tale.

I jot down what seems interesting of the reports that reach me. I know that they must be taken with great skepticism, above all when they come from "unimpeachable sources."

November 6th

I WONDER whether the Nazis are in good faith when they go on ranting about Badoglio and the King as *Verräter*—betrayers. Can they be so ignorant as to have forgotten that history is full of cases where one ally deserted the others? It was common practice in the eighteenth century, Queen Anne of England, Elizabeth and Paul of Russia, and perhaps even Alexander at Tilsit early in the last century, the Germans' own idol Frederick, Louis XV, and Maria Theresa. Did not Charles, the last Austrian Emperor, want to betray, and did not Napoleon III almost betray? Yet the Nazis howl as if the conduct of Italy was too monstrous to have occurred before in history. I ask what they would have done in Italy's stead?

November 8th

YESTERDAY Nicky and I lunched with Baroness Ritter at Quarto. In that huge Noah's ark, haunted by the ghosts of Demidoffs and Leuchtenbergs, of Thiers, and of Princesse Mathilde, the Baroness has inserted a Louis XVI apartment which she, herself a French-woman, occupies. It made me happy to pass some hours there in the midst of proportions, colors, chairs, tables, pictures, the most livable with, that have ever been seen.

While we were at Quarto, about which there would be much more to say, our hosts here were lunching the German Consul. He has just returned from the north, where he had been with Rahn, the last Ambassador to the Quirinal, and brought back the news that Ciano was in custody and certainly would be shot.

Why? Because he voted against Mussolini at the last Grand Council? Would his father-in-law shoot him for that? Then why did he call the Council to meet, if it was high treason to express an unfavorable opinion?

Or is it the Germans who will shoot him for reasons of their own? It is an interesting point, because if they do, they will be treating this country as conquered and occupied—not as an ally on an equal footing.

The same question comes up in connection with the Jews. We heard from Rome a couple of days ago that Jews were being penned into cattle vans to be transported to Germany. The Consul yesterday said that two hundred Polish and German Jews had been found here huddling in the synagogue and had been carried to Naziland by the Gestapo.

I cannot make out whether there were Italian subjects among them. If there were, it would be another proof that Italy, republican Fascist Italy, was being treated as occupied territory.

I recall Hitler's threat that if Judeo-pluto-democratic America came into the war, he would see to it that not a Jew was left alive on the European Continent. From the way he is carrying out this threat, it would seem to be the most unfaltering and unchanging point in his policy.

I have always assumed that Hitler believed in the omnipotence of the Jews, a belief so absurd that it comforted me. If he could so miscalculate the forces he was opposing, and their whereabouts, as to waste energies upon helpless Jews instead of concentrating upon dangerously determined actual enemies, then he was fighting windmills, and could not possibly win the war. It is my conviction that, a small percentage apart, Jews are exactly like other people of the same class everywhere. Those with real power, the financiers, the promoters, the industrialists, the inventors, were employing their resources to at least the same degree as the most *viejos cristianos,* for the "Fatherland." Nothing in any country more bourgeois, more conservative than the average, well-to-do, well-placed Jew. He has not only the readiness to cling tight to his moneybags, to dread a diminishing of his income, to support "loranorder," but a special interest in showing that, although not quite as others, he is as eager to be on the side of the "nice" people. He wants to be on their side out of conviction or interest but also with the hope that thereby he will attain complete assimilation, and cease to feel that he is looked upon as not quite "one of us."

This may account for the Jews' scrupulously avoiding in their immense charities any discrimination against non-Jews. On the contrary, they would seem rather to favor Gentiles—as they so obviously do socially. These assimilated Jews, like Copts under British and Syrians under French rule, make no bones about preferring the company of their masters. Everywhere, the assimilated Jew avoids rather than cherishes his fellow scapegoats and is proud to serve a well-known or highly placed person, entirely *judenfrei*—with no drop of Jewish blood in his veins.

Neither in experience nor in serious reading have I come across a trace of organization by Jews as Jews, for any purpose not charitable or educational; until Zionism there was no political organization, and even since, no Jewish party in any state west of the Vistula. The greatest Hebrew combine I ever heard of was the Alliance Israélite Universelle, whose one and only purpose it was to better the condition of proletarian Jews in less "civilized" countries.

I had heard vaguely of this Alliance but it interested me little until I happened to spend some days in Rhodes seven or eight years ago. To my surprise and pleasure, almost all the cabmen spoke excellent French. I took them for Greeks of the island, but on inquiry it turned out that, although there was nothing in their look or behavior the least Semitic, they were Spanish Jews settled in Rhodes centuries ago, and taught French in the schools of the Alliance. Their Fascist lords, who would have liked to treat the natives of the Dodecanese as scarcely human, had little sympathy for these *parenti della Madonna*—relatives of the Virgin Mary, as Jews are frequently called in Naples—and were urging them to emigrate. Many went, and found refuge in South Africa. On a later visit I learnt that they were not only urged but forced to leave.

The Alliance Israélite Universelle I had occasion to learn much more about later. So far as I could discover, the worst charge that could be brought against it was that it spread the French language wherever it went. Nothing further from its intention than to unite Jews with the intent of increasing their political power in any country, let alone of forming a secret organization for international and even universal dominion.

Far from being internationalists, the great majority of assimilated, bourgeois Jews tend to be nationalists in the aggrandizing annexationist sense of the word. It was the Jew Disraeli who invented British Imperialism. It was Leopoldo Franchetti and Sidney Sonnino who egged Italians on to fish in the troubled waters of the Balkan coastlands. In France the three Reinachs were rabid patriots who invested a great part of their fortunes in Russian funds—the Russia that all the time was massacring Jews—because it was supposed to serve French interests. And personally I have never met a Hebrew of German nationality or descent who did not believe in *Deutschland über alles in der Welt*—above everything else in the world. Not only in the Fatherland but in America what did they not do in the last war to secure its victory! I am confident that the majority of Jews would have been good Nazis in Germany if they had been allowed to be. As a matter of fact, they helped the emerging party not a little. Here in Italy with rare exceptions they were Fascists, and some of them ardent and active ones. Jews everywhere tend to overdo patriotism for fear it should be thought they did not do enough. It is strange that they preserve an immigrant attitude, so many generations after migrating from the ghettoes of their native lands, where their ancestors have dwelt for centuries, in the case of Germany for thousands of years.

November 9th

THE ACCOUNTS that reach me of the Jew-hunt here the other day remind me of what I read decades ago about the rounding up of the stray dogs in Constantinople. They were hounded and forced into conveyances that carried them to a desert island on the Propontis, there to starve to death.

That, if not worse, may be the fate of the Jews seized, handcuffed, and sent off to Poland perhaps to be gassed. Why the expense and trouble of taking them all the way to distant Lublin when they could so simply be put an end to here! Or is it that the Gestapo has been trained to prolong sadistically the agony of its victims?

November 12th

THREE OR FOUR DAYS AGO, in a speech at Munich, Hitler declared that if the Germans lost the war he would not shed a tear, for it would prove that they were not what he had taken them for.

He had taken them for the heroes of Wagner's trilogy out for the *Herrschaft der Welt*—lording it over the earth. Far more even than Napoleon, Hitler is the victim of Romanticism. The former based his dreams on the vast complex and universalistic traditions of Rome, as idealized by the French Revolution; Hitler his on the Nibelungs and inmates of Walhalla, with their animal lust of energizing, and contempt for human values. He miscalculated the capacity of the Germans to face and overcome the rest of the world; for the Japanese can be of no efficient help, and the European allies are of small account. *Qui a plus d'esprit que Monsieur de Voltaire?* it used to be asked in the lifetime of the most brilliant writer of his century. Who is wittier than Voltaire? The answer was: *Tout le monde*—that is to say, a combination of everybody. So we may ask: Who is stronger than the German people? Answer: A union of all the other peoples. These, so long as they retain strength, will always combine to prevent one of them from enslaving the others. If Hitler thought that England was too degenerate, Russia too unorganized, America too indifferent to oppose him successfully, he is learning to know better. Too late to save him.

Hitler will be remembered as an adventurer more inhuman, more desolating, more destructive not only of other countries but of his own than the futile Charles XII of Sweden. The last, however, remains a fascinating subject of song and story while I see in Hitler's career nothing that will serve literature. The word "literature" reminds me that the Nazis promised that a Jewless Germany, freed from the corroding or dissolving influences of degenerate art, would produce wonders in the way of prose and verse, philosophy and history, painting and sculpture, architecture and music. If Nazis have produced anything in belles-lettres, music, or the fine arts worth reading, hearing or seeing, and enjoying, they have escaped my attention, although it has been close.

The same may be said of Russia. What has anyone brought up under the Soviets produced? The brilliant profusion at the beginning of their rule was due to suppressed energies, liberated during the brief moment between two tyrannies.

If Italy has been, in literature, more creative than the two other totalitarian countries it is because totalitarianism has been less serious, less thoroughly applied, and altogether less efficient. Yet even here translations, chiefly of American fiction, attract a far wider public than the native products.

November 13th

IN THE LAST German paper to reach me I read of two executions for the foul crime of listening to the London radio, and discussing its reports with friends and neighbors. It will be interesting when the fighting is well over to inquire as to how many in German-occupied lands, including the Reich itself, have suffered capital punishment for having listened to the enemy radio, and drawing from it material for criticizing war and policy; then to compare the number in Anglo-Saxon countries hanged or shot for the same reason. It would also be worth while to compare the number of native spies caught and judged in German and in Allied lands. The inferences drawn from such statistics might be instructive.

The Nazi papers, by the way, since the German occupation arrive irregularly. For ten days none came at all. Then arrived a sheaf from Graz eight or more days old, followed by the Munich edition of the *Völkische Beobachter*. It was days later before any from Berlin appeared. Now they come rather more regularly but take at least six days. All of which speaks for difficulties of transport and communication in the Reich itself. Otherwise why should the Graz dailies have been the first to reach me, while the Berlin ones followed a whole week later?

While I am here *alla macchia,* my own place has become a *macchia* for others. Among them is a woman, a great friend of ours, who received a mysterious telephonic warning to leave her home immediately. She thinks that the invasion of her apartment by Nazi and Fascist S.S., which followed shortly after, was due to the imposition here, as in Germany, of the Nuremberg anti-Semitic laws. As a matter of fact, being herself a fervent Catholic and baptized at birth by a Catholic mother according to current Italian law, she was immune, even if her father was a Jew and I may add one of a family that for several centuries, perhaps for a thousand years, has had distinguished members.

It turns out that she was wanted because of her intimacy with Marina Volpi, against whom the German authorities had a heavy list of charges, inspired by the German governess of her daughter. The S.S. were searching for proofs that our friend had contributed a million lire toward helping English escaped prisoners and Italian deserters. As it happens, she has not a penny to her name, and lives on a pension of three thousand lire a month. But the Nazi-Fascists seem to believe that no contribution under a million is accepted by their opponents.

I have reported this little anecdote because it proves that a person whom a given event most concerns can be utterly mistaken as to its causes.

November 14th

WINTER is creeping up. The sun still triumphs over the rising mists, but only for a few hours. Yesterday it was thick enough to hide the sunset. But the fragrant, spicy Japanese medlar is in flower and the hedges are profuse with roses, the meadows starred with dandelions. Think of this day and this hour in Berlin or London!

I am pleased that President Roosevelt's party has suffered a setback in his home state and its neighbors. Not that I disapprove his policy, or his conduct of events, but that he has had far too large a majority. I believe that parliamentary institutions can function only when the forces are nearly equal, and the ruling party has to fight for its life, subject to perpetual criticism and the danger of losing control.

Overwhelming majorities make possible the follies of the Chamberlain period, when back-benchers would get up in the House and yell at the opposition: "Why are you wasting our time with your talk? You can do nothing against our numbers!"

The universal prevalence of huge majorities in the years preceding the war may be interpreted as a sinister tendency to one-party rule and *Führertum*—dictatorship.

The Axis press and other enemies of Roosevelt not only rejoice at his discomfiture, hoping to profit thereby, but sneer at his being deserted by his own state.

Yet it is natural that a man should have more enemies at home, where his activity from the beginning of his career offended many interests, individual and corporate, than farther away, where he came to full notice only when he had become a figure of national importance, and where he was far less likely to encounter opposition on personal grounds.

November 15th

A WILD SOUTHWESTER. Rain in squalls dashes against window-panes. Everything creaks, groans, and clatters, as on a transatlantic crossing in the Gulf Stream in a southerly gale.

When we have thoroughly beaten them how should we treat the Germans? If I had my way it would be either as convalescents or as incurables. The latter I should segregate, isolate, and see to it that they did no mischief, whether by word or by deed. The rest I would put in charge of fellow countrymen of their own who had never been seized by the Nazi madness, nor yet grown too embittered and vindictive by Nazi atrocities committed against themselves, or their relatives and friends. I repeat what I have said more than once: that there is no way of punishing a people, even if we had a right to.

Have we that right? Let me confine myself to the Anglo-Saxon world. Did we not aid and abet Fascism in Italy as a bulwark against Bolshevism? When Hitler began to stir the Germans, declaring in *Mein Kampf* exactly what he meant to do (and as a matter of fact has done), did people in our countries do anything to oppose him?

The upper classes dared not touch him for fear of war or Bolshevism. The lower classes had no little sympathy with his promises and instalments of welfare for those of their own condition in Germany, and, besides, wanted no money wasted on armaments that should go to raise their own standard of life. So Hitler was unopposed not only when he marched into the Rhineland but even when he annexed Austria and raped Bohemia. Nor was anything done to prevent his open attack on a legitimate government in Spain. The never-to-be-forgotten parliamentary undersecretary of the time got up every few days in the House of Commons to deny that Hitler and his boon companion Mussolini were doing anything out of the way. And what shall we say of crimes committed against dissidents, lay and ecclesiastic, in army and navy, and the unparalleled behavior toward the Jews? Of course the last two counts come under the convenient rule of not interfering with what goes on inside another country. We certainly need not have flattered and caressed Hitler, the way the British Ambassador did in obedience to orders. Were they, I mean the Anglo-Saxon public, the English one in particular, unaware that the Nazis were arming portentously, and would run amok the moment they were ready? For years Winston Churchill was kept out of the cabinet, and for a while even out of Parliament, because he lost no occasion to speak of the wrath to come.

We could have stopped Hitler in time, as we easily could have stopped Mussolini, if we had wanted to.

So I question whether, in justice, we have any right to punish those Germans who could not help submitting to force that we had allowed to grow overwhelming and irresistible. Sinclair Lewis' novel *It Can't Happen Here* describes how a similar state of things might arise and flourish in America. How expect better resistance from the people of Germany, so untrained in resisting government!

We should occupy Germany thoroughly, north and south, west and east, particularly east. The occupation should have three tasks before it, to be carried out simultaneously:

Parliamentary government and a press free to criticize not only its own but the occupying authorities. Members of Parliament irreconcilably disaffected toward parliamentary rule or to the occupying authorities to be disqualified and silenced for a limited period. Newspapers bringing false charges against their own or the occupying authorities to be punished with heavy fines and in rare cases with suspension.

I daresay parliamentary institutions will work badly enough at the start. It is only by using them, and them alone, that people learn to rule themselves and need not be forced to a bloody revolution when a change of government, not to say regime, becomes necessary.

Parliamentary rule will always be unsatisfactory, as will the human lot in general. Yet parliamentary rule is the least bad that experience has discovered. It must be put up with, and made the most of.

Militarism has eaten so deeply into the soul of Germans that even among one's own enlightened, humanized acquaintances, whose horror of the Nazis exceeds ours, many keep longing for the triumph of German arms. It is not of what defeat may bring in its train to them individually and to their country as a whole, nor even out of patriotism as we Atlantic people understand the word, but for fear of being left without an idol, without a palpable ideal—like Heine's "Grenadiere" with their *"der Kaiser, der Kaiser gefangen"* Napoleon, Napoleon a captive. They will not face the fact that only the defeat of their army can bring about the end of Nazism.

And yet this religious cult of the army cannot be said to constitute an essential element of the German soul. Except perhaps among the squires beyond the Elbe as a class, and stray townsfolk

here and there in the rest of Prussia, militarism was in the eighteenth century less widely spread in Germany than in France and
perhaps even England if we include sea as well as land forces.
One does not get the impression that either the peasant or the city
folk hankered after soldiering. It would appear not only in historical works but in contemporaries like Seume that governments
had to institute man-hunts to procure recruits. For all Frederick's
victories, the impression one gets of Germany for the generations
preceding Waterloo is of an unwarlike, peace-loving people with
petit-bourgeois standards, given over to plain living and, not a
few, to high thinking. The moloch of militarism—compared with
whose lust the moloch of Carthage was as one to a thousand—the
moloch of German militarism was a child, almost an infant, at
Königgrätz, but a fresh and joyous youth at Sédan. At Verdun,
not full five decades later, he was already aged, dogged, and
grim. He died and was buried in November, 1918. The German
army of today has nothing in common with the armies of Sadowa,
Sédan, and Verdun except in destructiveness, wherein, as we have
had ample occasion to learn, it surpasses anything the world has
known hitherto. But it is no more an army in the old sense of the
word than the steel and oil trusts of America are chivalrous hosts.
It is an army of laborers. Soldiering exerts a limitless fascination over small boys, and over grownups who remain small boys
to the end of their days. I remember how I felt at the age of six
as, spell-bound, I watched soldiers drilling, and the rapture at
hearing the blare of the trumpets and the tramp of the horses
carrying mounted brass bands. I shall not soon forget the enthusiasm that a little while ago seized the whole Italian people over
the Abyssinian expedition. Relatively few realized that it was not
a crusade as painted by romantic artists and authors a hundred
years ago. Military glory was an irresistible lure, although it
ended in conquest brought about not with knightly, chivalrous
prowess but chiefly with the help of superior armament.

Nevertheless, I believe that when it is pointed out to Germans
of the younger generation that war is now nothing but a *Gross-
industrie* at the service of a ruling clique, and that armies are as

much organizers and overseers of this industry as in the Ford plant at Detroit, it should not be difficult to destroy this idol even as the great Irminsul of the Saxons, more than eleven centuries ago, was shattered by Charlemagne.

It might be brought home to them that, to all but specialists, the only German military geniuses that have impressed the rest of the world are Frederick the Great and Moltke. Compare this number, and throw in Blücher if you like, with the glorious galaxy of poets, philosophers, musicians, men of learning, men of science, men of creative enterprise that Germany has produced in the last few hundred years and particularly in the century that runs from, say, 1740 to 1840.

In that one century, when Germany was little more than a geographical term, when Prussia celebrated triumphs against other Germans with Frederick, and suffered humiliating defeats inflicted by Napoleon—in those short hundred years flourished Lessing and Herder, Goethe and Schiller, Hölderlin and Novalis, Kleist and Jean Paul, Hoffmann and the Schlegels, Kant, Fichte, Hegel, and Schopenhauer, Haydn, Mozart, and Beethoven, the Humboldts and the Grimms, Bopp and Niebuhr. Those years built not only the foundations but much of the superstructure that made Germany, throughout the nineteenth century, leader in every field of activity, even in the noblest. Well before 1840 were born Bismarck, Heine, Hebbel, Schubert, Schumann, Marx, Wagner, Mommsen, and they grew to manhood in the spirit of their age. What has Germany to show among her sons who came to full manhood after the triumph of militarism? Except in the quantitative sciences, industries and commerce, no personalities to be compared with their predecessors of the previous hundred and fifty years. The boyhood and youth of those born before 1840 was that of dreamers and prophets who looked forward only to a Germany of the spirit able materially to hold her own in Europe but not to claim and conquer the controlling position.

In the nerve-racking truce between this war and the last, Germans were told they must choose between Weimar and Potsdam. I would urge that we should encourage Weimar as we certainly did not after the last war. German genius of every kind should be given fair treatment.

November 17th

"THOUGH HE SLAY ME yet will I trust in him." Nothing more optimistic, more life-approving, more life-affirming has ever been uttered.

The more wonderful, as this comes from the member of a small community, nestling between warring empires. Its insignificance saved it for a while. It was finally crushed as carelessly, as capriciously, as on a wood walk we encounter an anthill and kick it to pieces.

Like the ants, the Jews never lose faith in life. No nation, no community; Hamans and Hitlers everywhere; they live on, and enjoy life.

November 18th

I DREAM of depoliticizing nationality. As a millennial association of certain capacities, certain energies, certain habits of mind, certain qualities of character, certain achievements, and certain traditions, a nation calls for nothing but sympathy, admiration, and affection. We welcome it in the symphony of humanity, we accept it, and can be loud in our praises.

But when the government of a nation begins to take advantage of this sympathy, this gratitude, to smooth the way for political influence with the eventual hope of conquest, we protest; we try to reason, but ultimately we fight. In justified indignation, we pour the baby out with the bath and end by denying that the invader ever had anything to give us, was ever more than a wicked barbarian.

Toward the German, this is the present attitude of countries occupied by them, or warring against them. Yet to Slavs Germany, centuries long, meant civilization, meant culture. To us Westerners, in England and America particularly, Germany meant philosophy, literature, learning, science, music. By the time this little war—*questa guerretta,* as some of my Italian friends called it in June, 1940—is over, it will be difficult to find Anglo-Saxons, let alone French, Belgians, Dutch, or Poles, to recall what humanizing contributions Germans in the past have made to the House of Life.

A parallel case is Italy's with regard to the Yugoslavs and Greeks. To her eastern neighbors, Italy spelt civilization, humanity, freedom. Italian was the speech of the educated classes in Dalmatia. They loved Italy with a nostalgic love. The dream of every cultivated Dalmatian was to spend years in Italy, attend its universities, know its people. All shattered by the advantage Italian annexationists thought they could take of this sentiment, to incorporate Dalmatia in the Savoy family estate. Italian influence will disappear from Dalmatia, the Italian language will cease to be spoken, will be forgotten as it is in Greek lands.

When I first traveled in Greece in 1888, in the remotest recesses of Arcadia I was constantly saluted in Italian. Perhaps the peasant who addressed me had no extensive acquaintance with this language. But he took me for a foreigner, a Frank, and a Frank was no longer a Frenchman but an Italian. In his mind a European was an Italian. How different today, although in candor it should be added that this is not due to politics alone. Greek peasants have been to America and will shout as you pass them: "Mister, I come from Tombstone, where do you come from?"

About Japan, I have written elsewhere in these and other pages. This Arcady, built up as daintily, as exquisitely, as devoid of evil intent as the construction of the loveliest of birds' nests, a heaven of Korin screens, Satsuma vases, colored prints, bronze Kwannons, was beginning to look like an illusion in the eyes of one who read the *Grass Roof,* with its story of the Japanese in Korea, and supplemented it with the picture of Japanese vulgarity given in *l'Honorable Partie de Campagne.* It has vanished now, this sham Arcady, and will not reappear except as what Japan has always been down to our opening it up, a cultural province of China. It will be long before we are ready to give Japan its due even as a spiritual, intellectual, and artistic province of China.

A touching attempt to base political claims on fable and song was made for my benefit by the wife of the Minister of one of the Baltic states. She spoke wistfully and most persuasively of her national folk songs. No other people on earth had such songs. They surpassed everything that mankind has achieved as poetry and music. It was unique. It was supreme. Therefore her little land should be aggrandized with the territory of her neighbors, and powerful enough to be relieved of the shameful duty of playing the ichneumon engaged in picking the teeth, not, to be sure, of the Nile crocodile, but of the Russian bear.

I cannot refrain from giving one or two instances of how it works the other way round.

On my first visit to Budapest toward 1890 everybody answered you politely, cordially even, when you addressed them in German. I returned ten years later for the millennial celebration, in 1900, I believe, and neither at the railway station nor in the street could you discover a person who would admit to understanding German. The same in Bohemia. We were within fifty miles of Prague, the once so German town, and wanted to know the way to a country house we were going to visit. A well-dressed, intelligent-looking young priest shrugged his shoulders when we asked him in German and shook his head. Addressed in French, he replied with alacrity, and the more volubly as he had, of course, understood our first question and had time to prepare his answer.

November 22d

HITLER'S BEHAVIOR toward the Jews, as if they were enemy number one to his people, has many different causes. The chief is, I take it, the one given in *Mein Kampf*—a book beside which Machiavelli's *Principe* is small beer. There, he insists upon the necessity of holding up to his subjects a fundamentally irreconcilable enemy, one who never slumbers or sleeps, for whom pity is suicide, against whom everything making for his complete annihilation is a sacred duty. Moreover, there must be no multiplication of enemies; for that divides and diminishes intensity of hate. So whatever is done against Germany, whether by Russians, British, or Americans, must be led back to the Jews who lurk behind the rulers of these unhappy, misguided peoples, who, but for these same Jews, would joyfully embrace Hitler as their prophet, *Mein Kampf* as their Koran, and Nazidom as their Islam.

But there exhales from Hitler's attitude toward Israel a hatred too deep for impersonal politics, a rankling that would seem the result of some humiliation that he had had to suffer, some intolerable bitterness that he had been obliged to gulp down in his formative days. When walking the slimy sidewalks of wintry Vienna, peddling postcards colored by his own hands, he was reduced to sleeping in a Jewish night shelter where he was sneered at for his haranguing loquacity, and perhaps as well for his being conceived not in a purple chamber, but belowstairs, in a Rothschild establishment.

If that were so, it would be the most interesting case in history of a petty offense towards a seemingly helpless individual ending in horror to the like of which civilized humanity offers no parallel.

About the same time that this butt of low-class Jewish wit, this future failure as a painter—of whom, by the way, we never should have heard if he had been a tolerably successful one—rose to power as the deified autocrat of all the Germanies, the *Dublin Review* published against the Jews an article by a Catholic priest of such poisonous virulence that it surprised me to find it in the organ of intellectual Papists. The chief charge was that a Jewish shopkeeper, in order to get the insurance, set fire to his own house, which fire communicated itself to other houses and caused serious damage to this priest's parishioners. The tone and implication of the charge was that every Jew was a potential incendiary.

Simplifications of this kind are almost universal, and it is in reaction toward them that Jews are apt to spring to the defense of any fellow scapegoat, I mean Jew, against whom a dishonoring or felonious accusation is brought. They know that prejudice flares up with the phrase "What can you expect of a Jew!"

A Cilian acquaintance of mine, of noble Spanish origin, was cold-shouldered by English high circles but made welcome in German society, invited to country houses and to shooting and hunting parties. In a measure, he became an active friend of the Central powers, and an active enemy of England. If I am not mistaken this individual succeeded as a mischief-maker not only far beyond his position in Spain but beyond his wealth or natural gifts. I half suspect that he took a considerable part in the negotiations which took place between Hitler, Mussolini, and Franco in a common effort to wipe Europe clean of English parliamentarism, beginning with Spain. Who knows! A little more hospitality on the part of the English and Scotch gentry and this person might never have stored up the venom against England that he was distilling for many years.

Whose breast is not filled with rage when he recalls how he, as a foreigner, has been yelled at by French customs officials, sized up with insulting looks by passport inspectors, annoyed and teased at post offices, left in the lurch by railway porters, rudely disobliged by the fanged watchdogs of the museums, the Louvre in particular? And yet the French are the politest people in the world. Imagine therefore what friendly memories one cherishes of treatment at German frontiers, and at the hands of Nazi police! I know of nothing worse except an Italian government official who is obviously swindling you out of your eyeteeth while protesting that he is only doing his plain duty: *"Faccio il mio dovere."*

Bad treatment of strangers visiting your country, any rudeness toward them, any attempt to make them feel small, not to speak of getting the better of them, may turn them into bitter enemies; and who knows what potential Hitler is in the number! Again, when you are in a foreign land, by condescension, by an air of superiority, by ostentatiousness of wealth, not to speak of worse behavior, you may be helping to produce an atmosphere unfavorable to your country which, in moments of crisis, may prove dangerous.

The fact is that you cannot shake off corporate responsibility.

Every person is responsible when abroad for his country, when at home for his coreligionists, if they are relatively few, for his class, even though it may be the ruling one, for his profession, for his trade. If a Protestant in a Catholic country, or a Catholic in an overwhelmingly Protestant one, you cannot produce an unfavorable impression, not to speak of committing a crime or misdemeanor, that will not be met with the cry: "What can you expect of a Catholic?" or "of a Protestant" as the case may be. So for your class or profession. You may make dangerous enemies by your conduct.

We feel a natural call to magnify a grudge by universalizing it. It is not enough that Hans, Patsy, Donald, Isaac, or the individual with a more aristocratic name displeases us. We instantly jump to the conclusion that his race, his religion, his class, can produce no better persons.

So if you must misbehave, do so in your own religion, your own class, your own profession—best of all in the bosom of your own family. Even there, however, the offended member will say: "He is a regular Jones in the midst of us Robinsons, and what can you expect of a Jones!"

November 30th

YESTERDAY I received a batch of the *Deutsche Allgemeine Zeitung* and perused the two of latest date. Like a ghoul, I pounced upon the deaths at the front. They were, with one exception only, childless, either because they remained bachelors or because, as was almost always the case, they were far too young to have families.

It makes one wonder what the quantity and quality of the German population will be like in, say, 1960. It will be seriously impoverished, owing to the childless death at the front of so many of her best. Nearly all offspring of historic and other ancient families have been cut down. No small proportion of these obituary announcements boast that the deceased was the last of his race.

This does not prevent the more heraldic families from proclaiming their faith in Hitler. Humbler gentry and middle-class folk rarely mention the Führer and simply affirm that their dear one departed, in complete confidence that Germany would win through. Some still say that he died for the "bigger Germany."

With never-failing *Schadenfreude*—a peculiarly German trait —the same paper gathered the information that the Anglo-Saxons were deeply disgusted with Badoglio. They accuse him of having misinformed them about Southern Italy and the difficulties of terrain to which they attribute the snail pace of their advance.

If Badoglio did misinform them it could not have been intentionally. If he did, it was because he himself did not know. But what of the Anglo-Saxons who before beginning it did not make themselves thoroughly acquainted with the theater of their campaign?

December 1st

I RETURN to the fact that while I am free of any belief in providence, predetermination, fatalism, from any astrological notions, from any faith in miracles or supernatural intervention of any kind, yet I am not free of superstition with regard to Friday and the number thirteen. A certain expectation of trouble haunts me during the month or the year that begins with a Friday, or the birthday that falls on a Friday. The same for the first glimpse of the new moon on a Friday, on a thirteenth or seen through glass. I have lived through whole years, not to say months, under a shadow of expected evil. Happily, the evil never came and I am still alive and as well and comfortable as one dare expect to be in one's seventy-ninth year.

The curious thing is that I knew nothing of these superstitions during boyhood, youth, and earlier manhood. It came upon me as suddenly as the feeling of dizziness upon looking down from heights, whether tower, unparapeted roof, or precipice with nothing between me and the bottom. I felt it for the first time twenty years ago when riding along the bank of a stream not so very far below, between Hosios Loukas and Livadia, in central Greece. A fortnight or so before, mounted on a swift pony, I flew along a narrow path on the edge of a cliff sinking many hundreds of feet down, in the wild country between Andritsæna and Phigalia, in the heart of the Peloponnesos.

December 2d

TWO OR THREE DAYS AGO the republican Fascist government met to discuss the Jewish question (among others, no doubt), and the only decision come to was that Israelites had to declare works of art in their possession.

Yesterday morning, to the surprise and consternation of almost everybody, the government radio came out with the following police order: "Jews, whether Italian subjects or foreigners, were all to be treated as strangers and alien enemies, to be segregated in concentration camps, and their property to be confiscated for the benefit of the poor who have suffered from air raids." So much for the *ukaz*, but the radio went on to explain that in Russia as enemies of the state they would be shot, but that Italians, being sentimentally kindhearted, put up with relegating "the descendants of Judas and eternal betrayers of Christ" to concentration camps, and with returning their property to the poor from whom it had been robbed.

It seems that the prefect is beside himself, threatens to resign if the execution of these orders is insisted on. It is to be feared that more personal considerations may make him reconsider this resolution. I cannot believe that Mussolini and his counselors would have given out such an order. They know too well what the reactions would be on the part of every Italian except possibly some anti-Semites.

One must conclude that this enactment must have been forced by the Nazis, by Himmler's emissaries, if not by himself in person, on the chief of police. So much for the independence of the present Italian regime.

A couple of days ago I read in the *Deutsche Allgemeine Zeitung* an article on Mussolini. It described the comfortable, spacious, rather old-fashioned villa in which he was living. At the entrance to the grounds, German S.S. and Blackshirts keep guard. At the door one S.S. and one Blackshirt act as sentinels. Mussolini was making a marvelous recovery from the hardships which he suffered between his dismissal and his liberation. He has thinned down but his step is brisker than ever, his eyes brighter, the toss of his head more alert.

He looks the image of decision to regain his power and increase it. Meanwhile, he has two doctors, one German and one Italian. They take care that he should not get tired; and to assure this, they allow nobody to approach him, except for the most urgent purposes, or to telephone to him. Indeed, there is no telephone on the premises.

In polite words, the article confirms what I had heard already, that the Duce is prisoner of the Nazis, who use him as a figure-head when they require one, but deal with Italy as conquered as well as occupied country.

December 3d

GIOVANNI COLACICCHI was here yesterday, and recounted that his brother-in-law was on a repair ship in the harbor of Gaeta when German troops tried to take it over. As it ran on steam, there was no time to leave port. A dogfight ensued but the Italians succeeded in sinking the vessel. The same officer told that in all harbors, some of the warships were invaded by the Germans, but as they ran on oil they could get away, and after severe tussles succeeded in throwing the enemy overboard.

Whether this happened just before or just after the proclamation of the armistice, I have not learned. It seems that when the armistice was agreed upon, the date of its publication was to depend on events. It had to be proclaimed because it could no longer be concealed. What happened seems to have been something like this:

Cavallero, the army chief, played false to Badoglio and betrayed to the Nazis not only the date and conditions of the armistice but the plans of the Allies, which included landings in various places simultaneously, with the assistance of Italian troops. By this betrayal the campaign had to take another pattern—a sorry one, I must add.

Badoglio must have believed and assured the King that he had the army with him, and apparently the Anglo-Saxons took him at his word and made their arrangements accordingly.

It turned out that the army chiefs funked, either because they knew that their troops were war-weary or because they themselves hated the British more than they resented the Germans. When the armistice was proclaimed, the High Command here in Florence, for instance, refused to believe it and left time for the Germans to occupy the place. The same happened in Rome and probably everywhere.

Treachery or war-weariness—probably a *combinazione*. The wild joy of all at the announcement of Mussolini's downfall and later of the armistice would point to a condition like that of Russia early in 1917. Treacherous perhaps, and inglorious certainly, the Italian High Command and most officers may have built better than they knew. By standing aside they may have saved the country from a social revolution. One may doubt of its success, but it might have been more serious than the republican Fascist regime.

December 4th

MY RETREAT has terraces concentric with the horizon, which is just far enough away to seem on a level with the eye. I command a full view of the sky southward and westward. I can watch all that goes on under its dome. The clouds are endlessly varied, from the most delicately evanescent vapors lit up with rose tints to massive layers of slate with a curious tendency to stretching out in long horizontal strips. I could wish I had Ruskin's *Modern Painters,* to read his treatise on clouds, which I now should study with an interest it never inspired me with before. I wish I had his vocabulary to narrate what goes on in the sky. As it is, I am

reduced to comparing effects with the way the great Italian painters reproduced them. The brightest and gayest skies are like Titian's in his middle years. When covered, milky, and pearly, they
remind me of the late Bellini. The cold, watery dawn could be
painted in gray and green by Bassano, a damp and shivering day
by the harsh lapis colors of Paris Bordone. As for sunsets, more
often than not they call up the late Titian and above all Tintoretto and one more enchanting than either, their English descendant Turner.

As I look down over Florence, the cathedral, Giotto's campanile, the tower of the Palazzo Vecchio appear romantically silhou-
etted, and at times startlingly near. The foreground is the usual
suburban higgledy-piggledy of houses, churches, gardens straggling at my feet in rags and tatters. Its mass does not disturb, and
would not annoy but for two cylinder-like gasometers, only taller
and slimmer.

I may not speak for the admirers of "abstract art" who no
doubt prefer gasometers to other edifices, as they generally are
the most geometrical objects in a landscape. My kind of person
is distressed by them and one may ask why.

I suspect that the reason is something like this: not alone because of sordid association and evil odors, nor on the other hand
because of the circular shape. We are not offended by the tomb
of Cecilia Metella and similar structures all over the ancient
world.

The reason may be found in the disparity between shape and
substance. Their shape, cylindrical and tall, recalls recipients,
whether of iron, bronze, or even tin, cast all of a piece in a mold,
not buildings compact of blocks of stone held together by pressure of weight and contact.

We can identify ourselves only with things that have weight
and can carry, and need adequate support. We can feel ourselves
into a block of stone, or marble, or wood, and realize what is
above us, to our sides, to our back. We cannot assimilate a shape
which seems to have walls so thin that they scarcely suggest having a third dimension.

That is, I take it, the chief reason, apart from associations, why we dislike gasometers and why we cannot enjoy a structure like the Eiffel Tower. We can admire this edifice only as engineering, as a geometrical design. It remains as much a mere drawing on the sky as if done on paper of ordinary size.

For the same reason I cannot abandon myself wholeheartedly to the enjoyment of certain Gothic masterpieces like Saint-Ouen at Rouen. The pillars are relatively so light that I remain unconvinced of their ability to carry a roof of masonry; and I am led to question whether the elements concerned are of solid stone, with which I can identify myself, and not of some light metal. So Saint-Ouen has always impressed me as an architectural design rather than a real building.

The effect may have been different when it had its glass and its furniture. Indeed, Gothic building, as it advanced, found its justification more and more as a framework for glass, as a sort of cabinetwork, or as a huge metallic casket rather than as architecture.

Probably our pleasure in good masonry, where each individual block fits into the other, is based on the ease with which we can live ourselves into it. Better still, when it is bossed as in many Renaissance and some antique buildings and substructures. It almost certainly accounts as well for the way I enjoy the huge beveled blocks at Baalbek, at Hebron, at the Wailing Wall in Jerusalem.

Architecture, as an art, deals with appearances, and not with the actualities of engineering. I approve therefore of the American skyscraper, which, as structure, is of the same nature as the Eiffel Tower, but is so masked with stone, or what looks like stone, that we get the impression of masonry that satisfies our demands for weight and support.

I mention our skyscrapers because they furnish a supreme instance of how necessary it is that a building, as a work of art, no matter how engineered, how constructed, should appeal through the eye to the senses and not to the mind alone.

December 6th

ALL THE WHILE that Russia has been fighting Germany, I have never heard of the colossal advantage she enjoys over her adversary, thanks to the Anglo-Saxons' keeping Japan too busy to attack her, as the warring enemy of her Nazi ally. As it is, the Mikado's empire can do relatively little for Hitler's Reich. The Anglo-American forces engaged in the Pacific could be far less effective against the Nazis, being chiefly sea and air forces, of which in their struggle with Germany they now have enough; while the Japanese armies if free to be launched against Russia might give the victory to the Axis.

December 7th

WHEN THE WAR is well over, Europe will be kept busy rebuilding and restoring all that has been destroyed or used up. That will furnish employment to millions, for years. Each country will have to find means to keep its laborers in working condition.

But what shall we do in America with our thirty, or is it forty, millions engaged in war work? We shall have to find paid occupations for them, but as our houses and office buildings, banks, shops, and factories will remain intact, we shall have to invent other employment for them than rebuilding and restoring. We shall be forced to engage in enterprises that bring no immediate return but greatly increase our industrial efficiency. We shall not only build dams adding to our electrical power, build or improve roads abbreviating and accelerating traffic, but direct most of our energies to improving industries to such a degree that we shall be able to offer better and less expensive goods, from airplanes to children's toys, from the most efficient machinery, swiftest and most comfortable cars, to standardized clothing and footgear.

Europe, busy rebuilding and restoring, will need our producers' and our consumers' goods. Europe will get more and more in debt to us. We know the state of mind of creditor to debtor, in all ages and climes. The moment he insists on payment he is the enemy, the enemy that must be got rid of. Did not a Harvard professor some eighty or ninety years ago murder a dunning moneylender? Think how bankers are hated by the farmers at home, and not only by farmers. Think of the universal hatred of the usurer, be he Semite, Greek, Armenian, or native. I recall being insulted in Italy in the years following the last war as a possessor of dollars. I recall also the ill feeling there was against us everywhere in Europe, over repayment of debts incurred in the last war. It reached its most violent expression in France and was openly uttered in England. The resentment I encountered there among acquaintances was greater than elsewhere. I go so far as to say that it may have influenced British policy.

Britain must already be deeply indebted to us. It will be more and more so in the years to follow—more perhaps than any Continental country. The good result may be that England will feel more and more as part of Europe and partner in its difficulties. For us Americans, the consequences may not be so happy. The British, sooner or later, may lead a crusade against us to free the world from the intolerable burden of debt due to us. *Delenda est America.* The late Neville Chamberlain seems to have muttered it more than once. His successors in the next twenty years may shout it from the Houses of Parliament.

The remedy is at hand; but human nature, even in America, is not ready to take it. The remedy is to cancel debts incurred during the war, and to furnish free of charge, to the extent of our ability, whatever is necessary to start up the industries of all European countries, regardless of what part they took in the war. Naturally, those who suffered most would need most help, as may be the case where Nazi occupation was most predatory and destructive. That, indeed, would be a "new order"—but I fear it comes under the rubric "if pigs had wings."

December 9th

GREECE may be excused for keeping control of antique marbles found in its soil. The Greece of today has no other art treasures, and can claim a right to retain the more significant finds. Cardinal Pacca did well to forbid the alienation of masterpieces that had been acquired at public expense by papal nephews, to enhance their own family position, while serving for the enjoyment and instruction of every man. Indeed, when I first wintered in Rome, some five and fifty years ago, I was told by the oldest inhabitants that before the Piedmontese occupation, galleries of papal origin, like the Doria, Borghese, Barberini, etc., etc., were always open for everybody to walk in and out, as if through a public square. The common people carried their sense of copartnership so far that, having no privies of their own, they used instead the vestibules and grand staircases of the great palaces.

On the other hand, the attempt of communities, big and little, to retain their own art creations, good and bad, great and small, for no better reason than that they were done by fellow countrymen or fellow townsmen long ago, is as narrowing, as self-immuring, as the rest of nationalism.

I have no little to say about the campaign and propaganda in favor of the Italian *patrimonio artistico,* but it would take me too far, and demand much more space than I want to give to any one of these notes and reflections. If common sense, rather than the parish pump, dictated in these matters, Italian cities, instead of thoughtlessly keeping endless duplicates of their own works of art to themselves, would exchange all except the very best and most significant with the equivalent from other towns in the peninsula.

You can have such a thing as too many Botticellis or Bellinis in one museum; and an exchange between Florence and Venice would be sensible, some Botticellis going to Venice and some Bellinis to Florence.

It is still easier to get overfed, as one does at Siena, with Sano di Pietros, Giovanni di Paolos, Matteo di Giovannis, Girolamo di Benvenutos, Beccafumis, etc., etc. Likewise at Perugia, Verona, Vicenza, one gets satiated with the abundance of local competence and incompetence in the realm of art, as one does even at Bologna and Ferrara.

In the greater Italian galleries you seldom see a Sienese, a genuinely Perugian (for Perugino was not one), or, excepting Paolo Caliari, a Veronese painting. The only approach to a pan-Italian collection of pictures, the Brera in Milan, was formed under Napoleonic auspices.

Duplicates of more representative artists should go abroad. Every noble and even attractive work of art that goes to a foreign land acts as a missionary, inspiring sympathy for the people who produced it, and eagerness to visit their land.

Italian towns have the excuse that their works of art are all native and that their alienation is no light matter.

But what shall we say of Nazi Germany! There Munich sold Raphael's "Bindo Altoviti" and Berlin recalled all Italian pictures that it had distributed in various provincial collections, including more than one masterpiece, from Königsberg to Cologne, in order to sell them. With the proceeds more Pachers, more Cranachs, more Altdorfers, more Hubers could be added to collections that already had too many. No small part of these acquisitions had the interest only of being stepping stones in the career of a painter.

This leads me to say, parenthetically, that in making purchases for public collections, the whole staff should be consulted and not merely the expert for the article proposed. He is too apt to confound artistic with archaeological interest, and to subordinate the first to the last.

Dutch and Spaniards may not be inspired by a wish to exclude foreign museums from acquiring their works of art—the Dutch certainly not. Yet I would urge the former, these most rational of men, to exhibit fewer Vanderhelsts and similar hand-photographers. They bore one to the extent of indisposing one toward such a marvelous picture gallery as Amsterdam's.

As for Spaniards, they seem to have lost their heads over Goya. This real genius was most unequal. Portraits even do not always do him justice. In the painted cartoons for tapestries he is vulgar and hasty. Filling hall after hall of the Prado with these sprawling and screaming compositions is doing him no service.

Public funds should not be spent on imitating the American

millionaire, honored and even glorified, for having acquired some twenty copies of the first-folio Shakespeare, thereby preventing libraries, where they might be useful, from acquiring even one.

December 10th

I CANNOT HELP identifying religion and nationality. A Protestant is not quite a Frenchman, scarcely an Italian, and certainly no Spaniard. A Catholic is not quite an Englishman, nor even an American. To be a real Bostonian, when I was a lad, one had to be a Unitarian. Now society in that part of the U. S. A. with which I am acquainted drifts toward Episcopalianism.

The tendency everywhere is toward the dominant church. Who hears nowadays of a French Catholic turning Protestant, let alone an Italian or Spaniard? Who has ever heard of a Berlin Jew of the upper classes turning Catholic or a Viennese one Evangelical?

I cannot therefore blame the Turks of today for requiring that to share in the privileges and duties of a citizen he needs to be born a Mohammedan. If he grows up and becomes an atheist all the better. A like notion may have lurked in the background of Italian Fascism, and sprung all armed from the head of Mussolini when, in deference to Hitler, he began his anti-Semitic campaign.

December 11th

A COUPLE OF DAYS AGO the *Regime Fascista* had a serious article on Christ and Israel.

After vague talk about a Christ that was not God and indeed in no ways superterrestrial and of *Spirito*—the equivocal term spread by Croce's followers, which may mean mind or spirit, but generally mind—the writer went on to say that Israel was the enemy of humanity. Japan alone was as yet uncorrupted by Jewry. Even Fascism had not escaped its contagion, as is proved by the fact that nineteen out of twenty-five, at the last meeting of the Grand Council, voted against its chief, the immaculate Mussolini.

The article went on to appeal to the human race in general, but to the Anglo-Saxons in particular, to stop killing each other in a war started, fostered, and prolonged by Jewry for world dominion. It is a war that is ruining a Europe from which most Jews took care to get away before trouble began.

In short, the article out-anti-Semitized the reasoning of the Nazis with arguments made in Germany but served up cold and fly-bitten here. Could the writer have believed a word of what he said? And what of his readers?

December 12th

I RECALL that, some five and twenty years ago, in Paris, W. L., then a young man, asked what was the matter with our world. I remember answering that most states were far too big and that all undertook too much.

The big states are overgrown, overheavy, overcomplicated, overworked. Attempts to prune them, to simplify them, to divide up the burden lead to authoritarian totalitarianism. They may end by breaking down, returning to anarchy, and at best to a feudal anarchy.

I recall, too, saying at the same time that the solutions offered were as a rule of too abstract a nature and applied (if at all) to economic man only; but that economic man had the same relation to the real man that a geometrical figure inscribed within the outlines of a human body has to the living, acting, selfish, acquisitive, ruthless, passionate, human individual.

I cannot rid myself of a suspicion that has haunted me for decades, namely, that we might attain results better or as good by letting things drift, letting things happen, letting them find their own level, and stop fussing. What could be worse than the consequences that accompany, if they are not the product of, our universal and constant intervention, so profoundly thought out, so ingeniously planned, so mathematically certain! Would more millions be killed on land, in the air, on and under the seas than will have perished before this war is over? And when it is over, what shall we be reduced to but to a poorhouse where we shall have to slave for bread and water, with nothing to comfort us except the certainty that, our overseers apart, nobody is better off than we ourselves are. Ever-present state interference in Germany, in Italy, and even in England and America has kept these countries out of civil wars. But I doubt if international war is any more desirable. Internal wars are fought to decide what class in the community, at a given moment, is most fit to rule. The decision surely is not more subject to accident than is international strife; and the strife is about something more concrete, more real, and more intelligible.

If there are more wars, they may be social wars, interest against interest, class against class. I am tired of sentimentalizing over the workingman, crooning over him, and coddling him, as if he were the only concern and care of the state. If it comes to a free fight, with power in his hands, he will not be sentimental toward us; he will not think of all we have done for him since civilization began; he will not be more merciful to us than he has been in Soviet Russia. Let us give every chance to the workman's son. If he has the gifts to take advantage of them, let us do our utmost to assimilate him and make him feel that he is, in every way, one of us. Let us avoid educating the proletarian who has no aptitude for being taught to reason, and from teaching can only retain catchwords. If he has the gift of gab, and malignant stars favor him, he may turn out a Mussolini or a Hitler.

December 13th

AFTER HIGH MASS YESTERDAY, at the SS. Annunziata, the Archbishop of Florence, Cardinal Della Costa, gave an allocution. Among other things he said that the chief dangers for society today were nationalism, racism, and tribalism. The church was only half full and the congregation consisted for the most part of the lower classes, some of the men in uniform. They seem to have listened with grins and even laughter, and whether it was of approval or of jeering, my informant could not say.

❁   ❁   ❁

At last a full account of what has happened to my house.

Soon after the coming of the Germans, the art authorities furnished placards warning that the place was under their special protection and not to be occupied.

Nevertheless, it was not long before German officers appeared and inspected the house to see whether it would suit them. Berti Anrep received them nicely, and they let themselves be persuaded that they had better look elsewhere.

Later other Germans showed up, this time medical officers with a view to taking up quarters at I Tatti. At first it was five or six with their orderlies; then it was the entire staff, comprising at least fifty persons. That would have been a disaster indeed. In the first place, it would have meant moving Mary, in her helpless invalid condition, from her nest, her special bed, her familiar surroundings, to an impersonal nursing home. Then it might have entailed rough handling by common soldiers, and damage not soon repaired, given the conditions we shall be left in when the Allies arrive.

While the Anreps were already packing up their belongings the Germans suddenly decided that Poggio Gherardo, the neighboring place, suited them much better and, taking possession of it, ordered the tenants there to clear out and to settle down in my house instead.

The first thing the jolly boys did there was to throw all the furniture out of doors and windows, letting it rattle down hill. Then they installed a pig in what used to be the dining room. In short, they made themselves at home.

Poggio Gherardo, as a place, may go back some eight or nine hundred years. The present house must be of the seventeenth century. There are wide corridors and spacious rooms. It now belongs to the Aubrey Waterfields, British subjects. When Mussolini declared war against England, the estate was sequestrated and a Fascist Senator chose to occupy it on a nominal rental, although he disposes of two houses in town. At a moment's notice he was bidden to remove himself to I Tatti, where nine rooms were assigned to him, my study, bed and dressing room, music and dining room and drawing room downstairs, and three rooms on the second floor. All this for the Senator, his lady companion, and three servants.

The first thing he did on reaching the Tatti was to sit down and write five foolscap pages of claims for damage, addressed to the occupying authorities. Nearly one page was filled with his titles— Grand Officer of the Kingdom, Grand Officer of the Order of Sts. Maurice and Lazarus, ex-Undersecretary for Agriculture, etc., etc. His claims were of two sorts, moral and material. The moral damage consisted of disturbance inflicted on an old man, who for his services to the state merited a well-earned repose. He would, however, set up no claims for damages because, although he was known to high-placed Nazi officials, and through them could get a hearing, he did not want to trouble the glorious occupying forces, for he had an admiration amounting to reverence for the German army. For material damage, he expected to be repaid, and that consisted of furniture that had suffered in transport, and the cost of bringing it over.

It seems that the occupying authorities pay claims of the last kind, provided of course they are made by Italians and not by enemy aliens, as indeed they pay rent for Italian houses they occupy. One of the reasons, by the way, why they look out for places belonging to foreigners, and under sequestration.

The above-mentioned Senator's claims for damage remind me of what happened to Aline Sassoon, in the early days of the automobile. She was motoring in the Scotch Highlands, and at the approach of the car sheep were scattered. The owner claimed fifty pounds for moral damages to this flock.

The claimant in this case is only sixty, nor does anybody understand just what were the services that entitled him to a well-earned repose. He seems to have picked up quite a bit by creeping and crawling.

He has been living for many years with a lady some fifteen years his senior. She dominates him completely. She still has a husband, it seems, in a high mountain village on the way to Rome.

It was famous in its day for its highwaymen and, if we may trust Horace Walpole, for possessing, among its relics, a complete set of gnashing of teeth, and a bit of the blessed fig tree which Our Lord cursed.

Alda Anrep, who, with husband and son, is living at I Tatti, had to receive this lady and was told by her that we should strew roses, roses all the way where the Germans were going to tread, because they were saving us from the worst horror known to man —an Allied occupation.

This same lady has a very grown-up son. His only title to fame is that he counts as a fervid anti-Semite.

I learn, by the way, that the Mussolinian radio every day belches out a chapter of the anti-Semites' law and prophets—the "Protocols of the Elders of Israel."

December 14th

THE FASCIST RADIO and the Stefani agency yesterday made a declaration to the following effect: In times of trouble and uncertainty, as all history teaches, not only are political prisoners liberated but many criminals get loose.

Such criminal elements have gathered into groups, arrogating to themselves police powers, and committing regrettable acts, for which they have no authority. They pay off private grudges, or want to get hold of other people's property.

They must be dissolved at once, and nobody must exercise police functions except a national guard of *carabinieri* in combination with Blackshirt militia.

One may ask: Why have the prefect and other authorities now in power made no effort to stop these gangsters? Why have they not until now dared to disown such a hemomaniac as according to all accounts their chief, a certain Capitano Carità—charity!— seems to be?

Dreadful things have indeed been going on, apart from Jew-hounding. In Florence alone there are several places to which people are taken, tortured, half killed, and let out, some to die almost immediately. The pretext nearly always is that the victims are Communists, i.e., anti-Fascists.

December 15th

ITALY, the Italy of the resuscitated Mussolini, of the Mussolini who in 1934 said all he could and all that need be said about anti-Semitism, namely, that Italy was no place for it, has followed Germany and declared that no Jew can be an Italian, that all Jews are to be considered as foreigners and, while the war is on, as alien enemies.

Now there are no countries in the world that have benefited more by the Jews than the Italy and Germany of the last century and a half. Here they have not only contributed to finance, to commerce, and to every kind of material welfare, but fought for the liberty, independence, and unity of the country. When somebody at the beginning of the racial laws took their defense the Fascist answer was not to deny what the Jews had done but to assert that they had done it for their own advantage. As if anyone ever did anything against his own advantage, the term taken in its widest meaning!

I need not attempt to say how loyal, how helpful Jews have been to even the Fascist regime here, and how much they did to create a Germany that made it possible for Nazis to carry on the war they are fighting so wonderfully.

The hardest thing for Italian and German Jews of the better class to bear now is to be deprived of the feeling for the country and people with which from early infancy they have been taught to identify themselves. Many were baptized at birth, or were brought up with no sense of difference between themselves and their fellow citizens. Suddenly, for no fault of theirs or of their forebears, they are deprived not only of home, country, and of national identity but massacred as anthropomorphic microbes, or at best driven out with no land to receive them, no people to welcome them. They are too many and the world everywhere is too full of them, for the bitter truth is that no community can afford more than a certain number of Jews. Sad is the lot of these *Schlehmils* who have not sold, but been brutally shorn of their shadows.

December 16th

HAVE JUST READ Charles Louis Philippe's *Bubu de Montparnasse.* I cannot attempt to apprize it as writing, although even as a layman, and no expert critic, I could find much to say about the unexpectedness and freshness of the style, its suppleness, its ductility, remaining so classical while neither neglecting nor hiding anything. I may venture, however, to speak of the book as literature; and literature is the art which creates, or discovers, types and characters, enlarges, widens, deepens our feeling for humanity, our sense of the universe, and of our place in it. From that point of view, *Bubu de Montparnasse* is a masterpiece. It introduces us to a Paris of poor and lonely students who come up from the country to train for a profession, soft-boiled, tender, aspiring, and encounter another Paris, the Paris of the hard-boiled, the tough *souteneurs,* and the prostitutes. It is not the Paris that we American tourists or even artists know, the Paris between the Louvre and the Bois, nor yet the Paris of the studios, but of the lower and lowest classes of the Boulevard Sébastopol and its variegated, multicolored, crapulous night life.

The heroes of the book, if it has any, are Pierre Hardy, a tenderfoot and tenderheart, and the tough-tough in the slang as well as in the ordinary sense—the *souteneur,* the blackguard who exploits prostitutes for a living, Bubu de Montparnasse. He victimizes a little woman whom he debauched and so sealed to himself (in the Mormon sense of the word "sealed") that she neither could nor would get away from him, despite his slapping her, cuffing her, and treating her as his mere convenience. And yet she is a little woman who in sheltered circles would have made a dear wify. Pierre Hardy meets her streetwalking, takes her to his bosom, and might have ended by marrying her. Bubu, who has been in prison, appears unexpectedly with other toughs, male and female, and snatches her out of Hardy's bed.

The hard-boiled in this story have it all their own way, and the soft ones knuckle under. Yet the author has understanding and, if not sympathy, at least charity for everybody. Even these brutes are not wholly inhuman, are capable of pity and affection, if not of love. In none of them is the sense of better things wholly dead.

Bubu is an *Übermensch,* a superman. He is solid, he is chesty, self-possessed, without scruple, without a thought of how his conduct may affect others. "He walks abroad without a care while others toil; he can get the better of everything about him; he walks like a man to whom the street belongs, as if it were his Louvre. He felt ample and free in his thoughts, in his vital parts, in his ideated life, in his life as he lived it. . . . He takes Berthe the florist, picks her up lovely and virgin, and turns her into an instrument for his pleasure and then of his profit. He feels his muscles, he taps his chest and says: 'I am Bubu de Montparnasse.' "

He is the stuff of which is made the late American gangster, the Italian *Ardito* and *squadrista,* now giving his last kick, the German S.S. men and their equivalents in Spain, Rumania, and elsewhere. They come to the top in moments of social upheaval, and rule and ruin their victims as have Fascist and Nazi leaders—to mention the two worst gangs, the two who unfortunately have made history, and done so much to unmake our world.

I wonder whether Céline would have written his *Voyage au Bout de la Nuit* if he had not read Charles Louis Philippe. His book is still farther away from our Paris—as far as Belleville and even farther, places from which our Paris looms in the distance, no more to be approached or even envied than Olympus was by ordinary mortals. In a sense I find *Au Bout de la Nuit* more of a revelation than *Bubu.* As no other work does it make me feel how much mere animal happiness can underlie the most horrible conditions of life, and make it worth living.

It would be interesting to compare Stephen Crane's *Maggie: A*

Girl of the Streets with *Bubu*. Crane was dead before the latter was published, nor is it likely that the author of *Bubu* was acquainted with Crane's story. They have much in common, both being tales of toughs and prostitutes. But the contrasts and not the resemblances attract me. The Irish-Americans are pugnacious, brutal, utterly without self-awareness, energizing with no thought of consequences, and ending dead drunk on the dung heap. The girl Maggie, a flower of that dung heap, too delicate, too tender to live in her surroundings, makes away with herself. Not even in her does mind count, and in the others there is no sign of it. In the Parisians there is intelligence among the coarsest and toughest, as well as in the least tough and least bestial, as in Berthe, Bubu's bread-winner and pleasure-giver.

December 17th

YESTERDAY I saw an elderly Englishwoman married in Genoa to an Italian and having grown-up Italian children. When Mussolini made war on the British Empire, she was sent to a concentration camp somewhere in Umbria. Influence procured her liberation, but not permission to return to Genoa.

When Mussolini decreed the return of all income held abroad by his subjects, American women were compelled to do it as Italian citizens. Long before he joined Japan against us, American women married to Italians were already treated with suspicion, cold-shouldered and made uneasy, no matter what their social condition. They had to keep out of the way, lie low, almost in hiding.

December 18th

MANY IN THIS COUNTRY, I learn, believe that it was Roosevelt's master stroke to get the Japanese into such a corner that there was nothing left for them but to attack us as they did at Pearl Harbor. After this the American people, hitherto still uncertain, still hesitating, could not help hitting back and thereby entering the war, who knows how much earlier than it would have otherwise. The delicate question remains whether such a Themistoclean thought ever passed through Franklin Roosevelt's head. Did it through the minds of Irish and Jewish secretaries?

December 19th

I WAS READING recently how Andrea Dandolo turned the Fourth Crusade aside from its idealistic purpose of liberating the Holy Land from the Moslem yoke. Instead, he induced it to conquer, impoverish, and ruin the only Christian power that might act for Europe as a shield and buckler against the invading Turk, Seljuk, or Ottoman.

It struck me as a parallel to what happened more than six centuries later when the Italian *Risorgimento* was taken over by the Piedmontese. These greedy and insatiable annexationists trapped the movement into serving their own ambitions, to satisfy their will to power, to prestige, to swagger. When His Sardinian Majesty visited London just after the Crimean War, did he not go about begging for a *petit agrandissement de territoire!*

The *Risorgimento* might have ended in a cantonal federation of the Swiss type. It could have remained liberal, humanitarian, and enlightened. Its population, its moral and material resources would have placed it at the head of the smaller powers. With them, it could have confederated to defend every decent, every civilizing, every humanizing principle. Instead, it let itself be annexed by Piedmont, which thereby could realize its multisecular dream of claiming recognition as a great power.

As a great power, Italy with no material resources, with no reliable army, with no adequate authority enabling it to play the part, was driven to take up a sorry role.

It had to trouble the international waters so as to fish in them. It had to encourage the evil courses of the effective great powers, so as to establish precedents for its own rapacious conduct, should it have the chance. So much has the Italian soul been imbued with the lust for conquest, for increase of territory, for prestige, that few Italians disapproved the imposition of their rule over hundreds of thousands of Germans and Yugoslavs in the Tirol, the Triestino, and Istria. Even after the last war Salvemini, afterwards persecuted and driven into exile as opposed to aggrandizement, assured me that these new subjects would profit by the benignity and humanity of Italian administration. After the bombardment of Corfu certain anti-Fascists announced with great complacence that in international matters they would always be found on the side of their government. When Nitti, the very bugbear of Italian nationalists, returned to report about the settlements after the war, he made the memorable declaration that Italy at last had the keys to her house, and that in consequence nothing of an international nature could happen anywhere on earth in which she would not have her say. I do not recall whether it was in public or privately that he made the declaration that against America he held in his hand a powerful weapon. It was stopping the supply of Italian labor!

The other fatality of the *Risorgimento* was Garibaldi the cowboy, the gaucho, the chesty Don Quixote who when all is said and done found but windmills and sheep to face him. As when the French arrived in 1796, or the Nazis three months ago, Garibaldi and his Thousand encountered no serious resistance; and everything fell before him as he marched from Palermo to end in the net spread for his capture by the Piedmontese. His successes and the assistance of the French in Lombardy, costing all together some five or six thousand Italian lives, left them with the conviction that they could make successful wars at small outlay. Thus they attacked a scarcely defended Libya, and Abyssinians armed with superannuated muskets, bows and arrows, and javelins.

Along the same lines there would be much to say about Mussolini's policy in Spain, as well as in attacking France when he thought she was finished and that in a few weeks England too would yield to the Nazis. But of that on another occasion.

December 20th

A FEW DECADES AGO the Bostonian psychiatrist Morton Prince
wrote *The Dissociation of a Personality.* It spoke of a pious, good,
rather ailing young woman called "Miss Beauchamp." When her
health was worse than usual, she lost her more constant continuous personality, which gave place to a naughty, even malicious
will-o'-the-wisp of a creature, whom Prince called "Sally."

This Sally would eat and drink things that made Miss Beauchamp sick, boasted, swaggered, strutted, swore in a way that
would have horrified the other; or took her a tramp of, say, fifteen
miles, wearing the body out to a frazzle, and then leaving poor,
utterly exhausted, and helpless Miss Beauchamp to find her way
home. Fascism has played Sally to Italy's Miss Beauchamp. The
great majority of the Italian people is as peace-loving as any in
our world, humane to others and hating adventure. Nevertheless,
the Fascio made it bombard Corfu, invade Abyssinia, intervene
with all its available resources in Spain, in order to spread its own
madness further and to extend its dominions over the whole Midland Sea. And finally it made it stab France in the back, when this
seemed safe to do so.

Sally-Fascio is still gibbering, gesticulating, and misbehaving
revoltingly; but her days, perhaps her hours, are numbered. Who
will pay but poor Miss Beauchamp–Italy, and it will be a long and
heavy bill. It will take this unhappy land and its people decades,
generations perhaps, to obliterate the effect of its misdoings in
the last ten years. I pity innocent Italians and Germans who were
misled into consenting, or terrorized into submitting, to the actions of their governments. If only they could learn that it is every
citizen's business to watch his rulers, who should be good house-
keepers and not conquering demigods, peaceful participants in
the House of Life and not gangsters panting to exploit it!

*   *   *

I hear that the Vatican has a representative at Moscow and is
pleased with the way he is being treated. It is rumored also that

the Pope summoned Weizsäcker, the German Ambassador, and told him that if his government insisted on applying here in Italy all the Nuremberg laws against Jews he at Christmastime would radiophone a discourse that they would not like. It seems that in consequence an alleviation of these mad monstrosities has been promised; but I have not heard yet that anything more humane has been done.

Far from it! But first, let me jot down that it is now ascertained that the bombs that fell upon the Vatican buildings a little while ago were not thrown by Anglo-Americans, nor even by Germans, but by Mussolinians starting from their airfield at Viterbo, with the intention of smashing up the Vatican radio installation.

December 21st

NEARLY TWO MONTHS AGO my hostess began to talk of preparing a plum pudding for Christmas. I expressed the hope that she would invite me to partake of this Yuletide dish. She looked at me archly and said that of course I would be as I should still be here. I submitted skeptically, but here I am and the Allies are fighting in the Abruzzi for ditches, for crumbling slopes, for precipices, for crags, or merely marking time. Meanwhile, people in the Italy occupied by the Germans, and their bootlickers the neo-Mussolinians, are losing faith in the Allies, doubting whether they ever will come, and drifting towards a sort of reconciliation with their former masters, hoping that these will turn out no worse than they were previously.

It will take great events to justify the Allied campaign in Southern Italy. At present they seem to be fulfilling the prophecy of Churchill, when he spoke of what it would be if they had to conquer Italy inch by inch.

*　*　*

I have been reading for months past about Italy and the Near East from Constantine to Dandolo—from 300 to 1200. It confirms the conviction I have had for forty years at least that if parliamentary rule had nothing else to be said in its favor, it was yet the

least bad regime, because the only one that permitted a change
of ministry without confiscations, mutilations, massacres, and civil
wars.

*   *   *

A claim for racial purity can be made in good faith only by
those who know no history and forget human nature. Apart from
the obvious fact that sex ignores race, ignores class, ignores religious differences, not to speak of such newfangled dogmas as
nationality, and that infiltration of heterogeneous blood was even
more abundant in the past than at present, we know that in every
migration the immigrant and conquering males have taken up
with the native women. We know that in historical times transfers
of populations have taken place under Assyrian and Babylonian
rulers as in our day under Stalin and Hitler. Stalin has been churning all the races of Asia and Eastern Europe in one churn, and it
will be interesting, in generations to come, to study the result.
Hitler has called back Germans from the heart of Russia, from
Yugoslavia, from Bulgaria, as well as from the Baltic provinces.
Does he really believe that these peasants and tradespeople have
suffered no mixture with other races?

The noted publicist Hermann Keyserling jokingly asserts that
he is a descendant of Genghis Khan. Many of his cousins on his
mother's side have the same Mongoloid eyes and skin. They
scarcely go back to Timugin. More likely to a licit or illicit alliance
with native Estonians among whom the Ungern-Sternbergs settled as conquerors.

So much for conquests, migrations, and transfers of population.
It is not all. There is still another flow of foreign blood into the
veins of settled populations from the earliest times down to nearly
our own day, in Turkish harems till the end of the sultanate. I refer to slavery. It was for thousands of years the most uninterrupted
and profitable trade. Nobody in antiquity or the earlier Middle
Ages was immune from the liability of being sold into slavery. If
we may trust report, even a Plato did not escape it and more than
one philosopher—Epictetus, for instance—remained a slave or
was so born. I need not expatiate on facts which are easily accessi-

ble in books. What must have been the result? Not to speak of the upper-class women who abandoned themselves to slaves physically and morally superior to their husbands, the huge slave population ended by merging with the natives and injecting into their veins blood from every white and perhaps from every black, even every yellow, race. I have seen Moslem women in Syria looking like French great ladies, I have seen Van Dycks hoeing in the fields of the Hauran. At Constantine I have seen Jewesses blonder than any Scandinavian. Near Ghadames I conversed with Arabs as pink-cheeked as any beef-eating English farmer. On the other hand, I know Italians who look as Hittite as any Syrian, Germans of many quarterings who look as Jewish as if they came straight from the Pale. One need not speak of Arab, Berber, and even Negroid types in Sicily, Spain, and above all in southern Portugal.

The Nazi may protest that he had no southern slaves, that he was never invaded by yellow warriors. The latter claim is certainly not true. What of all the Eastern tribes that stampeded across the length and breadth of Germany in the train of Attila and other conquerors! Did they piously spare the Teutonic females and avoid fecundating them? Later, Westphalian cadets with no place for them at home wound their way across the Elbe and occupied Slav territory. They dispossessed the native gentry and married their daughters. In the Balticum they brought no peasantry with them, and most probably it was the same in the trans-Elbe region. Probably the lower orders of those territories are Teutonized Mazurs, Poles, and Lithuanians, everything but pure-blooded Germans. Not so long ago when they were in a rage with a neighbor they were still sending him not to the devil but to the Teuton. *Es hole dich der Teutsche.* Even if "Teutsche" was only a euphemism replacing "Teufel" it would not be intelligible if not heartfelt!

December 23d

READING Crispolti's *Pio IX, Leone XIII, Pio X e Benedetto XV,* I note that the author, like all Catholic publicists in France

and Italy, tries to defend the last-named Pope against the charge
of having been pro-German during the last World War.

I used to know a man who was born, so to speak, on the thresh-
hold of the Vatican and all but brought up in its precincts. He
knew all that was going on during the reign of Benedict XV, and
assured me that he was uncompromisingly pro-Austrian and therefore pro-German. Should the future be interested in this Pope it
will not find it easy to get at the facts. Scholars will discuss, po-
lemicize, and conclude in accordance with their prejudices and
call their conclusions "history."

The same friend told me that Benedict XV fell head over heels
under the influence of a certain Gerlach. Consequently, Roman
Black society raved over this fascinating, aristocratic, wealthy
young prelate. He entertained the cardinals magnificently, he was
prodigal in alms-giving, he was most devout and scrupulously attentive to every ritual prescription.

He came to Rome highly recommended by the Archbishop of
Cologne. Yet it turned out that this personage who said mass,
heard confession, and administered the Holy Sacrament, even to
the Pope himself, was no priest, not even a Catholic but a Protestant and a Prussian secret agent.

The acquaintance from whom I learnt this remained an unquestioning, pious, practicing Roman Catholic. All the same, he had
no great opinion of the perspicacity or character of even the highest clergy. We were talking one day of the difficulties in bringing
back Anglicans to the bosom of the Church. We discussed many,
and finally I mentioned papal supremacy. That, he said, was the
one and only insurmountable difficulty. Every other could be in-
dulged or smoothed over; not that one. No non-Catholic could see
through papal actualities as this true and loyal son of Holy
Church.

December 24th

WHEN THE AIR WAR CEASED to favor Nazis and their junior
partners it became mere terrorizing on the part of the Allies. The

last German papers speak of it now as the *Judenkrieg*—the Jew war.

Who began it? Who used it with every material accompaniment to overwhelm Holland, Belgium, and France? Who gloated over devastations in London and the total destruction of Coventry? I recall the German press stating with satisfaction that forty-three thousand English men and women lost their lives during the first German air campaign. It was all the fault of Churchill, who alone prevented the dear, over-the-water cousins from joining the family of pure-blooded Teutons.

Judenkrieg—in a sense it does answer to the description in the Apocalypse of what would happen when Antichrist came to reign.

Not a little of Nazism runs parallel with, if it is not copied from, the meanest kind of ghetto Judaism. We need not enumerate other items of the rabbinical dream. For the most part it is a *Zukunfts-musik*—a music of the future—promising the messianic triumph of Judaism over other nations. These would submit or disappear. The effective program of rabbinism is the segregation of the Jew. As that is getting more and more difficult, the individual Jew in hundreds of thousands if not in millions refuses to be segregated in a ghetto. Once out of it, the Jew ceases to be a Jew in everything cultural and remains one, if at all, only zoologically and to some extent, no doubt, atavistically.

Hitler, following Mussolini here as in so much else, but effectively and not merely as a *stato di progetto*—as a program, as a pious wish—compels every German subject out of his own country not to live in a ghetto but to remain ghetto-minded. I mean to say that he has to bring up his children in schools where everything, even the alphabet, is taught with Nazi intent. He has to attend frequent Nazi gatherings. In these conventicles he is commanded to remain true to the Nazi faith, to extirpate Jews, and to worship Hitler as God, as Lord of all, just as Israelites adore Jehovah. The individual German is carefully watched, and woe to him if he utters a word against the faith or shows himself lukewarm.

From the very beginning of air war as practiced by Germans, in

Poland, in the Netherlands, in France, and most of all over London and other English towns, I felt sure they would lose especially if we Americans came in, as indeed I never doubted we should. Anglo-Saxon mechanical resources, Anglo-Saxon mechanical skill, Anglo-Saxon sportsmanship would take to it and carry it beyond competition.

This has already happened. The Nazis can put up no adequate defense against our air attacks. Let infantry-minded people sneer to their bile's content, I for one believe that we could win the war from the air alone.

If I had my way I should go on pounding at Berlin until panic possessed its denizens—I deliberately say "denizens"—so that they ran hither and thither all over the Fatherland spreading hapless, despairing dread and woe, far and wide. Against millions in such a state no S.S., no Gestapo, no Himmler nor even a Hitler could prevail. The armies at the front, if they did not catch the disorder, would soon be left without food, without munition, without clothes, and have to give up the game.

In making this proposal, am I so bloodthirsty, so heartless, so inhuman? I am none of those things. I am abstract. Anyone who knows me or who has read these notes must be aware how much I appreciate and love the kind of German who, until a not distant past, contributed so much towards building our House of Life. In actual life I am almost caressing to individuals who come into my presence. The moment it is not Hans or Bodo or Waldemar in the concrete but Nazis in general, human pity, feeling, sympathy can disappear and give place to an abstraction with no human content.

December 25th

I REFERRED YESTERDAY to the way abstraction can dehumanize one. I recall that in the last war I was wondering whether that was not the reason why Germans for the great part, as individuals so kindhearted and so ready to feel with others, can turn into mechanized executioners, as impersonal as a guillotine, the moment the Fatherland, the state, the army orders them to go against abstractions labeled French, English, Russian, etc., etc.

I have been tempted at times to ask whether this unusual readiness of Germans to submit to abstractions in every field, not of action alone but of thought as well, was not in part at least due to their indulging too much in symphonic, relatively timeless, music. Such music easily puts one into moods whence the concrete disappears almost entirely, where the mind is filled with exhalations that cannot be condensed into verbally statable concepts. It cannot remain unsatisfied; yet the vaguest abstractions suffice.

Wagner must have felt something of this danger, for he furnishes a verbal basis for the symphonic and undramatic intervals of his operas that keep the listeners tied down to the words of the libretto. Pious Wagnerians attend to it as closely as to the score. There is nothing of the sort to keep one from opiatic vagueness in the symphonies of a Beethoven, a Brahms, a Bruckner, and their foreign followers César Franck and Sibelius.

*   *   *

I learn that the Nazi authorities have had the libraries of their archaeological and historical institutes in Rome packed, put into railway vans and started on their way to Germany.

Why have they done so? What risk of destruction did they run that could not be obviated either by depositing them in the precincts of the Vatican or in one of the many safe subterranean halls in which Rome abounds? Rail at the present moment is far from safe, even for Germans. These cases may be subjected to bombardment, to being sidetracked, to being exposed to the wind and the rain, and eventually to falling into the hands of the enemy.

Of the libraries belonging to the German historical institute, I know nothing. The library of their archaeological institute I know to be the completest of its kind in the world. It contains every printed word regarding Greek and Roman antiquity. It has many an item that could not be replaced. It has been the paradise of every student for generations.

The obvious reason why the Nazis have ordered its removal and return to Germany is the fear that if it fell into Anglo-American hands it might be used to replace libraries destroyed by them in Holland, in Belgium, in France, in Poland. It looks like a confession on their part: they are aware of the damage calling for retribution that they have committed.

December 26th

Both the Pope and the Cardinal of Florence have spoken courageously and clearly. The interesting thing about both discourses is that the substance of them has been summarized in the press subject to this regime. Another sign of something is that the *Osservatore Romano,* the Vatican daily, is again being sold at newsstands. After the armistice it disappeared. Has the rump of Nazi Fascism suddenly become aware that its days are numbered, and that it would do well to start acting in a way that might make people forget its recent behavior?

How lawless, brutal, even bestial it has been, including foul torture of its victims, has been clearly referred to in the allocution of the Florentine Cardinal.

Another explanation is that Nazi Fascists are trying to ingratiate themselves with the Vatican in the hope that it may induce the Allies to treat, instead of insisting on unconditional surrender.

Interesting, too, is the account given this evening by the Mussolinian radio of the Christmas dinner offered by the commander of the German forces in one of the great hotels of Rome to Allied prisoners. What a contrast, this radio took care to say, with the conduct of the Allies, who even Christmas Eve went on pitilessly bombarding German towns. "Peace to men of good will." Dare Nazis claim immunity on that ground?

December 27th

I cherish dreams about human society. A persistent one is of a vegetative society where the individual will bloom and wither like a flower. A perfect society, toward which we are striving, if we could attain it, would by definition leave no room for improvement or change.

Some such ideal must have been in the mind of Confucius and his disciples, for almost all Chinese have attempted to realize it. The Jesuits likewise tried it in one way in Paraguay, where the population was to be lifted to the state of superior animals; in another way in Europe, where the upper classes were to be trained, drilled, and shaped to a superb magnificence, to a high degree of classical culture, to missionary zeal, fixed, stable, and moveless.

I vaguely recall mystics, English ones in particular, comparing paradise to a garden in which the souls were the flowers.

I confess this vegetable ideal of society makes no small appeal to my artistic sense. And I cannot help dreaming of a society in which every individual would be a work of art, of ethical as well as aesthetical art. My life long, from earliest awareness I have admired and loved nothing so much as beauty of conduct, goodness as a natural function, truthfulness likewise, with an ever-present sense of its being no isolated phenomenon but the responsible part of the universe.

I am wandering away from the subject, a vegetative humanity, society as a garden. But flowers and fruit nowadays are being constantly improved, grafted, combined. Why not try the same with mankind?

Why not, indeed? The trouble is that in the case of human beings we start with an idea, an ideal, a dogma even of what they ought to be, how they should behave, what they should think and say. If only we could treat them the way gardeners deal with plants! They do not say: "You must, you shall be and do so and so." No, they study the nature of the plant until they ascertain which improvement can be attempted; and they often succeed not only in bettering its health and its appearance but even in producing combinations superior to any of their ingredients.

In other words, we are far too unempirical in our attitude toward society, and far too much guided by fears, or hopes, or intellectual and political constructs, ecclesiastical or sociological, economical or tribal, class-conserving or class-resenting.

To conclude: just as plant improvement must rest on botany, the improvement of mankind must rest on anthropology.

December 28th

IT IS SURPRISING how many Italian Jews of the highest class have taken to agriculture, investing not only capital but their energies in the enterprises, most of which have prospered. And now under this ghost-Mussolinian regime, the proprietors have had to take to the bush and their estates are confiscated.

One of the accusations brought against Jews is that they will not take to the land, cannot be farmers. But until very few generations ago where would they have been allowed to become tillers of the soil? I recall from my childhood in Lithuania hearing of Israelites making most urgent and piteous appeals to be allowed to take up land and farm it. The Russian government turned a deaf ear.

In Hitler-ridden countries one of the first and most insistent items of persecution against the Jews is to confiscate the land they are trying to work.

     * * *

An acquaintance who knows the Vatican and what goes on there told me once that unless God was behind it, it could not possibly go on. Such was the incompetence, the foolishness of most of its officials and the confusion and even disasters they produce. He is at one with the Jew in Boccaccio's tale whom his Florentine friends could not reason into conversion but who returned from Rome a Christian, saying that unless God upheld the Church as he saw it there, it could not possibly go on.

The same acquaintance related an anecdote that was new to me: Cardinal Consalvi, Pius VII's Secretary of State, opposed some terms of the Concordat arranged between the Pope and Napoleon. The Emperor was furious and had the Cardinal brought to give him a piece of his mind. He ended up by saying: "I can destroy the Church if I want to." "Sire," answered Consalvi, "we have not succeeded in doing so in eighteen centuries."

Later, I remember, we talked of the Jesuits and he assured me there were priests of that order working as engineers and foremen in Russia on the chance of being able to put in a word in the right place for the one and only Church. For the glory of God and the Church, His instrument, the individual Jesuit had to do whatever he was ordered to do, including even deviation of conduct. We have heard all this and it is always being denied. So it was interesting to get it from a stout Catholic who not only admitted it but approved it and was proud of it.

December 31st

I HAVE READ Charles Louis Philippe's *Marie Donadieu*. I do not begin to understand his attitude toward the heroine. She is one of the most voluptuous creatures in literature and yet somehow not gross, not carnal, not exciting, nor yet repulsive. I understand the self-searching, self-excavating, self-delving hero better, him but not his talk. Most of it is over and beyond my head. He anticipates Lawrence in his views of sex but with endlessly greater depth as well as delicacy. One thing about Philippe's hero I envy: when he talked, people did not feel as if listening to him but to someone inside themselves.

1944

January 1st

A RADIANT icy day with gemlike details in landscape as in the backgrounds of the Van Eycks, Roger van der Weyden, and their followers. Out of the wind, it is warm yet invigorating. Where the northeaster is free to approach you, draw your wraps about you. He comes straight from the Eurasian steppes of Russia. There, how lake and marsh must be frozen over, and fighting will be possible over vast territories hitherto dividing armies.

I am reminded at this time of the year of days spent with Edith Wharton in her château at Hyères. In sheltered parts of her many-terraced garden mimosa was in flower. More exposed spots received the arctic blast as here.

I am reminded as well of the January and February, 1891, that I spent at Monte Oliveto Maggiore. Day after day, week after week without a speck of cloud in the sky. My rooms had the sun all day. In the evening a fire of dry twigs kept me warm. In the daytime, icy though sparkling, I drove about in a light two-wheeled cart, uncovered, of course, rather thinly clad, not minding the cold, eager to explore every church within reach. I could go a fair distance, to Montepulciano, to Asciano, the Montalcino, and to Siena itself.

What jolly evenings we passed, the Abbate di Negro and I, before the crackling fire, when he told me numberless good stories about his early days in Rome under Pope Gregory!

Four and fifty years ago, and as present as today! What is this strange thing time which caresses, gnaws, and devours us, which nevertheless memory can ignore or conquer?

January 2d

ACCIDENT has put in my hands the verses Byron wrote on Napoleon's fall. They anticipate by many years not only the odes of Victor Hugo but the entire book dedicated to the Emperor by Chateaubriand in his memoirs. They outline and sketch the attitude most of us still have toward the ever-fascinating Corsican; and in the lines entitled "Napoleon's Farewell" they prophesy the return of his spirit. Surely no anticipated prophecy has been so well fulfilled: "Yet may thy heart leap to my voice. . . . Turn thee and call on the chief of thy choice."

January 3d

YESTERDAY, talking of the belief in the evil eye, I suddenly remembered what happened to us at Bitonto in Apulia. My wife was with me. We had barely left the station when a swarm of children began to follow us as we walked, joined by others, as well as by women and men. They streamed into the cathedral after us, they crowded up, they got between us and the object we wanted to look at. Sight-seeing was out of the question.

Suddenly we had a happy idea. I began to roll my eyes, not fixing them on anybody in particular. My wife turned to the crowd and said: "We are very sorry to have to warn you that my husband is a *jettatore*—has the evil eye—but he is the kindest of men and would be distressed if he harmed anybody he happened to look at."

No sooner said than the people began to stream out of the church as fast as the wide-open doors would let them. For the rest of the day we were left severely alone. No wonder the great Hohenstaufen wrote:

> *Bitontorum*
> *Tot caput asinorum—*

Bitontines, so many heads of asses.

January 4th

THE SPECTER-FASCIST PRESS does not call us Americans any more but Unitedstaters—*Statunitensi*. The last atrocities we and our British allies have committed in Southern Italy are too dreadful to relate. We have deprived Fascist bigwigs who for years held high positions and replaced them with anti-Fascists. And instead of designating the mayors as *podestà* in authoritative medieval fashion, we have returned to the "liberalistic" title of Syndic. The worst atrocity is still to be mentioned. Naples is teeming with typhoid fever. Are the Anglo-Unitedstaters devoting their energies to stamping it out? Not a bit of it! Why, they are distributing cans of macaroni with tomato sauce.

I wonder what inspires the tone of diffidence toward Russia discernible in Roosevelt's holiday utterances. Surely no doubt as to fighting Germany to a finish. Can it be that when Roosevelt, Churchill, and Stalin met, and Japan was the chief object of discussion, it proved a bone of contention? Did the first two try to wangle from the third that the moment the Nazis were brought to their knees the Soviets should immediately join us against the Japanese? Stalin may have hesitated, fearing that his people would be exhausted and eager to relax. Perhaps we want only to use the airfields and harbors of Pacific Russia, and perhaps Stalin is asking, in return, more than we are ready to give.

I used to get bored with acquaintances who read the French Swiss dailies, and would come and shake their heads, and express great fear of Russia's imminent defection. At times I would lose patience and turn the subject.

Great, therefore, was my satisfaction, while reading Ambassador Davies' book on his mission, to discover that the Soviets had had their minds open to the immensity and urgency of the Nazi threat long before we ours, and that this conviction inspired their conduct in matters international.

January 5th

I AM NO THEATERGOER, and never have been, except in early boyhood; then I used to get crazy with expectancy and so dizzy that when I got in sight of the stage, chandeliers and balconies whirled round and round for some time, before I calmed down to enjoy, and not merely to be possessed.

Since I have been elderly, the rush of air in turning doors in America, the annoyance of the petty, grasping *ouvreuses* in Paris, and the fact that I would lose most of the first act before my ears had learned to grasp the talk on the stage—all contributed to making me fight shy of the theater. Add the fact that in Florence it was a Sabbath day's journey to any theater, and that when one got there one might be chilled to the bone, ill-disposed by the cold smoke of cheap cigars, and presented with acting seldom bad, but rarely to any mental or moral purpose.

Nevertheless, I regret that only now have I made the acquaintance of Alfredo Testoni's *Cardinale Lambertini.* I might have seen it acted by Zacconi, who, I am told, did it to perfection.

As a presentation of character, as the picture of a society, as wit, as humor, it is a play that one may venture to place somewhere in the same Hall of Fame as Shakeapeare's *Merry Wives of Windsor.*

Not that it is as merry or as farcical, but that it is as much the revelation of a character and a picture of life. The high society of a typical Italian town in the mid-eighteenth century is conjured up before our minds in a way so convincing that almost we cease to be spectators and become part of it. I scarcely can recall another presentation as good of its haughtiness, its fatuity, its emptiness, its reducing life to sex, swagger, and heraldic flash. In the midst of it, towering high above it, the Cardinal-Archbishop, a prince of the Church but an enlightened eighteenth-century great gentleman on a level with a Montesquieu, and with the noblest of the progressive man-loving thinkers in France and England. The way he dominates his high and mighty fellow Bolognese, the way he persuades them, the way he gets round them, the way they baffle him, is brought home to us, almost as if we were in his skin, not in ours.

There is but one false note. It is De Brosses, who is portrayed as a French fop, with silly curiosities and far too keen about women. He was anything but that.

January 6th

HAVING REACHED the shady side of my seventy-ninth year, I regret at times that I cannot hope to see the outcome of this gogmagoggery of a war. One can vaguely, faintly imagine the lineaments of new territorial combinations, new cartographic shapes, new political unities; one can even guess at the outlines, articulations, and mechanisms of a new social order. What I cannot conceive is how it will affect the *Weltanschauung*—the attitude toward the whole of existence, the cosmos as a pattern—of individuals; nor can I admit, if serious change there must be, that it will be permanent, as for instance Christianity after paganism, and not a mere passing phase.

How many important utilitarian discoveries and inventions have I seen appear: electric light, the telephone, the motorcar, the wireless telegraph, the radio, aviation, and the cinema. They are conveniences by which I profit every day. Yet I should not be surprised if, after a little, I could not be as happy without them. As a matter of fact, they have not become part of my world. I can recall being steam-minded. As a small boy, I saw a locomotive being stoked and watered, after slag and liquid had poured out from below. The identity with animal processes made it easy to assimilate steam. Of how electricity works I have only the vaguest notions. Little boys of five are more electricity-minded, motor-minded, air-minded than I am. Left to myself I could only switch on the light. I could scarcely call up on the telephone. I never use it. All in all, I belong to the pre-machine age.

Surely people who are born to electricity, and know all about the workings of telephones, automobiles, aircraft, wireless, must have a different outlook upon the world from mine! I can see that they do, yet to me their tastes, their appetites, their absorptions seem like aberrations. The songs they like to hear, the print they enjoy reading, the pictures and sketches they admire, their society ideals and performances are as foreign to me as if they came from the heart of Africa, far more than if from China and Central Asia. A polite truce reigns between us based on their side in the feeling that I am not worth troubling about, and on mine, on the conviction that they, or their descendants, will return to my House of Life, which alone offers a permanent home for the soul of man.

No age is understood by its participants; for life muddles and confuses, if it does not exclude understanding. Only when it is over and past can a later age attempt to understand it, an age that feels mirrored in it as we are just now in the last centuries of antiquity. So it does not follow that contemporaries appreciate or recognize their creative, or even their merely effective, personalities. A society may be much more transformed by an individual obscure in his lifetime like Marx, destined to inspire a Lenin and a Trotsky, founders of a new world order, than by blustering, bluffing, warring, massacring, brutalizing figures like the mad Mahdi or a Hitler or a Mussolini. Just yet we cannot see who will rise up and lead us after the war, nor by what signs we shall recognize them.

How many understood Jesus of Nazareth as He passed by? The greater part of humankind after full nineteen centuries still fails to understand Him. One may ask how many have understood Him, how many, free of prejudice, have as much as attempted to understand Him.

Sören Kierkegaard asked whether it would have been easier for one who frequented Jesus to understand Him than for us today. He argues the case at length and concludes that unless he had

JANUARY, 1944   205

faith it would have made no difference. And every reader of
Kierkegaard knows that for him faith meant his relation to Deity
and that this relation constituted his cosmos.

My cosmos was in essence and potentiality complete when I
was thirty, if not earlier. I have been able to assimilate numberless matters that fitted into this scheme of the universe. Others
I discarded altogether, such as spiritistic and occultistic phenomena. The uncanny activities of dowsers and radiosthenists I
shunted for the present.

At this point I must relate a singular occurrence. I was invited
to take tea with Professor Toesca, of the University of Rome.
There I found Professor Mercati, a well-known Byzantinist and
brother to the Cardinal of the same name. He is a famous dowser
and can find water wherever it is to be found, not only on the spot
but from a photograph of the place where water is to be expected.
Likewise, he will discover metals. Toesca put a number of photographs taken pell-mell of pictures by old masters face downwards
on the table, and invited Mercati to assemble in different piles
those that were by the same painter. To my no small astonish-
ment, I might almost say to my stupor, he with the guidance of a
wand or pendulum accomplished the feat fully as well as any of
us who have spent years, a lifetime, on the practice of connoisseurship. The fact was there. I could not ignore it, but in no way explain it. I had to leave it as, before Franklin, did the observers of
electrical phenomena.

I can, after a kick or two, accept the new theories about Nordics
appearing in Greece and in Asia Minor as early as the beginning
of the second millennium B.C., and the even earlier identity of the
civilizations prevailing in Mesopotamia and in North-West India.
I not only accept these discoveries but assimilate them, and hence-
forth they are part of my universe. Not so with the world of science and philosophy.

I remember being among the earliest readers of Bergson's
Premières Données and *Matière et Mémoire*. I worked hard to
understand them and perhaps did; the more so as I enjoyed the
acquaintance of the great thinker and could ask him for enlighten-

ment. But it dropped off the rolling platform that was carrying me along, and left me as much of a Kantian as if I had never heard of Bergson.

Likewise with Einstein. I enjoyed the advantage of having friends who could claim the right to understand him. They did their best to explain him and left me with the confused sense that I had grasped something, although I could not say what. But it would be foolish to pretend that what I had snatched of Einstein became part of my cosmos.

I cannot mention Bergson without recalling our first meeting. He had read me, which made me happy, and remarked that much of my work was concerned with discovering and establishing identities. But what were identities and how did we recognize them? I remember looking at him fatuously, and answering that it was by comparing detail with corresponding detail. Of course; but that was not what he had in mind, and I have never got over being ashamed at the puerility of my answer.

Before meeting Bergson, I read everything of Nietzsche's I could lay hands on. For some time he absorbed me completely. It coincided with occupations and meditations that prepared me to write my *Florentine Painters*. Even that essay bears few traces of Nietzsche's transvaluing influence. The male bodies of the Olympian statues and the Parthenon pediment are as beautiful as thoroughbred horses, as stags and antelopes and gazelles; but I do not crave for a humanity as unconscious, as unaware of itself as these quadrupeds. Far from being the first degenerate, Socrates remains for me the earliest superanimal, and thus the first superman in Nietzsche's despite.

As an organism that took in and gave out, as an instrument, I was complete at five and twenty, and this instrument has worked and preserved its identity for more than fifty subsequent years, in the face of all the forces pulling and pushing, forward and backward. It has changed little if any, although much it dealt with has disappeared, and much that was not there before has taken its place.

So I say with Ogni Ben in Browning's "Soul's Tragedy": "Forty-seven leaders of revolt have I known." I have lived through no end of fads and isms, not to speak of blasting winds of doctrine, like Sovietism, Fascism, Nazism, from which we are still suffering. I have seen such turns of fashion, such crazes come and go, and visual topsy-turvydoms like *surréaliste* painting and visual atheisms like "abstract art."

I come back to my beginning, and venture to doubt whether, if I lived some years longer, I could hope to descry what movement was going to decide the future and what on the contrary was merely a passing seizure leaving nothing behind but a weakening of the social machine, and a shaking up of our House of Life.

Luckily, we live on what is unchanging in human nature and not on its fads and fashions, whether visual or mental. To a limited degree, I can penetrate to what is under them and ignore them when they seem bubbles and mere vapors; or, if promising, leave them to fitter and better-attuned minds to be pursued and understood.

For the greater part of my eighty years I have been meditating on the future of mankind, and have accustomed myself to the idea of a society where there will be no want, no forced labor, no prestige values. It is probable that idiosyncrasy among men is so thoroughgoing that individuals exist for every kind of occupation.

Aldington in his autobiography, speaking of the last war, tells how much he feared his Tommies would resent having to remove and get rid of the ordures of the camp, when a noncom came forward and assured him that a friend of his would prefer it to any other job.

Assuming that certain communal and even national tastes exist, for which volunteers in sufficient abundance may not be found, conscription might have to be enacted. It would be no greater hardship, and one year's labor, at say one and twenty, would suffice.

For the rest of their days individuals would be free to dispose of their time as they pleased. Some of it they would give to a trade they enjoyed. Some few hours a week will suffice to supply them with the material needs of life, whether vital or luxurious.

How will they put in the rest of their time? The gifted will be able at last to devote themselves to the pursuits urged by their daimon. But the mediocre, the dull, the languid, the lazy, how will they get on with nothing they are obliged to do for a living?

The problem of the future would seem to be above all the problem of how to put in one's leisure, what to do with idle hours. In a desultory way it has been dealt with by industrial and mercantile organizations. By Ford, for instance, in America, and half a century earlier by the firm of which my friend Herbert Cook's forebears were the proprietors. On a nation-wide scale, it was first attempted by the Italian Fascist government—unless, indeed, there too the Soviets came first.

The Fascists deserve praise for the intention, and I tribute it the more willingly, as it is the only praise I can give them. In practice, however, they turned their *Dopolavoro* into mere propaganda, into putting megalomaniac ideas into the heads of working people, into inducing them to hate other nations, into a cult of Fascism, and into insisting on loyal adherence to its chiefs.

❖   ❖   ❖

My imagination is baffled when I try to picture a society with no prestige values, whether of inheritance, gifts, or occupation. Ideologically that is what we are tending to, and it may not take centuries before elaborate efforts are made to realize it. The result should be interesting. Anatomy and physiology will oppose; and it is to be feared that they will win through, for they are coeval with mammalian life. The instincts with which they have endowed us will prove masters of any scheme our so feeble intelligence can frame.

Let us play with the notion—not yet an idea—of a society without prestige values. The scavenger would be a hygienic expert or functionary, on a level with any other. So would the courtesan. She would cease to be a whore or even harlot, and be an hetaera. Even humble females would no more be looked down on for keeping shop than society ladies who do so today. Every activity not manifestly harmful would be as well rewarded as any other.

In a sense, there would be no rewards. The pooled products of everybody's labor would be for everybody to use freely. As there would be no prestige connected with possessions, and consequently no love of display, no manifestation of "conspicuous waste," people would want only what they could enjoy by way of houses and furniture, of clothes and ornament, of food and drink, and other physical needs. There would be less jealousy if love was purged of prestige, and sex relief was admitted as a physiological necessity, like food, and as distinct from love. Love would be purified and sublimated, if it ceased to be what its essence still is, a call of nature, and became a spiritual as well as physical interpenetration.

Unfortunately, jealousy is not confined to sex. It will be hard to get the better of it in persons who resent every inequality that does not suit their heart's desire. Few are able to admit superiority and, instead of secretly, if not publicly, resenting it, are ready to welcome it, to enjoy it aesthetically, and when it ethically deserves it, to worship it. Resentment is unhappily at the bottom of more social discontent than economical difficulties. When these last are overcome, as in the course of time they may be, inequality of physical make-up, of mental and moral gifts, will remain and fester in many natures.

Nevertheless I go on dreaming of a society based not on theological, sociological, or any other abstract dogmas and pre-established principles, but on the pooled product resulting from the functioning of the individuals composing it. In a sense we have it always; for despite ideologies, human nature resists change and, given time, assimilates every ideal pattern of life, even the Christian one, to what it can realize.

January 9th

AM I MUSICAL? Hand-readers tell me that I ought to be. When half my present age I must have looked it, for I can remember, on one of my periodical returns home, being cold-shouldered by fellow passengers on board ship for refusing to perform at a concert. They would not believe that I could neither sing nor play an instrument.

I doubt whether I have an ear or a sense of rhythm; and I certainly have little musical memory. I catch an air as easily as the next man. When it comes to symphonic or other concert music, I seldom grasp a composition at a first hearing. I get a sense only of whether it is worth pursuing further. At times, it leaves a longing to have it repeated immediately. And when I can experience a piece often enough, my feeling about it ends, somehow, by being what the authorities approve.

Music does various things to me. First and foremost, it liberates trains of thoughts. Then it encourages musing and daydreaming. Best of all, it conjures up worlds of marvelous possibility, conditions of ecstasy, visions of magical radiance, of a universe permeated by divinely intelligent goodness, and of a Beyond surpassing all present powers of imagination.

Only the greatest poetry, the noblest architecture, the sublimest scenery can compete with music in arousing such feelings. And it is perhaps more poignant, more penetrating, more permeating than any of them, or all of them put together. It certainly is more transporting.

It is singular how associative music can be. I was walking one day in January, 1891, from Buonconvento to Monte Oliveto Maggiore. For no assignable reason—perhaps I had heard it recently at a concert—I hummed as I went Schubert's Unfinished Symphony. Since then, and to this day, I cannot hear or even think of that composition without vividly recalling that walk, its incidents, and who was with me. It was the late Charles Loeser, well known as a collector and art critic in my time.

January 12th

THE LAST *Völkischer Beobachter*—the Nazi party paper, journalistically excellent—and the last *Deutsche Allgemeine Zeitung*

—the organ of the respectable German bourgeoisie—bring interesting matter. They dwell and insist on the kernel of Hitler's last speech: that the Allies were not fighting for victory but for the annihilation of Germany, for the extirpation of all Germans.

Who accuses others confesses what he would do himself. This monstrous idea that the Anglo-Saxons want to leave no German on the face of the earth could have arisen only in the mind of a person like Hitler, who has tried, and not unsuccessfully, to deal that way with Poles and Jews.

In both these German papers the Jew remains enemy number one. Poor, poor England—fearful pressure is being brought by American Jews to induce, to oblige, to compel her to withdraw the ban on further Zionist immigration into Palestine. Can old England resist and stick to her policy of reconciling the Arabs at all costs?

But, oh joy, the wave of anti-Semitism which reached America some time ago is rapidly rising and cries of "Down with the Jews" are being painted on walls everywhere, particularly in New York. Although the policy is to ignore feeling against Israelites, Mayor La Guardia has had to take note at last, and to implore his fellow townsmen not to listen to anti-Jewish propaganda.

The Englishman, the American, the anti-Fascist Italian may now and again disappear from the German press. The Jew never. The last Jewish atrocity is that Litvinov and Maisky have got themselves appointed on a committee for the after-war settlement. Maisky a Jew? I never knew that.

But sooner or later every individual opposed to the Nazis is sure to be designated as pluto-demo-bolshevik-Jew.

Indeed, I am surprised that these same papers, when speaking of the skirmish between specter-Fascist armed forces and "bandits" in the neighborhood of Florence, making out that these last have been scattered like chaff, and their chief captured alive—I am surprised that they designate him as a Russian simply, and do not add that he is a Jew as well.

This skirmish, by the way, did not turn out so well for the Nazi-protected Fascists as their papers try to make out. The "bandits" took fourteen prisoners to the three or four taken by their adversaries.

"Bandit" is a term applied easily by Italians. Thus the Abyssinians opposing Mussolini's invasion were bandits, and so of course were the troops of the legitimate Spanish government, against whom the same Mussolini was defending civilization, "loranorder," as he had for so many years previously.

January 15th

AT A QUARTER TO SEVEN this morning the sun had not risen. To the east the morning star was darting its rays in a sky bluish green at the zenith; overhead the moon, about to enter its last quarter, was pouring down its refulgence.

Toward noon it was almost hot in the sun and not cold in the shade. We climbed the hill covered with bottle-green cypresses, and oaks retaining their leafage bleached to the color of pale bronze. On the other side of the top, we got into real woods. I mean among trees with plenty of undergrowth and not, as above I Tatti, each stem growing out of the rock, as if it too were a mineral, jade and emerald. Paths crisscrossed every way. Indeed, the whole of Italy is cobwebbed with the traces of immemorial treading of human footsteps. Returning, I reveled in the sight of the oranges glowing golden on their trees—real oranges growing in the shelter of the house. What a paradise! A few minutes later a heavy bombing shook us up.

January 21st

MY THOUGHTS still run along the lines pursued in the pages I started writing the 6th.

How will the future deal with boredom, the accidie and the more "common or garden" *ennui* which grips a society when nothing happens to stir hopes and fears, nothing to excite and absorb,

and worse yet, nothing to satisfy youth's craving for adventure—
of youth and those who through a lifetime remain youthful.

Some few years after Waterloo the nieces of Metternich went
to him in a body and begged for another war. Life in peacetime
was so dull. No exciting news. No hairbreadth escapes of friends
in whom one took a peculiar interest, no brilliant dances for the
shining youth on leave from the front.

In the middle decades of the last century, again and again, the
cry was raised, *"La France s'ennuie"*—France is bored—and it
frightened Europe.

The whole world may feel like that when wars are no longer
possible. Would there still be adventure? Where? How? The earth
will have been explored in its entirety: land and sea, mountaintop
and ocean floor. Adventure will have to take to interplanetary excursions, or to invention, and the solution of problems. The first
may be feasible someday, sooner perhaps than we now expect. As
for the others, they will be confined to the few who have the gift
and character. They will be mathematical and out of reach for
people like myself. It is not likely that historical scholarship will
survive. Who will look back to a past when self-interest, passion,
and sentiment ruled the world? For an *élite* there will be abundance of adventure along intellectual lines. What will the rest of
the community do, who have no brains for such occupations, and
find no happiness except in a sphere where courage and physical
aptitudes count along with brains?

Hitherto even the most quiescent communities, say the Con-
fucian Chinese, have found outlets for adventure in conquest and
hazardous administration. They wedged their dominion into the
Islamitic world as far as Kashgar, lorded it over the vast Amur
Basin, colonized or imposed their civilization on Korea, on Japan,
on Indo-China, on Siam. This could be achieved only by the material as well as spiritual superiority of the Chinese.

But our midget of an earth will soon be too small for large-scale
energizing, in the material sphere. Wars will have been demon-
strated to be utterly absurd and survive, if at all, as a sport, as an

excuse for betting and gambling. And man's last gesture may be a wordless yawn.

There comes back to me a summer afternoon when I was enjoying the cool on the veranda of a cottage neighboring on the park at Versailles. Suddenly there appeared a shortish old man, all bald head, with malicious eyes and a quizzical smile, who, when we were introduced to each other, spoke with a warm, husky voice. He stayed but a few minutes and, in connection with I remember not what, remarked that in the Middle Ages people were more amused than in our own time.

I was in my early forties. I had read and reflected, and this observation of Henry Adams was like a spark on tinder. It flared and lit up so much that hitherto had remained vague and murky, because I had been taking too deterministic, too solemn, even too pompous a view of the past.

Fledglings of puritanism that we were, we had given ourselves up to studying history as a spiritual combat against evil within and without ourselves, and thought seldom of *panem*—of bread—and never of *circenses*—amusements.

By amusement, however, neither Adams nor I had in mind circuses and other deliberate entertainments. What we meant was living keenly, zestfully, relatively free to work as one liked and to loaf when one pleased. It meant not to be the slave of fixed hours, and of so much output per hour. It meant to run risks, to allow for ups and downs—in short, to leave room for variety, excitement, and some sense of adventure.

We retain this kind of life in the slums. Cobblers, tinkers, chimney sweeps, plumbers, clothes-menders, small shopkeepers of every kind in these purlieus, can alternate work with play and are not obliged to take either in impalatable, in indigestible doses.

Though frequently exposed to cold, disease, hunger even, as indeed most city dwellers were in the Middle Ages, may they yet not be happier, more zestful, more eager, in short more *amused,* than the same number of people in their comfortable well-supplied mansions and country houses?

Once upon a time a woman of my acquaintance who was trying

to uplift working girls in the East End of London asked a class of them what the words "bore," "being bored," and "boredom" meant.

None of them knew the words except one, who thought it referred to being lost in deep thought. This happened some fifty years ago. By now uplift may have taught slum girls what it means to be bored.

It is interesting to reflect that accidie—no appetite for life— never attacked city dwellers of the Middle Ages with their helter-skelter, higgledy-piggledy manner of life, but haunted the over-organized, clockwork-monasteries.

I have known women who lived opulently with the income derived from their incomes yet not knowing how to get through the day. Too old to attract, too shrewd to be trapped by adventurers, they would snatch at this or that diversion, but in no sense of the word were they amused. To be amused by art, by ideas, or even by society, one must have the appropriate gifts, and few of the overrich have them. I verily believe that charwomen get more out of their lives than these millionairesses.

Nor is the condition of the average well-to-do American woman much better. Often she has no housekeeping or children to occupy her; and where she has both, they yet leave her with a leisure that she does not know what to do with. If she is energetic, she may go into business or push a gentleman friend. More likely, she will go into politics and, as a *rentière,* campaign against Franklin Roosevelt, or in favor of something else which she understands little. The average female of the same class, apart from joining her in cursing the President and his Jewish and Irish advisers, will look forward to the fad lectures she will hear, the discourses she will not understand, but above all to the bridge parties of the afternoon.

I recall staying at an hotel in Boston—in cultured Boston— where the average *rentière* women of the possessive classes would come by hundreds and occupy all the sitting rooms at small tables. There they sat. Not a word was spoken. Not a sound was heard except the hushed thud of the cards as they flapped on the tables.

Killing time, instead of employing it as the very substance of life lived and not merely got through with, is surely the sin of sins. And that is what overleisure may lead to!

Happily, it is conceivable that the majority of mankind will evolve, through inheritance and instruction, tastes for art creation of every kind. As women, in leisure hours, knit and embroider, man may develop talents for the arts as well as for the sports that we take to naturally. When so many will be working with no expectation of material reward, intent on the same problems, who knows what genius may be revealed, and what masterpieces created! Already, in almost every civilized country, hobbies are rife among individuals with a certain leisure. As leisure increases, these hobbies will find more opportunities for spreading out and flowering into something more artistic, more creative, at once more penetrating and more expansive, pushing further and further back the flaming frontiers of the human universe and turning aspiring man into a hopeful rival of the Demiurge.

January 22d

I READ nearly all the German papers that can be had: the *Deutsche Allgemeine*, and the *Börsenzeitung* of Berlin, the *Hamburger Fremdenblatt*, the *Kölnische*, the *Münchener Neueste Nachrichten*, the *Wiener Journal* and the *Völkischer Beobachter*.

All have the same news, the same propaganda, the same sneers and insults directed against Anglo-Saxons in general and against Churchill and Roosevelt in particular. These take the shape of quotations from the English and American press. I assume that they are neither falsified nor even too much distorted.

Now, the readers of most of these papers are anything but uneducated. They belong to the upper layers of German public opinion. How is it possible that they do not distinguish the attitude of these particular Anglo-American journals as of opposition? Is it likely that many German readers of these extracts ignore this and do not envy countries where, in the midst of the bitterest war, people are free to say what they think, to criticize their government fairly and unfairly, to poke fun at their rulers?

It may be therefore a questionable policy to carry on a campaign with quotations from writers of the countries against whom the campaign is directed, even if the writers include such hoary Victorian jokers as Bernard Shaw, and malaprops like Margot Asquith.

The intelligent German readers may go so far as to ask why the Russian press is never quoted for carpings and insults against Stalin and his regime. They may come to the conclusion that Soviet subjects, like Nazis, are not free to say what they think, and that no daily dares print a word of opposition.

January 25th

EVERY DAILY appearing in the Reich and in its hernia gives considerable space to Jews and to Roosevelt. At times the President of the U. S. A. is an out-and-out Jew. More often he is only Jew-haunted and Jew-minded.

In the papers I received yesterday there was an account of Roosevelt's last "swindle." It consisted of the monstrosity of giving each soldier that left for the front a copy of the New Testament for which he had written a preface.

The daily anti-Jew article rubbed its hands with glee over Japan's behavior toward the few sons of Abraham, Isaac, and Jacob still found in the wide-flung empire of the Sun God's descendants.

The Nuremberg laws were being applied strictly to all those "human microbes" in Japan's recent conquests. But that was little. The real business was tracking and extirpating the insinuating, penetrating, sinister, world-hungry, antihuman, antinational Jew-mindedness that had already taken hold of influential classes, in the Far East even.

Before this war began E. M. Forster spoke of the Jew-consciousness with which Hitler had inoculated us. How true it is for all of us, from Honolulu eastward, through America, through Europe, through Asia to Meshed in farthest Persia, we all know. But we were left to believe that Ainus, Japanese, Koreans, Chinese, Siamese, Tonkinese, Javanese, Formosans, etc., etc., were unaware of the existence of Jews, let alone knowing of their hellish, devouring, destructive, grasping, clutching, all-conquering propensities. They too are now made Jew-conscious. I am sure there are members of that so-called race who will ejaculate: "What an ad!"

I am seeing friends who, unlike myself, have no drop of Jewish blood to taint their veins. They are at least as much horrified over the treatment of Jews as I am, and can get it as little out of their minds.

The hunt still goes on. The other day forty new agents were appointed in Bologna to ferret out Jews still in hiding. Even a Dominican of Hebrew origin had to flee his monastery for fear of arrest, and found his way here.

The other day a parish priest of this diocese was arrested for harboring a Jew. The Cardinal of Florence intervened, declaring that he himself was the culprit and requesting to be jailed in place of the priest; which, of course, resulted in the liberation of the prisoner.

I heard an amusing anecdote yesterday. Children in a Sunday school were being taught that no child was a Christian until it was baptized. "Are they all Jews before?" asked one little girl.

What was Haman to Hitler! He never hoped to kill more Jews than were to be found in the one hundred and twenty provinces of the Persian Empire. Hitler's ambition embraces the whole earth. He has made a good beginning with his present Reich, where it is calculated he has massacred some three million. This number must include those of Poland as well.

Poles have hitherto ranked with Jews, as mere vermin to be got rid of at any cost. All of a sudden they have become objects of tender solicitude. Stalin threatens to include an entire million in the frontiers he means to make for Russia. And his hypocritical allies who made war to defend Poland against Germany permit this monstrosity! Truly, the Nazis are softhearted. Stalin wants to annex one million Poles. They have put several millions out of misery.

January 26th

THE ANGLO-AMERICANS have made a landing on the spot where Aeneas landed three thousand years ago. According to last accounts they are already at Velletri and have thus achieved, in a couple of days, what it took the Trojan hero so long to accomplish. The terrain still sets the same problems that it did of old. Lord Allenby soon after the last war told me that in his campaign against Jerusalem the David of the Book of Kings was his best guide. All this will be changed when war will be confined to the air.

January 27th

IF MANKIND SURVIVES another five thousand years, making progress slow indeed, yet progress, we now living and acting will seem to people of that distant date to have belonged to what we call "antiquity." Should anyone question this, he will be advised to look at the place Jewish and Greek expressions, Jewish and Greek feeling and thinking went on occupying; how much that combination of Jewish religion, Greek metaphysics, and Roman imperialism known as Christianity dominates us still; how much our literature, no matter in what offspring of Greek, Latin, or antique barbarian speech, still carries on the values, the traditions, the historical references, and the rhetoric of antiquity. Our ethical axioms, the courses of conduct to which we consent, even if they do not enjoy our reasoned approval, will seem singularly like those of the ancient Oecumene. They will point to our preference for Greek and Latin literature, to our cult of Homeric notions of virility and war, and to an even greater and more formative regard for the Bible among Protestants and its derivatives among Catholics; point to our creeds and prayers and hymns.

Time and time again I have asked myself when and how the break would come. A full hundred years ago a Parisian *gamin* cried out, "*Qui nous délivrera des Grecs et des Romains*," and the cry was not to a wilderness. Some fifty or sixty years later Viennese politicians shouted, "*Los von Rom*"—away from Rome— Rome as the administrative seat of Catholicism. The ejaculation was not taken too seriously but attracted my attention. It was followed some two or three decades later still by the revulsion of Professor Strzygowski from the visual art of the Mediterranean world and its "hothouse products." He favored anything that did not glow with the heat and did not smell of the honey and brine of the Midland Sea. He ended by finding little to his taste in the world's architecture, except the timber buildings of Galicia and of more and more northern climes. As for the figure arts, nothing pleased him but Runic and even more primitive scratchings in lands close to where Shakespeare's Lapland sorcerers gather.

Despite the considerable influence he had not only in all Germanies but in France and England as well, I would not let the Viennese professor have the honor of directly inspiring Hitler, Goebbels, and Himmler, or the practitioners and interpreters of "abstract art" who surpass him by turning altogether away from representation to find satisfaction in geometrical pattern only.

Art and its interpreters are like the swallows that do not make a spring but prelude it. Bode's behavior over his "Leonardo bust," and the way the whole of Germany was marshaled to support him, gave, before the First World War, a foreboding of what was cooking up in Berlin and Potsdam and how they would conduct hostilities and propaganda.

Nazism, and the present conflict, are continuations and realizations of the means and ways of the last war, with overwhelmingly improved instruments of combat. Nazism is, in a sense if not in essence, a barbarian revolt—let us hope not a revolution—against the humanistic values thought out by the best Greeks and their Hellenized disciples in Alexandria, in Rome, and even in Judea. Its anti-Semitism is but the spearhead of its anti-Christianity, and is based on resentment against minds subtler, quicker, and more cognizant of fact as well as value. It would rage as furiously against Catholics as against Jews if they were as small and as vulnerable a minority. Nazism is the last phase of the intermittent, ever-renewed attempt of partially Romanized Germany to shake itself free of Mediterranean influence.

Despite the horrors committed and damage done, it does not look as if these descendants of Hermann, Attila, and Genseric would have their way.

More probably the present phase of the antique world, the harmony of Greek, Jew, Roman, and assimilated barbarian known as Christianity, and identical with European civilization wherever found, will gradually give place to a society which has outgrown, forgotten, or discarded it.

No longer is Greek regarded as essential in education. It is already being pursued only by students who mean to make a profession of teaching it, or of using it as philologers and archaeologists. Latin will follow before long. Hebrew disappeared from general culture generations ago. Little by little their literatures, including our rituals, will sink into the background and disappear along with institutional Christianity itself.

What will replace them? I for one cannot conceive. Our languages will cease to be understood even earlier than our ideas and feelings. Our literature will be as dead as Hebrew is today. If aspirations toward the good and the beautiful survive, what shape will they take, what expression will they find in the visual and verbal arts, and in music? We can no more imagine it than even an Alexandrian, let alone a Periclean, Greek could foresee Chartres or Rheims Cathedral, the plays of Shakespeare, the music of Beethoven, Wagner, and Strauss. And I speak of art only. What of the material world, and all that will have been invented—inventions and discoveries that may change society even more radically than the arts! Underneath it all, the least changed will remain man himself.

January 28th

ANOTHER REFUGEE, a lady of the best society, has found shelter in this house. She arrived after adventures worthy of the late Greek romances, with a babe six months old that, on foot, she carried for many hours over stony paths. She had to avoid roads where the ghoul-Fascists might have arrested her.

Her husband has had a prominent position in one of the African provinces where apparently a good deal of anti-British propaganda was current. One of the chief accusations regarded the Suez Canal. This lady seemed to believe that the canal being "internazional" meant that everybody could pass through it free of charge. Nevertheless England made Italy pay so much for every ton, and so much per person for every ship, and every soldier or civilian going to and from Eritrea, Abyssinia, and the seat of empire. She had no idea that the canal was a private concern, and that although nobody, in peace or war, could be stopped from passing, everybody had to pay, from England as well as from other countries.

Italian imperialism rests on a most unexpected ignorance and a total disregard of the questions of labor and transport. One of the bitter complaints after the last war against France and England was that Italy had not been given the coal mines of Eregli. Now, Eregli is on the southern shores of the Black Sea. I tried in vain to tell my Italian friends that even if they owned the mines they would have to supply machinery, pay engineers and workmen, and send ships to fetch the coal; that apart from giving employment to a mere handful of Italian subjects, the economic advantages might be questionable.

The pusillanimous conduct of the Chamberlain cabinet over Abyssinia, and later over Spain, led the Italian press to believe that England was in her decline, and that she would not be able to hold India much longer. Who, then, should take up the task England had carried out so incompetently, so greedily, so wickedly, who but Fascist Italy?

It was not only newspapermen, with no notion of the facts, and obliged to write what they were told, but in one instance an eminent Indianist. This scholar, who, with British protection, encouragement, and assistance, could study Indian problems and must have been aware of the difficulty of solving many of them, except with patience, and in the course of many years—this gentleman, when convinced that both France and England were collapsing, did his best to make Mussolini see his duty in taking over the white man's burden in India.

It seems our new lady refugee was made unhappy when she heard me say Abyssinia would not be returned to Italy.

It never occurred to her apparently to ask: What rights so ancient, so well grounded did Italy have to that Empire? It apparently had not entered her head that it was inhuman and immoral to fall upon your neighbor with superior arms, in order to enslave him and exploit his resources; that Italy had no claims on Abyssinia, and that in fact the conquest of that country was one of the sources for the state of feeling that led to this war. This same lady believes that absolute government alone is good government and that all revolutions are due to intellectuals.

January 30th

IN O'MEARA's *Memoirs of St. Helena* Napoleon is constantly harping on Castlereagh's stupidity. The English working classes are famished and yet their government does nothing to encourage manufacture and trade. The British, who stood the brunt of the long war against him, should have demanded advantageous commercial treaties from Spain, who owed so much to England, and from the latter's allies, Prussia and Russia. Not a bit of it, and the last two are excluding British goods.

Then, how foolish to have given back Java to the Dutch and the Isle de Bourbon to the French—the French, who should be prevented from occupying stepping stones to India. Napoleon seemed to believe—I have no doubt with secret joy—that England had ruined herself fighting him, and was too far gone and too stupid to recover. The future was Russia's, as indeed so many believe today.

He harps on England's getting nothing out of the war against him, and it seems to him the depth of stupidity. It does not occur to him that grab and grip were even in his day archaic and already superannuated policies, and that Great Britain might be wise in refusing to keep all that fell to her while fighting.

Even now, it is the rarest of experiences to discover a Continental European who will not tell you that England is out for nothing but more and more territory—and that despite the surrenders that incurred Napoleon's contempt, and the later cession of the Ionian Islands and of Helgoland.

O'Meara's chronicle of Napoleon's complaints over his treatment by Hudson Lowe is distressing. The moment an official tells you that he is only doing his duty, you may expect the worst. He may merely be stupid, resentful of superiority, unconsciously enjoy taking it down a peg and bossing over it. He has nevertheless immortalized himself: as much as the creature who, to secure his name for posterity, burned down the Temple of Diana of Ephesus. But Napoleon was a chatterer. He had to talk, and O'Meara had to act as go-between and complaint-carrier. Great, perhaps, and fascinating, certainly, as was Napoleon, a gentleman he was not. *Un monsieur ne se plaint qu'une seule fois*—a gentleman complains but once.

February 1st

EXCEPT in the human sphere, the irrational is being pushed back all the time. It is already so far from us that, for practical considerations, it no longer counts.

I have marveled that one could undertake to treat man in the lump as rational. Yet our ethics and politics are based on the notion that he is. Nature we regard as irrational, and are never indignant with her for the havoc she commits. An eruption of Etna with accompanying earthquakes kills fifty thousand human beings and overwhelms the work of years; turns the prosperous farms, the busy towns, the smiling landscape into a desert of grim lava under a malignant sun; and we feel no indignation. Nature is irrational and the irrational is irresponsible; you cannot get indignant with blind, unconscious force.

And is man in the lump more aware of the consequences of his actions, more responsible and therefore a subject for indignation? For indignation is based on the idea that its subject could have acted otherwise.

Man in the lump is little, if any, more rational than a herd of buffaloes on the stampede, as it used to be described when I was a small boy and buffaloes still roamed free in regions now thickly settled by Babbitts, their bosses, and dependents. The individual man may be more rational, but nothing like so much as, despite universal experience to the contrary, we expect him to be.

We do this so as to hold him responsible for his acts, to stir up indignation against him, and to punish him accordingly.

As far as mankind was concerned, whether in the mass or as individuals, this has been our attitude until some generations ago.

A gradual change has come over us since the publication of Ossian and the Percy *Reliques* on the one hand, and on the other the rise of Romanticism in Germany.

Literary critics have called it the awakening of wonder. It was rather the dawn of a suspicion that man was not a rational being. The awakening came slowly, and is perhaps only now being commonly recognized.

At first it took the shape of awe before hitherto unsuspected depths and passions lurking in the human breast. It found, or tried to find, expression in Novalis, in Chateaubriand, in Scott, in Byron, in Tieck, in Chamisso, in Jean Paul, in La Motte-Fouqué, in Hoffmann, in Pushkin, in Lermontov, and of course in the galaxy of the French Romantics.

This recognition of the individual's irrationality would have done little harm to the European world as a whole. But it quickly passed over to an admiration for the heroic, that is to say for outbreaks of energy no matter how directed, as well as for primitive societies where heroism could be continually displayed. It stood for a life wild but free, indifferent to consequences and therefore noble; the kind of life that the contemporary British official in Palestine—his imagination fired by the ultraromantic Lawrence and contrasting it with his own cribbed and cabined one—fancies the Bedouin is always living.

Unfortunately, admiration was followed by nostalgic longings to return to a similar state of society and to the actual cult of the irrational. It no longer sufficed Wagner to celebrate passionately, tenderly, magniloquently the victims of a love philter; he had to go further and sing his contempt for reason as embodied in Mime, and rational order as incarnate in Freya, and belch out delirium over brainless derring-do in Siegfried.

From Wagner and Nietzsche, and the former's son-in-law the ex-English Chamberlain, to Hitler and Rosenberg, with their blood and soil, was but a step. Nazism and its affinities are based on the cult of the irrational as the ultimate reality. Hence the return to a primitive, or at least archaic, tribal solipsism, and the politics, morality, and inhumanity of the jungle—in short, the spirit of a Siberian tiger provided with every up-to-date mechanical, theatrical, and propagandist instrument of combat.

Nazism in the collective sphere is paralleled by Freudism in the case of the individual. For thousands of years reason has endeavored to tame the wild beast in our bosoms, to chain the mad dog, to extirpate the vermin. Now we are urged to let them loose and disport themselves in the sun, even if nominally it is with the purpose of getting rid of them. I confess to little faith in the promise. The immediate result is an excited interest in what goes on beneath the belt to the exclusion of head and members. It is as if in a household everything was ignored—proportions, architecture, comfort, furnishing—and that nothing counted but drains, more drains, and ever more drains.

How far is man, as an individual, rational? Where does he begin to be invincibly irrational? How far can sex and amusement be safely suppressed? Ascetics of the last five and twenty centuries thought, enacted, and tried to enforce the reduction of the last to zero and the first to the grudgingly admitted necessity of continuing the race.

We have successfully revolted against puritanism, and the present tendency is to study problems of sex and recreation with no respect for theological or moralistic prejudices. The results could be hopeful, if a dragon did not lie in the path. It is the tendency of totalitarian societies, and of many economists elsewhere, to turn sex not into a fountain of joy, of inspiration to poetry, to painting, to music, to all the other arts, but into an industry for the production of cannon fodder or of consumers for manufactured goods.

To my knowledge, the question has never been studied of just how much man, whether in the mass or as individual, is affected by catchwords and phrases. That we are highly verbo-toxic seems certain to our rulers, if not to ourselves. The press was powerful, yet how feeble compared with a monopolized radio, in producing crowd-mindedness! The individual who resists, even when not subjected to police persecution and social ostracism, is left out in the cold, angry and gasping. A state-directed and exclusive radio may succeed in plunging or, shall we say, doping its subjects into a condition of mind as unquestioning as that of any archaic society. Nazism has achieved it. It can fall upon its neighbors, overcome them, slaughter them by the million, and enslave the survivors with as little protest from the all but totality of Germans as ever reached the ear of a Babylonian conqueror in the third millennium before our era. Not only Nazism but any other authoritarian society must end in a return to archaic conditions of a more and more primitive kind. The circle will be ultimately rounded off; the irrational will have triumphed, and there will be no further question of reason.

But there is Russia. I have read a good deal of what has been published in England and America, France and Italy, about Soviet politics, Soviet society, Soviet economics.

Only two books seem to throw a certain light on the country that is now warring so successfully against the Nazis. Ambassador Davies' observations are largely concerned with industries and preparations for meeting the onslaught from Germany that Stalin was expecting. Interesting as he is, he has little to say about the sociological, and nothing about the inner life of the Russian masses.

The other book is by Littlepage, an American mining engineer who confines himself to describing what he saw. He saw all sorts of peoples and clans torn away from their hunting, their nomadic, their agricultural pursuits and tribal organizations; flung far from their habitual haunts, and forced into mines and factories along with groups of different speech, different religions, different customs; and although many perished, many others ended as good workmen, excellent mechanics, as well as detribalized and standardized Soviet subjects.

Talk of the "melting pot" in America! It will take generations before Irish and Poles, Italians and Jews will get out of their several ghettoes and be Americanized.

Stalin's policy, cruel, inhuman, reckless of associations of attachment to soil and blood, of tradition, of family ties even, is by far the most interesting social experiment ever made. It treats men and women as mere clay or as chemical elements. It remains to be seen whether, in the long run, they will remain as inert. One of my few regrets at being so near my seventy-ninth year is that I cannot expect to see the result of Stalin's undertaking. He may succeed in detribalizing, in deregionalizing the variegated populations of his vast empire—if indeed that has been his intention. He may reduce the human beings dwelling between the Baltic and Pacific to the same condition, speaking the same language and uttering the same catchwords, with the same fervor. Will they stay put?

Not likely. They will develop a governing class not only in administration, in industries, in business, in politics, but no less in the realm of mind, in the sciences, in thought, in literature, and in the arts. Will this ruling class not grow too selfish, too self-appreciative, too arrogant, too exclusive, too possessive, as similar classes have done in the past—as they did in Russia to such degree that the masses could easily be roused to massacre them?

Revolutions are necessary because ruling classes lose grip, fail to rule for the common good, and have to be swept away. To give the sweepers adequate enthusiasm for their distressing task, one has to dope them into ecstasies of conviction that they are creating a paradise upon earth: no hunger, no disease, no jealousy, no envy, no spite; only brotherly love, disinterested activities, freedom for the exercise of the highest, most individualized functions; every creature encouraged to strive for his own perfection.

If this is so, if mankind is destined to go through the same phases eternally, no matter in how many generations or centuries or even millennia a full circle is completed, then man is not a subject for history but for anthropology.

Indeed, I have often asked myself whether history has begun. Political and social history certainly not. The histories where the rational gets the better of the irrational are the histories of the sciences and of the arts. Yet such is the lust of writers and readers for blood and thunder that no history is read much, no narrative is considered to be real history, unless it mythicizes politics and war.

The corollary should be—I fear it is seldom drawn—that most so-called history is read not for instruction and enlightenment but for entertainment. It is either as attractive narrative, like most of our classical histories from Herodotus downwards, or it attempts to rationalize the past, as started by the authors of the Biblical Books of Kings, pursued by Polybius and Tacitus, St. Augustine and his host of followers through the ages, and the Hegel-inspired historians of the last hundred years.

For which reason I am at times induced to approve the Chinese, who will hear nothing of the past except actualities. Or I tend to fall back on memoirs and letters, which tell what at any given moment people were feeling and thinking about the events that were taking shape in their presence. I end by having more respect for them than for the documents so revered by philological historians.

A fear often takes hold of me that we may not be meant to be rational. It looks as if man is an animal who like other animals has to spend his long life fighting, with the difference, however, that at the same time he is, as Bergson had it, a machine for creating gods and of course myths.

It is not improbable that once mankind ceases to battle, and to believe in life-sustaining lies, religions, superstitions of every kind, it may cease to live.

We are too far from such an eventuality to regard it as practical politics. At present we must fight the irrational tooth and nail.

February 6th

A GERMAN OFFICER who has just returned from leave reports that cities like Cologne and Frankfurt, which he saw with his own eyes, are reduced to heaps of ruins. The shops are empty. He asked for a uniform and was told that he could take what he found. He found nothing. He saw, in midwinter, recruits practicing in clothes barely suitable for summer. The soldiers were being well fed no longer. Even for the officers, the food was poor and far from plentiful. The only comforting recent event, he said, was for Germans that they had struck oil both in Hungary and in adjacent Austria, so that they no longer fear a shortage or even stoppage of petrol.

Here in Florence, open trucks arrive from the "Gustav line" with wounded Germans lying on straw. They look pitiable, wan, greenish. The town is full of their troops going southward. They may not remain more than three days. Everybody praises their correct behavior.

Which is not the case with the ghoul-Fascist regime. These continue to arrest generals all over the place, and priests who have sheltered and fed English prisoners. On the other hand, Fascist bosses are being attacked and at times with success. There is no little sabotage. Reports are rife that the bands in remoter places no longer ask but demand obliging proprietors to give them not only food and clothing but money as well, considerable amounts.

The same officer told us that Hitler has apparently taken Florence under his special protection, and issued orders that nothing shall be done to draw upon it the terror of the Anglo-Saxons. It seems that Hitler was profoundly impressed by the town. When taken to the Piazzale Michelangelo, he stood and looked down on the churches and palaces with the Arno running between them to the plain toward Pisa. He stood lost in deep feeling from which he found himself again with the ejaculation: "At last I understand Feuerbach and Böcklin!"

The realm of beauty, of art even, exists for Hitler as it does not for his precursor Mussolini. What a mystery is this demon of a Hitler, the incarnation of the irrational, yet with something fascinating that makes one wonder.

February 9th

YESTERDAY toward midday high up out of a dazzling sky appeared formations of Allied aircraft, which bombed and bombarded with detonations that sounded like thunder.

It is difficult to find out what they were after, or even what they hit. Apparently nothing of military use. Rumor has it that they struck an orphan asylum.

The Axis-minded will go so far as to say that the flying machines came for no other purpose.

Many of the Axis-minded who now recognize the evils of Fascism and the bestiality of the Nazis have been so successfully "vaccinated against the truth," to use Michelet's phrase, by Axis propaganda against the English, that they snatch, seize, and grasp eagerly at anything that makes the English out to be no better than the Germans.

We all are miserable sinners, and it is easy enough for those so disposed to pick out and isolate cases of English conduct that are reprehensible, and to insist on them with so much emphasis that they swell to the bulk of Nazi atrocities.

To win the war, these Allies must inevitably resort to the arms of their opponents, *à corsaire corsaire et demi,* and thus give ground for their being charged with as much devilishness.

What gets me is the Axis propaganda about the war in the air.

At the beginning of the last war, in 1914, I heard Lord Desart say that of course nobody would commit such a crime as bombing civilian populations from the air. The Germans began it, and in this war the Nazis won with it their world-shaking, disconcerting triumphs in Poland first, and then in Holland, Belgium, and France. Upon which, they set about deliberately to destroy London, and succeeded in almost bombing Coventry out of existence. From its name the Germans made a verb and boasted that all other British towns would be "coventrized." When the statistics of some forty-seven thousand killed by their onslaughts appeared, the Germans gloried in the figure, and snarled that it was the fault of Churchill for daring to resist them. In Axis lands, no public protest was raised against these massacres and destructions. I doubt whether so much as a twentieth part of their populations minded. The overwhelming majority were delighted.

Italian Fascists were day by day hearing and reading of the continuous bombarding of Malta, with no thought of the killed or wounded, and no regret for the destruction of peculiarly beautiful masterpieces of their own architecture. And when Mussolini begged humbly for the permission, graciously granted by Hitler, to join with several hundred machines in the air war against London, Fascist bosoms swelled with pride.

This state of mind and heart regarding the air war would have gone on as careless of humanity, and as indifferent to destruction, and would have increased in compliance, if only the earlier air triumphs had continued.

February 11th

THE AMERICANS who a few days ago bombed the environs of Florence made a victim of Lina Cavalieri. This at one time notorious beauty lived here for years, it seems, and in sufficient obscurity for me never to have heard of her presence. Latterly she got frightened of remaining in town, and went to occupy a villa in the Pian dei Giullari region, out of harm's way, as she thought. There her fate overtook her.

In O'Meara's memoirs Napoleon speaks of chance and luck, and how in his earlier career as a soldier, always directing or taking part in battles, people were shot down next to him, while he never suffered more than slight wounds.

To return to Lina Cavalieri—I had forgotten her and supposed she no longer existed. At one time in Italy, and then abroad, she excited some curiosity. She was of the humblest possible origin: it was believed that her father ran the privies of the Roman railway station. She was discovered by Carlo di Rudinì and trained by him for the role of *femme galante*—the high-stepping *cocotte*.

Rudinì, by the way, was a first-class trainer for society splendor and success. Did he not change the small-bourgeois D'Annunzio from a gifted poetical genius into a flashy man of the world?

I cannot recall how the Cavalieri lived before she reached the skyscrapers of Manhattan. I seem to remember that she kept a beauty parlor in Paris. In New York she was taken up by Bridget Guinness, an exquisite creature whose house before the last war was all but the center of New York's smartest society. Bridget— as all called her, whether they had or had not a right to—got it into her charming, irresponsible head to make Lina's fortune. She threw her at the tousled, half-crazy "Chimpy Chanler," and he married her. The wedding was soon followed by a divorce.

February 14th

MY HOSTESS lunched yesterday in the company of the editor of the most authoritative Tuscan daily, the *Nazione*. His name is Mirco Giobbe, the first part certainly Yugoslav and the second probably Venetic. He claims, however, to be a Roman and to have been at school with Ciano. He talked freely; and she is a precise as well as a lively reporter.

Of Ciano he said that Edda Mussolini made desperate efforts to save her husband. Nothing availed. It seems that orders for his death came from Hitler and were peremptory. I recall that on the second day after Ciano and the other four were shot, the Fascist press came out with notices and articles discreetly but clearly regretting the execution.

The editor regarded the execution as necessary for winning the war—and he was certain they would win it. Presumably the example would make the chiefs of other satellite countries think twice before they attempted to get out of the Nazi camp.

He confessed that he had been commanded to prepare a special edition of the *Nazione* to celebrate the repulse of the Anglo-American forces venturing to land with felonious intent on the sacred shores of Latium. He had no little difficulty in keeping back the publication. This is on all fours with the Duce's going to Libya, prepared to ride into Alexandria as conqueror on a white horse.

He went on to say that the Germans could not leave the Pope in Rome. If they did, he would order American Catholics to vote for Roosevelt, in the impending presidential elections.

I tried to point out to my hostess that in the first place Roosevelt, so far as I knew, had not yet decided whether he was going to stand again. Moreover, if His Holiness gave out such a command, it does not follow that all Catholics would obey. The certain result would be that most still practicing Protestants and Jews, as well as pious freethinkers, would thereby be induced to vote against Roosevelt.

But it is not easy to get the attention of Continental Europeans, when one tries to talk to them about American politics as an actuality and not as suits their prejudices and wishes.

She inquired of the editor what the shooting affray of a few afternoons ago in Florence had been about.

When the resurrected Fascists returned here, as a cynically transparent mask for a Nazi occupation, they could trust neither the militia, nor the *carabinieri*, nor the police to do their bidding. They proceeded to empty out of the reform schools boys of criminal propensities, armed them to the teeth, mounted them on cycles, and ordered them to act as police. These are having a grand time, ordering people about, insulting, threatening, and at times carrying out their threats.

It seems that the other day they had been banqueted and came out the worse for drink. While marching through one of the principal thoroughfares, some of them fired off guns and pistols, upon which the others, in their booze, concluded that they were being shot at from the houses they were passing. A general *fantasia* succeeded, and some of the cheery lads rushed into the houses to discover who might be shooting at them. In one they found a most respectable professional man in his bath and killed him outright, shouting as they left: "We have done for him."

It appears that the German commander of the district asked the specter-Fascist general of the same district how many troops he could dispose of. "Seven thousand," was the answer, "but they are unarmed and unless you supply them with guns and ammunition they are of no use." The Germans, for fear that they might turn against themselves, will not trust them with arms.

The same journalist defended the bloodthirsty, sadic Captain Carità because he was so "sincere" and in *"buona fede."* What crimes, O sincerity, are condoned and even approved of when done in thy name! Carità may not be torturing or killing for financial profit or even place: he simply may be satisfying his lust for the agony and blood of his fellow men.

The editor expressed his conviction that in France the only person left to collaborate with the Nazis was Laval. Similar statements have reached me again and again from German sources.

February 15th

THE *Völkischer Beobachter*—the *People's Observer*—is the official daily of the Nazi party, and is edited by its John the Evangelist, Alfred Rosenberg.

On the 7th of this month it published an illustrated broadside about Siena, and in big square letters announced that this abode of art in every field and every kind, this treasure house not inferior to Florence, had been almost totally and deliberately destroyed by the terroristic Anglo-American air gangsters.

I did not believe this piece of news, seeing the Italian press and radio did not start up the hullabaloo they would have made

if it had been true. They only spoke of damage done to the Os-
servanza across the valley to the north of Siena; and even that
seems doubtful.

Nevertheless, to make sure, I had inquiries made at the office
of the art superintendent. There nothing was known, it not being
their business; but they did not regard the report as probable.
Their indifference, by the way, speaks either for a lack of interest
in monuments and works of art for which they are not personally
responsible, or perhaps for a sense like mine: that the Anglo-
Americans are not likely to go out of their way to destroy buildings and their contents when they have no military value.

On further inquiry it turned out that Ranuccio Bianchi-Ban-
dinelli had been at Siena days after the publication of the Nazi
organ, and that he had seen no sign whatever of damage from the
air.

We can add that whatever devastation Siena has suffered in
the fifty-six years that I have known it has come entirely from its
aediles, eager for novelty at all costs.

February 17th   B. B. to X . . .

DEAR FRIEND, thank you for the political letter. I cannot leave
it unanswered although I can scarcely more than indicate briefly
the subject I would like to discuss with you. If we could talk
things over calmly, quietly, fully, and *ohne Feindschaft,* I should
probably take back or modify some of what I shall now write
down, and clarify the rest. I fear our opportunity for such talk
is still far away. So I jot down what spontaneously comes to my
mind.

To begin with, let me remind you that for several years I have
been urging my Italian friends to master conversational English.
Few Anglo-Saxons understand and speak any language but their
own. Even then many of my Italian friends will be handicapped
by the fact of not having the material means to receive the Anglo-
Saxon warriors and dine and wine them in the midst of attractive
society. It might easily happen that such hospitality dispensed by

the wrong kind of people will greatly appeal to these warriors who, impressed by their titles, may turn to them for advice, and believe that they can trust their recommendations. Thereby the more politically minded people who will come after will find themselves sidetracked.

You must expect little sympathy from the Anglo-Saxon occupation for ideas of redistributing or diminishing the legal rights of private property. You may propose taxing its incomes to the extent of 90 per cent and you will perhaps encounter no opposition. On no condition must you question on principle the "sacred rights of private property."

So much for the occupying forces. Now as to your fellow citizens. I fear you underestimate the force of passive resistance that can be developed by your possessive classes. They have ceased to be a governing aristocracy, but by their mass they can still afford a stout—let us hope not overwhelming—resistance to threats against their hold on property, if not of privileges. You should therefore be cautious in the language you use with regard to private property, particularly in land, and the rights that go with it.

I would propose reconciling landowners, industrial, and financial interests by introducing and fostering a spirit of compromise. The trouble with most Latin politics is dogmatism, turning politics into theology. Discuss with your adversary, no matter how little, at first, he seems inclined to listen. Propose meeting him part of the way. Make it clear to him that it is his only chance of not losing everything.

A like course might reconcile many of the least stupid property-holders, and at the same time rally Anglo-Saxon public opinion to your side.

If you offend and frighten property-holders, not to speak of attempts at using violence, there is serious danger that this time they will throw themselves into the arms of the Vatican as twenty years ago into those of the Fascio. The Vatican, with its cohorts of Jesuits and other praetorians, has a beautiful, liberal-sounding, comforting, and reassuring program ready—a sort of Dollfuss regime—and is on the watch, hoping that the leftists will drive other parties to its motherly embrace.

And, dear friend, you must let me say a word about my own position. You will easily believe that, given my advanced age, having no heirs of my body and my entire income in America, I am fairly free from fears about my own possessions in Italy. You will not suspect me of property-holding sympathies and prejudices, on personal grounds. I can assure you that if I had my way I would have property attached to service, to usefulness to the community as a whole. But I would proceed not only without violence but gradually.

My own deep-rooted instinctive desire is to preserve cultural values, humanistic standards, and freedom of thought and speech for every individual in a community.

I do not trust a proletariat to care for these matters, let alone to foster them. It would take long to explain why I have such a dread of the proletariat, and more still of its "intelligentsia." I fear it, and I would oppose in every way the prevailing tendency to regard the proletarian and his interests as the chief concern of the state.

I know what the proletariat is like in America, where the factory hands are being exploited by hundreds of Mussolinis and Hitlers. These "Führer," these "Duci," are just as arbitrary, just as despotic, and just as ambitious as over here. In America, happily, there is among the *burjui* a strong enough civic spirit to defeat them, chiefly by yielding to what is feasible in their demands. In England, likewise, demagogy is checkmated by the readiness of the possessive classes to anticipate exasperation of the working classes by giving in to their more reasonable demands before it is too late.

Luckily, Italy as yet has a percentually small, an almost insignificant proletariat, and by proletariat I mean workers engaged in heavy industries and to a limited extent the manual workers, excluding the peasantry. I would not encourage it to believe in its own supposititious rights and in its dominating importance. I am inclined to believe that it is your and my only serious long-

range enemy. Remember: Fascism, Nazism, etc., etc., are ultimately based on plebiscitism, and the plebiscite is invariably an
appeal to the proletarian spirit.

If there is a serious difference between me and Italian leftists
it is over that. Other differences could be easily reconciled. I fear
the fanatical sympathy of the Italian intelligentsia for a proletariat which threatens in our day to play the part of the third- and
fourth-century soldieries. I dread abstractions of every kind when
applied to politics, I dread fanaticism over formulas and systems.
I dread Soterism, messianism, the *Führerprinzip*, the expectation
of getting good government quickly.

Life and political thinking have taught me, as they have others,
that government is the art of the momentarily feasible, of aiming
at the least bad attainable, and not of the rationally most desirable.

I must end with a word about my own possible usefulness as
interpreter between Italians and Anglo-Saxons.

To begin with, there is my age. This not only incapacitates me
for hard and continuous work but exposes me to the charge—
perhaps well founded—of being an old fogy, unable to understand the problem of the hour.

Then I fear that of the Anglo-Saxons coming here, the very
few who know of me at all as a political thinker consider me an
ideologist. The reasons for this they will have forgotten. For
twenty years I have been telling them that Mussolini meant disaster, meant war, and that his ideas were incompatible with our
world order. They have been compelled at last to fight an ideo-
logical war but retain the vague memory that I was inopportune
and therefore not practical in politics.

I should have the further disadvantage of being the "man on
the spot." It is a cardinal principle of Anglo-Saxon policy to put
no trust in the "man on the spot." In foreign, particularly in Latin,
Slav, and Moslem lands, the "man on the spot" tells of things that
in England and America could not happen. So the Anglo-Saxons
believe that they cannot happen anywhere and the "man on the
spot" exaggerates, and talks nonsense.

Despite everything, I shall be happy to do whatever I can to help you to heal Italy of her sickness and to get her into a convalescent condition.

February 19th

ITALIAN FRIENDS are more and more disgruntled and indignant with the Anglo-Saxons for bombing their cities and being so slow in coming to free them from German occupation and its foul specter-Fascist parasite. They naïvely demand to be treated as the prodigal son for whom was killed the fatted calf, in the shape of all the good things they have been deprived of and to receive them unrationed and almost gratis.

They demand that much to reward them for being sick of the war, and not wanting to continue the fight. The Anglo-Saxons should therefore treat them not only as allies but as privileged ones, because they are Italians—*quia nominor Leo.*

They cannot realize that ever since war-weariness lay hold of them, the chief problem has been how to get rid of their former allies, the Nazis.

The Germans will not go. They seem inclined to make serious sacrifices in order to remain in their positions. The Italians are doing nothing to evict them. They leave it to us.

But the Anglo-Saxons must refrain from using the one arm in which they have developed crushing superiority. They must not bomb towns which the Nazis are using as strongholds.

Propaganda is converting more and more Italians to the conviction that it is cowardly, inhuman, wicked to use aircraft. The Germans should be met with the bayonet and not with aerial armaments.

Absurd stories are being unofficially whispered, told, and printed of the terrible and willful havoc made by English and American bombs. It seems to be turning Italians who were ready to receive us with flowers and hymns into soreheads who conclude that there is nothing to choose between Nazis and Anglo-Saxons.

Perhaps it is as well. An occupation can never be satisfactory, and Italians were expecting a paradise to follow an Anglo-Saxon one. After a lowered opinion of the snail-pace victors, there is a chance that they will be agreeably disappointed.

February 20th

MUSSOLINI issued a decree yesterday telling recruits who do not answer the call to the colors that if they do not do their duty in the next few days they will be shot wherever found, preferably in their own homes. What better confession that the youth of the country either wishes to ignore this regime or simply is war-weary and wants the end of soldiering, and that they take to the woods rather than to the recruiting office. Yet the Nazi press had been rejoicing at the alacrity of the numerous forces that were running to the defense of the Duce!

The same press from day to day fills its columns with quotations from *Fortune, Time,* and other periodicals in America, from the *Daily Herald,* the *Daily Worker* in England, and similar publications complaining of abuses and expressing dissatisfaction with their several governments. Yesterday I read of a member of Parliament who got up to accuse Churchill of conniving at various malpractices. Would anyone in Naziland have dared to make a similar charge against Hitler, and would any German publication be allowed to make the complaints and criticism that fill columns of the Anglo-American press?

February 21st

YESTERDAY there died, as he was stepping out of his cottage to take the noontide sun, an old peasant of over eighty-six, the head of the family that has been working the neighboring farm for three hundred years and more. Ever since I have been here I have found him on my walk along the terraces cushioned with grasses and wild flowers that lead to his dwelling. He was as merry and talkative as Wordsworth's Simon the old huntsman. He enjoyed being alive, and was always smoking his overpowering

Virginia stump with keen relish. Sundays he came out in holiday attire and went to mass on foot. There was a man who said "yes" to life. He had nothing to complain of. He accepted old age as inevitable, and suffered only from its bodily inconveniences. He was well treated by sons, daughters, and in-laws. They showed no sign of wanting to get rid of him.

How different from the end of peasants, too old to work, as described by most French writers since Balzac! How much less cruel than what was the custom fifty years ago, and may still be in Calabria! There the old couple, as soon as they could work no more, left the farm and took to the road. When I protested, such a couple replied that it was quite right, that their fathers and forefathers had done so.

My hostess tells me that this dear old man did not hesitate to fill a big basket with plums of no very pleasant kind, putting on top a layer of better looks and taste to take to market. When he was dividing walnuts into the share going to her, and the one he was going to keep, he weighed each one and passed to her the ones with no kernel.

The Florentine peasant is a civilized, in a sense cultivated, individual. He is human and kindly, but he knows his rights and his perquisites. He is aware that his landlord does not approve, and if nothing is said he will behave charmingly. Woe to him who starts opposing what the *contadino* regards as his rights. He gets nothing out of him, and for himself a sore head.

Every profession has it perquisites and privileges at the public expense; only what is considered right in one's own day and one's profession, group, or class changes from time to time. Thus sinecures for aristocracy and gentry were a matter of course: their morality was questioned by nobody. The paymaster of the British forces in the eighteenth century used the big sums entrusted to him as his own property for the time being, to employ to his own advantage. In our own days, bankers take as perquisite a day's interest on sums deposited with them.

It is beautiful to watch the peasant at his work. When digging up the tough clay with his spade, his movements express directed energy that no work of art has surpassed. The chocolate-colored furrows after hoeing look as if they had been treated by a jeweler rather than an agricultural laborer. As a matter of fact, Tuscany scarcely knows agriculture—horticulture only, if not something still more delicate.

The old man who died yesterday wanted to live to see his grandson, who was either prisoner of the Allies or collaborating with them in the south of Italy. The mother of this boy dreams of him all night long. To her the war is a question of how soon she will be able to see him again. At the same time she and the whole family are as pro-Ally as I am, have their radio, and listen to it with excited interest.

It is, by the way, not easy to discover Italian peasants, or even artisans, who do not believe in the victory of the Allies. Without the propaganda of the specter Fascists, they would not even resent the bombardments.

I mentioned the mother of the boy who is with the English. It is a pleasure, like listening to music, to see with what zest and keenness she digs and hoes and picks olives or does washing. One icy day I asked her how she could stand dipping her hands and arms up to the elbow into the cold water. She would not hear of sympathy; on the contrary, she was enjoying it. The other members of the family are scarcely inferior in spirit. They employ a young woman as help, who is supposed to be wild and half-witted; but her head, her eyes, her entire face, are as beautiful as Sebastiano del Piombo's women in his early Giorgionesque phase, as in San Giovanni Crisostomo in Venice, or the Fornarina of the Uffizi.

When I think of Italy's future it is on the peasantry that I fall back, on the peasantry, the independent artisans, and small shopkeepers. They still are the majority, and if only the intelligentsia does not succeed in addling their pates Italy may be the first country to recover after this man-quake. I envy Italy this peasant, artisan, and small tradesman population. We have too little of it in America, and of peasantry nothing of our own. I mean to say that the descendants of the Fathers and pioneers, just because they had the blood of pioneers in their veins, could never become peasants. For by peasants, as I probably have said earlier in these notes, I mean a person so attached atavistically to his bit of soil that he would rather suffer and endure than quit.

Our farmer never hesitated to leave his acres on the chance of bettering himself by selling or even deserting his ancestral holdings and going west, then selling that farm so as to acquire with the proceeds a much larger estate still farther west. The result is that we not only have no peasantry but no places to which, generations after generations, persons can turn to, as to home. Possibly the Polish and Lithuanians who have taken up our deserted New England farms may remain a peasantry. If they do, it may be because they do not get assimilated, do not become Americanized, and remain priest-ridden Slavs.

Stalin, if we may trust what we hear, is determined to get rid of the peasant in Russia, and of turning him into a proletarian. I wish I could live long enough to see how this experiment will turn out. Can it succeed, and with advantage to the peasant and his country?

February 23d

SOFT SNOW in huge flakes, like bunches of grapes, has been falling for hours. I have just returned from our usual morning round. I could have wished the snow harder, for I still enjoy crunching it underfoot, as I enjoy crunching crusts with my teeth.

The entire landscape was translated into black and white like a Chinese painting—even though close at hand, a touch of gold hung to the drooping mimosas as in the Far Eastern pictures a touch of russet to the trees. The distances were mysteriously lit up with shy sunlight behind misty vapors circling in the sky. What a miracle, what a transfiguration! Yet none of our friends seem to appreciate it. For most of them, nature and life are not a miracle; only a fancied departure from nature and life seems miraculous.

February 24th

I HEAR from various quarters that my book on *Italian Painters,* written for the most part nearly fifty years ago, is still being read in Italy and in France but no longer in America and England. This smallish volume may count as the nearest approach made by me to giving a fillip to thought on art matters.

Which leads me to ask what use I have been since I was forty. By that time I had written the book just mentioned and I had completed and published the systematic work on the *Drawings of the Florentine Painters.* I had already made many attributions. It is true that in later years I perfected and refined the method in a way that enabled me to reconstruct the careers of Filippo Lippi, of Botticelli, of Antonello da Messina, of the young as well as of the old Giovanni Bellini, and others. Since forty I have been the chief instrument for directing a stream of Italian pictures to America. I have collected a library which may turn out of some utility to students of art and civilization who come after me. As a contributor to thought I doubt whether my death soon after fifty would have made the slightest difference.

When only three and twenty myself, I happened to hear the then well-known journalist, amateur artist, and husband of a peculiarly Rossettian Greek wife, the Schenectady American W. J. Stillman, say that he did not care a pin for what was written by men under forty.

At that time forty seemed an immeasurably remote age after which one would be relegated to vegetative obscurity; and Stillman, who then was absorbed in Italian hand-to-mouth politics, and was defender in chief of Crispi both in England and America, may have had in his mind only what is written on day-to-day affairs. I recall how bitterly I resented his declaration. What was to do in the endless years to pass before I too was forty and could say my say?

Stillman was as wrong as only a journalist can be. It is historically demonstrable that, with rare exceptions, genius and even talent appear long before forty, and achieve their utmost before the end of the fourth decade. There are glorious exceptions, of course. Rembrandt certainly and Frans Hals as well. Titian and Tintoretto perhaps likewise. Possibly also both Bellinis. In the field of literature it would have been a great loss if Shakespeare and Goethe, Plato and Sophocles, Cervantes and Tolstoi had died at forty. And what of Kant and Hegel?

I remember having been told years ago by one of the few great mathematicians of our day that in his pursuit genius revealed itself around the twenties, when it made its most valuable contributions to the advance of their art. In lyric poetry Coleridge, Wordsworth, Byron, Keats, and Shelley were dead before thirty or had given their most specifically best at that age. In music there are Mozart and Schubert, in Italian painting we have Giorgione and Raphael, none of whom lived to be forty.

In the case of Raphael I doubt whether we need regret his early demise. As for Michelangelo, who knows what we might have been spared had he disappeared on the completion of the Sistine Chapel ceiling. True, we should be without the fascinating nightmares of the Medici Tombs; but how many distorted, heaving, bulging monstrosities we should have been spared, not so much of his own as of his followers, whether architects, sculptors, or painters down to our own day almost!

February 25th

IT IS WHISPERED about that the Allies are preparing two landings in full force, for the end of this month. As this month has only four days before it, I have my doubts about the date. So much for the time; and as for the place, one is to be on the shores of the gulf of Lyons and the other in the neighborhood of Trieste.

An Allied force in Istria would attract partisans from Slovenia, Croatia, as well as the Serbian Banat, and could annex Tito's army. It could, if properly prepared, and in sufficient strength and intelligently conducted, begin a march towards Vienna: with results as effective as Sherman's ride from Atlanta to the sea.

✿ ✿ ✿

Hitherto Himmler has stood for all that was most unscrupulous, inhuman, and thorough in ridding the Nazi cosmos of dissidents, of Jews, of Poles, of unsubmissive Dutch, Belgians, Norwegians, etc., etc. His name was a name of dread, of horror, of terror, and widely advertised as such by Nazi propaganda.

All of a sudden this same propaganda has taken to speaking of him as a friendly, affectionate, even tender and most paternal person who thinks of nothing but inviting all who suffer, old and young, and little ones in particular, to come to him for comfort and security.

It reminds me of the broadside portrait of Mussolini appearing years ago in a Sunday issue of the *Daily Mail*, or was it the Sunday *Times*? There, instead of the ferocious prizefighter that he tried to look like, he was represented as if he were a young grandfather leading by hand his tender flock to church on a sweet Sunday morning.

What can be the object of this transfiguration? Has he been marked out to succeed Hitler in case the first Führer should disappear? Are the Nazis preparing to turn on humanitarian tunes in their propaganda orchestra, now that force is no longer with them?

It seems that the Nazi authorities have ordered the present Duchess of Aosta to quit Florence and to go where she wished, provided it was safe from the Allied occupation. She protested that she did not want to leave. They have allowed her to remain for the present, warning her, however, that at the next summons she might not have more than an hour to get ready in.

Why? The only explanation that occurs to one—the explanation offered by the person who reported this piece of news—is that the Nazis want to keep firm hold on the baby boy the Duchess had some months ago. Consequently, in case of victory they would not countenance the resurrected regime of Mussolini and his republic, but restore the monarchy in the person of this infant of the Aosta branch. They could then rule Italy through men of straw who acted as regents. In that case the dowager Duchess of Aosta—author, I believe, of many of our woes—would at last be able to sing *Nunc dimittis*. She would have seen the ambitions of a lifetime, the plotting of many decades, brought safe to port and crowned with success.

* * *

A cyclist fired as he passed at a German soldier and disappeared. The Kommandantur at once ordered that in the ward where this happened cycling should be forbidden on pain of being shot at.

The German paper tells of *Selbst-Schutz* organization for self-defense formed by Germans in North Schleswig, the local police being unable or unwilling to protect them. I ask against whom? Of course, against the native Danes.

* * *

Governments last as long as the undertaxed can defend them against the overtaxed.

* * *

Continental folk easily fall into saying that the various English tribes do not know how to carry on war. This opinion is confirmed among Italians by the way the Allies have been campaigning here the last eight or nine months. It may be true that they, the Anglo-Saxons, do not know how to make war, but how is it that they win them? Is it because, as was said by Berthelot or Clemenceau during the last war, that war had got to be too complicated an affair to be successfully conducted by soldiers? Do the Anglo-Saxons win wars because they are not soldiers?

February 27th

THE GERMAN PRESS of the last few days is devoted to Monte Cassino and its destruction by those barbarians, those air gangsters, those terrorists, the Anglo-Saxon aviators. They publish declarations signed by the Abbot and confirmed by Kesselring that not a single Nazi soldier was to be found within the monastic buildings. But, even if there was not a single German trooper within the walls of the enclosure, there must have been any number of pillboxes and bunkers just outside. Nazi tactics during Allied air attacks are well known. Ex-Premier Vittorio Emanuele Orlando has seen again and again their armored cars rushing during air raids toward St. Peter's in Rome. Here in Florence a canon of the cathedral, who lives across the way from it, tells me that they hug its walls when the alarm sounds.

The Nazi newspapers are filled with press quotations from all over the world, not only of their friends but neutrals like Spaniards, Portuguese, and Swiss, including—to my no small amazement—the *Zürcher Zeitung*.

I wonder how many of the writers, let alone readers, of such stuff had ever heard of Monte Cassino; and of those who had heard of it what percentage had any notion of what the place was worth artistically.

From the artistic point of view, excepting the library and perhaps some precious utensils, brought to Rome months ago, there was nothing in the mother house of the Benedictine order that recalled its founder and its sovereign abbots of the Middle Ages. The buildings and decorations were no earlier than of the seventeenth century and in no way remarkable for that period. There are in Catholic countries hundreds of structures far more valuable. What connoisseur would dream of placing it beside the Escorial or Sankt Florian or Melk!

The outcry is cynical propaganda. It is based on the queer axiom that a Mussolini is free to demolish and disfigure whatever he pleases in a city like Rome, to make hideous gashes, to bottle up spaces, to furbish up and even to forge ruins, and to receive nothing but prayer and praise except from a few soreheads; while the accidental destruction of this or that bit of ancient building by Allied bombardment is a crime against civilization, against humanity.

Mussolini's ideal was Haussmann's Paris. In pursuit of it he cleared away the Borgo and made St. Peter's the end of a vista

like the one afforded by the tiresome avenue leading up to the
Paris Opera House. Had his reign lasted another ten years, little
of Sistine, of Baroque, of Rococo Rome—the human Rome—
would have been left standing, nor much of medieval. He might
have thought twice of making away with the ruins of the Caesars,
but they also would have gone ultimately and nobody daring to
pipe a protest.

There is more reason to deplore destructions at Cologne, and
elsewhere in the Rhineland, of Romanesque churches. Yet there,
too, even the most cultured people may be unaware that those
structures have been as much repaired as the stocking so darned
and redarned that nothing remained of the original fiber, in this
case the original masonry. As a matter of fact, most of them, all
of them, can be rebuilt to look no less old than before present disasters.

Far be it from me to deny that architecture owes much of its
beauty to the caress of time, to what we call patina, which in
America a few decades ago we appreciated so much that we had
houses built "weather-beaten." I deplore damaging, let alone destroying, old buildings. Yet let me ask how much of Cologne Cathedral was old enough to have acquired the weathering, the
patina. As a matter of fact, the nave and façade are forgeries of
the last century.

It would take a book to say all one might say about the preservation of ancient monuments, and the cultured cant and hypocrisy regarding them. I cannot undertake to do it here. I will say
a word about the attitude of modern aediles toward the problem.

They act on the notion that a building remains unharmed, is
brought back to its pristine state, if it is freed from other structures choking it or encrusting it—in short, if it is scraped down
and furbished up. Then they isolate it so that you can examine it
inch by inch, as does the archaeologist. When you protest, they
grow indignant with your captiousness. You cannot make them
understand that there is no such thing as an isolated building
abstractly itself, like a marble or ivory reduction of the Tower of
Pisa or of the Taj Mahal standing on a table, that a building is a

part of a complex of masses and profiles, deprived of which it changes almost as a head or a hand cut off from its body. The same aediles will insist that only what interests archaeologists— for the archaeological reasoning they can follow—is of any value, and that if they demolish a whole square and preserve everything that serves the momentary pursuits of the scholar they have cared for every interest of culture. I well remember after the demolition in Florence of the Mercato Vecchio, perhaps the most beautiful and characteristic product of popular Florentine art—a complex of bulk and shape in freestone, in marble, in bronze, in glazed terra cotta the like of which Europe had never seen—when some- one had the courage to protest, Count Torrigiani, the syndic, indignantly replied that every bit of sculpture and painting of artistic value had been scrupulously saved and deposited in a museum.

What I have in mind will be made more intelligible to others if I cite an example near to all of us Americans. A century and some decades ago the Episcopalian community of New York built a house of worship which we know as Trinity Church. It stood monarch of all it surveyed, pointing heavenward with no struc- ture close at hand or big enough to take away from its impor- tance. Go now to look at it. You will have to search. In the hud- dled midst of huge skyscrapers, it remains intact but lost, like an obelisk at the bottom of a well waiting to be pulled up and placed under the open sky.

Ninety-nine per cent of the good people whose propaganda-fed horror of air destruction is vociferous would not as much as think of saying a word against the jobbed demolitions of old towns so as, in the words of the proud inscription that runs over the arch of the life-diminishing *piazza* which replaces the Florentine Mer- cato Vecchio, "to bring it back from old mustiness to the life of our day"—*dall'antico squallore alla vita moderna.*

Not only would they not raise their voice to oppose such van- dalism but would probably be outraged if others did. Only a little while ago the principal Tuscan daily, the *Nazione*, among various charges against Anglo-Saxons, reminded its readers that those barbarians had had the brutal impudence to interfere and prevent the good Florentines from pulling down their Ponte Vecchio, old, squalid, moldy, and replacing it with an up-to-date bit of engineering. Worse still, owing to the same barbarian intervention the higgledy-piggledy, shapeless, sordid stretch across the Arno between the last-named bridge and the Ponte S. Trinita had to remain a plague to Florentine eyes, instead of giving place to a cozy public garden with consumptive palms, green benches, lanterns of the same color, and conveniences named after one of the twelve Caesars.

February 28th

MONTE CASSINO will be rebuilt and with no regard to expense; for "money is no object" when Catholic piety is appealed to.

Instead of erecting an exact copy of the mediocre edifices that we have known, why not do something more interesting? I remember how grateful I felt to discover on Mount Tabor in Palestine that they had put there a close copy of the fifth-century Church of Turmanin which had been taken to pieces by progressive natives for its masonry to serve as material for roads and bridges. (Did I not with my own eyes see an Arab as elegant as a Van Dyck carting away stone, brick, and mortar from Mschatta, a once-noble palace in the land of Moab?) I would propose nothing less than replacing the Monte Cassino of our day with the copy of old St. Peter's. We know enough of that venerable and noble structure, the church, its forecourts, its terraces, its approaches, the interior with its colonnades and transepts and mosaics, to be able to reconstruct it.

It would look new at first. There is a difference between architecture and scenic edifices. The first constructs for the future as well as the present; the second, for the brief present only, a present as brief as the duration of exhibition buildings.

Stop to recall what Louis XIV would have seen of Versailles!—the palace and terraces raw with freshness and hard with newness; the trees like matchsticks and looking for all the world like one of our young cemeteries.

After what has been said it will surprise no one, although it may shock many, who will stone me for a Philistine, if I venture to say that most edifices of the past could be rebuilt with little if any loss of their ultimate artistic effect as shape and mass. The more so as most temples, churches, and palaces have been measured inch by inch, centimeter by centimeter, have had plans and elevations and cross sections most accurately recorded, not to speak of the water-color and photographic reproductions of the chiaroscuro effects.

Most Romanesque and Renaissance structures could be rebuilt and after two or three generations look to all but prying archaeologists as if they were the original edifices.

The case is different with later Romanesque, with ripe Gothic, with Rococo, where much delicate carving and real sculpture occurs. These cannot be replaced; for the hand of our stonecutter has been so mechanized that it cannot deviate from the geometrically correct to breathe life into stone animals and plants and make them look as if they had flesh and sap and circulating blood.

To come back to our starting point, nothing of late Romanesque as at Aulnay or on the façade of Chartres, or of ripe Gothic like Rheims or Rococo as found so often in France and in South German lands, was to be seen at Monte Cassino or, for that matter, in the porch and neighboring part of San Lorenzo in Rome.

Now that, so carefree, I have let myself go in a rollicking mood, I want to confess to one of my many cherished dreams.

It regards San Marco in Venice.

Under irresistible Gothic influence, the soft, shadowy effect of what certainly was the Byzantine interior was dissipated by the huge rose windows to the west and to the south. I would have these gashes that flood the basilica with glaring light bricked up, leaving only smallish, narrow, arched openings.

Inside as well as in the narthex and north corridor, I would remove all mosaics later than the end of the fourteenth century.

Byzantine mosaic confined itself to accentuating ribs and intervals of structure with architecturally appropriate figures. It left narrative compositions to the darker and otherwise less conspicuous parts of walls or chapels. Even the arrangement severely followed the verticals of the structure.

Nothing can be less suitable to the wall spaces of San Marco than narrative compositions like those of a Campagnola or a Titian, and least of all the sprawling designs of a Tintoretto. As decoration they are scarcely better than modern newspaper illustrations stuck onto walls.

I would remove them and replace them with an undifferentiated gold ground, than which nothing is more impressive and more transfiguring.

As for the outside of S. Marco, the later ribbons and laces do not disturb me, but the hideously inappropriate recent mosaic over the central door and the only less evil older ones in the lunettes above I would not tolerate. Why, seeing that happily Gentile Bellini in the masterpiece representing the Corpus Domini procession that has San Marco for background has reproduced the original mosaics, still intact toward 1500, in accurate detail— why would it not be possible to copy them? As for the central lunette, I would cover it with various marbles that took the color and tone of the façade as a whole.

March 1st

RUMORS FROM ROME say that the Nazis mean to defend it with might and main, that the Pope expects to be carried off to Germany, and that notice has been served to the refugees in the Vatican that their safety can no longer be guaranteed, for the Germans would not respect the right of asylum. I can believe none of this and yet it is possible. The Nazi propaganda machine can undertake to put even the kidnaping of a Pope in a light that will sanctify their conduct in the eyes of their hypnotized sympathizers, particularly of those fervently devoted Papalists, the Spanish pro-Germans.

March 2d

RECKLESS BELIEVERS in equality tell us that seeming "inferiority" is a matter of chance, of circumstance, of opportunity, etc., etc., and not of essential physiological formation. The so-called "inferiors" will catch up with us if with might and main we help them, and assuming—a large assumption—that they will let themselves be helped.

What of us in the meantime? Shall we stand still, waiting for the others to catch up? Surely not. We go forward or disappear, or as good as disappear. Between those who keep going forward and those who are catching up, there still remains an interval. I will not take as examples the African blacks; for they have but lately begun to benefit from the blessing of our civilization. Let us rather take the North Germans, free from any taint of "Negroid" Mediterranean blood. For well over a thousand years they have been submitted to strong Mediterranean influence in the shape of Christianity and humanism. Have they caught up yet?

March 4th

I CANNOT CONSULT the big Oxford dictionary to ascertain when the word "international" was first used. I recall hearing it as an epithet for activities of a praiseworthy nature, "international society" for this, "international organization" for that, all meant to bring people together in friendship and to promote humanitarian ideals.

Suddenly, under the pressure of anti-Dreyfus propaganda, it began in France to be a term of abuse and as such spread not only to Latin countries but to a certain extent to Germany, Scandinavia, and even England and America. To be internationally minded was to be a *déraciné*, a *sans-patrie* with no roots anywhere, without a country, a danger to the community, a Jew, a Nihilist, etc., etc.

At the same moment, by the way, for the first time in human

history the word "intellectual," hitherto a term of praise, became
one of reproach, of contempt even, as leading to "international-
mindedness." A Montesquieu in the middle of the eighteenth
century could say that God had made him a human being and
politics alone had made him a Frenchman. A Goldsmith at the
same time could write *The Citizen of the World*. A Goethe remained international-minded to the end and after Jena regarded
without dread the possibility that the Germans might be scattered like the Jews among the nations.

As a matter of fact, internationalism characterizes the horizontal as distinct from the vertical groupings of society.

The vertical groupings are of the clan, the tribe, the nation.
Just now the last are the only ones to count, and standing alone,
perhaps as mere survivors, they risk being overwhelmed by the
horizontal tendencies of society.

The horizontal tendencies manifest themselves with increasing
force in every activity and every association except the political
ones.

Royalty constitutes an "international" ready to take employment with any country that still believes in its usefulness. High
society, less and less designated nowadays as "good society,"
recognizes its own across frontiers, linguistic barriers, and even
color in the case of the yellow peoples. Officers of army and navy
are as ready to fraternize, act for common interests, and enjoy
common gossip as to be up and at each other's throats the moment the vertical powers unleash them. Great financial and industrial interests are notoriously hostile to barriers, lose no chance
and neglect no means to leap over them. One need scarcely add
that but for personal envies and jealousies, science, learning, art,
literature, music, theater, and, most obviously, the radio and the
cinema ignore politics, that is to say vertical divisions, except
when they are engaged or prostituted in their service. The most
rabid nationalisms sympathize if they do not join hands with like-
minded groups in countries hostile to their own, and in a latent
state of war with it. And I have nearly forgotten to name the most

horizontal of entities, the most international of institutions, the all-pervasive Roman Catholic Church.

But fanaticism, like misery, makes strange bedfellows; and nationalism, when it found voice with a theology, mythology, and ethics all armed in the France of fifty years ago, tried hard and for a time succeeded in using the French religious orders and clergy to fight internationalism in one of its least aggressive phases, in the shape of those scapegoats for economic sins called Jews. Of this later.

Clearly what those who succeeded in turning the epithets "international" and "intellectual" from terms of praise to expletives of vituperation had in mind was a blind horror of these qualities when found in individuals who put them at the service not of the heraldic, the possessive, the institutional and governing classes, but of the unsatisfied who were clamoring for a seat at the banquet of life, or in those terrible individuals who, in ripe years, had not got over asking "why" and saying "I want to know." You could defend tooth and nail the German army, the British House of Lords, and the French Academy as Paul Bourget used to do with no small intellectual skill; you could sing the praises of the Jesuits, Redemptionists, and similar associations; you could be as clever defenders of "international law and order" as Joseph de Maistre and in our own day Brunetière, Jules Lemaître, and other powers, thrones, potentates, and prophets of the French Academy and French press, and nobody would reproach you with being an "intellectual" or an "internationalist." If, however, you said a word in favor of those anti-Jesuits, the Latin freemasons, or in defense of socialism, of the "lower orders" in general, of oppressed and massacred Armenians, then you were an "intellectual," an "internationalist," to be boycotted, to "have your life made difficult"—to use the hallowed phrase of Mussolini, for years the idol, the "defender of the Faith" of the upper social ranks everywhere.

It is a question whether anti-Semitism was at the bottom of the anti-Dreyfus movement in France or only incidental to it. But it opened the sluices to a pent-up hatred of the Jews that took one by surprise. It was not, as in other countries, confined to humble shopkeepers and an occasional swell or paradox-monger, but raged among the gentry high and low, and their sons in the army; was voiced by most Academicians and aspirants to the Academy; was served by gifted caricaturists and of course music-hall singers. In fact, the Dreyfus affair practically turned into a Jewish affair.

As I am not writing reminiscences, I shall not jot down what I could call to mind of my experiences during that passionate period of French history when Frenchmen were divided into two camps as opposed as any in the past, and only saved from civil war by the conditions of society and government at the moment.

All honor to France that the struggle ended in favor of humanism and that the blind reactionary forces that elsewhere—in Spain, for instance—would have led to their complete victory were almost wholly laid low and silenced. It took the bestial bludgeoning that France received in June, 1940, to bring to the fore, not to power nor to govern, but to execute the mad Nazi will and to realize the measures against liberals, intellectuals, internationalists, all more or less qualified as "Jews," that the anti-Dreyfusards wanted to actuate fifty years ago. But the France where this could happen has fallen lower than ever before in its history as an organized nation, in enjoyment of its present frontiers; even lower than when Jeanne d'Arc came to save it after a similar collapse five hundred years ago.

March 6th

THE ALLIES have stopped sending war materials and other supplies to the Turks. The Allies are at long last tired of Turkish hesitation to join their dance.

Why should the Turks join it? What could the Allies offer them to make it worth their while to partake in a contest which, whoever won, bode them no good? They are still an army with a people to support it, and keenly appreciate another people given over to supporting an army, as do the Germans. They put no trust in navies and airplanes, being duffers in both these ultramodern services. Besides, why should they want to see Germany's power destroyed? They do not share our indignation and our humanitarianism, having acted before and being ready to act again like the Nazis at their worst. For them the diminution of Germany spells increase of power and authority to the contiguous, all-powerful, hereditary enemy Russia.

What have the Allies had to offer the Turks to induce them, despite sympathy for Germany in its militaristic Nazi phases, to join in its destruction? It does not seem that they want more territory, in Iraq, Syria, Palestine, Arabia, or in any part of the far-flung Ottoman Empire of a hundred years ago. They seem to be interested only in holding tight to Asia Minor and its coasts.

From a military point of view that Turks can understand, the only appreciable bait the Allies could have held out to them were the islands that hug their shores and approaches, Lemnos, Lesbos, Chios, Samos, Cos, Rhodes. But these are overwhelmingly Greek in population, and Allied public opinion would not tolerate their being allocated to them.

So this Turk, so sympathetic to the English as a "Gentleman" has played off the Anglo-Saxons against the Germans, the latter against the former, and put the war to profit. If only Italy had had "realistic politicians" to rule it, neutral Italy too would have made a good thing out of this shindy, and still better, Italy would have been the center for everything required by civilized life, would have been courted by everybody, would have won credit and authority as a real great power and not the sham one she has been.

❈   ❈   ❈

The Nazi press tells of six thousand Japanese, four thousand military and two thousand civilians, in an island of the Pacific having committed suicide rather than surrender to Americans. I cannot share in the admiration of such incandescent patriotism.

It is running amok against one's self in good Malay fashion. For one must not forget that the backbone of Japan is Malay, and that Malay savagery and ferocity still smolders there under a thin coating of Chinese culture and a thinner coating of Western civilization.

"Then you believe in the persistence through the ages of racial characteristics?" someone will ask. Yes, I do when the race has occupied the same territory for many centuries, submitted other ethnic elements to its unquestioned will, and for a thousand years remained in almost airtight seclusion. That is the case with the Japanese but, for instance, not with the Jews, scattered over the face of the earth, suffering, despite every possible defense, all kinds of physical infiltrations as well as moral and intellectual influences and taking part in the life of other communities, as the Japanese until recently did not.

This collective suicide, so highly praised by German propaganda, must rouse the envy of the Nazi leaders. They too would liked to reduce religion to patriotism and to a faith that, if it could not move mountains, could inspire self-immolation. For an operative religion is a faith for which one is as ready to die as to live.

Our civilization must dread such religions, such ages of faith, particularly as the totalitarian nations do not hide but glory in proclaiming, almost as the Japanese do, that the spirit of the nation is its God and that they mean to treat other peoples as manure, as drudges, as raw material for exploitation.

March 7th

MUCH SOCIETY TALK, whether of the drawing room, the table, the club, or the café, satisfies a physical need that we share with our chattering anthropoid forerunners in remote ages. Heard at a distance, it is confused, unintelligible, and encourages thoughtful children to expect that if only they could come close enough to a cackle of geese they would understand it, as they do human beings when near enough.

Several dialogues going on in my presence, each regardless of the other, either deafen me with their clamor or annoy me because I overhear snatches of talk sufficiently interesting to prevent my giving entire attention to my interlocutor. I enjoy conversation as much as ever, provided it is only between two persons, the others listening until their turn comes. Let me add that I am as ready to listen as to speak. I do not, as I did no doubt in the past, use the other person's talk as a springboard for my own.

The younger one is, the more the interlocutor is a mere incentive. So eager are young and youngish people to find utterance and be heard that they scarcely care what they say, so long as it satisfies two demands of their nature, namely, talking and self-assertion. From the moment they have blurted out something, they will argue till they have the last word regardless of sense, as when Hogg and Shelley quarreled over Goethe, tooth and nail, and ended by confessing that neither of them had read a word of him.

So much of the talk I hear, or overhear, silences me. At my age I have no physical exuberance forcing me to jump up and take part in a conversation which, I know, is not intended either to inform or to enlighten, but merely to enable one to let off steam, to salivate intoxicatingly, and to enjoy one's own wit and its effect on others.

So I sit silent and hear all sorts of things said, and statements made that I know are inexact, or false, or absurd, and I feel no itch to play the sage and to try to put matters straight.

Young and youngish people seldom want that. They want to exercise their own functions, their own powers, and to use us elders as supply stores for facts, anecdotes, ideas even. And not infrequently, these same facts and ideas, after a few days, will be served up to us as discoveries we failed to make.

With writing it is not quite the same. When young, you were so charged to the muzzle with things you wanted to say that say them you must. Later you discover that not only your happy thoughts—your Einfälle—but even your more serious trains of meditation and reflection have been anticipated again and again, numberless times. If you had known this when about to explode into print with your own ideas, naïvely believing that they were as new and fresh as the dawn of creation, your animal spirits might have got too damped, and kept you from utterance. Within a year of eighty, my present age, one seldom is carried away by the conceit that one has a communication to make or a message to give not heard of before. In a sense this is a mistake. True, the fundamental ideas are few, long recognized, and rarely subject to serious mutation. Yet the way a person with the experience, reading, and the thought of a lifetime presents an idea may make it more palatable, more assimilable to younger contemporaries than previous, and perhaps more penetrating, versions of the same idea.

In writing there is thus no excuse for stopping because of age. In talk the physical facts are so much against us that one sympathizes with Walt Whitman, who, when sitting out on the piazza and invited to join the chat of young people indoors, said: "No, dearie, I love to hear your laughter, but I do not care for your talk."

So much for me and others nearly as aged. Something similar happens to human societies as wholes. Our society of today has taken in, and assimilated, what it could grasp and understand of a given train of thought: for instance, what the propagators and opponents of nineteenth-century enlightenment and liberalism had to say. It transpires that, like young people, the crowd of to-day has snatched only at the crude, brutal, paradoxical ideas of the last century, reduced to catchwords that the Mussolinis, the Hitlers, the Rosenbergs enounce with loud-speakers and million-mouthed oratory. Gobineau misunderstood by uneducated persons who have never had a volume of Gobineau in their hands; Darwin misunderstood by individuals who knew him by hearsay only, or through premasticated popular articles; Nietzsche misunderstood and reduced to the one word "Superman," furnish the unanswerable appeal to demagogy. There was no stemming such cataracts of verbosity and its effects on the average lord of a vote, on the plebiscites based on unmitigated universal suffrage. Those who know better are reduced to silence.

Nineteenth-century liberalism appealed to trained, instructed, well-informed reason, and naturally could not thrive in countries where the majority of voters were not politically fit to hear, let alone listen to and understand, such a summons. Hence its eclipse until the day when again the competent few will take government into their hands and educate the many to an appreciation of

what politics means, what obligations it imposes, and how it is to
be conducted.

Nineteenth-century liberalism had not emancipated itself
enough from eighteenth-century rationalism and illuminism. It
failed to take account of original sin, that is to say the animal, the
wild beast still caged in man and pawing his mind. That was the
chief if not the only error of nineteenth-century liberalism. It
might ask with Brünnhilde when against orders she tried to spare
Sieglinde and Siegmund from the wrath of Fricka: "*War es so
schmählich, was ich verbrach*"—"Was it so mean, what I have
done then."

My sympathies go out to Brünnhilde even if it led to her being
put to sleep for twenty years, as indeed liberalism has been for as
many and more years. Its awakening is sure to come, and for so
long as man remains human, and not merely the cleverest of the
anthropoids, he will return to reason after wallowing first voluptu-
ously, and then miserably, in the mire of the irrational, and in the
slaughterhouses of violence.

March 9th

THERE IS SNEERING at Allied bombardments and how seldom
they hit a bridge or any other aid to traffic, and how wicked it is to
go on pelting at Prato and Ponte a Sieve.

Florentines are atavistically ungrateful, and factiousness stupe-
fies them, or they would realize that the Allies want to prevent the
Germans from sending by rail men and armaments to attack them.
They keep on bombarding Prato and Ponte a Sieve, two important
points to north and to south of Florence itself. The two or three
raids on Florence that have done some slight damage, and cost
some few human lives, have not touched the heart of the town
and have been peripheral if not merely accidental.

Insistent reports din my ears with descriptions of what Allied
bombing has done to towns like Pistoia, Arezzo, Pisa, not to speak
of Bologna and Milan. I find it hard to believe them. Take the case
of Pistoia. I have been assured that it is in total ruin, nothing

left of the great square with its cathedral and frowning medieval buildings. Well, there happens to be a servant here whose home is near Pistoia and who has just come from there. She reports that, excepting what was hit near the station, everything is intact, particularly the great square. On the other hand, a person as responsible as a university professor of art history should be, goes about saying that there is nothing left of Arezzo. If that was the case, how is it that the Piero della Francescas in the Church of San Francesco, so near the station, have suffered no damage, nor the scarcely less important sculptures on the façade of the Pieve, nor the cathedral? As for Bologna, one would suppose that its brick chimneys, like leaning towers, would be the first to fall under heavy bombardment, but I gather they lean towards each other as for centuries past. Pisa likewise is said to be in ruins and as good as deserted, yet excepting its flimsily constructed Campo Santo none of its artistically valuable buildings seems to have been greatly affected.

I am eager to know what actually is the case and how far these destructions have gone; whether intentional, as the Fascist-minded insist, or unhappy accidents, as the rest of us think. As soon as I am free and have a car, I mean to visit the towns above mentioned, see what really happened, and draw up a detailed report. My expectation is that much will have been lost but nothing like what the Fascists claim.

March 10th

OVERPRODUCTION. Ever since I can remember Chicago has dreaded a bumper grain crop, sure to bring down the price of wheat and to ruin not only speculators but hard-working farmers as well. In most recent years our Southern states have harvested millions of bales of cotton that they have burned either because they could sell them only at figures so low that they might cheapen prices for years to come or else not at all. Similar calculations led Brazil to burn millions of tons of coffee.

In the last hundred and more years the human crop in Europe-

American acres has been so abundant that for much of it, and of good quality at that, no market could be found. Worst of all, this was not a passive crop like cotton or wheat, coffee or tobacco, but one bursting with energies which, pent up too long, might ferment and spoil it altogether. Nature, Providence, the economic process, or by what other names we invoke the powers whose domestic animals we seem to be, had to find a way of decimating the herds and of getting rid of the millions of individuals it could not market. Ancient methods of keeping down the human crop— namely, pestilence, the obligatory celibacy of the nunnery, monastery, and clergy, the toll of a perpetual petty state of warfare, the insecurity of life—had almost ceased to operate. Other ways had to be found. They were discovered in more and more modernized warfare with its ever-increasing wholesale slaughter.

Tennyson's "Charge of the Light Brigade" celebrates an instance of such slaughter, and the sensitive human poet concludes that "someone had blundered." That someone did not blunder. He was a domestic animal obeying the invisible masters of our species and herd.

The Crimean War was on a small scale. Ours of the Secession, lasting four whole years and ending only after the South had been devastated by generals acting on the principle that you should leave the enemy nothing but eyes to weep with, marked a definite advance in ridding peoples of their unmarketable, that is to say unemployable, members.

Parenthetically one may ask: How one can think of unmarketable members of a society claiming a territory so vast as in 1861 was already the United States of America. In the first place this huge domain was thinly settled west of the Alleghenies. Beyond the Mississippi it was only beginning to be occupied. The whites of the South were not over many. Only in the New England states, marching with southeastern New York, was the population at all dense. Schenectady, not a hundred miles to the north of New York City, little before this date, as we know from W. J. Stillman's autobiography, was a border town with redskins in and out as familiar figures.

If the land was so unexploited how can one think of its being unable to market, that is to say to employ, its entire population? I need not remind readers, most of them much better economists than I am, that a nomad civilization can employ perhaps one person to a square mile, while an intensive society like Belgium can make use of hundreds in the same area.

To return to the evolution of the slaughtering establishment by which superfluous individuals are eliminated, we cannot praise Sadowa or Sédan for effectiveness. They incurred relatively small loss of life. The dire necessity of diminishing population and using up energies increased alarmingly between Sédan and the Marne. Meanwhile the instruments of destruction had not been idle. Far more shattering explosives had been invented; the range of artillery had been greatly increased, as witness the Big Bertha; the air war was trying its doves' wings, and the submarine became a great power. The expenditure of energy was enormous. Individuals were killed by the million. Before the First World War was over the countries engaged began to boast of the quantity of lives each had lost; and I was assured that one government, at least, deliberately exposed its troops to certain slaughter so as to be able to enlarge claims based on the number of its dead.

And yet the last war, the First World War, was child's play compared with the one of which we are now enjoying the well-advanced fifth year. The Nazi press calculates the Russians killed as mounting up to fifteen millions. It is no doubt grossly and deliberately exaggerated. Assuming it to be exact, then surely the German mortality cannot be less than half that quantity. Perhaps five million dead—the war is not over—may not be far out of the actual figures. Compared with these, the dead of the Anglo-Saxons are relatively few, yet still a respectable amount.

This war is the first in which all the energies, positively all, without exception, are being employed by the imperceptible powers that breed us and herd us in expending the greatest output of energy that can be summoned to rid us of the greatest number of individuals. As the war is proceeding, more and ever more are taken over from productive to destructive occupations. As "nature" works by overwhelming excess, the loss of life, the waste of energy accruing before the war and its aftereffects of disease and listless confusion are over, will go beyond, the original purpose of destroying unmarketable individuals and their irrepressible activities. The same something has so constituted mankind that it behaves like the child who enjoys building a sand castle and equally enjoys kicking it over and trampling it down.

The word "Moloch" still gives a shiver to us who were brought up on the Bible and who at the same time have some acquaintance with Carthaginian history. Yet it only means "King." Moloch was the King of the Semitic city to whom, in moments of great distress, babes were sacrificed as burnt offerings. A cruel and wicked practice, surely.

But wait a moment! How many do you suppose were the dear innocents thus devoured by the superstition of a relatively primitive, only partially civilized, and certainly not Christianized community? Let us say ten, twenty, forty, sixty, and, at most in moments of deepest distress and utter hopelessness, a hundred at a time. Bear in mind, however, that much as babes and sucklings may touch a mother's heart, they were creatures in whom society as yet had invested little by way of nurture, culture, and training.

And we? Today? What do we do to propitiate and satisfy and satiate our Moloch, our King of the City, our indwelling spirit of the race, of the people, of the nation; when with our voices, our radios, our loud-speakers, he screams and shouts and yells for aggrandizement, for space in which to act, for monopoly, for the slaughter of heretics within, and the massacres of all gentiles whether still resisting or already submitted?

We sacrifice to him as holocausts our youth, our manhood, sparing old age only because it is not to his liking. We send our young women and mothers into fields and factories. Every able-bodied person, regardless of nature or sex, is put to preparing Moloch's fiery furnaces or to offering victims to his godhead. And how infinitesimal is the number of victims sacrificed by Sidonians, Tyrians, and Carthaginians as compared with the millions upon millions that nowadays Teutons and Anglo-Saxons, Latins and Slavs

offer up to their respective Molochs and Baals, Kings and Lords
of the State!

The Semites of old were more true to themselves, more genuine
than we are today. They made no bones about it and talked no
nonsense. Their Moloch was no God of Love, no well-wisher of
his people. They were his slaves, his chattels, and when they
served him well, obeying his behests, singing his praises night and
day without interruption and feeding him with an abundance of
blood and fat, he did them no harm, nor prevented nature from
producing plentiful crops, both vegetable and animal, including
man-fruit, human children. But woe to his worshipers if they displeased him in word or deed no matter how unintended, how innocent. He addressed them in the only language at his command:
pestilence, plague, and famine. The Sidonian understood, and
paid his dismal tribute to the "furnace blue."

We send off our millions to our Molochs, pretending that we are
noble, heroic, self-sacrificing, ready to die for the good of humanity, for a higher civilization, for the love of our kind. The real reasons are not those. They remain either deliberately hidden from
view by propaganda or buried too deep in human nature to rise
to the awareness of the average patriot.

March 12th

SEVERAL DAYS AGO I wrote that the Allies were bombing Prato
and Ponte a Sieve to the north and south so as to spare Florence.
Yesterday forenoon Florence itself was bombed. The bursting of
the shells was deafening and made everything tremble. It sounded
as if vertically overhead, and directed at one's person.

I was disappointed and distressed, for I had hoped that Florence would be spared. A gentleman who with me was watching
the spectacle said he could not understand why the Allies had allowed the Germans so long to use the town as an accumulating
and distributing center, not so much for railway as for road traffic,
without doing anything to stop it. The Germans, he thought, were
taking advantage of Allied respect for Florence, thereby recogniz-

ing that their enemies aimed only at military objectives and not, as the Axis propaganda pretends, at terrorizing and destroying.

Later in the day the B.B.C. spoke of what had been done over Florence and why, offering reasons identical with those given by my Italian friend.

Meanwhile I remained agitated and nervous with fear of what might have happened to Santa Maria Novella and other noble buildings in the vicinity of the railway station. Happily, no edifice of the least historical importance has been hit. The B.B.C. said the Allies had sent their most expert bombers, noted for their accurate aim. As a matter of fact, they spared no skill in making sure that no building of architectural value was harmed.

Which does not mean that there were no human victims. Nor can I understand why, on leaving, they let fall bombs, as animals their droppings. Such bombs seem to have hit hospitals and houses at San Domenico, and done harm to life and limb.

March 16th

INDIGNATION of spectro-Fascist press with the Pope, for not fulminating against Anglo-Saxon bombardments of Monte Cassino, Castel Gandolfo, and Rome itself. The leader writer of Farinacci's paper, probably the ex-seminarist and anti-Semite Church Father Preziosi, complained that although the Primate of England spoke out, as likewise the Primate of France, the Primate of Italy did not. No one should know better than Preziosi that the Holy Father is not the Primate of Italy any more than Marcus Aurelius was the Emperor of Italy. The Pope, it is true, is Bishop of Rome, but not Archbishop of Italy. If he is Archbishop, it is of the *orbis terrarum*, and an ex-seminarist and ex-priest knows that well. He is in bad faith, as are most intelligent and educated Axis propagandists.

Which reminds me that Virginio Gayda died the day before yesterday, killed, it was reported, by an Allied bomb. I first read him at the beginning of the last war, in touching appeals to liberate Italians from the oppressive, stifling, asphyxiating Austrian rule. Not so many years later, ten years at most, he became the chief defender of Fascist imperialism and ended by being the mouthpiece or rather the pen of Mussolini. A British diplomat assured me that Gayda used to weep on his shoulders, and swear he did not believe a word he had to write, and that he was in indignant despair at having to do so.

Hullabaloo over bomb that fell plumb on the Mantegna chapel of the Eremitani at Padua. Few can regret their destruction more than I do, and I hope that early reports are exaggerated for propaganda purposes. But even if it is a fact I would not weep my eyes out. They were not oversuitable for the space they covered and their coloring was not harmonious. The best in them can be enjoyed in the highly satisfactory photographs of them that now exist, with an abundance of detail.

How many of those who now put on sackcloth and ashes for the destruction of the Eremitani Mantegnas have as much as heard what happened in Rome at the beginning of the last century. There then reigned a saintly Pope, Pius VII. He had the laudable idea of increasing the Vatican museum by adding a gallery known ever since by the name of his family, Chiaramonti. To procure ground for this gallery a Quattrocento chapel had to be demolished, and the interior of this chapel was frescoed over with compositions by Mantegna in his maturest years.

No voice was heard, no word of protest raised against this vandalism. Drawings after the frescoes might have been made, if fragments could not be preserved, as might have been done had anybody cared. Manifestly, nobody gave a thought to flinging to oblivion an important series of paintings by one of the few greatest Italian artists.

Not so many months ago Mussolini pronounced that he preferred museums crowded with flags taken from the enemy to any filled with masterpieces of art.

March 17th

I HAVE A TASTE for reactionary and illiberal literature, provided it is well argued. Not only do I enjoy the writings of a Joseph de

Maistre, a Gentz, a Barbey d'Aurevilly, a Léon Bloy, a Maurice Barrès, but the documents and letters of a Metternich and a Bismarck. Never has anything so backward as the *Memorandum* of Solaro della Margherita reached me before.

For twelve full years he ruled the dominions of His Sardinian Majesty, and the *Memorandum* is his account of it.

He approved the support given by his King, Carlo Alberto, to the comic Duchesse de Berry and, when himself in power, encouraged the Carlist effort in Spain. He wanted to interfere in favor of the *Sonderbund*—a reactionary secession movement—in Switzerland, and praised Nicholas of Russia for helping to suppress the Hungarian rebellion. He would have liked to help Francis Joseph in trying to put an end to revolutionary activities in Lombardy.

He abhorred aspirations toward Italian unity, which he suspected of being less a national than a liberal movement subversive of law and order, of rank and privilege, and, worst of all, of the Church in all its manifestations and activities. He would not have kindergartens because they were the invention, he thought, of a Protestant named Owen. He hated agricultural societies. In the first place what did they know and what could they do that was not known and done already, seeing it was a pursuit that went back to Adam? Then he smelt liberalism behind these idyllic pretexts. He went so far as to disapprove of liberal Churchmen, including, of course, the tendencies of the new Pope, Pius IX. In short, he did his best to restore and perpetuate a seventeenth-century Baroque society and government, with the Church supreme and the gentry prospering under its beams and happy in the radiance of their sovereign.

Internationally, apart from interfering when feasible in favor of reaction, his two ideas were both unfortunately inherited by united Italy, namely, to stickle for her dignity and to add to her territory. He confesses that these have been the main pillars of Piedmontese policy and they have gone on dictating Italian policy to our present day, at what cost and with what results we can now judge. He goes so far as to suggest that his King, Carlo Alberto, who dismissed him for his illiberalism, was as little liberal as him-

self. The King was playing with Italian yearning for liberty because he meant to use it to get the better of Austria. When this
was achieved, he would divide the peninsula between himself and
the Pope, throw off the mask, and return to principles and policies
of the good old times, before the French Revolution of accursed
memory.

Solaro della Margherita's critical sense may be gauged by his
belief that the Talmud teaches ritual murder, of course not obeyed
by civilized Western Jews, but still practiced in the Near East, as
instanced by their murder of a Capuchin missionary in Damascus.

This was the man who was allowed to rule Piedmont before
Italy threw herself into its arms, as, in our day, into the embrace
of Fascism.

Talking of reactionary mentalities, I was told lately that the dispossessed Italian dynasties not only hankered to return but were
by no means without hope of taking up their thrones again. They
live with Astolfo's brains in the moon. With the King of Sardinia,
who outlived the Revolution and the Napoleonic period, they have
no language but the cry of *"ottant' ott' "*—that is to say, 1788.

March 18th

THE GERMANS have given up the pretense that they were treating Florence as an open city, and are said to be putting back air
defense at every suitable eminence around the town.

Florence was surrounded by Mussolini with *autocentri,* airfields, and barracks, some of the last rivaling Mauretanian Lambe-
sis in imposing grandeur. Now they are crowded with German
troops, as are schoolhouses and other public buildings, while no
room in any house in the suburbs or environs is left unrequisi-
tioned by the Nazis. In short, Florence is now the distributing
center of men and ammunition for the whole of central Italy. And
yet they have the impudence to call it an "open city."

A hat factory belonging to a friend some twenty miles from
here has had orders to use up all its reserves of raw material to the
last scrap for hats to be sent to Germany. The director, who had

to deal with the German officials, asked them to lunch and, having put them in good humor with food and drink, ventured to say that what they were doing to his establishment was utter spoliation. They did not deny it, but seeing he had been so nice they would recommend him for some sort of repayment. "With the money received, you may be able to procure fresh stock, and if luck is on your side, you may get away with it before we are in a position to return and requisition it once again." How much I prefer the German who says "There it is" to the propagandist who says "It is not"!

March 19th

REFORM, reform, reform—institutions, constitutions, laws, decrees. None that can be enacted will help much. Our fundamental difficulties are not political but anthropological, and even zoological. They spring from the depths of human nature, of animal nature. Their sinks are not easily drained, scoured of their bestiality, and made fit for humanity. Much can and will be done. Much can and will be done, but it will take centuries, not months or even years.

The remedy to our afflictions lies outside the range of "practical politics" and, as its application can in no way profit the ephemeral politician, is not likely to be taken up by him, unless he is at the same time a lover of mankind, ready to sacrifice himself to the improvement of their dense, confused, and devil-driven minds.

Vichy France, assuming it to be sincere, wants to re-educate its subjects, and realizing that the process must be retarded to assure its genuineness, has decreed that Spanish shall be first, and for most the only, foreign language taught to French youth.

The expression "ephemeral politician" makes me think of D'Annunzio, the verbal Garibaldi who spoke as if he expected to conquer with catchwords and tinkling cymbals, as the other did with derring-do. His words were taken out of his mouth by Mussolini, who fed them to his followers, and with these verbosities expected to beat England and America when he challenged them to war.

The closest parallel to D'Annunzio that France in my time could offer was Maurice Barrès. The distance between them was perhaps more national than individual. Barrès had incomparably greater originality as a writer, a wider horizon, a more penetrating depth, and to my palate greater beauty of language. Moreover, he was an active journalist and politician. Yet not even remotely did he dominate France as D'Annunzio did Italy—a land seemingly as subject to the cult of the hero, the savior, the Duce, as France in the main is opposed to it.

March 23d

YESTERDAY morning five "deserters," that is to say young men who had not answered the call to the levy, were executed. It seems to have been a hideous affair. In vain General Adami Rossi, head of the regular army here, was entreated to commute the sentence. He ordered recruits of the regiment to which these victims should have belonged to act as a firing squad. Whether they did not want to aim or aimed badly, the poor victims were an hour being murdered.

This same General Adami Rossi at Siena had similar deserters tried in the great square while he smoked cigarettes and yawned as if it was none of his business. When the so-called trial was over, he drew out a paper previously prepared and read out the death sentence. He also insisted on having representatives of all the military services present to watch the performance. They were to be taught the lesson of devotion and duty to the flag, and the consequences of disobedience. The result seems to have been that loathing and horror filled the breasts of the bystanders. They went away each coloring his version of the massacre, and preaching hatred of the proceedings.

Those, by the way, who answered the call to the levy are given no arms, but ordered off to labor, digging, carrying heavy loads, breaking stones, etc., etc. If, tired and faint, they fall out, they are driven back with kicks and the butts of rifles, just "as if they were Jews or Poles," added my informant.

It is reported that the Eremitani chapel at Padua with the Mantegna frescoes was bombed because the nunnery next door had been occupied by the Fascist army headquarters. So it was not because of a stray shot, as I had supposed, that these paintings have been destroyed.

A commission has been called by the Fascist prefect consisting of the Cardinal, the art superintendent, and other notables to enlighten and calm the townsfolk about the persistent rumors that the basements, cellars, and crypts of public buildings from the cathedral to the Uffizi, from San Lorenzo to the Pitti, are filled with explosives and other war material that may invite enemy bombardment. The same commission eventually might guarantee that the conditions for treating Florence like an open city have been fulfilled.

The Germans want Rome and Florence to be accepted by the Anglo-Saxon invaders as harmless places of refuge for the principal works of art of the entire peninsula. It would suit them to take shelter in the midst of masterpieces which the "terrorist air gangsters" would respect.

Qui trompe-t-on ici? How can Florence and Rome be made open cities when both towns—even if not a single Axis trooper, gun, or bullet remained in them—are hugged in the embrace of Axis armies and armaments? Surely the Germans must know that their opponents will not consent to this proposal. Why, then, do they make it? To induce their sympathizers to believe it will not be their fault if Italy's "art heritage" perishes.

So far as I can make out there are three different bands in the bush, harassing the specter Fascists. There is the *tricolore* monarchical one, there is the Communist Garibaldi lot, and there is a riffraff of all sorts of undesirables ready for anything. The first two work together, but will have nothing to do with the third. The first two get supplies by air from the Anglo-Americans. It seems that a box containing six hundred thousand lire descended on a group of Germans and that a huge box containing chocolate, coffee, and tinned edibles landed in the public square of Figline.

The attitude of some Italians to the Anglo-Saxons is that the lat-

ter must and shall win the war; but if in the process they give
signs of stupidity, of incompetence, of failure, they feel less distress at the consequent prolongation of the war than pleasure in
the thought that after all the Anglo-Saxons are not as superior as
all that.

March 26th

THIRTY-FIVE S.S. have been ambushed and killed somewhere
in Rome, and the Nazis have had three hundred and fifty hostages
shot as reprisals, ten Romans for one Tudesque. Very merciful on
their side, for, in their heart of hearts, one German is worth a hundred at least, if not a thousand, Italians, none without a touch of
"nigger."

In the concrete, each of the Romans slaughtered and even each
of the S.S. ambushed has my sympathies. In the abstract I cannot
but welcome the event, for it will convince Italians of what they
never would believe: that the Nazis acted in this way in every
country they occupied.

March 27th

NICKY READ ALOUD Goethe's dedication to his *Faust*. It moved
me to tears. It was not so much the beauty and humanity of the
verse as the thought that only little over a century ago the Germans had a Goethe and that the same people now has a Hitler.
Caliban triumphing over Prospero, and enjoying the enthusiastic
adherence of tens of thousands where Goethe could not muster
hundreds.

What an *Umwertung aller Werte*—change of values! I wonder
what the inventor of that phrase, what Friedrich Nietzsche, would
think of the result!

Between the two wars, the most humanized Germans understood the contrast between Weimar as the focus of the Goethe
cult and Potsdam-Essen as the symbol of the materialistic impulses of their people, the worship of efficiency and trust in force

even though it slay them. They came as suppliants to the python-slaying Apollo but forgot the Sminthean, the vermin-killer. And Apollo, as incarnate in Goethe as ever God in man, did nothing to prevent the tribes and hosts of verminous man-shaped monsters from overcoming and enslaving the humanized, the Apollonian Germans.

*   *   *

Italian friends listened to Winston Churchill's speech of yesterday evening, and came away not only disappointed but contemptuous. No word of comfort, no promises of a speedy conclusion to our troubles, but instead, talk of tables and chairs, and other homely articles of furniture and housing.

It is sad that so many, perhaps most Italians of the upper if not governing classes, have been brought up to believe that politics deals with prestige, with magnificence, with power, with conquests. In the speech Churchill made yesterday they not only miss the rhetoric to which they are accustomed but think it infra dig for the "head of the government" to insist as he did on housing, on cottages, on furniture and similar domestic matters too humble, too trivial for the attention of a statesman.

Italians and Germans, indeed most Continental peoples, will not have it that government is only housekeeping for as many millions as compose the nation.

*   *   *

A gentleman from Lucca brings the news that there they have shot seven who failed to appear at the call to arms. All could have received a pardon but only two asked for it. The condition, however, was to join up and to be sent at once for labor either to the front or in Germany.

He tells me that the plan of the Germans and their Quisling is that the moment a given region is invaded by the Allies, the males shall be sent either to the front or to Germany while women and children are collected into concentration camps. This has been whispered already from house to house, from man to man, from woman to woman, and is creating consternation.

The same informant reports that in the mountainous region between Tuscany and the Modenese there have been pitched battles between the Quisling Italians and the "bands," and that it was going so badly with the first that they called in the Germans. Over a hundred of the Communists—officially all who resist are Communists—were taken. As to their fate there is serious disagreement. The Fascists want to shoot the ringleaders only, but the Nazis insist on shooting all.

Finally, he said that at Lucca the person responsible for the worst excesses is an idealist. God save us from idealists in politics!

March 28th

NATIONALISTIC PROPAGANDA seldom fails to infect the victims of the oppression from which liberalism would free them. The riots fomented by baboos and landlords in India are a case in point. They have—the British, I mean—many difficulties in attempting to rule a subcontinent inhabited by hundreds of language groups and thousands, perhaps, of castes. No effort more serious than the effort to free the peasant, the workingman, the small shopkeeper, the officer-clerk from the oppression of the hard-hearted landowner, his accomplice the bloodsucking lawyer, and the indifferent industrialists; to alleviate the lot of the working classes and the condition of the poverty-stricken "cultured proletariat." Yet propaganda periodically rouses these suffering millions to protest against British rule and its efforts in their favor.

The same in Egypt. There the Turkish and Turkicized Arab landowners exploit the peasantry, treating them as no better than cattle. Their hygienic conditions were revolting. Their standard of life was scarcely neolithic. The English tried hard to improve their lot. In vain, and when Zagloulites in the course of their campaign against the English started markets outside the towns, the fellahin flocked to them.

The same in Palestine. The Jewish settlers committed the crime of raising the wages of agricultural laborers, not out of philanthropy but because they needed the peasant and could pay him. They wanted the land of the peasant-proprietor and were ready to pay his price—not the pitiful one offered by the wealthy natives.

These are the fundamental reasons for the bitter hatred the "Arab," that is to say the Palestinian effendi, cherishes against the Zionists. The literates (seldom of Arab origin, some trained at Oxford and Cambridge) have been won over or hired by the effendis with the result that not only have the feelings of the Arab-speaking middle class, gulping propaganda from the papers and hearing it on the radio, been affected, but those of the peasantry, whose lot the British administration and Zionist economy were improving.

To what extent the German peasant and workman have been turned against their liberators by Nazi propaganda it is hard to judge at a distance. Here in Italy, Fascist revivalists have had, so far as I can judge, no effect on the peasantry and little on the workingman. The first may feel that they are untouched by government, and the second has not had his head stuffed with "things that ain't so" by superior schooling at the expense of his good sense.

Even before the last war, these interests had induced the Italian nationalists, few as yet, to coalesce their aspirations. Their party was made up at that time of romantic schoolmasters, of a small number of writers and journalists, and of some of that vast horde of titled Italians who resented it that abroad they did not receive the same welcome as the subjects of more prosperous countries. The moneyed powers started party dailies where they could spit out their hearts—as the French say—while rousing the people, that is to say the newspaper-reading classes, to indignation over the fact that they had neither coal, nor iron, nor cotton, nor copper, nor wool in sufficient quantities to enable them to compete in big and heavy industries with more favored lands, like Germany, England, France, and the United States.

At this point it may be asked what this has to do with the Hindu raia and the Arab fellah. In this way. The Italian nationalist, in so far as genuine, was as much the victim of interested propaganda as the Hindu and Arab peasant and office drudge. It was all the fault of the great powers, England in particular, who not only had fabulous resources at home but snatched everything abroad, leaving nothing for Italians. Finally came the cry that poor Italy was strangled, asphyxiated in its narrow seas by England, who would not let her get out into the air to breathe, to live, to conquer, to profit by the slave labor of natives and the wealth of grabbed territories.

I remember going to a music hall in Paris during the last war when the French government was making propaganda for England and hearing a song of many stanzas recounting the hardships, troubles, and miseries of mankind; each ended with the refrain *"C'est la faute de l'Angleterre."* "It is all the fault of England" is the universal cry when things go wrong for a nation, as it is "all the fault of the Jews" when things go wrong with individuals. But Germans, Italians, Russians, French even, do not seem to realize that by whining, whimpering, and howling this complaint they are recognizing England's natural hegemony, that England is the ruling power, that England is a St. Nicholas owing everybody a Christmas present, and even a living or better still a kingdom and, most imperative need of all, a people to oppress and enslave.

Continental European sympathizers with the victims of British tyranny and misrule would be left without a hobby if their own governments were running Judea or Egypt. No meetings of protest, no agitation, no newspaper opposition, no flaunting of authority permitted, and no cry of the oppressed would reach their ears.

March 29th

Frontally, Nazi propaganda has relatively little effect on more liberal Italians. When Hitler made the alliance with Stalin and the apostles of Nazism in Italy preached to their flocks that the Bolsheviks were no longer Bolsheviks, my acquaintances and friends paid little attention; nor did they when the Russians again became tooth-and-claw cannibal Bolsheviks, the moment the Führer made war on them.

A subtler German propaganda, emanating chiefly from French Switzerland, kept insisting that Stalin would seize the first favorable moment for making a separate peace with the Third Reich, and probably enough for joining it in war against the Anglo-Saxons.

When his successful steadfastness proved that this kind of propaganda would not hold water, it became subtler still and began to moan over the fact that the Western powers were letting Stalin have all the innings, and that the victory of his arms would end by making him dictator over Europe, if not over the whole earth. The English and Americans had better make haste to share his laurels.

As a matter of fact, people who talk that way know no more than the rest of us what the Soviets mean to make of their victory, assuming that it is theirs alone. Still less do they know what capacity Russia will have after the war to realize imperialistic or Communistically apostolic ambitions.

Let us assume the worst: that Russia alone has won the war (as many Italians now seem to believe), that their military power will be at the service of a will not only to rule but to impose their Communistic religion on the rest of the world.

I am Pangloss enough to fancy that if Russia does come out as the greatest power at the end of this war, the others, England particularly, will automatically look for partners and buffers. They will realize that through a Germany too crushed to rise again the Soviets can as easily sweep over the Continent as the Nazis did in the early summer of 1940. In self-defense and instinctively, they will tend to restrain the wild, thoughtless vindictiveness and fanatical hatred of so many who have suffered from Nazi onslaughts and Nazi oppression, Nazi provocation to war, and Nazi methods of carrying on war. Anglo-Saxons and even French will be compelled to see that without a German buffer state Russia would soon be at their own frontiers. This conviction would lead them to do everything in their power to restore to Germany sufficient mass and solidity to serve as a bulwark against Soviet aggression.

Before the last war and particularly during its course the balance of power was much discussed, disapproved, and decried by many idealist lambs in Anglo-Saxonia, too innocent to recognize the German wolf under his sheep's clothing.

Every regime that has attempted to dominate Europe has encountered, no matter after what flashy triumphs and even thrillingly glorious victories, the successful opposition of all who held to their independence and would not be absorbed by another power, no matter how magnificent. Instinctively they turned to England, and as instinctively England went to their aid. Why? Because for three centuries and more England has shown no wish to annex Continental territory. Like other states, she asks to be left in peace, free from blustering threats and probabilities of aggression. So she has headed coalitions against Philip of Spain, against Louis XIV, against Napoleon, and now against Hitler.

England's conduct, as well as that of all the peoples who hope for her victory, is instinctive and spontaneous. We see it even in private life. Where there are three and one is disposed to be overbearing the other two automatically join against him. So in business, in public life from ward politics to international affairs, we instinctively clutch at anyone who will help us against the menace of the moment.

There is nothing more natural than the "balance of power" as international policy.

March 31st

I AM SURPRISED that so little indignation appears on the surface against the systematic enslavements carried on by the Germans. On secure authority I have it that the Nazis mean to carry off a million and a half Italians to work in Germany. They have already required a definite contingent from each town: for instance, thirty thousand from Florence and ten thousand from Siena. When I recall the indignation felt a hundred years ago in England, and in our Northern states, over slave raiding in Nigeria and how it eventually led to our Civil War, one of the most maddening and horrible in history, I cannot help suspecting a singular incapacity for indignation on the part of Italians. Indeed, Dante is witness to it, or he would not have let Vergil embrace him with such rapture because he had given way to those feelings.

Here are episodes described by a correspondent quoted earlier in these notes. They may be subject to the personal equation but are true to the idea if not the detail:

"One of the worst things done yet is this deportation. We have seen trucks passing crammed full of unfortunate people standing up pressed against each other, among whom there were ladylike-looking women in handsome fur coats. One of these cargoes came from Rome and unloaded its contents in Piazza della Signoria for a brief respite. The poor victims with ashen faces and sagging limbs leaned stupefied against the Palazzo Vecchio. They had neither eaten nor had a drop of water since they left. The gaping crowd was stirred to pity, two thousand lire were collected, and food was bought and distributed before they were brutally packed in again, to be carried to an unknown destination. My daughter was passing through Piazza Vittorio when suddenly all the issues were blocked by 'republicans,' and every able-bodied-looking man or woman was seized and packed in a truck. Women shrieked and kicked, men were roughly handled. Two days ago the same thing happened in Via della Vigna; another time they walked into all the restaurants and carried off men and women. A few hours after they are packed into a sealed car and taken off to Germany."

The same friend describes her experience of a bombing and follows it with a characteristically burlesque episode:

"But I must not sadden you only with tragic news and shall tell you of a most comic scene that happened during the first bombardment of Florence in the refuge of one of the better-known palaces. One of the ladies living in it rushed down, florid, over-blown, decked out in all her jewelry, which she wears all the time now, terrified, dashed into the vast and dim cellars into which poured a few minutes later all the prostitutes from a neighboring brothel. They were clutching around their persons more or less bedraggled kimonos, and were followed by half-clad clients and by the *padrona* clasping the cashbox to her ample bosom. As the

bombs fell, the lady got frantic and, extracting her rosary from
her bag, fell upon her knees before a marble statue that glim-
mered pale in a remote corner. The prostitutes followed suit and
they wailed their Ave Maria in mournful chorus. As everyone's
eyes got used to the semidarkness, it was perceived that the statue
was a naked Bacchus, clad only in a most visible large tin fig leaf."

Another friend, one in a position to receive the confidences of
German officers, writes that they speak of how everything is crumbling on their side, and of the indescribable horrors going on under the Nazis. How I pity these officers, whom automatizing discipline compels to act as the instruments of a gang they abhor,
more perhaps than even we do, we who are no Quislings helping
the Nazis in their worst behavior toward fellow men.

April 1st

FINISHED Goethe's *Faust*, part one—for the how many-eth time,
I wonder, since my first reading more than sixty years ago.

As a composition it is so disappointing that I doubt whether I
shall want to peruse the whole again. The real drama, that is to
say the love of the hero and Gretchen, is not sufficiently realized,
not adequately developed, not given enough body, is only indi-
cated, brilliantly and beautifully but intermittently, in episodes.
And these episodes are either too short or too long—too long as
compared, for distance, with the Ophelia passages in *Hamlet*.
How much more Shakespeare would have made of it we can see
from the way he treated *Romeo and Juliet*, which is as brief a tale.

Nor can I find characters as distinct from types in this first part.
Faust is the young intellectual, tired of climbing the Mount of
Purgatory, I mean life; and while waiting for his second wind,
belches his disappointments. Mephisto is the smart, youthful
cynic. Gretchen is the young girl trapped by her own impulses
and innocence into a tragic passion.

To give the play—if indeed play it can be called—substance,
Goethe stuffs it with irrelevancies like the scenes in *Auerbach's*

Keller, and the *Walpurgisnacht.* I confess that this time the first did not amuse me and the second bored me.

Goethe's *Faust* is not a plant with roots deep down in the earth and branches reaching to the heavens, as are the tragedies of Aeschylus and Shakespeare. It is a Christmas tree hung and decorated with gorgeous fruits and flowers and toys of many kinds. There are beautiful verses like the dedication, the ballad of the King of Thule, Gretchen's "Meine Ruh ist hin," the Easter walk, and the marvelous last scene, although that is just a trifle prolix. Then, all the profound and so well-ordered sayings which Goethe his life long kept pouring out.

The truth seems to be that Goethe, perhaps the greatest man of letters and one of the completest of human beings, must have had a short breath as a creative artist and may have lacked staying power. Without changing its pattern he could not carry through an undertaking that required development. Thus even the second half of the first part of *Wilhelm Meister* lacks the Mozartean radiance of the first half. As for the second part, it is of course a casual collection of episodes little if at all concerned with Wilhelm. Nor can we seriously consider the many episodes and interludes of the second part of *Faust* as illustrating the protagonist's evolution from youth to old age. You may regard them as symbolical if you like, but symbols in poetry can never be more than exhalations.

In a sense Goethe's most considerable effort at a composition is his *Elective Affinities,* a relatively commonplace, modern, in some respects up-to-date novel, the kind done nowadays more delicately, more subtly, by Charles Morgan and his peers.

Goethe was, at rare times, a divinely lyrical singer, in earlier years a fair playwright, always a wonderful gnomic poet and a great man of letters, seldom a creative dramatist or narrator of the highest order. I say this with no intention of belittling him, but only to define him as an artist, as the artist within the man of letters, the scientist, the administrator, the comprehensive human being.

❖　❖　❖

Gretchen in her prison cell sings the ballad of the *Machandel-boom*, the juniper tree, of which the Grimms give such a gruesome Low-German version in their *Tales*. Loeper, in whose edition I first read *Faust* more than sixty years ago, cites a parallel in a Provençal folk song. It begins like this:

> *Ma maire m'a tuat*
> *Mon père m'a mangat*
> *Ma sure Margaridate m'a pleurat*, etc., etc.

How account for this? Scarcely by recent importation from Germany. More likely the ballad was brought by the Goths who invaded the South of France and in Septimania, the strip of territory between the Rhone and the Pyrenees, remained a sovereign people till the end of the sixth century at least.

It would be interesting to inquire what contribution the various tribes which occupied what is now France made to its history: the South, with its Gothic conquerors penetrating a society composed of Celts and Iberians, Greeks and Romans; the Northeast, the Paris Basin, with its Franks and Normans penetrating Romanized Gauls; the West, Vendée and Brittany, with Gauls Celticizing who knows what. For the Celts scarcely began to invade Gaul before the end of the sixth century B.C. Whom did they encounter when they began to occupy this territory? Basques in the Southwest, but farther north, whom?

According to all we can descry of the past, the Goths were of all barbarians the most disposed to accept the Hellenic universe, then already in Christian garb. Their mingling with the Celto-Greco-Roman elements may account ultimately for the Albigensians, for the Trouvères, for the revival of sculpture. Who knows? Perhaps these inquiries have been made with interesting results. But the individual counts for so much and it is seldom that he can be explained. Chateaubriand, Renan, Briand were Bretons. What have they in common? A gift of words?

April 2d

AMERICAN BOMBERS have killed some twenty and wounded ten times as many innocent inhabitants of Schaffhausen and done much damage. Unfortunately, this Swiss town lies on the ragged edge of the Reich. I can account for this unhappy event only in this way: The Allies must have known that, taking advantage of the vicinity of the frontier, the Germans using it as a shelter placed as near to it as possible plants or stores, and the Allies at last could not stand it any longer.

❋   ❋   ❋

I hear that government offices are now open only till 9:30 A.M. The air visitations of the Allies are effective in disorganizing work and diminishing output. Many are pleased, as they do not like to toil for the Germans. The lower orders, now that spring has come, flock to the nearest heights, take food, and spend the day picnicking. One of the many by-products of war.

April 3d

REREADING Labriolle's *Réaction Payenne* has led me again to wonder what might have happened if, instead of reigning a bare three years, Julian the Apostate had ruled the Empire, for thirty.

The doctrinaires of historical necessity and historical inevitability, if any survive, will scarcely deny that in thirty years Julian might have achieved what, in less time, the Bavarian and Austrian rulers did in the last years of the sixteenth century.

These princes found a Germany running fast towards Protestantism. They succeeded in bringing back to Rome, to a post-Tridentine, asceticized, Jesuitized, sectarian Catholicism, not only the South and the Rhineland, but Nordic Westphalia as well. The wars ended with the agreement that the sovereign of each state could impose the religion he pleased. *Cujus regio, hujus religio.* What clearer and completer denial of historical inevitability than this decision: that the prince could compel his subjects to run into the mold and take the shape he pleased, for that is what religion means. It means the shaping of character, conduct, politics, institutions, of the whole of life, in short.

What Bavarian, Austrian, and other rulers could do for Romanism, Henry VIII and Elizabeth for Anglicanism, could surely have been done by Julian for his beliefs. The majority of the Empire was as yet not even avowedly Christian and the minority was pagan at heart. This was particularly the case with the landowning and other ruling classes. The Emperor would have found enthusiastic adherents among them, and as for the inglorious company of time servers, they would have turned with the wind toward the sun.

In thirty years he might have succeeded in having his way as much as Constantine did in as many. He evidently meant to imitate what was best in the organization of the Christian parish and would have taken away from Church and diocese the care of the poor while alive and of their decent burial when dead—two important functions the Church inherited from the Synagogue. He would have created a ritual in which the worshipers were not dumb bystanders but participants in soul-stirring responses and hymns.

Furthermore, he would have succeeded in drawing to his religion most of the best talents of the time. That would have been better than wasting them, occultating their minds in hair-splitting theological speculation based on perverted history and undiscussed metaphysical premises held together by the impeccable logic of the madhouse.

True, Julian was goaded to fanaticism and to the disgusting monstrosity of hecatombs, as well as to a grimly facetious persecution which might have been carried further had he lived. On the other hand, given his intellectual powers and administrative ability, both as soldier and as statesman, it is by no means improbable that in the long run success and good sense would have got the better of him. He might have ended by letting the Christians alone. Deprived of patronage and other material and honorific advantages, they would have been reduced in the course of three decades to the number of genuine adherents—a small number, perhaps.

One cannot even attempt to formulate what kind of religion Julian might have succeeded in establishing. It would have had to be more than mere ritual; it would have had to promise life hereafter, and learn to console and comfort here below. It would have produced a theology and, almost certainly, one based, like Christianity, on Neoplatonic metaphysics. It would, however, have been unburdened with the products of a staggering attempt to harness its theology not to vague symbolical fairy tales like the Greek myths but to presumed historical actuality as related in the Old and New Testaments.

Be that as it may, certain advantages would have accrued from which we should be profiting even now.

In the first place, Julian's religion would have respected antiquity. It would have cherished the buildings and works of art, and prized the masterpieces of literature. Not only the great and glorious but the dreariest and silliest "Julianism"—let us so call it —would have saved poems, plays, histories, memoirs, biographies, scientific and philosophic treatises which Christian indifference and even hostility allowed to perish.

Furthermore, it might have saved the Eastern world from the horrors of a monachism which furnished *squadristi* or *Stosstruppen* to ferocious partisans like "Saint" Athanasius and "Saint" Cyril of Alexandria. It certainly would not have allowed a Cossack hetman like "Saint" Ambrose brandishing his *nagaika* to satisfy his lust for power by humiliating and massacring Arians, Jews, etc., etc.

Julianism would have prevented the monopoly which led the Church to actuate a totalitarian authoritarianism the like of which the world had never known before or since, till our own day in Russia and Germany.

Julianism might have induced the Church, already so arrogant, so masterful, so unevangelical, to return, with the genuinely faithful, to its sources and its primitive purity. It might have compelled it to drop theological controversy harnessed to power and instead to cultivate the Christianity of the Gospels, and to behave as a struggling and not as an all-powerful institution.

One could write volumes on this subject. If I were twenty-nine instead of seventy-nine it would tempt me. As it is, it must suffice to draw attention to this fallow field of history.

If Akhenaton had reigned half as long as Ramses II—the Nilotic *Roi Soleil*—he might have freed Egypt from the strangling grip of the Theban priesthood, and anticipated by a thousand years the best that Jerusalem and Athens were going to teach. If Philip of Macedon had not been assassinated he would have turned his arms westward to Hellenize perhaps the whole of Europe penetratingly, instead of leaving the task to be half done by Romans. If only Alexander, his son, had lived thirty or forty years more! If Antiochus Epiphanes had succeeded, Hellenism would not have been addled by Judaism. There was no historical necessity for any of these misfortunes and failures, nor for hundreds of others. But for Mussolini and his peculiar temperament Italy, in the face of manifold opposing reasons, would not have engaged in this war and be suffering her present humiliation and distress. If Hitler's mind had not been possessed by infantile stories about the Jews, he would not have made their extirpation one of the most urgent, if not the foremost, of his tasks.

No, we must stop thinking and writing about human history as if it were geology or astronomy. It is, on the contrary, crossed and recrossed by the unforeseeable and incalculable, and subject to accident, to individual character, to caprice even.

April 9th

IN THE LAST ENTRY I referred to the disparagement encountered by attempts to rewrite history. I suggested that they could be defended as criticisms of a past held responsible to some extent for what is unsatisfactory in the present.

Writing about the future does not interest teachers of history, but it escapes the disapproval of those solemn seniors. Besides, it is more excitingly fanciful. And yet most attempts to paint the future are merely utopistic pictures of what the author would wish the present to be. In sober fact the future is seldom more than an epithet, an adjective of an optative kind, applied to the present, whether to modify, intensify, or emphasize. Naturally, I have in mind a future stretching indefinitely before us: not the future of tomorrow, the next day, or the next month, when, short of accident, we, as individuals or communities, shall be achieving this or that action already well on the way in our minds, if not yet materially manifest.

The future in the sense we usually give the word is, I repeat, optative, is εἴθε γάρ, is *utinam*, is *would that*, always some desired or imagined improvement of the present or, indeed, and that more seldom, a warning against actual practices expected to affect us in a future so near that it is all but present—as the butter in the churn.

From the present we cannot get away, and it is more honest-minded not to pretend to. This, however, should not prevent us from attempting to understand how a given moment in the past seemed and felt to those who were living it. Nor should it discourage efforts at drawing conclusions about the more remote consequences of activities and policies of today. Thus Jules Verne made anticipations of the submarine that as yet are but half realized; and Wells's *War in the Air* was a prophecy more than fulfilled in the war now going on. It is far more risky to try to foretell the effect of current policies. What will England be like when this war is well over? What class at home will have the say, what will be our position abroad? What authority will the United States have in international affairs and, assuming it to be great, what use will it make of it? What understanding will it have of its responsibilities? What individuals will emerge capable of handling events so much more complicated than any we have dealt with hitherto?

April 10th

A FRIEND returned from Berlin reports that the town is in ruins; many façades remain standing but with nothing behind them. As the noted Berlin humor slumbereth not nor sleepeth, it now calls the town *Trümmershausen bei Potsdam* (*anglice* Rubblehome near Potsdam). It seems, however, that the capacity of its denizens for organization is so great that life is livable even under continuous bombardment from the air. He went on to say that, despite everything, the humbler classes retain a boundless faith in Hitler and his ability to save them.

He had occasion, this same friend, to visit the salt mines near Heilbronn, where quantities of things precious by way of art or history have been stored away in galleries of an even temperature and free from damp. It made me happy to hear that the marvelous art treasures of Germany are being so well cared for and kept safe for a better day. Let us hope for a generation better fitted to appreciate them, and to learn from them.

Fascist propaganda has suddenly discovered that Rome is a holy city, and therefore not subject to the ordinary course of war.

It seems that Allied bombs fell here and there in the outskirts of Rome yesterday, Easter Sunday. Fascist Catholic sentiment was profoundly shocked. I will not ask here how Fascism, a new totalitarianism, can live together with the immemorial totalitarianism of the good Catholic. They sneer bitterly at the indignation expressed by Anglo-Saxons over the Mussolinian invasion of Albania on a Good Friday, while these same Anglo-Saxons do not hesitate to bombard the "Holy City" on the same Christian anniversary.

These Fascists forget, or perhaps never understood, that the Anglo-Saxon horror was not over the violation of a holiday but the violation of the right of a small nation to be safe from the aggression of a bigger one, and that bigger one a nation which had already assumed, of its own choice, the role of protector. The Anglo-Saxons were bombarding the outskirts of Rome in the routine course of a war that they did everything decent to prevent, which nevertheless the Sultan of Italy, obeying his Nazi Calif, insisted on making. But one of the results of Fascist propaganda is that it renders its victims incapable of appreciating differences and distinctions not produced by bayonets.

April 12th

IN THE FACE of all that has happened, Florence and, I suppose, other towns not occupied by the Anglo-Saxon ogres are placarded with the following appeal to the citizens: "Sea, do not give us back our dead, do not give us back our ships, but give us back our glory."

This to a population so war-weary that the majority would rather go into concentration camps or let themselves be sent to forced labor than fight. This to a population aware that they have no voice in affairs, and that the Germans leave them to stew in their own juice, or to let pothouse fight pothouse, unless their own safety is concerned; to a population knowing that the other day, for the killing of thirty-five German Gestapo men, at least three hundred and fifty Italians, happening to be at hand, were shot dead; to a population well aware that the bands, so-called "brigands" or "Communists," who haunt the neighboring hills, were more than a match for the republican Fascists, seeing that these have to ask the Germans for a thousand men specially trained to cope with guerrilla tactics.

It seems that the public considers these placards a most wonderful and poetical appeal. It makes one despair of the near future for Italy. If only the dear people would take to heart the words of Renan in the preface to the *Prêtre de Nemi:* "The party who cherish dreams of a transcendent future for their country are their country's worst enemies"!

April 13th

WITH INCREASING INTEREST and attention, the Nazi press devotes itself to calculating and speculating what the afterwar will be like in Allied lands, in England particularly. As might be imagined, these Pisgah sights are of the murkiest kind. Are they intended to act as a card of comfort to the German public by assuring them that it will be bad on the other side, even if that side wins? Or is it a roundabout way to satisfy curiosity about the future without letting it dwell on their own—on what will happen to them? The Anglo-Saxon reader may not know that in Naziland it is strictly forbidden to print anything about Germany after the war. The more intelligent Germans will read between the lines and, with the help of what they are asked to believe about the Allies, will draw conclusions about themselves.

* * *

The King of Italy, no longer Emperor of Abyssinia and King of Albania, declares his irrevocable intention to hand over his legal powers to his son, the Prince of Piedmont, the moment the Allies occupy Rome.

I have never met or even seen this Prince. From all I can gather he is a good soldier, a veritable soldier.

That is what I object to. The morally if not legally responsible head of an up-to-date commonwealth, whether King or President, should be trained in ways that cannot be acquired in a military school or in commanding a battalion, a division, an army. In all these OBEDIENCE is the rule. You obey those above you, and order about all below you. This is no training for the presiding officer of a parliamentary regime. In such a regime not command but persuasion is the only technique which will produce results. You cannot dragoon, you must convince. The experience of a good drill sergeant, of a colonel, or of a general will not stand you in good stead. On the contrary, it will unfit you for the task.

In all history I cannot recall an instance of an eminent soldier's successfully ruling a country governed by free discussion. Even the Duke of Wellington is no exception, although he comes near being one, perhaps indeed because no Briton has had the gentleman in him completely replaced by the soldier. In our times MacMahon was a pitiable failure, and in our own country General Grant was worse than a failure.

The presiding officer of a community, and pre-eminently so a lifelong presiding officer, that is to say a king, should be taught history, anthropology, law, and the effective use of words.

A further objection to the soldier-king is that he will tend to give far too much weight to military matters, sacrificing more vital national interests while giving the army undue prestige in the eyes of the public. It should enjoy no more consideration than any other body serving the state, and should be as subordinated to its pedestrian, workaday welfare.

April 14th

THE NAZI PRESS is full of deep sympathy and profound understanding, manifested by the echoing voice of all Europe—"Europe," be it noted, meaning that part of this continent under German occupation—for Ribbentrop's admonitions to the Rumanians and the other once satellite, now commandeered, countries.

In this allocution, the Nazi Minister for Foreign Affairs told his vassals that they must not expect the Allies to quarrel among themselves, to make separate peace, or to do anything else to the Axis advantage. As for England, where would her Asiatic possessions now be if Germany had not made war to bridle the power and ambition of Stalin!

I begin to see the line of defense the Germans will take when they have lost the war. It will be something like this:

We alone have understood the danger the barbarous and brutal Slav is to European civilization. We knew that a Russian invasion was imminent. In vain, we urged the Western powers to join us in a crusade against them. Neither France nor England would listen. Not only that, but they declared war against us, we who were sacrificing ourselves for the sins of the world, who were preparing our defensive-offensive campaign against the Slavs. We were driven to defend ourselves against the people for whose defense we were getting ready to fight. Our might enabled us to put an end in no time to French opposition. England escaped our benevolent attentions, and continued to be a thorn in our side.

A moment came when we could afford to ignore the West and turn eastward. Continuing the campaign to which the invasion of Poland was but an overture—so misunderstood by the Poles that we had to massacre millions to save the rest—we invaded

Russia, and in no time reached the gates of Moscow and before long were on our way to the Caspian.

Thus far reason had prevailed. Then the irrational began to oppose us, and little by little, with the help of the uncomprehending English and their colonials, the United States foremost, we were forced out of Slav territory and saw our own Fatherland invaded not only by Stalin's forces but by his Anglo-Saxon auxiliaries as well.

That is all that you are—Stalin's auxiliaries. For centuries we have been a shield and a buckler for you against the Scythian and Sarmatian hordes. With your help they have conquered. We are at their mercy. No longer can you count on us as a bulwark. Power, as we know to our cost, has its momentum. Will you let it overwhelm you after it has steam-rolled us into a highway for the invader? What are you going to do about it? Will you have the sense, before it is too late, to save us from an enslavement which may compel us to help enslave you? No more talk of Nazis and anti-Nazis! We all are totalitarians now, and for many a day to come authoritarian as well.

What separates us now?

The answer may be: the humiliation, the despoliation, the blood of hundreds of thousands of Jews.

April 15th

THERE LUNCHED HERE yesterday a gentlemen fresh from the distant bourne which Rome has become. He told us of the three hundred and fifty seized in the quarter where thirty-five Germans had been killed, and sacrificed to their shades by the Teuton brutes. Men, women, and children, among them the eighty-five-year-old widow of Tittoni, in his day a figure in European politics. It was with no little difficulty that she was saved from the holocaust.

In many streets of Rome have been prepared gates which the Nazis can shut at a minute's notice to control the population.

The same gentleman, a Sicilian by origin and a lawyer by profession, had two versions, new to me, of why the armistice was announced on the wireless three weeks earlier than agreed upon.

One version is that De Gaulle, out of spite at not having been admitted to the discussion as an equal, gave it away. The other is that the Allies, not trusting the Italians and fearing these might use the terms for bargaining with the Nazis, hastened to publish it.

I jot both down, to me equally improbable, as instances of how difficult it is to know how and why things happen. The evidence, so called, is confused and conflicting. Tired of discussing, historians settle down to a conventional statement, to Napoleon's *fable convenue.*

In a long-drawn conflict like the present one, the opponents adopt and assimilate those qualities of each other that make most surely and swiftly for victory. *Fas est ab hoste doceri*—it is just to learn from the enemy.

We Atlantic peoples will come out of this war as totalitarian certainly and almost as authoritarian as the Germans. Necessarily so. The only thing that may differentiate us from other totalitarians and authoritarians is freedom of speech, a free press, a free radio, etc., etc. That may save us.

April 19th

LONDON AND NEW YORK send missionaries to China, to Africa, to the remotest and wildest parts of the earth, to inculcate the Gospel by the example of their own standard of life. Likewise we send expeditions to study the manners, customs, folkways of the Trobriand and Easter Islanders, and other fashionable haunts of overexcited anthropological curiosity.

Many, myself included, question whether missionaries are not wasting our money and their energies, doing the objects of their zeal more harm than good. We believe there are no end of Trobrianders, Easter Islanders, and other neolithics, not to speak of paleolithics, in our midst: in our slums as well as in every grade of

society, the fashionable not least. We should prefer our missionaries to sacrifice themselves rather in humanizing these savages
or barbarians, these fetish worshipers in our own ranks.

Anthropology should begin at home.

By anthropology I mean the study of usages, practices, manners, customs, beliefs, superstitions, etc., etc., that do not readily
submit to rational treatment but remain as they are, mobile or
fixed, and find brilliant defenders armed with all the learning that
up-to-date research can apply.

I could wish that our anthropologists grew serious and, forgoing
aquatic picnics among Pacific islands, would devote laborious
years to the study of all that is naïvely taken for granted, and no
less tenaciously than irrationally held, by the average matron,
the average businessman, the average cleric, the average lawyer,
the average soldier, sailor, administrator, butcher, baker, etc., in
our own societies, high and low, low and high.

Something of this kind must have been in the mind of the late
Professor Sumner of Yale, with his sociological investigation and
publications. Far from being a Philistine as Van Wyck Brooks
designated him, we should honor him as the great scholar and
pioneer that he was. What he meant to initiate was an inquiry as
to what in our own people was too fixed, too immovable to yield
to immediate philanthropic effort or legislative decree; what
among "the heirs of all the ages in the foremost ranks of time"
remains as little subject to persuasion and even to force as any
other irrational energy, say a certain volume of water in motion
or turning to steam.

You know enough about the nature of water not to argue with
it, preach to it, or appeal to its better instincts. You let it alone; or
if you must deal with it and want it to take a more convenient
turn, you provide ample space for its career by canals, sluices,
safety valves, and other devices.

Human nature in a given moment, at a given place, is scarcely
more subject to reason or persuasion. It took a community of half-
educated, I mean untraditional, folk to legislate alcohol out of all
but therapeutic use. Anglo-Saxons can prevent control of prostitu-

tion, although, in India at least, the British army has it. To take a
higher flight—religion is a human necessity. Few are they who
can burrow through the muck and grime and hard-caked filth of
superstition, or shake off the admirable and appealing doctrines
of Christianity, to reach a sustaining vision of their own. The rest
require some sort of comforting assurance against fear, and an
outlet of enthusiasm. If you take their childhood's creed and rites
away, they will hanker for others and find them in Nazism, in
Communism, and worst of all in nationalism. The average man
can no more be deprived of access to some sort of mass emotion
than steam of an outlet.

The anthropological study of ourselves in all classes and layers
should be as indispensable to the statesman as the study of Roman
and other laws to the lawyer, and anatomy and physiology to the
physician and surgeon. Otherwise your legislation will be a mock-
ery and your attempts to enforce it a tyranny which human nature
will expel or at best alter to its own requirements, as we Westerners have done with actual and not verbal Christianity, or East-
erners with Buddhism. The reformer, the legislator, who enacts
improvements and laws suitable to people as they should be but
not as they are, will always succumb to the demagogue, the Mussolini, the Hitler, to the Fascism, to Tammany Hall, with their
cynical acquaintance with human nature at its worst, and their
playing down to it. In a moment of great distress and uncertainty,
they invariably conquer with appeals to the lowest morality and
the meanest intelligence. Far be it from me to urge imitation of
the various Fascisms, or the politics of Tammany Hall. On the
contrary, I believe in the possibility of humanizing that beastliest
of all animals, man. Only you must know what you have to deal
with, and use appropriate measures based on the knowledge of
what you can do with him at a given time and place. You must
not act, as reformers generally do, in accordance with what man
should be, but with the intellectualized experience of what he is.

There are in effect no worse enemies of society than the crystal-
clear, incorruptible idealists. They ignore the animal in man, and
recognize only a highly rational being who easily should be con-

vinced and persuaded to change his ways and conform to their program. They invariably disappoint the masses, leaving them at the mercy of the sly, the greasy masters of appealing catchwords and gross promises, the Duce, the Führer.

The anthropologist should prepare as thorough and searching a diagnosis as possible of a community. On this, the statesman with infinite patience, and despite discouragements, knowing what he has to start with, what he can count on, what pace he can take, could build, and with one step after the other, feeding, amusing, comforting, and in extreme moments flattering, attain results desirable in themselves and able to serve as levers for further effort.

April 22d

SOME EIGHT DAYS AGO Gentile was assassinated. Returning from Florence to his "refuge," halfway to Settignano, while the chauffeur was opening the gate of the drive, four youngish men approached the car and asked whether the man inside was Giovanni Gentile. When he answered that he was, they shot him dead.

It was given out at once that the assassins were "intellectuals." I could not see why these should be in such haste to kill Gentile, in a moment like this. True, he has been the partiarch of the Fascist church—for Fascism like Hitlerism is more religious than political—he has been as well the philosopher who attempted to justify the ways of Mussolini to men. Yet I never heard that, as Minister of Public Instruction or as influential person, he had ever been unjust, let alone cruel to individuals. On the contrary, he was helpful and good to everybody.

It seems that Göring's "merry men," while sweeping the lower slopes of Monte Morello clean of "Communists," killed the favorite secretary of Gentile, who was spending the Easter days with his mother in a villa at Cercina. When Gentile learnt this, he threatened to go to Mussolini and tell him what was going on here, that it was sheer anarchy and misrule.

Thereupon, as is by no means unlikely, Captain Carità, who

under S.S. protection still runs the province, had him assassinated.

At the same time that Göring's merry men were clearing the slopes of Monte Morello, they were "murthering and ravishing" in the deep valley at its bottom, and on the opposite slopes of Monte Senario. The Cardinal of Florence happened to be on a pastoral visit to Vaglia and had immediate reports of the killing, the robbery, the devastation committed by these merry men. His Eminence has not kept silence. He may get the Germans to hold their hand. Will he rouse the Florentine possessive classes, the Tuscan aristocracy, to effective indignation? That is doubtful. It is so much safer to keep quiet!

April 23d

I DO NOT KNOW to what poverty economic pressure will reduce us. Nor do I foresee how deeply our people will let themselves be doped by the propaganda of universal providers, electioneering speakers, and soapbox orators promising plenty and pleasure if only we shut our eyes and, except to them, our ears as well, and let them lead us to the stall or sty, cinema or circus, that we dream of as paradise, as the Garden of Eden.

Assuming, however, that the spiral of history will continue to function, this war may be followed by much the same distaste for "enthusiasm" as prevailed in the first half of the eighteenth century.

The translation of the concept "enthusiasm" into recent speech has been in Italy *idealità* and in the Reich—more honestly cannibal—"the greater Germany," both leading to wars as vile, as mean, and as bloody as the religious wars preceding the Treaty of Westphalia.

I do not expect that all enthusiasm will disappear. Some of it certainly will accrue to the benefit of that residuary refuge of the soft-minded, the Roman Church, and drops may irrigate the barren land of Protestant religiosity. With rare exceptions, members of the influential classes will turn toward reasonable ways of looking at society and its problems, try to discover its pressing needs and how to supply them, while endeavoring to make political questions rationally intelligible to all members of the community, teaching them what are its problems, and which the most promising solutions.

Rationalism in ethics and politics is necessarily optimistic, for it believes that the effort to improve avails. It will instinctively give attention to the elements of goodness in things as evil as original sin has made us. The cumulative effect of finding so much gentleness, humanity, and good sense in the common people—objects of aversion and disgust hitherto—led to the sentimentality that found its voice and its advocate in Rousseau. Its rising tide carried the ruling classes back to enthusiasm, as manifested in the French Revolution, followed by the Napoleonic Wars.

Those years—a bare quarter of a century—were succeeded by as many of divided interest: the ruling classes, as exemplified in Metternich, Charles X, and the Vatican tending toward a cold, dry, and restrictive outlook on society and politics, while the romantic intellectuals reacted indignantly and created the liberalism of the middle decades of the nineteenth century.

Dare we hope that the period of rational politics which we may expect after this war will not be followed by a wave of sentimentality, ending in another tidal wave of enthusiasm?

April 28th

NATIONALISTS keep insisting that the Italian forces which refused to join the Germans and the recruits that take to the woods rather than join the republican colors do not do so because they prefer the Allies to the Axis but simply because they have had enough of fighting.

Italian nationalists began as early as the fiasco in Greece to speak contemptuously of their countrymen as soldiers; and as the Allies were keeping quiet and the Soviets in seeming flight, the same nationalists concluded that the Germans were invincible, a superior race, a race of heroes, of supermen. Nazi victories kept confirming them in this opinion until it became a conviction—

nay, a faith they have not yet given up, nor probably ever will.

How is it that these nationalists, dreaming as they did of Roman glories and the reconquest of its ancient empire—how is it that they do not realize now, at long last, that with such unwarlike material as they say is furnished by the Italian people, military glory and conquests are out of the question; and that they miscalculated and led their country not to magnificence, splendor, and world exploitation, but to abject defeat? Years ago, before the filibustering campaign in Abyssinia, it was reported that Mussolini ejaculated: "This people will never make good soldiers." Knowing this, why did he start a series of wars intended to turn the Mediterranean into an Italian lake, driving the English off its waters, and penning up the French, or even pushing them back to the hinterland of Provence, after expelling them from Africa?

Surely Renan is right when in the *Prêtre de Nemi,* as already quoted here, he says that the worst enemies of a people are those who encourage it to dream of glory and magnificence. How dangerous to trust in Duci, Führers, messiahs, except as Orthodox Jews do who forbid human interference and leave all to God.

*   *   *

Here in Florence the mood of some, if not all, Germans is apparently not cheery. Officers up from the south do not hesitate to declare that the Allies deliberately mark time and do not come forward. The same Allies will fight desperately to win a certain position and after hours abandon it.

The common soldiers in their *Soldatenheim*—soldier's home— speak of decapitating Hitler and shooting Mussolini.

The Germans are getting seriously afraid of the bands occupying the heights all around. These seem well organized and armed. Their soldiers feel no eagerness to meet them, and it is rumored that they are thoroughly drenched with spirits before they are sent out.

April 29th

THE SENSE of antecedent probability is the sixth sense. We are not born with it as with the five senses, but acquire it through education and training, experience and practice. Every mature person uses this sense in his job as well as in whatever else interests him deeply and uninterruptedly.

Here is an instance. The late R. van Marle, the author of some twenty volumes on Italian painting, was asked during the First World War to replace, at a few hours' notice, a friend who was going to give a lecture on bees. He did so, and observed that one of his auditors kept jumping up again and again as if startled out of his wits. The lecture no sooner over than this individual came forward and, introducing himself as a beekeeper, wanted to know whence the lecturer had drawn his facts. Van Marle confessed that he got them out of Maeterlinck.

You may say this was a case of professional knowledge. If you like, but it also proves that the beekeeper's sense of antecedent probability, acquired through experience, did not prevent his admitting the bare possibility that Van Marle's statements might have something in them. He would have been ready to discuss them, although the conclusion would not have been far off.

Most cases of antecedent probability are less obvious than the one just cited. They are dimmer, vaguer, more diffused, harder to substantiate. Take my own case.

An Italian picture is put under my nose and I am told it is a Leonardo, a Raphael, a Titian, a Botticelli, as happens often enough. My sixth sense, that is to say my previous experience of the painter in question, runs to the window, as it were, to see, and almost immediately decides for or against the attribution.

Many years ago in Washington a picture was shown to me as by Raphael, and I turned it down without a moment's hesitation. It created a scandal: that I was so hasty in my judgment, did not take time, did not submit the painting to an elaborate analysis, etc., etc.

While there are works of art sufficiently close to the masters to whom they are ascribed to be a thorn in the side of a scholar for years, and even for his lifetime, in most cases his sense of antecedent probability saves him from doubt and the need of further investigation.

But miseducation can do as much as education to establish a sense of antecedent probability. It can do it all the swifter as it does not count on experience and firsthand knowledge but on mere statement, so oft repeated that it gets fixed in the memory like a jingle, like Mark Twain's at one time universally known "Punch, brothers, punch." It answers to the well-known saying of the Duchess in Alice: "What I say three times is true." The sort of misinformation now called *"bourrage de crâne"* (Michelet spoke of it as vaccination against the recognition of facts, and our Josh Billings as filling heads with "things that ain't so") establishes a sixth sense that makes its possessors capable of seeing only what that sense permits them to believe probable.

The domains where a miseducated sixth sense has the easiest time finding the greatest abundance of tasty food for its prejudices and furies are religion and politics, particularly in time like ours, when it is far from easy to keep them apart, so closely are they intertwined.

I recall that during the First World War English and French dailies were sold at all newsstands in Germany. There was no danger that the average Hohenzollern subject would believe a word that did not accord with his sense of antecedent probability. That had been seen to by propaganda against England as the chief criminal. A series of deliberate calumnies first forged by Jesuits against Queen Elizabeth, taken up by the Spaniards of Philip II, then by the French of Louis XIV, and enlarged as well as intensified by Napoleon were forced, cut and dried, into the politically anticritical mind of the good and true Teuton. Then, as so much more now, everything that could or might reach him from the other side was only "an English lie."

Anti-British propaganda has not only affected Germany, where it has been rife for the last sixty years, or Spain, where it has been

preached for nearly four centuries, but Italy in a measure unexpected; seeing that it has been applied only since Mussolini's
plebeian fury over the sanctions against his rape of Abyssinia,
and considering how much friendship with England had been,
ever since the *Risorgimento,* a principle of Italian policy. There
was an old rhyme: *Con tutti guerra salvo con l'Inghilterra.* The
people who have acquired this perverted sixth sense smell out
anything told by the Allies, unless indeed it is in accord with
Axis news, as *bugie inglesi*—English lies; and nothing from an
Allied source will convince them. They will have to be re-edu-
cated, and given another sixth sense, more open to facts as facts—
at least *our* facts.

I could fill volumes with instances from Germany, Italy, and
Spain, not to speak of France and French Switzerland, of people
in this as well as in the last war whom no arguments, no display
of facts could move. It goes to prove the eighteenth-century
rhyme: "A man convinced against his will/is of the same opinion
still."

I will cite but one further instance. We were at Madrid in the
winter of 1916–1917. One evening we went to have tea with passionately reactionary, ultra-Catholic acquaintances. My wife, who
had just joined me from London, was asked whether people there
were not starving, whether there was no lack of water, whether
Londoners still had gas and electricity. My wife assured them
that three or four days previously they were suffering from no
such privations, although of course they could not enjoy the abundance of prewar days. Our Spanish friends looked pitifully in-
credulous.

April 30th

I HAVE FOLLOWED the Nazi press ever since the beginning of
this war. Never have the Germans attacked. They made war on
Poland to save hundreds of thousands of their brethren from
being massacred by Slav savages. They made war on Russia because they knew that the Soviets were on the point of attacking

them. As for England and France, it was they who started hostilities; and it was only to defend them against destruction from the Allies that the Nazis occupied Norway and Denmark, Holland and Belgium. If some stupid and treacherous persons in those small countries conspired against their German protectors, they had to be dealt with and at times rather harshly.

Look at the aims of the Nazis and those of their opponents. The former are fighting to establish a reign of peace and good will in Europe to begin with, and on the rest of the earth later. They meanwhile have the greatest regard for occupied territories, caring infinitely for their welfare to the extent that the necessities of defense against inexorable enemies will permit. The Germans are bleeding, not to death they hope, but bleeding to protect the European part of Europe from Slav bestiality, Yankee imperialism, and English lust for power. And what are these fighting for, if not to destroy the Reich and reduce its population to slavery and famine, to be trod under the boot of the Soviets, oppressed by the haughty and arrogant Briton, and exploited by the Yankee-Jew? Surely no good and true German will fail to see whither his approval, his devotion, his affection should be directed.

The good and true reader of the *Völkischer Beobachter,* the *Münchener Neusten Nachrichten,* the Berlin *Börsen-* and *Allgemeine Zeitung,* the *Kölnische Zeitung,* the *Hamburger Fremdenblatt* (to name those I most frequently peruse) will understand, when this war is over, that he has been beaten but will not believe that justice, humanity, and civilization gave us the mandate to beat him. He will remain soreheaded, morose, more than ever believing in force—has it not overwhelmed him!—and plotting in his heart, as so many Germans after the last war, to get force on his side.

One of the chief afterwar problems will be how to convince this good and true German victim of Nazi propaganda that it was our bounden duty to keep making war on him, no matter at what cost and what suffering, until his rulers stopped behaving like the neolithic cannibals that in their twentieth-century jargon they boasted of being.

It will be no easy task. To bamboozle is not easy, to debamboozle is almost impossible. This phrase of Maynard Keynes, applied to President Wilson, is as true not only of Germans but of Spaniards and Italians in this war. I fear there is nothing to be done with grownups but to let them die off. We must concentrate effort on young people, and see to it that our version of events reaches them in detail, and in the most convincing terms. We cannot prevent their parents' trying to rouse them to revenge. In the schools at least let them be taught our version of the story.

Propaganda is but one of the means, and the grossest, of producing a sense of antecedent probability in envisaging events and interpreting information. There are others, scarcely less effective in intervening between us and actuality. Education as distinct from training should endeavor to emancipate us from this kind of tyranny.

Even as I was writing this, I received the last German papers. They speak complacently of having put three hundred thousand Jews into concentration camps in recently occupied parts of Hungary. Old and young, men, women, and children, none excepted but physicians and apothecaries. Then the Nazi papers boast of all that is being done to de-Judaize business and professions of every kind in Hungary.

May 22d

THE SLOPES OF ETNA afford landscapes enchanting to the eye as well as to every other sense. In their season the fragrance of orange and lemon blossoms is almost overpowering. The wheat grown there is of such excellence that it is held too good for local consumption and exported abroad even out of Italy. In every respect this region is a garden of the Lord, a paradise. Not only materially but spiritually it is the heart of Sicily. Catania, its center, is the intellectual capital of the entire island. Its university is one of the best in Italy. It has been the home of Verga, the great novelist, the adopted home of De Roberto, whose *Vicerè*, in the opinion of Edith Wharton—no mean judge of the novel—

should rank with the highest literary achievements of the last century, as the most creative Italian romance after Manzoni's *Promessi Sposi.*

Once in every fifty years or so this Eden, this paradise, is visited by destruction. Etna vomits torrents of lava which overwhelm the countryside, and belches up clouds of cinders which cover it with a sinister snowfall. Farms, villages, towns, cities, are burnt and buried, thousands perish.

Undiscouraged, the inhabitants of this region begin all over again, as we do after so relatively mild an "act of God" as a winter blizzard. Forgetting Etna's rages, or believing that they will not return in their day, they go to work and enjoy the exercise of their functions as if nothing could disturb or interrupt, let alone put an untimely end to them.

So with future persecutions of the Jews as by Hitler defined. They may occur again and again, and even be worse than the present one, which is the most violent and destructive in the three thousand years and more of Hebrew history. This time many have been able to escape to countries the Nazis could not reach. Where would they flee to from America, for instance, or from a world state where the entire earth would be subject to the same decree?

Life itself is, as Victor Hugo put it, a death sentence with an indefinite reprieve. Death is always imminent. A friend seldom leaves me for more than an hour without my wondering whether I shall see him again. And I refer to periods of steeped peacefulness, not to the man-quaky conditions of today. Nevertheless we do not long for "easeful death" to put an end to our anguish and fear of dying. Christians or Jews, we no longer canalize all our energies toward making a pious end, but "enjoy weeping in this vale of tears."

May 23d

So, ALTHOUGH I do not believe in the likelihood of a satisfactory end to anti-Semitism within our historical horizon, and can offer but the coldest comfort to the victims of the present outburst of the *Furor Teutonicus*, I can promise the Jews pleasant intervals between massacres and, further, that these intervals may be extended. The conditions under which for so many centuries the Jew has had to live have endowed him with unusual zest and capacities for life. Let him use them, yet "walk in the fear of the Lord." If only he can avoid waxing fat and kicking like the Deuteronomist's Jeshurum and worse still kicking the inferior of his own "race" while cringing and fawning on his non-Jewish social superiors, and bribing his way into their society with expensive gifts and lavish entertainments!

The Jew still has a mission. This word I must let go at its current value. To discuss the contradictions implied in the attempt to define it, unless indeed one accepts it as appointed by divine providence, would carry me too far and involve me in fruitless controversy. The Jew's first mission was to give the white race its religion. Christianity is detribalized Judaism in nearly everything but its Neoplatonic and Gnostic theology. Its expansion over the earth is the fulfillment of prophecy. It is so much the Jewish dream of spiritual dominion come true that in a future not too distant it may be hard to believe that Judaism and Christianity were not the same religion, answering to the evolving needs of successive ages. Strange that the contemporary Jew takes no pride in an achievement the effects of which surpass those attained by Greece and Rome together!

In the future he should cultivate the qualities that anti-Dreyfusards and other anti-Semites have reproached him with. He should not identify himself with the rest of the nation in its chauvinism, in its overweening self-satisfaction, self-adulation, and self-worship. He should be in every land the element that keeps up standards of human value and cultivates a feeling for proportion and relations. He should be supernational as the Roman Church claims to be. Who blames the Church for being so, except mad anti-Papists? The pity of it is that its hold on the governing classes, and even on its clergy, from archbishops and bishops down, is not strong enough to cope with their nationalism. For instance: Mussolini's filibustering expedition against Abyssinia enjoyed the enthusiastic approval of the Italian clergy and, I fear, of Pope Pius XI himself.

The Jew should try to check stampedes of opinion and mitigate mass movements of animal fury. Thereby he would prove himself a patriot; for patriotism, it cannot be too often repeated, signifies love of our country, whereas nationalism teaches the hatred of other countries. There the German Jew sinned. Who wrote the hymn of hate against "Engelland" at the outbreak of the last war? A German Jew. Who tried to get to America with a film displaying faked British atrocities? Another German Jew. Who encouraged the Emperor William in his naval and colonial ambitions? Again a Jew, Ballin, who, however, had the pluck to kill himself when he realized what it led to. The German press was, to a considerable degree, in the hands of Jews. Did they do anything to stem and check militarism, imperialism, annexationism? Who whipped the dogs of war more than the Jew Harden? Who preached nationalism more than the Jewish editor of the *Magdeburger Zeitung*? Who served German propaganda and intrigue in neutral countries during the last war better than that editor's brother, both bearing an illustrious rabbinical name?

Most of the German Jews I myself have met or known through others were fanatical nationalists and remained so as prosperous immigrants in America. Until we went into the First World War many of them, far and beyond anything done by non-Jews, made propaganda for the Reich and organized every species of assistance that our easygoing laws tolerated. Even since the triumph of Hitler, there have been Jews who have let themselves be declared "edel-Arier"—honorary Aryans—so as to serve the Nazis with might and main. What insanity on the part of Hitler to have combined his (or his people's) passion for power with an exterminating war against the Jews! In all Europe, except perhaps France and England, in nearer Asia as well as in our country, not a few might have been his propagandists, his defenders, his helpers.

May 26th

THE JEW WHO, soul and body, heart and mind, has got away from the ghetto and acquired the methods of up-to-date science, scholarship, and thought along with the mental attitude and acquisitions that they have achieved, can be more easily dispassionate and objective than so-called Christians, alias Gentiles, alias Aryans, especially in things human, in fields where traditional and personal prejudices run wild, like philosophy, history, criticism, literature, and art.

This same Jew has learnt not to resent condescending, sneering, or even outrageous remarks about his "fellow scapegoats." He has read plays, romances, and novels where the Jew is seldom manifested as an ordinary citizen. Generally he is described as less honest, less sociable, even less kindly, while at other times, though rarely enough, he is too good to be true. The same enlightened Israelite has learned to appreciate high qualities in literature, or merely witty and humorous writers, despite what they bring up against his own people.

In reading history he will appreciate the fine qualities in statesmanship of a Titus, a Trajan, a Hadrian and of thousands of others later who were wolves to Jews. He will even admire the political and administrative as well as theological gifts of ferocious Church Fathers like Ambrose of Milan, who was anything but a saint to Jews, or of Athanasius and Cyril of Alexandria. Christian saints, when dealing with Jews or speaking of them, have seldom if ever seen anything but their bad qualities and odious characteristics. These are so easy to find everywhere in every people. For instance, while I am writing this, we who are in this war attribute these defects to our adversaries regardless of race and religion. Their being so universally applied to the Jew does not prove that he monopolizes these faults but only that the feeling towards him is still hostile, although not always actively so. Excepting Francis of Assisi, it is not easy to discover an eminent saint who cherished "Christian" feelings toward the Jew.

Men of letters have been almost as prejudiced from first acquaintance with this intractable people. Even Goethe remained
cold towards them and received icily Rahel Levin, the person
who among his own contemporaries did most for his fame and
popularity. No doubt he could not get over the tales heard from
nurses and schoolfellows about the denizens of the *Judengasse*
of Frankfurt, his home town, denizens of that miserable ghetto
whence swarmed Rothschilds, Erlangers, and many others down
to the Blumenthals and Seligmanns of our own day.

The enlightened Jew has learnt to forget his "own tribesmen"
when judging of events and persons and literary creations. What
Frenchman, German, Italian, or even Anglo-Saxon can claim as
much fairness in deed and word toward enemies of his own nation!

May 27th

AT TIMES I ask myself where lies the difference between the
enlightened Jew I have been trying to make out as so objective—
to use the word much abused by Germans with their constant
claims to objectivity—and the non-Jews of the same grade. Of
course I omit mental and moral characteristics of a kind that escape unprejudiced investigation, whether introspective on the
part of the Jew himself or studied from the outside by the anthropologist or ethnologist.

I would suggest that the chief difference is in the attitude toward Jesus. The individual brought up as a Christian sucks in
with his mother's milk a feeling toward Jesus that he never gets
over, unless, indeed, it is changed to one of half-educated dema-
gogical revolt. No matter how much he has shaken himself loose
from the rites and practices of his bringing up, he retains for
Jesus a tender reverence of love and awe combined, which renders him incapable of approaching His personality and career as
he would approach any other historical figure.

The enlightened Jew can and does, but with piteous results.
What would he not give to know everything about this greatest

and sublimest genius of his race, greatest and sublimest in influence, in effects, in results. Were these merely due to chance,
because the yearning and wishful thinking of the times conjured
them up out of the mist of confused and confusing religious aspirations, crystallizing around Paul's certainty that Jesus, who
was crucified and died, had risen from the dead, and thereby, in
a world hungry for the afterlife, assured survival for every man?

There certainly was more, as can be guessed rather than perceived from the Gospel narratives. Sad it is that the synoptic ones
—the fourth scarcely counts in this connection—are but the
murky record of what struck the humble intelligence of Galilean
villagers and fishermen. They believed in Him for his cures and
miracles, and were simple enough to desert Him when these
failed, yet to return when convinced that He had risen from the
dead. Of His aspirations, His qualities of mind and heart, His
teaching, His sublime irony, they who saw Him as through a
glass darkly, understanding Him only as one possessed of a
power—a *barakah,* as the Moslem calls it—spoke to others who
probably had not known or even seen Him, in a way that has
come down to us in the Gospels. They allow us to see Jesus as we
decipher a stained-glass figure seen not from within but from out
of doors.

If only Jesus, like Socrates, had had a Plato among His listeners!

Yet the sayings reported, few and contradictory as they are,
suffice to make one marvel. He who had on the one hand such
penetrating and clear-eyed insight into human nature, and on the
other such freedom from prejudice, such a sense of values, and of
all that man needed to be completely humanized, must have been
beyond what any Jew had known or seen before Him; must have
been the fulfiller of the law and the prophets in so far as they
were spiritual and not tribal. What would one not give for a life
of Him written by a contemporary Israelite, an enlightened Phar-
isee or an unworldly Sadducee. We hunger and thirst to know of
His origins and childhood; for neither the fairy tales of the Gospels nor the rough folkloristic anecdotes of the "Gospel of the
Infancy" come anywhere near to satisfying us. We want to know

about His boyhood and youth. Did He impress the Temple with His wondrous precocity, and if He did, how was it that they lost sight of Him? Then the years before His brief activity begins— how were they spent, under what influence did He come while in Galilee? Did He know the Greeks and had He an inkling of their ways of thinking? And what really happened toward the end?

We have Hebrew and Aramaic records of messianic apparitions nearly contemporary with His. If He alone deserved death at the hands of both Temple and Synagogue, He must have been more alarming. Why, then, this stillness, this *Totschweigen,* as the German has it, about Him? Jewish lore, whether doctrinal, biographical, or legendary, betrays not a single trustworthy reference to Him that is not centuries later.

The explanation must be that Jesus was regarded as a national danger for preaching doctrines that Temple and Synagogue recognized as harmful to their faith and opposed to their interests. Their faith, against which Jesus seems to have rebelled, was a narrowly tribal one, consisting mainly of rites, ordinances, usages, and practices that would isolate the Jew and prevent his being assimilated by the Gentiles as the "lost ten tribes" had been. Their interests lay in the moneys brought by pilgrims to the annual feasts, as well as those collected by apostles sent out for that purpose to every land where Jews dwelt, lands covering not only the Roman Empire but beyond.

Parenthetically, let me explain that "apostles" went abroad to gather what the Synagogue's daughter, the Holy Roman Church, came to call "Peter's pence." Even Paul, in order to justify himself before the surviving disciples of Jesus in Jerusalem, had to claim that he was serving in that capacity. Preaching was incidental, but Paul took every advantage of the opportunity offered him by his apparent mission to speak of his visions, ideas, and aspirations. The real basis for the rapid growth of Christianity was not, as writers since Augustine have believed, the existence of the Roman Empire but the ubiquity of the Jew in and out of the Empire.

To return to Jesus and the constituted authorities in Jerusalem, these could have had no reason for getting rid of Him unless He held and published doctrines that were opposed to their tribal faith and their money interests. It is probable that Jesus Himself did not realize the bearing of His mission as clearly as His persecutors did. To them it must have meant that He intended to destroy the Temple, and to by-pass Mosaism as a religion merely tribe-preserving. The events proved that they were right.

There may have been another reason besides for the way the Synagogue ignored Jesus. I do not have in mind the fear its doctors may have had of hostile ears and eyes. There were Jews in numbers beyond the reach of the Church Fathers who guided and governed the ex-Roman Empire. Under Parthian, followed by Sassanian and succeeded by Mohammedan rulers, they could safely have published what they pleased. Yet we discover no word, no sign betraying acquaintance with the historical Jesus, scarcely with His name, in the Babylonian Talmud, the most important of all rabbinical writings.

The second cause for this deliberate ignoring may have been the horror felt by the Synagogue at the attempt, following so soon after His death, to deify Jesus. It began with Galileans and was greatly advanced by a citizen of Hellenic Tarsus, named Saul and afterwards Paul, all of them influenced, no matter how indirectly and how unconsciously, by contact with Greeks. Hellenes had always been ready to declare divine the unknown fathers of princely mothers. One of them, Euhemerus, taught that all the gods were deified historical figures. Hellenistic rulers assumed godhead without shocking opinion. Later on Roman emperors, first at their demise and then in their lifetime, were deified and worshiped as gods—practically if not theologically, for to all but a few the genius of the emperor was the emperor.

The Jew, unless strongly influenced by Gentiles, never deified —not even his most revered teachers, prophets, guides, and warriors; not even Moses, not even Joshua, not even David, not even Elijah. On the contrary, if we may trust the scholarship of the last hundred years, the Israelite's instinctive tendency was in the op-

posite direction, to reduce gods to men, as he did with his patriarchs, as he did with Samson.*

The Jew returning from the Babylonian captivity brought with
him such a horror of the blasphemous claim of a mortal to godhead that he was ready to submit to martyrdom rather than to
pay divine honors to a creature of flesh and blood, no matter how
powerful, how exalted. The horror increased with time. The wise
Roman understood this, and exonerated the Jew from the worship
of the emperor's genius to which all other inhabitants of the Empire were subjected.

Imagine, then, what the deeply religious Jew must have felt
when the individual who had proposed detribalizing Judaism,
and consequently was crucified, began to be worshiped as a god
by His followers, and identified with Jehovah. A blasphemy so
revolting that it could only be met with total silence.

And so to this day, ready as it is to annex every individual that
it can claim, Jewry has not yet turned toward Jesus.

May 30th

I COULD WISH that some rich Jews would turn away from showy
altruism and establish a school for the study of Judeo-Christian
relations from the birth of Jesus the Galilean to our day; the behavior of Jewry to the emergent Church, and the reaction of this
Church from its cradle to its full growth, its many centuries of
monopolistic splendor, rising too often to arrogance, and its breaking up into numbers of sects, whereof the Church of Rome, although by far the most dominant, is yet but one.

Seldom, I fear, would the publications of these scholars be
pleasant reading. In their books, these scholars should avoid Ger-

---

*In this connection let me quote in paraphrase from the *Selbstgespräche* of
Heinrich Homberger, p. 81: "What makes Jews distasteful to demigods like Liszt,
Wagner and Co., is beyond question that they have no awe for them. They feel
that the Jew sees through them to their earthenness, that in short they are found
out to be mere mortals."
So in Jewish legend Moses had to escape from Egypt not because he had slain
an Egyptian but because he had happened to see Pharaoh satisfying the call of
nature, which, as a god, the same Pharaoh pretended not to be subject to.

man-mindedness and write as French and English historians used
to write, before they too were enmeshed in Teutonic philology.
They should write for every well-educated person to read and not
merely to exercise their own faculties of acumen and subtlety
while displaying prodigies of learning in the presence of fellow
athletes.

If not pleasant, it would be instructive reading; and by explain-
ing what reaction followed what action, it might go far toward
removing misunderstandings, perhaps might end with inducing
the Papists and Orthodox to insist in their myth and ritual less
and less on the passion and death of their founder, the root of so
much anti-Semitism implanted in the preconscious minds of innocent infants.* The cry of *Los von Rom,* of *qui nous délivrera
des Grecs et des Romains,* precursors of German Nazism and
French collaborationism, may again and again threaten everything
that in our civilization comes from both the classical and Hebrew
worlds. We shall have to pass over differences in order to save
with Christianity that heritage of the Mediterranean past which
modern barbarians resent as bitterly as ever Kleist's Hermann did.

May 31st

IT WOULD NOT BE FAIR to end without a word about assimilation. It is inevitable. The emancipated Jew will not return of his
free will to a mental and spiritual ghetto, nor can he be forced to
it. The Jew still remaining in this ghetto aspires to get away unless his mediocrity, petty ambitions, material interests, or indeed
his nationalistic religiosity keeps him there. Out in the world, he
finds it increasingly irksome to follow the isolating, antisocial precepts and ordinances concerning food, clothing, ritual, cleanli-
ness, and sexual life, and no less difficult to follow the nobler enactments regarding worship and the study of the Torah. He ends
by compromising with his religious habits, usages, and beliefs,

---

* A good start toward the goal has been made by James Parker in two readable
and informing books, published by the Soncino Press, London: *The Conflict of the
Church and the Synagogue,* 1934, and *The Jew in the Mediaeval Community,* 1938.

and dropping them one by one, till little is left except a vague Deism.

At the beginning of the Nazi persecutions of the Jews, one of the most reputed German-Jewish intellectuals told me that it would take another two thousand years before complete assimilation could take place. On the other hand, a remarkably intelligent German gentlewoman assured me that it would have happened before the end of the present century if only Hitler had not started his mad campaign.

There have been and there may be again Hitlers not only without but within Jewry. The Synagogue that maltreated Uriel da Costa and Spinoza at Amsterdam was composed of so many little Hitlers. A true precursor of Hitler in preventing assimilation was the prophet Elijah. A rather open-minded king of Israel, Ahab by name, wedded a Tyrian who not only did not worship the tribalized Jehovah but brought with her a civilization at least materially higher, and tried to induce her husband to adopt it. Against this threat of assimilation, Elijah with his young dervishes raged furiously, rousing the backwoodsmen to revolt and to murder Jezebel. The worst they had to tell of her was the story of Naboth's vineyard. I ask what would happen nowadays to an individual who stood against the sovereign in the way Naboth did?

Elijah's nationalism did not avail. The northern tribes were too closely related to their Phoenician brothers and Aramaic cousins in blood, in speech, in thought, in feeling, to escape the lure of their more attractive ways of life. Soon their existence as an independent state was put an end to. The politically minded were dragged to Assyria and there for the most part disappeared, dissolved into the kindred population. Of the remainder the more enterprising must have gone over to the Sidonians and Tyrians, contributing who shall tell how much to the building up of Carthage, to the splendor and misery of Semitic power in the Western Mediterranean. The others remained on the land and became the Samarians, who until the sixth century were a numerous community scattered over the Empire like their brothers, the Jews. Between them fraternal hatred raged.

The Judeans meanwhile clung to their rocks jutting up between the Dead Sea and the lowland. They were comparatively safe from intrusion, and as late as the fifth century B.C., Herodotus, who took such an interest in Egypt and Persia and all that lay between, did not know of their existence, neither their tribal name nor the name of their city, Jerusalem. And yet he may have traveled over the road connecting the two empires that passed almost within sight of that same city. Foreign influence touched them too little to prevent their integrating into a close-knit community, impenetrable and impermeable. Even when they too lost their independence, and their leading families were dragged into captivity, many returned from Babylon and established the Temple state—a political entity not rare in Syria and Asia Minor—that lasted till the destruction of Jerusalem and did not wholly perish before the second-century rebellion of Bar-Cochba and its bitter consequences.

But were these Judeans Israelites? In the farewell address put by the Deuteronomist into the mouth of Moses so little is made of Judea that its mention seems like an afterthought prefixed later. Deborah in her glorious song does not name it at all. They may have been latecomers, surging from the Arabian desert and not taking easily to city civilization. Among them Elijah's fanatical tribalism prevailed, producing a ghetto state from which emerged the Judaism that, for good or for evil, has had a "dynamic" formative influence on the white man's world which is still operative and likely to be so for many years to come.

Persecution from without did much more than compulsion, that is to say persecution within to prevent assimilation. But for the violent impatience of Antiochus Epiphanes there would have been no Judas Maccabaeus, and Hellenism might have made sufficient headway to affect the history of the entire white race. Incipient rabbinical Judaism might have been far too enfeebled to beget two daughters like Christianity and Islam.

Although arrested, assimilation was not killed. I suspect that not only the Books of Wisdom in the Bible were done under Hellenic influence, but that even prose masterpieces like Esther,

Ruth, and Tobit, so un-Semitic in form, were written by Hellenized Jews. In Alexandria Philo's head was turned by Plato, the metaphysical, theosophic Plato, the mystagogue Plato, not the delicate ironist and poetical visionary, the ethical and political thinker and king of prose writers. Called to book by his mental habits, that is to say his conscience, or perchance by tribal bonzes, Philo made the acrobatic attempt to reconcile his Platonism with Judaism, and foisted on the world not only the allegorical interpretation of the Bible but the "Logos" and a cloud of ever more misty thought connected with that alluring word. It should be remembered that without them Christian theology could scarcely have taken the senseless shape it has, regardless of the Jesus of the Gospels, and in opposition to His spirit. It was Philo's application of allegory to the Old Testament that enabled the Church Fathers to oust the Chosen People from their inheritance and to assert that they, the Christians, were the true Israel. The rapid expansion of Pauline and Hellenistic Christianity and the opposition encountered in the Synagogue led to cruel hatred on both sides; and then, on the victory of the Church, to legislation that limited the Jews' activities, confined them more and more, and finally cooped them up in ghettoes. There they festered and by the end of the eighth century persecution had reduced them to such isolation, not obligatory, but self-imposed, that they would not even use the Greek or Latin alphabet as hitherto but wrote their vernacular in Chaldaic or in cursive Aramaic, as still in our day is the case with Yiddish. For a thousand years to come the ghettoes in Christian lands would not permit acquaintance with the Latin character. As late as towards the end of the eighteenth century Salomon Maimon, wishing to acquire it, had to have recourse to Robinson Crusoe expedients.

And yet the outer world seeped in and the ghetto oozed with Neoplatonic, Gnostic and Manichaean notions—some of which got coagulated and shaped into the Zohar and other cabalistic writings—while many a Catholic superstition and practice found its way into the Jewish home.

How much more difficult for the Jew out of the ghetto to remain uninfluenced by the civilization of the people about him! If he uses their language he cannot avoid its reaction on his mind and heart. This language is based on Christianity, as, of course, is the rest of our civilization. Every practice as well as every law, every ethical standard, every attitude toward our fellow men is based on Christianity or colored by it. No one can escape its pervasive, penetrating, absorbing influence.

The more advanced do not attempt to oppose it. The others must follow. Unless persecution retards it, in our country assimilation cannot be so far away, is in fact already here, although more in deed than in name.

We make as much of Christmas as the rest of our fellow citizens, and of the other Christian holidays and Sundays scarcely less. Unconsciously we follow the customs and folkways of our neighbors and, unlike St. Paul, who boasted of being more Jewish than other Jews, we aspire to be no less American than other Americans. And we genuinely feel so. Even our sewing women speak of our "Pilgrim Fathers" as if they were descended from them.

But to be an American or indeed a Briton, Frenchman, or any other European, is to be a Christian. Not, of course, as the member of a church or suscriber to a creed or dogma, but as a participant of a civilization that we can no more shut out than the air we breathe.

A year or two ago Benedetto Croce published a pamphlet entitled "Why We Must Call Ourselves Christians." It will surely appear in English translation before this is published. I recommend it to my readers. They know that this eminent philosopher, literary historian, critic, and interpreter is emancipated from specifically Christian theology, prejudices, aspirations, rituals, and usages. Yet he feels that he must call himself "Christian."

I often used to meditate on the fact that before Hitler rendered Jew-conscious Yakuts and Tibetans, Kamchatkans and Japanese, Javanese and Eskimos, Andaman Islanders and Hindus, it would not have occurred to any of these far-flung nations crawling over the earth's rind that a European Jew—I mean European in the cultural, not in the geographical, sense—that a European who happened to be a Jew was not a Christian.

Christianity as the product of European history is inescapable unless a ghetto were still to be had. You cannot establish such insulators in Western lands. And yet the alternative remains: complete isolation or assimilation.

June 1st

WE ARE READING Shakespeare and Racine side by side. I enjoy the Frenchman for what he is. But how different! Always the heroic, superman, grand, magniloquent, even when declaiming—and he is always declaiming—sentiments of exquisite tenderness and subtilty. He never derogates from his statuesque perfection. I love the music of his verse and his world freed from physical and economic wants and restrictions, a world of people at liberty to give vent to their passions with nothing to consider except similar qualities in others, as much "above the clouds" as themselves. They give me something of the same sensation that I get from Cosimo Tura's pictures—only they are not contorted, and distorted, and they live in noble architecture more to my taste.

Think of Frenchmen brought up from early years on this heroic eloquence. Surely it must falsify values of real life and inspire them with rhetorical sentiments that make them incapable of looking superpersonal affairs, international affairs, for instance, straight in the face.

Shakespeare, on the other hand, seldom heroizes his characters. They remain human, no matter how much raised above other human bipeds by situation or individual qualities. The comic, the humorous interludes bring one back to workaday existence however tragic and superhuman the theme may be.

But what a puzzle Shakespeare remains! We have now read his comedies as well as *The Tempest* and all the Roman plays except *Antony and Cleopatra*. They are best when most lyrical—*As You Like It, Midsummer Night's Dream, Romeo and Juliet,* some scenes in *The Merchant of Venice,* and others everywhere. I cannot understand Shakespeare's inequalities. *Coriolanus* is so dull and *Timon* so ranting, yet they were composed after *Julius Caesar* and after the great tragedies. How account for such a fall! Perhaps Shakespeare was sick and tired.

As must have been the case with Dickens when he wrote the *Tale of Two Cities,* which we are finishing. It is rant, sob-stuff, and bad Carlylese throughout, with but few touches of the Dickens who wrote *David Copperfield.*

June 3d

A MONTH has gone by without my jotting down a word about current events and the gossip they exhale, which, let me add, suffers no slight "sea change" before it reaches me. It reaches others, even those placed near actualities, in shape little more defined and of closer correspondence to what happened.

For three weeks no daily or weekly has arrived from Germany. I cannot believe that this failure is due to difficulties of transport only. I have had a letter from Stockholm. It had to cross the Reich and its suburbs and yet reached me in ten days. It would look as if the Nazis had reason for not wishing their troops in Italy to read the press of the Fatherland, and to learn what goes on and what is thought there.

One of the last weeklies that I perused was *Das Reich.* Therein Goebbels, taking as usual the pose of the philosophical historian, spoke of the uncertainties of war and that this one had turned idiotic, with no reason for going on. But if continued it must be, the Germans were ready to defend the Fatherland against the Anglo-Saxon mercenaries who were not fighting for their homes, their wives, their children, etc., etc.

Between the lines, one read an appeal to the Allies for a peace of compromise. The same desire lies behind the insistence that they are ready to carry on the war ten years—in short, that they will never yield the fortress, Germania.

Not so long ago they spoke only of the Fortress Europa. Since then it has shrunk a bit, but this dungeon they mean to keep. Yet I am told that they are not sure they can. They even speak of Soviet troops' sweeping across from the Carpathians to the Rhine. Perhaps this fear is cast upon the waters with the intention of its infecting with a dread of the Cossack all who live to the west of that stream. Again propaganda in favor of compromise.

The "Atlantic Radio" is generally so jammed that one gets little out of it. That little tells of dreadful conditions in Germany and growing discontent, even within the Nazi ranks. The wisdom of pumping so many foreign workers into the Reich is being questioned, as well as the miscellaneous employment of untrained women and girls.

I hear that in Naziland there must be some twenty million foreign laborers and that one seldom hears German spoken in the streets. It seems that the most pliable are the Russians, some of whom are employed as "noncombatants" on all fronts, as they certainly are here in Italy. Next come the French. Of Anglo-Saxons one never hears.

Press gangs seize people here too, not only men but women, and pack them off to do slave labor in Germany. The Nazis are determined to get their one and a half million Italians to replace as many Germans for the front.

When the smash comes, how will these twenty and perhaps more than twenty million workers from occupied and satellite countries behave? Will there be sufficient police to deal with them? Do the Germans rely on their being too reduced by semi-starvation and hardships to take action? Or do they count on the Allies' occupying their country so quickly that the slaves will have no time to organize a vindictive revolt?

The Germans complain that their Far Eastern twins, the Japanese, do not prevent Chinese coolies from going by the hundreds of thousands to Siberia to replace Russians drawn to the front. I wonder how many other coolies work for the Japanese. It would be absurd to suppose that the lowest-rank Chinaman had political preferences.

❋   ❋   ❋

Meanwhile, here the last call not to dinner, but to arms, combined with the threat of the death penalty to those who do not answer, has resulted in some thirty thousand appearing at the recruiting stations. They were treated like returned prodigals and one case under our notice is characteristic. It is of a youth who having been enrolled six months ago had deserted, and was in hiding. Tired of remaining cooped up in his room, he answered the call of military authorities. They, who a few months ago had taken him as fit for the front, now invalided him with the order to appear again after 360 days precisely.

This would give a certain substance to what is said and believed by his defenders: that Mussolini has insisted so much on getting Italians liable to service into the army, in order to save them from being sent as coolies to Germany. I have my doubts, seeing a similar apology was offered for his declaring war on France. It was to save Italy from being occupied by the Nazis and from the consequences of such an occupation as already exemplified not only by belligerent countries like France, but by one which, like Poland, had not wanted war, or by neutrals like Holland and Belgium, which had not so much as dreamt of it.

*　　*　　*

The contemptuous attitude of Nazi-minded Italian bourgeois toward the bands seems to be unjustified. No doubt many are no better than what these moneyed, comfortably situated people say. Others are a thorn in the flesh of the occupying troops, whether German forces or Fascist riffraff. They help to pull up rails, wreck trains, destroy bridges, and they keep in touch with the Allies, who, like Elijah's raven, supply them not only with money but with arms and ammunition for defense, receiving in exchange precise information about Nazi-Fascist doings. These bands fight when necessary, and I understand that the Germans are far from sharing the contempt for them that some Italians express.

A German press agent has been here and, speaking of the Allied bombings of Germany, insisted that they are largely done to

terrify. Then he went on to explain them on the ground that Anglo-Saxons were convinced that a German policy of terror can be
defeated and destroyed only by proving that it could be out-
trumped by superior terror.

The same press attaché said that American prisoners cannot
be made to answer questions about fighting or war. Not so much
out of reticence as lack of interest. The war has to be fought to
an end; but their preoccupation is only with what is to happen
afterwards, how work will be found for thirty million now engaged in war industries, not to speak of how, when returned to
strictly economic conditions, they are to be cured of the wasteful
habits there acquired.

For the last weeks the numerous poor in Rome have lived on
the edge of starvation, as no supplies could reach the town, isolated as it was by American aviation rendering traffic, whether
by rail or road, too dangerous to be attempted.

To such a degree rises the Italo-Nazi cult of the German forces
that their retreats south of Rome are described as voluntary, occasioned by deeper insight into the strategic problem, never as consequence of the enemy's superiority. Why should I be surprised,
I who remember reading some years after the last war, in one of
the most respected Italian dailies, that Caporetto was the greatest
victory of that war? How this was argued I cannot recall. It suffices that it was declared with no paradoxical and no comic intention, in a responsible organ of Italian public opinion.

June 5th

YESTERDAY Rome was evacuated by the Germans, whose radio
boasts of this forced retreat as a great victory. A few days ago
they were still insisting that Rome must be held at all costs. Military necessity required it, and prestige demanded it—prestige
of which they know so well the value. But Hitler, the completest
cynic who ever ruled, knows that his subjects do not recall today
what he insisted upon yesterday, and that he can safely urge at
this hour the opposite of what he said four and twenty hours ago.

When Mussolini declared war against the United States, it seemed fantastic that Italy should be making war against us who never had stood in its way, never opposed its interests, never did worse than sending our heiresses to enrich the penniless gentry, and our tourists to spend their money here. At home we received them and treated them fully as well as other immigrants. Moreover, when Fascism was young it took American methods for its model, sought our friendship and found it, and some of its most showy measures were taken to impress us, as for instance trains that arrived on time, roads made fit for fast driving, museums free of charge, Herculaneum to be excavated, etc., etc.

All this went by the board in Mussolini's theatrical rage against the British, unaware that in the present historical horizon America would not fail to run to the aid of an England in danger.

And now, more incredible still, American and British troops, after beating the toughest, most highly trained, most expert army the world has ever seen, are marching in triumph through the streets of Rome, "the Holy City," as the godless Fascists have had the impudence to call it.

Mussolini has decreed three days' mourning, despite the Nazi pretense that they freely abandoned Rome, a burden they were happy to unload on the Allies.

The Roman population seems to be of another mind. Much cheering, hugging, smothering with flowers is of course the tribute that a Mediterranean crowd offers to any conqueror. The majority, however, has welcomed them as liberators from abuses, from oppression, from torture, not to speak of fast-approaching starvation. It is rumored—but denied by the Nazi-minded—that jubilating Romans packed full the Square of St. Peter and were blessed by His Holiness. I can believe it. He too must feel relieved; for to the last minute he risked being dragged captive to Germany.

As the end of Nazi-Fascist tyranny approaches, it grows more and more beastly and wicked. Credible accounts reach me of revolting tortures, physical as well as moral, that they inflict. The boss of the Arezzo district seems to have been the worst yet. Even defenders of the Mussolinian faith acknowledge this, but add boastfully that he has been transferred. Yes. Nobody left to wreak himself on, he has gone to fresh woods and pastures new.

At the same time equally credible reports come through of thoroughly trained, completely equipped, well-organized groups, waiting for the signal to act against Nazis and Quislings. It would make me happy if Tuscans proved able to rouse themselves from their lethargy and "do their bit" in freeing themselves from the corrupting, un-manning and dehumanizing rule under which they have cowered and quaked for over twenty years.

June 6th

THE GERMAN RADIO brings news of Allied landings in the estuary of the Seine, as well as on the Cherbourg peninsula.

No doubt an infantry and artillery invasion of the Fortress Germania and its outer defenses is necessary to convince people who believe in bayonets and cannons only, that the Anglo-Saxons too can use these obsolescent arms.

As for me, I am more than ever of the opinion that for free people, like ours, the air is the most suitable and effective arm. Our young men are natural mechanics, are sportsmen to a daredevil degree. They should be encouraged to volunteer in aerial forces; and these should be sufficiently strong and ready to inspire fear in the hearts of future Hitlers, not to speak of verbal warriors like Mussolini. We could then guarantee Abyssinias, Albanias, Polands, Hellenic kingdoms against aggression and nobody so rash as to beard us. If the Anglo-Saxons had had five years ago the air armies they have now, would Hitler have ventured his throw? He made it because he relied on his mastery of the air. Neither he nor his chum Göring knew what they were doing. As a matter of fact, "Unser Hermann" seems to have retired from war and politics, and to be devoting himself to collecting works of art. Does he expect to retain them when the war is over? Is he acting automatically out of habit, or to impress his victims, the German people, that he does not doubt of victory and the Reich's ability to keep what it has seized, robbed, and raffled in every occupied and satellite country?

There will be a cry on our side for restoration of all the Nazis have taken; and I should approve of making them give up to the farthing's worth everything they have snatched. What has been destroyed or lost in consequence of their predatoriness, I should make them repay not with Mediterranean masterpieces but Teutonic ones, German, Flemish, Dutch. Of these, claimed by Teutomaniacs as flesh of their flesh, the museums of the Reich have more than enough. They could spare a percentage of their Van Eycks, their Roger van der Weydens, their Van der Goes, as well as their Master of the Death of the Virgin and similar fifteenth-century Rhenish and Hanseatic artists. I would leave them their Dürers, their Holbeins, their Cranachs even, but not all their Baldungs. Italian, Greek, and other classically inspired works I should let them retain in the hope that their civilizing, humanizing influence will affect them as it did their grandfathers and great-grandfathers.

June 7th

TOTALITARIAN WAR as conducted at present, with conscript armies and labor, nobody of an age and health "to do his bit" exempted, is a return to primitive savagery, when one tribe or clan sought to exterminate another standing in its way, and every neighbor north and south, east and west, was held as standing in the way, even as now.

Seeing that no individuals except invalids and dotards are exempt from work of some sort to achieve victory, why go on making the pretotalitarian difference between soldier and civilian? Soldiers are still treated as a class apart and above, way above, civilians.

As an instance let me cite my own case. I am a civilian prisoner in Italy. If I were a soldier, I should be corresponding with relations in about a tenth of the time. The same Red Cross that brings the trooper news from America in two months or so takes two

years or eighteen months at least to bring me twenty-five words
from my sisters.

It is not the fault of the so well-instructed Swiss institutions. It
is our censorship. A letter sent through the Red Cross is forwarded
to an inquiry office, where it is kept a year and a half or more.
Why? Either to exhaust the possible effects of treasonable communication or because the office takes time. Our censorship is so
cautious that it will not even allow the delivery of a cable sent
from Switzerland saying that So-and-so is well, unless it makes
sure that So-and-so is not bodily in an enemy country.

Censorships seem to be carried on in our countries, and here
in Italy, by unpaid amateurs to start with and then by hirelings
for the most part with no training and even less intellectual
preparation. I could tales unfold!

The only censorship which, since the beginning of this war, has
worked with dispatch, discretion, and common sense has been the
German one. Whether from the homeland or from occupied territories, letters have reached me in reasonable time; moreover, the
correspondents have been allowed to write what they pleased
about the difficulties and follies they encountered and to criticize
what they pleased, provided of course that they kept away from
military matters.

June 8th

INSTEAD OF DICKENS and his distressing *Tale of Two Cities,* we
are now reading the ferocious historical books of the Old Testament. What is Torquemada or any worse persecutor, if one there
be, of Christian times compared with that nationalistic archfa-
natic the prophet Elijah! But the stuff has an incomparable grip
of human reality at its average worst and best. It never talks of
actions and feelings of which we do not feel ourselves capable.

At the same time we go on with Shakespeare and Racine.
Othello is too poignant, too painful, and almost makes one wish
Shakespeare had some of Racine's marmoreal coolness and dis-
tance. The Frenchman never reaches emotion except through

tranquillity. This morning we finished *Macbeth,* which did not lacerate me at all. It is far enough from actuality to carry one on the wings of wondrous verse to the sunset and back to the sunrise and forward, without churning up one's insides. What poetry is there, not only as idea and image but as verse! Truly, Shakespeare was the greatest transmuter, the greatest verbal alchemist that ever wrote.

Pity he never took a Biblical theme. What might he not have done with it—say the story of Saul and David, and Jonathan, and Samuel!

June 9th

I SCARCELY KNOW a German who does not want the victory of his army, and I certainly know no German who does not yearn for the downfall of the Nazis. The same German wants both and seems incapable of thinking things out to the end, and saying that if the army wins the victory will not be theirs but of the Nazis. In fact, if the German army won the war it might start Nazism on its run for a thousand years, as predicted by its Brigham Young, I mean Adolf Hitler.

With my Italian friends it is not the same. They are too intelligent to believe that the end of Fascism would follow the triumph of Axis arms. They are courageous enough to sacrifice military glory to rationally human politics. In the upper classes, however, there remains a minority who, while not desiring the triumph of Hitler and his hosts, still seethe so much with hatred of England that they will not allow the superiority of Allied arms. They chafe over every move, pointing to Allied stupidity and contrasting it with the miraculous intelligence of the Germans. For these, their sympathies remain so strong that in their hearts they would like them to smite the Anglo-Saxons, to drive them into the sea from Italy, and to prepare for them a worse Dunkirk in France. They go on believing that there will be returns of fortune, and that somehow German military genius will prevail. Yet in these same hearts there is no desire for the imposition of Nazi-Fascist rule upon their own or other countries. It is singular how incapable of mental integration people remain, particularly in matters political, and how comfortably they squat on both horns of a dilemma.

Human incapacity for integration is notorious, and an historical account of it would fill a library. In the restricted matter of political thinking, or rather feeling, integration seems not to exist for most people.

Perhaps it is just as well; for the few who cherish and cultivate it arrive quickly at state worship and totalitarianism as by Fascists and Nazis practiced and preached. Better far the "muddling through" which accounts for the political superiority of Anglo-Saxons up till now. I begin to fear that in America particularly we are getting too impatient for an integration that, if hurried, will be premature, and even disintegrating, in the end.

June 10th

IT IS RUMORED in Florence that bands, alias brigands, alias rebels, have occupied Siena and Perugia. I wish it were so. I should like them to give the lie to the stories that reach me according to which these boys took to the woods out of distaste for soldiering, and sheer cowardice.

Graziani, head of the specter-Fascist army, has issued a decree that Italians drafted as laborers to Germany will be considered as soldiers at the front. If without permission they return to Italy, they will be treated as deserters.

Senator Contini and his son have been arrested. Major Carità made a perquisition in their country house, accusing them of harboring weapons and supplies for the bands. He found none but carried away a diary which he pretends has incriminating entries. He will release them on the payment of three million lire, at present rate of exchange something like twenty-five thousand dollars.

Jewish acquaintances of mine have been threatened with the

worst if they did not immediately pay a ransom. They have com-
promised on half a million to be paid at once and as much again
next October. The last item is mere face-saving, of course.

These figures prove how modest are Italians in their financial
expectations. The case is different in the realm of fancy—the valuations of art objects, for instance. Their journalistic imagination
mounts sky-high and, being seldom called back to earth, puts
prices on pictures at figures that have no relation to what they
would fetch at Christie's, or at the Hôtel Drouot.

June 11th

SIX YEARS and more have passed since I have perused an Italian
newspaper. Most of this time I have been an assiduous student of
the German press. This is in essence no less mendacious, no less
sneering, jeering, and vulgar than the Italian. But it does not offend me so much.

Why? The reason must be that German abominations do not
touch me so closely, because Germans are remoter from me than
Italians. After living for fifty years in the midst of Italians and
with them, everything they do and say comes home to me almost
as if they were my own people.

Now it is well known that the bad behavior, the stupidity, and
above all the vulgarity of one's own people sting and smart and
touch us to the quick.

Some of my disgust with the Italian press is due to the fact that
Italians seem to regard as indecently naked a substantive that is
not wrapped up and swaddled with adjectives. In the case of a
suspected adversary no epithet is too absurd. Thus when Richard
Norton some thirty-three years ago led an archaeological expedition to Cyrene, the Italian press, including the so authoritative
Corriere della Sera, incapable of believing that the enterprise did
not mask annexationistic intentions with regard to territory considered by them as an Italian reversion, applied to him every term
of abuse, of which the least was "codfish." Who knows what that
conceals! I have never been able to discover.

June 12th

THE FEW WORDS jotted down yesterday about our tolerance of
vulgarity in another nationality that it is hard to put up with in
our own reminds me of a matter that has been in my thoughts for
fifty years and more. It is this.

I first read Dante with Charles Eliot Norton at Harvard in
1885. I could not utter a phrase in Italian, and knew it as one
spells out a dead tongue. Nevertheless, the *Divine Comedy* made
me breathless as it loomed up before me, and I panted to reach
up to it.

Three years later I was residing in Florence, learning its living
spoken language. For an hour or more every morning I conned my
Dante.

After a while I began to be aware—and this awareness grew
upon me as the years went by and my familiarity with the workaday speech of Tuscany increased—that although I understood its
greatest poet better and better and loved his passages of pure
poetry ever more feelingly, yet a certain glory was departing from
his trilogy. Not merely that so much of it lost interest and progressively bored me, as I realized that Dante had compressed his
spiritual universe only less than his physical one into a limited
compass, and made it too much like an ingeniously contrived
clock whose scope it was to ring out perpetual praise of its Maker;
not that alone.

There was something else.

When we read a dead language or a living one that we do not
speak, few or any words or phrases we encounter are linked with
commonplace, or mean, or sordid, or disgusting associations. That
fact removes them from the workaday atmosphere into a more
refined spiritually, a purer and nobler one. Single words in a foreign tongue may have a splendor in our eyes that those who ordi-
narily use them do not feel, or deliberately avoid feeling. We
know of the old lady who took such comfort in hearing or uttering
the word "Mesopotamia," or about the sentimental German who

on her first visit to Italy read out the word *latrina* as her train stopped at a station, and was enraptured by it.

Which reminds me of the Chinese diplomatist who, on being introduced into a Boston drawing room, discovered there conspicuously displayed Kienlung vases, beautiful indeed as ceramics, but destined in China to more humble and intimate use.

Familiarity breeds insensibility, and every Western language since the early Renaissance has periodically tried to refresh itself first with wholesale draughts of Latin and Greek, more recently with borrowing from each other, and in the last hundred years with increasing doses of slang, thieves' lingo, and shoptalk; so that at the present rate, classical English and perhaps classical French as well may cease to be understood except by the learned in some few generations.

It is well known that the less we are acquainted with a foreign language, provided we know it at all, the more likely are we to interlard our talk with it. When we get to be nearly as much at home with that language, its vocabulary and idiomatic expressions, as with our own, it ceases to enjoy the fascination of being *"Herrlich wie am ersten Tag"*—glorious as on the day of creation.

There can be no doubt but that subjective remoteness—it need not be objective—lends enchantment to speech as to space. We recall Ruth Draper's fashionable lady who in her overcrowded, futile life finds no leisure for her snobbish aspiration to read Dante, and getting no further than *nel mezzo del cammin* discovers there a height and depth of meaning that the equivalent phrase in New Yorkese would never have yielded.

And our continued employing of Biblical phraseology, stigmatized as Wardour Street English, or of the *style noble* in French —what is it but the effort to get away from Wardour Street and the Boul' Miche?

This train of thought leads me to wonder whether—returning to where we began—English-speaking readers of Dante do not overestimate him, as we all perhaps overestimate Latin and even Greek writers, because of the glamour shed upon him by unfamiliarity with the language in which he wrote, as certainly is the case with the admiration foreigners have for Byron.

On the other hand, our so eerie American slang and its equivalent French *argot*, as faintly displayed in Céline, is an attempt to steer clear of the commonplace and overfamiliar by ducking under it instead of rising above it. I enjoy it, and shall not be ungrateful enough to pretend to denounce it. Yet I cannot refrain from saying that its psychological foundation is ignorance or neglect of idiomatic English or French, both competent enough to express anything we can have to say, provided we are able to exploit their resources. Slang, no matter how brilliant, is but froth and bubble over the placid depth of classical speech.

June 17th

ANNIVERSARY of Bunker Hill! When I was a small boy it meant a holiday comprising a pilgrimage to the monument, and pleasant hours spent in play with boa-constrictor cordage in the Charlestown Navy Yard.

Nearly seventy years later I am here in Italy under German occupation, but with the Anglo-Saxons approaching, and their guns almost audible.

Meanwhile, Fascists are skedaddling and evacuating as fast as they can. One hears of fifteen thousand going—a veritable exodus —men, women, and children. Why are they going, what are they afraid of? They must feel guilty, well aware of what they have done, and what reprisals to expect. If they stayed, most of them would be agreeably disappointed. Few have anything to fear from our authorities, and not too much from theirs. No doubt they dread payment in kind—and what kind!—from neighbors they have maltreated or humiliated.

Celle, near Pistoia, the magnificently romantic seat of our friend the bibliophile De Marinis, has for months been preparing to house the German General Staff and its chief, Marshal Kesselring. It would seem that he is there now, incog, but his real presence betrayed by the distance kept by all who approach him. They say he spends hours together staring at the landscape, rapt in thought and looking the picture of misery.

A fluke brought me ten days of the *Neue Zürcher Zeitung* and as many of the *Deutsche Allgemeine*. The differences and contrasts are interesting. The German daily boasts, blusters, jeers, sneers, insults, rejoices in what to us is iniquity, while the Swiss dispassionately looks around the circle of the earth, espying what can interest a humanized man, under present conditions. Nothing escapes its observation and its humane as well as rational comment. I know no other daily so universally well informed—almost as if war opposed no difficulties to collecting and publishing disinterested information.

Not all of it from our side is pleasant reading. Plans for the future, social, economic, international. How I dread self-satisfied dogmatism not alone on the part of the new lords risen from the coal mine and the locomotive, but of the Cambridge paragons, the Robespierres of finance. They know what they want. Who does not? But they have no idea what it will cost to get it—how much more than any return on the investment.

A young officer has joined us, fresh from a German concentration camp situated near Brest Litovsk. He wintered in a log house, with the cold and snow driving in through the chinks, but yet keeping fairly warm. For food they had twice a day—they, Italian officers—five boiled potatoes. They had soup consisting of hot water with lumps of grease thrown in. They had to do their own washing, which they hung up to dry in the hut they occupied. No books, no dailies, no radio, no news of any kind, no writing paper, seldom a word or a parcel from home. No contact with any human being outside the camp. Death, if they succeeded in approaching a German female, death for the Italian and the female as well. Utterly cut off!

When the armistice between Italy and the Allies was declared, the superior officers, from army chiefs down, with rare exceptions, funked and disappeared. They would take no responsibility and give no orders. A million and a half Italian troops who, if properly

led, still had fight in them, were carried off like sheep to Nazi concentration camps. Half a million of them are already dead of starvation and hardship.

This same officer blames the King of Italy as the first deserter.
I have no clear opinion of this so unintelligible personage. Is he a
monster of indifference, a chicken-livered egoist caring for nothing but his throne and his dynasty—if even for these?

I nearly forgot to mention that the *Deutsche Allgemeine
Zeitung,* organ of the Berlin upper classes, continues to rejoice
in the progressive de-Judaizing of Hungary. I supposed it would
stop with finance, great commerce, and the professions. Not at
all! It goes down to the petty trades and careers. It would seem
that in Hungary as in Poland the humbler Christian natives followed no occupation but shepherding, farming, and soldiering.
All else was left to the Jews.

What will happen to these putative descendants of the Hebrew
patriarchs is of small interest. But how will life go on in Hungary
when the Israelites are not allowed to exercise any of their usual
occupations? Who will shoe horses, who will build and repair
houses? Who will sell bread and salt, who will make shoes and
clothes, who will drive them when they have to go to town, who
will doctor them or supply them with medicines? It would seem
that without the Jews, Hungary would fall back into a neolithic
condition. The magnates have Vienna, Paris, and their shooting.
But the rest of the Hungarians!

June 18th

FINISHED Marie Bashkirtseff's *Journal.* Most of it is boring, endlessly repetitious. But she was precocious to an unusual degree
and at twelve, although she feels like a *Backfisch*—a flapper—
she writes like a gifted grownup.

She is possessed by the ambition to excel, whether in love, in
society, in music, or in painting. It haunts her night and day. As
she has no inhibitions—a rare thing seventy years ago—she puts
down everything she feels and thinks. And she puts it down in

straightforward, clear language; but she never refers to anything below the belt.

Having done with flirtation, and her voice giving out, she turns to painting, frequents Julian's studios, enjoys the instruction of Tony Robert-Fleury and, toward the end, of Bastien Lepage. With the last, she gets on intimate terms, adoring him as an artist, and all but loving him as a man. She is touched by his suffering, as he is dying, although he was destined to outlive her, if only by days.

She never loses sight of her rank, her wealth, her privileges. Yet she sees through the vapidity of society, and particularly of her set in Russia. Indeed, writing between fifty and forty years before the Bolshevik revolution, she describes a society that can give no reason for being allowed to live on, to be borne at such expense to the community at large.

She can have generous outbursts of extrapersonal feeling, as over the death of the Prince Imperial and the end of Gambetta. About this so mysterious figure she writes eloquently, appreciatively, convincingly. Perhaps out of admiration for him, she has outbursts of enthusiasm for the republic, and finds words of scorn for its reactionary opponents.

The most important part of the journal is concerned with her zest, her ambition, her passion as a painter. She feels that she could be one, must win recognition, and whether or not, do, excel, and achieve what will satisfy her.

I could wish, by the way, that the glib writers on the artist in general, and the painter in particular, would read her journal. They would understand better what it means to be a painter, what an effort, what a torment, what an agony it is to become one. How little philosophy, metaphysics, sociology, cosmology, ontology, etc., etc., enter into his occupations and preoccupations. How absorbed the painter is day and night by the question of "how," and how seldom by "what," how much by technique, and how little by anything else. Never a word about the subject matter as concept or idea, but always as something to exercise your technical ability.

She was learned after a fashion, seeming to have some acquaintance with Latin, well-read in the classics, in translation probably, reading history intelligently and delighted to discover that Stendhal was fascinating and Zola almost great. Later, after perusing Vogüé's articles on Tolstoi, she devours *War and Peace* and finds no higher praise than to say that he was as good as Zola. She enjoys Turgenev and has the good taste to prefer the *Mémoires d'un Chasseur*—the stories of a squire out shooting—to his society novels.

Two quotations from her journal will give a fair idea of her.

On September 5th, 1882, she writes: "I am a crazy creature plus awareness."

And on August 1st, 1884: "Will you believe it? Well, I am neither painter, nor sculptor, nor musician, nor woman, nor daughter, nor friend. All in me becomes material for observation, for reflection, and analysis. A look, a shape, a sound, a joy, a sorrow are instantly weighed, examined, proved, pigeonholed, taken account of. And when I have talked or written I am happy."

June 20th

FOR MILES TOGETHER the highway to Bologna is crowded with German soldiery tramping, motoring, employing carts, any and every obtainable vehicle, in their trek northwards. They take along all they could lay hands on, mattresses, blankets, woolens, clothes, pots and pans, spoons, knives, forks, pieces of furniture from houses they have occupied for months perhaps; every kind of foodstuff, oil and wine particularly. Not inanimate things alone, but cows and calves, oxen and horses, mules and asses, rabbits, geese, chickens, anything alive and edible.

Yesterday forenoon the clerks serving the railways were seized and without ceremony dragged off to the station to be sent north.

The Germans are not only destroying what may serve the Allies but taking with them whoever might help to rebuild the country they are evacuating. The same policy led them to take Blum, Daladier, and Weygand from France to be interned in Germany, and from Italy Cini, and millions of men from the various countries they occupied. That policy, by the way, dictated the treatment allotted to a million and a half Italians suffering and dying in Nazi concentration camps.

Assisi is in our hands and I envy my friend F. Mason Perkins for being liberated from the Fascist-Nazi incubus, which, no doubt, has been weighing crushingly on him, as on the rest of us.

As the day of liberation approaches I begin to have a new set of fears. In what condition shall I find my house? How long will it be before I can occupy it with comfort? What will be the behavior of Americans and British when they occupy Florence? Will they be pedantic or humane, gullible or sensible? Will they avoid the glib sirens on the wait for them, and their male instigators who believe you can get anywhere with an American if you feed and drench him and flatter his simple soul?

What I fear most is this: a legend has grown up and prevails here, the Lord knows through no action or fault of mine, about my political importance as an American. They cannot believe that at home, to the extent that I am known at all, I count only as an art critic. As a citizen, alien born, I should be of the second class, but living abroad and selling no American products, I rank at best as of the third class. I have no political acquaintances whom I could influence, I have no authority. Catch Italians believing a word of that! Every effort to enlighten confirms them in their conviction.

So I expect to be besieged by acquaintances and their relations, clients and dependents of acquaintances, expecting me to procure them exemptions, favors, privileges from the occupying Anglo-Saxons. As I shall rarely succeed, they will go away thinking that I, who could, would not help them.

With this I do not mean to say that Italians are greater believers in "pull" than the rest of us. I recall numerous cases of favors procured in France and even England by people in "high society" that it would not be easy to procure for the rest of us. And I need scarcely refer to what a Congressman, let alone a Senator, can procure for his constituents from the administration at Washington.

Human nature is not different from country to country. Under similar conditions and like pressure, it acts in pretty much the same way everywhere.

June 21st

PEOPLE GO ON saying: "Whatever you may think, Mussolini and Hitler are makers of history." There have been other such makers whom we do not admire for what they made. There was Ravaillac, who stabbed Henri IV and made history. There was Princip, who shot Francis Ferdinand and thereby started the First World War. There was the shoddy assassin Ante Pavelich, who murdered Alexander of Yugoslavia and also made history. Then there are the spectacular Asiatic conquerors, Genghis Khan and Tamerlane, to mention only the most notorious. But what kind of history did they make?

*   *   *

The dreamt-of world state, if not unfailingly liberal, might afford no escape to dissident individuals from the wrath of a Hitler who with his paladins had seized universal dominion.

Hitler has shown what is the position of an outlaw in every land submitted to his occupation or his hegemony. Imagine their fate if there had been no countries these could take refuge in.

My dream is not of a centralized world state but of an earth whence state has disappeared, and municipalities only are left, co-operating peacefully and happily with one another.

June 22d

FOR THE FIRST TIME in years I have been perusing not this or that play of Shakespeare but all of them in the accepted chronological order.

I venture to put down a few of the impressions made on me by this rapid survey, without stopping to ponder over the problems suggested, or to puzzle out the enigmas and obscurities of the text.

First and foremost the lyrical quality. Ariel-like, swift, leaping, dancing, surpassing anything I know except perhaps Aristophanes in his *Birds,* Shakespeare seems to lose no occasion for dashing off in lyrical ecstasy. And it is as a lyrical dramatist, first and foremost, that the plays mark him.

He is good at the stage business. He is better far in his deeply penetrating insight into human nature, and his charitable, kindly acceptance of its mixed fry of good and evil. He is still more marvelous in his gnomic sentences and passionately dispassionate reflections. Yet in each of these fields others, if only a few, have done as well and perhaps better.

Shakespeare reigns supreme as the poet of youthful, exuberant gaiety, of fairylike insubstantiality, of high spirits and joyousness.

I never before realized how much Goethe owes him in this respect. Not in this respect alone; more still, and not always happily, in the comic, facetious, and farcical episodes in his plays. *Faust* particularly has few episodes, few lines even, that do not smack of Shakespeare.

As much and more may be said of Hofmannsthal.

After his lyrical supremacy what impressed me most in this gallop through his plays is Shakespeare's genius for fooling, clowning, billingsgating, vituperating, mocking, jeering, etc., etc. What a vocabulary! There again, I can think of no parallel in European literature since Aristophanes.

None of these last heights could Shakespeare have attained if he did not have a supreme, unique gift of words. Others by the thousands and, in the course of the ages, by the millions may have felt, thought, imagined what he did, but were mute comparatively though great after a fashion. There has never been another European who could find not only adequate words but evocative, radiant, illuminating, transfiguring, as well as penetrating and revealing words for whatever idea, fancy, fact, reflection passed through his head.

After his supremacy in the world of words, what struck me most was his political wisdom, his political charity, his acquaintance with the crowd, and his singular insight into the demagogue. Take Thersites: Shakespeare has no little sympathy with him, and states his case eloquently and convincingly. At the same time he sees through him down to the envy which inspires him. His victors never fail to find noble words for the vanquished, not even Mark Antony for Brutus, not even the cold-blooded Octavius for the same Mark Antony.

Shakespeare seems to me more Shakespeare in *Macbeth* and *Lear* than in *Hamlet*. The last has no doubt his best-expressed and deepest thinking. The others rise higher and sink deeper, are endlessly more tragic, I venture to say Wagnerian, and despite Wagner's advantage of orchestra and voice, of the words interpreting the music and the music the words, they surpass even his *Tristan*. Far from filling me with horror as *Othello* does, *Lear* and *Macbeth*, like all sublime tragedy, lift me up into the peace of understanding.

Othello horrified me. Not the Moor, but Iago. No violence, no brutality affects me as does villainy, plotting, planning, out of jealousy, envy, and love of evil; compassing the despair of the innocent, and driving them to deeds of violence against others or themselves. Unconsciously, unwittingly we do evil enough. Life is at the expense of others. The more reason to avoid malignancy, by which I mean deliberate evil-doing, cold-blooded, carefully thought out mischief as a fine art, almost forgetting its end, while rejoicing in iniquity.

This reminds me to speak of Shakespeare's relation to Italy. So many of his plays take place there or have Italians among their *dramatis personae*. It is easy to account for it, without recourse to the improbable supposition that he had a personal and intimate acquaintance with that paradise and its people. As a matter of fact, most of the stories read in England at the end of the sixteenth century were Italian, drawn from Boccaccio, Cinzio, Bandello, etc. With the gift for living himself into others and their situations, with his command of words, the author of Shakespeare's plays could have had no difficulty in conjuring up an Italy as glamorous as, since then, many of us northerners have found it.

Parenthetically, let me add a word about the Elizabethan attitude towards Italy. English and French, let alone Spanish, history is no less full than Italian of deeds of treachery, villainy, monstrosity, and blood. Think of the later Plantagenets and Tudors, and what they could do!

None of them ever said it. That is the reason why Italians seemed such devils to people capable of doing as ill, and perhaps worse. The Italian put it into words: Machiavelli the inhumanity of statecraft, the storytellers deeds of darkness in private life.

The Anglo-Saxon has a dislike for self-consciousness and for putting into words, in clear phrase, and in logical exposition activities "human, too human," pursuing which, he cannot bear to have put before him in language that discloses the gulf yawning between his ideals and his conduct. Because he is but vaguely aware of what he is doing, he can flatter himself that he is always acting, or trying to act, up to the standards with which his class and station have fitted him out.

As for Shakespeare's deep tender humanity, where in literature can one find the like of the scene in *King John* between Arthur and Hubert, commissioned to blind him? I know nothing to compare with it, not even Oedipus and Antigone at Colonus. Nor the increasing depths of self-abasement and self-pity, yet never mean, petty, or sordid, as uttered by Richard II from the moment of his return from Ireland to the end. To the very end, as if pitying not himself, but anyone placed in the same situation. For depths of doubt, sorrow, despair, and resignation I can think of nothing to place above it or even beside it.

To these cursory and necessarily superficial impressions about the work I would add one, and one only, observation about the author. He must have been brought up a Papist. No born and trained English Protestant at that time of fierce controversy, clashing propaganda, and persecution could have had such a familiarity with Roman Catholic ritual, practice, folklore, as well as dogma and church policy. Who has stated Vatican claims through the ages as his Pandulph in *King John!*

Finally, let me mention his love of romance and the romantic, his feeling for the glamor of the Orient. Few great writers have understood as he the magic of evocative names.

Curiously dull I find *Coriolanus,* and *Timon* is somewhat ranting in its pessimism. One might think they were written in a fit of despairing depression and that the author came out of it saddened yet serene, with diminished *joie de vivre* but no loss of faith in humanity and hope for its future.

June 23d

I HEAR that the Cardinal has received assurance from the Pope himself that the Allies will do their utmost to spare Florence, and that only the most pressing military necessity will lead them to bombard it.

It was gossiped that before they evacuated Florence, the Germans would blow up all the bridges. Then that a commission went to Hitler imploring that they be spared. Now it seems that the Ponte Vecchio and the S. Trinita bridge will not be touched. The last is the most elegant and artistic thing of its kind in Europe, and its destruction would indeed be a loss, more than a dozen Monte Cassinos.

June 24th

GERMAN SOLDIERY, ever since the occupation, have been quartered on the estate of friends in the environs of Florence. There has been a continuous coming and going. Yesterday or the day before as a company was leaving the captain sent his orderly to ask for a puppy which belonged to the *fattore's* little girl. He was begged not to insist, because since its birth the little girl had been devoted to it, and it would break her heart to lose it. The German captain replied that he would have it, and if it was not sent at once he would come and take it at the pistol's point.

June 26th

MY SEVENTY-NINTH BIRTHDAY! Little did I expect to celebrate it still "in hiding" when I came here almost ten months ago. I then thought to be from home eight or ten days, and no more. Then for Thanksgiving, and thereafter for Christmas surely. On New Year's Day my hostess prophesied that I should be here for my birth-day. I laughed heartily. Easter passed, so did Whitsun, and here I am on June 26th.

There is nothing in which I have been so much out of reckon-ing as the time factor. All through this war I have been out in my calculation. For instance, I remember feeling that from the day we Americans entered the war, it would last but a few months.

It served to keep up my spirits and I hail my error as *felix culpa* —happy error.

*   *   *

There has come to my notice the document of an agent sent in 1936 by Hitler to the Vatican. Hitler felt that a good part of the Catholic clergy, not to speak of the laity, would adhere to him if only they had papal approval. He felt, too, that what stood most intransigently between him and the Vatican was the racial ques-tion, namely, the exclusion of Jews from humanity and humane consideration and their treatment as inferior animals to be de-stroyed pitilessly, or to be used when use could be made of them.

Hitler wanted to bring the Vatican to his way of thinking, and his clinching argument was that, if not now, two or three centuries hence the Vatican would agree with his ideas as it does now with Galileo's.

The person who during the Jewish persecution had the charge of justifying it to the Tuscans has been lodged in my house during my exile. Now he has run away, and I shall have the room he oc-cupied not only cleaned and disinfected but exorcized.

This individual engaged a peasant to take him and what he wanted to carry with him in a cart. On the way to Firenzuola they were stopped by German warriors who took everything they had except the clothes on their backs, all the propagandist's lug-gage and whatever they found in his pockets, the peasant's horse and cart and, what affected his peasant's soul most, his *fede,* his wedding ring.

This reminds me of the sacrifice made by Italian women on the occasion of the filibustering Abyssinia expedition. It was "voluntary," of course, as voluntary as the volunteers who were made to go to Spain. No doubt many gave up their wedding rings—superstitiously sacred to Italians of all classes—with passionate fervor and the hope of serving their country in its attempt to oppress another country. But the great majority, in all classes, did it out of fear and even out of snobbery. Among the last was a lady of enigmatical descent married to an American of high standing. I knew her to be anything but favorable to Mussolini and his ambitions. Yet she, an American citizen, came to Italy on purpose to throw her wedding ring into the crucible. Let us hope it served to preserve and improve her position in the best Fascist-minded society!

June 28th

LATE LAST NIGHT, and again from six this morning, the dull thud of distant guns, some of them shaking the house. It reminds me of evenings spent in the eastern quarters of Paris during the spring months of 1918, when the Germans were only forty miles away.

The peasants with whom I have been exchanging "good mornings" all say *che finisca presto*—may it finish soon. In these four years of war, I never heard them express a wish for a happy issue, or anything similar.

The head of the specter-Fascist forces here, Adami Rossi, a general of the royal Italian army of whom I have already spoken as a man of blood, guilty of many, if not most, of the atrocities committed here, now proposes that all hotels should be blown up by the Axis troops before they leave, so that the Allies may find no lodging.

The other day, stretched full length on the sidewalk at Rifredi —a suburb a mile down from here—were found the bodies of two women. They were recognized as two Jewesses who had been sequestered for some time by the Hitlerites. On the slopes of

Monte Morello, a few miles from here, were found the bodies of four women. Their dress and shape were of the prosperous classes. Their faces had been made unrecognizable.

I heard months ago, but could not believe it, that Italian Jews who happened to be in the Dodecanese or elsewhere under Axis occupation in Greece were brought home and handed over to the Gestapo, who took them to Como and drowned them in the lake. Now I have had the same information on the best authority.

I fail to understand why they were not made away with where found, instead of putting their murderers to the expense and trouble of bringing them all the way to Como. I inquired but got no answer. I can only think of some Odinite sacrifice that might be propitiously performed at Como alone.

We do not even begin to conceive what may be lurking in the heads of uneducated brutes like many among those to whom Hitler has given authority.

June 29th

READING SHAKESPEARE recalls me to the intention I had of long standing to jot down a few words about euphuism and slang, its stepsister, its opposite, its reverse, its wrong side on the carpet.

Slang, like euphuism, is due to an inability to say what one wants to say in the vocabulary and phraseology of current educated speech. "If you cannot say it sing it," said the young woman to the shy and stammering lover. The euphuists try to sing it, the users of slang and—shall we call them dysphuists—bawled it, croaked it, spat it, flashed out phrases like rockets, luridly illuminating a world as murky as the one of the euphuists was dainty and gingerly.

The last have always been a handful, speaking a *Côteriesprache,* as Carlyle called it. The Tudor and Jacobean euphuists were not only on the lookout for a language that could be a vehicle for what they had to say but one which was cryptic enough to be unintelligible outside their circle. This kind of elegance always has existed when and where there was an exclusive society. Like "thieves' talk," it served their ends and shut out the rest of the world. It raged in London just before the last war under the leadership of highly gifted young men and women of the most cultivated sets in smart society.

Slang has humbler origins. It arises among the young and spirited who have had no chance, occasion, or leisure to learn the classical use of their tongues. To express themselves, they wrench current words and phrases out of their setting, and invent new ones. Some are so vivid, so iridescent, so poignant, or so picturesque that they appeal to the better-educated and are incorporated into their own speech.

In that way slang, the humble stepsister of euphuism, turns out to be the fertile if rather earthy daughter of the spirit of language; while euphuism is apt to be too refined, too remote from life, to result in anything but sterility.

*   *   *

Cannonading continues under a sky as crystalline, as pure as has ever been seen. But for this continuous thud, one could describe the landscape with Goethe's "Über allen Gipfeln ist Ruh"— the horizon is still—but the cannonading sounds nearer than it did yesterday.

From dark to well on in the morning, a continuous roar and rattle of traffic on the north road leading to Bologna. I should not have known whether is was going up, that is to say to the north, or down. The wide-awake *contadina* I encountered on my walk told me it must have been up and not down, because the rattling and rasping was of motor vehicles climbing and not descending.

*   *   *

Finished Montesquieu's *Grandeur et Décadence des Romains*. Written fully two centuries ago, it is more like what persons like myself think about Roman history than anything that has appeared since. Only in his treatment of the Byzantine Empire does he fail to be up to date, not so much, however, in spirit as in detail.

I happen to be more interested in the way past events are mirrored in the centuries intervening between their occurrence and

our own day than in the events themselves. No doubt some German unknown to me has written an unreadable book on the fame
Rome enjoyed in the eighteenth century. I do not know where to
look for it. So I am left to speculate. What was it, and when was
it, that Montesquieu's rational view of Rome was replaced by the
mythically heroic one that has reigned since, and is still reigning
today?

It must have begun before the French Revolution, for that was
inspired by the Plutarchian view of Roman history. Then it must
have been the reading of Plutarch that made the difference between Montesquieu's rational and critical view of Rome, and the
romantic one of the French Revolution, the Italian *Risorgimento,*
and Mommsen's Caesarism.

June 30th

THE HOUSE SHOOK after midnight, as if the cannonading were
overhead. Yet it could not have been nearer than sixty miles as
the crow flies.

Less traffic on the Bologna road. Have the Nazis exhausted their
enforcements? Have they stopped trooping northward?

Kesselring, the chief of all German forces in Italy, has given out
an order in which acts of sabotage and activities of the bands are
censured as cowardly behavior which, if not stopped, will, to his
sincere regret, mean the death of ever so many people who will be
shot in reprisal even if perfectly guiltless. And yet Kesselring is
reported to be a devout Catholic and Christian. How reconcile
this order with his religion? It raises the question of the German
army chiefs. Most of them disapproved of Hitler and all his ways.
Yet they have been serving him. "Oh no, not him, but the army"
—that army which has a people to feed, clothe, and arm it, "the
army that must prove its invincibility." "And no matter at whose
service and for whose advantage?" "No matter."

Nothing left for us, if we mean to have peace for some time to
come, but to prove that this army is not invincible; to demonstrate
that it served inhuman purposes and that it must not be allowed

to retain any halo of romance or glory, that on the contrary we must detail its servile conduct, obeying every Assyrian behest, letting itself be the instrument without which the Nazi attack on humanity never could have taken place. It can but redound to the eternal disgrace of the Junker class, to which the army chiefs belonged, that they abetted and aided such a monstrosity.

Talking of monstrosities, the official Nazi press, as quoted by the specter-Fascist one, gives it out that, if perish they must, they will see to it that all Europe perishes with them; that they reserve in their quivers poisoned arrows of a malignity undreamt of by the Allies, which they will use at a last resort.

Declarations like these and Kesselring's may account for the fact that the Nazis, with their Gestapo and S.S.'s, are viewed with horror wherever they go. The minority here that is still with them, and cannot deny their atrocities, does not attempt to excuse them but insists that it is the way war is made and that in similar conditions and occasions the Allies if they know their business would act in the same way.

There lurks the poison that Michelet characterized so well as *vaccin contre la vérité*—inoculation against the truth.

Have been perusing recent issues of *Forschungen und Fortschritte*, a German periodical that kept one up to date in all fields of scholarship, exact science, and philosophy. It has become more and more imbued with the intellectual perversity of the Nazis.

The decline, the corruption even, was fostered by the tendency of German writing, whether historical or metaphysical, to trouble the waters with such curls and swirls and plunges and involutions, convolutions, and obscurities that when you took great pains to find out what there was to fish up, it turned out to be some accepted idea that had been stated in a few clear words by a Schopenhauer or a Mommsen, a von Hartmann or even a Treitschke, a Burckhardt or a Wölfflin.

Young Germans of my acquaintance seem to enjoy this muddy, faintly translucent style and cannot understand my exasperated intolerance of a writer like Srbik. They may understand my disapproval of his attitude as an historian although they themselves are rarely free from his awe-inspired state worship; they cannot follow me in finding his prose turgid, involved, and obscure.

These epithets apply to most German writers of recent years, including some whose popularity is by no means confined to Nazi-land, whose names I prefer to leave unmentioned.

July 2d

A PASSIONATE flower-grower friend has sent up as a birthday present orchids so rare that it has taken twelve years of watchful attention to bring them to full florescence. I have enjoyed the twist and droop as well as the shape and color of the petals. How little that is, compared with the passionate understanding on the part of the lady who cherished them through twelve whole years!

❀   ❀   ❀

There have fallen under my eyes the papers of a Fascist propaganda agent during the filibustering Abyssinian adventure. He reported to both Duce and Führer, to Mussolini and Hitler.

In France, he saw riffraff only or madcaps like La Roque and, with the exception of Chautemps, nobody of any consequence. All express great admiration of the Duce and hope for the success of his adventure. Nearly all give vent to hatred of England and their loathing of the League of Nations. Some offer advice as to how to circumvent Britain's game.

In England, he does not seem to have seen Sir Mosley (*sic*), but he saw members of the Imperial Policy Group most of them admirers of Mussolini and in sympathy with his ambitions. At least so this agent thought. He reports that among them there were six and twenty M.P.'s and has letters from one of them.

Clearly, this agent must have been accredited by the Duce to do what he could, both in France and in England, to make friends not only for Fascism but for its imperialistic ambitions. High and deep moral indignation against so many governments, sixty or more in number, leaguing themselves against one lamb, innocently munching grass!

The success of this agent seems to have been small in England,

even if he did win over some few cranks. In France, on the other
hand, he met with a sympathy rather frightening in its hatred of
England and its eagerness to stop at nothing to do it harm. I wonder if the hatred of England will not be more difficult to stamp
out in France than in Germany.

July 3d

THE GERMANS, on the plea of saving them from Judeo-American
predatoriness, want to take along with them as they leave all the
valuable and admired masterpieces of art to be found in Florence.
They must be aware that, owing to the constant bombing of lorries
on the highroads, these masterpieces run serious risk of destruction on their way to the north. Why, then, do they want to carry
them off? I can scarcely believe it is the vindictive desire to deprive Florence of them. They surely believe the Americans will
do what they, the Germans, would if victorious: seize all works of
art as booty.

German troops are snatching whatever they can lay hands on
and not only in obedience to orders and for army purposes. They
do a great deal of freebooting quite openly and the officers must
be aware of it. If these do nothing to prevent it, the rank and file
must be out of hand and no longer amenable to discipline. The
other day the counselor of the German Embassy at the Vatican
was made to get out of his car. Still worse, the Vice-Duce, Pavolini,
was treated in the same way, while the offenders drove off with
his car of magnificent state, as they did with the counselor's more
modest vehicle.

The German soldiery in Florence hold open market of their
stolen goods, from motorcars and fine clothes to eggs and radishes.
They sell at a tenth of value, and with the proceeds rush to the
shops to buy underwear and other dire necessities.

Under my windows I hear the lowing of cows and calves. They
used to be shedded hundreds of yards away. For fear of their
being carried off, they now are kept all but in the house.

On the other hand, a villa near by occupied by the German

Red Cross is being treated as satisfactorily as possible, under the circumstances.

July 4th

THE GLORIOUS DAY!

I wonder whether our Sammies sweating under the midsummer Tuscan sun recall the day—the day when the Yankee sons declared their independence of the British sire. Let us hope that the companionship in arms will rub out the last trace of ensuing ill-feeling, and make the ordinary American private realize that he is member of a great constellation of communities, if not of one consolidated commonwealth.

Suddenly there rises to conscious memory, as if coming up with a submarine from the depths, the recollection of my first Fourth of July. I had just come from quiet, neolithic Lithuania, a boy of ten. The heat, the sweat, the scorching sun, the noise, the clatter, the penny whistles, the firecrackers, the magenta-colored toy balloons, the pink lemonade, the sticky balls of popcorn, deadly fatigue, stumbling feet, sleepy weariness—that was my first Fourth of July on American soil.

I never again was exposed to this annoyance. On that day I was always at a safe distance from a celebration.

The nearest parallel to this distressing experience was twelve years later when, induced by fellow students in Paris, I went through a Quatorze Juillet. I witnessed the parade at Longchamps, marching and shows, and the evening with the sweaty dancing in all the squares of the *Quartier*.

No, decidedly, I lacked the exuberance, the abandon required for hearty participation in mass festivities. Besides, I had an instinctive distaste for "man in the lump" and fear of their feelings. The more so as I could not resist feeling with them.

With shame do I recall as a student in Berlin being caught in a crowd when, with bands playing and banners flying, Crown Prince William was returning from a review at Tempelhof. They cheered and cheered and I got a lump in my throat, and tears in my eyes. I was horrified, for I disapproved of William's conduct toward his dying father and despised his popularity. Yet I could not resist mass emotion. Nor can I even now. Wherefore I have done my best not to find myself in a crowd.

July 5th

MY OWN HOUSE is sheltering a major of the regular (not the "republican") army, who with his troops was swept down to Cassino by the Nazis when, expecting a landing, they rushed southward to stop the advance of the Allies. There his men were disarmed and set to roadmaking. His story proves that these highways were finished in time to be used by the Allies, and that in the monastery of Monte Cassino the Germans stored arms, ammunitions, and explosives sufficient for a campaign. The Allies had no alternative but to blow it up.

I receive a letter written June 25th by a friend who farms his own land on an estate some ten kilometers this side of Siena. It is occupied by the Germans and their antiaircraft guns are placed within a stone's throw of his house. The privates snatch from the peasants everything they find: food, horses, mules, donkeys, cows, calves, pigs, etc., etc.

He went to Siena to ask the protection of the Kommandantur, and was told by the German in charge that he could do nothing, that the troop was out of hand, that they stopped officers on the road and at pistol's point made them get out and leave the cars to them.

Siena itself has been deserted by the specter-Fascist authorities, big and little. A kind of municipal police remained to represent law and order.

July 6th

SOON AFTER last midnight, two officers sent by Marshal Kesselring woke the Cardinal-Archbishop of Florence with an imperatively urgent request. It was to get into a car and rush to

Rome, there to get a promise of the Allies that they would not occupy Florence, or even pass through it, but treat it as an open city
as by the Germans defined.

The German definition of an open city, as illustrated by their
conduct here, is a city where they can have their Kommandantur,
their S.S. organization, their Gestapo, their armored cars, their
arms and troops, excepting a tiny bit in the center where they may
not lodge but pass and repass, shop, stroll, and loiter.

This is "open city" for Germans, for the Chosen People, for the
Herrenvolk which has one law for itself and another for the rest
of mankind. From the Allies, the Germans demand and expect
that Florence shall harbor no offices or officers, no troops, no armaments, no armored cars, no cannons, and above all permit no
transit.

If the Allies do not consent to this, Marshal Kesselring threatens
to defend the town of Florence square by square, street by street,
house to house.

As in the days of Attila and Pope Leo, Totila and St. Benedict,
the Church remains when military and civil authorities disappear.
Both friend and foe here (and by foe everybody, except the dregs
of Fascism, means the Germans) appeal to the Cardinal to advise,
to help, to save. I wonder if a like appeal to the Church could take
place in France, let alone England or Germany.

I forgot that a few days ago a man old enough to be the father
of a gardener on this estate was shot by the Germans. It was for
neglecting his duty as watchman on a telephone line.

The Germans are not missing a trick to leave behind them a
hatred which this time is mingled with contempt. For now they
seem to be mere pilferers, petty thieves, marauders, and assassins.

My heart aches for all the *Unsereiner*—Germans of our own
kind—who will suffer for this not only materially but morally.

July 8th

THIS MORNING, as the peasants were driving into market with
their produce, Germans stopped them, pulled them down, and

went away with fruits and vegetables, cart or wheelbarrow, horse
or ass.

Yesterday three vehicles stopped in front of the principal fur-
rier's. One had German officers, the other German soldiers, and
the third German police. They proceeded to sack the shop, laying
hands on all they found, chiefly the furs deposited for summer
keep by the ladies of Florence.

July 9th

FINISHED R. C. Muschler's *Philipp zu Eulenburg*, an excitingly
interesting book. It consists of three elements: the character and
career of an artistically and poetically gifted German gentleman,
who was at the same time a Prussian nobleman; his intimate
friendship with the impulsive, wayward, conceited, irresponsible,
but fascinating Kaiser Wilhelm of our day; and the story of how
he, Eulenburg, was brought to a miserable end.

He was creatively musical and poetical. He was statesmanlike
as diplomat, and intimate adviser and moderator of his sovereign.
He was a perfect husband and a delightful, perhaps too indulgent
father. He was a loyal, helpful friend. His relations with the Kaiser
—which, by the way, offer an unrivaled view of German affairs
international as well as national, and a picture of court and society
—ended by rousing envies which account for his fall.

But for that envy of his seemingly so starry, so radiant position,
what could the accusations brought against him have availed?
They were of having committed homosexual acts some twenty
years previously, and of having perjured himself by swearing that
he had not.

The plot against him was directed by that spider Holstein, notorious as the chief weaver of German international intrigue, and
by the unscrupulous, brilliantly sensational journalist Maximilian
Harden. Although the first hated Eulenburg out of envy and jealousy, both aimed not so much at him as at the Kaiser, meaning
to expose the latter's lack of judgment, decency, and taste in having a "degenerate" for his closest friend and chief adviser.

The Kaiser behaved like a sneak, and his Chancellor Bernhard von Bülow like a skunk.

Only a few weeks before the accusation was publicly brought against Eulenburg, the Emperor was on the most affectionate terms with him, and insisted on bestowing on him the highest decoration at his command. From that moment, without waiting for private explanation or public trial, he dropped him in the most cowardly fashion. To use common parlance, he got such a scare that he shrunk away, and hid his face from the friend who hitherto had meant most to him, the friend to whom he owed most. The Kaiser could have hushed voices and stopped proceedings if a craven fear had not got hold of him.

But his court circles and his Chancellor were actuated by other sentiments than cowardice. Bülow, who owed the success of his career to Eulenburg, not only did nothing for a benefactor to whom he had often and recently expressed his gratitude and affection, but worked against him, helping to prepare his fall, advising William not to interfere with the proceedings and seeing to it that they were as severe and harsh as possible. In the court, in society, in the Foreign Office, not a soul to stand up for him. Quite the contrary. All rejoiced in his fall.

Why? Moral indignation? Surely not. In the first place, the charge was far from proven and was of a "crime" supposed to have been committed twenty years previously. Twenty years ago —"I have never done it since I left school." Besides, excepting the Rhadamanthine spouse of the Kaiser, who in high court, military, literary, or journalistic circles cared? Oscar Wilde was at that time read in Germany as nowhere else before or since. Portraits of him faked up to look the happy pederast were exposed in all bookshop windows. Far from being frowned upon, homosexuality was not discountenanced. In the army, on the contrary, Greek friendship among officers was smiled upon as leading to greater efficiency.

The England of Dilke, Parnell, and Wilde was pruriently puritanical, cantingly hypocritical, and while personal grudges and politics may have contributed, it was offended public opinion, the bellowing of the herd, that made it impossible to employ them in any realm of the commonweal. This was a kind of self-mutilation. What was lost by excluding Dilke and Parnell from affairs I cannot gauge. In the case of Wilde I venture to believe that he would have transformed the theater of the English-speaking world, and might have been the Congreve of our time.

In Germany, on the other hand, the fall of an Eulenburg was due to nothing but envy and jealousy—the *invidia* of which Tacitus spoke nearly two thousand years ago.

Envy is the master passion of the German. One seldom opens their diaries, correspondence, or memoirs without being struck by the outrageous role of envy. What an iron discipline or love of the task must it take to get teamwork out of such characters!

We know already what part this hellish ailment played under William. Not yet, what ravages it has committed under Hitler. No doubt these gangsters felt from the first that they must hang together or hang separately! Someday we may learn what part envy and jealousy played in the inevitable and invincible struggles for power among the Nazi paladins.

July 10th

SCARCELY a doctor to be found. Who has not been pressed for Germany is in hiding. Thus the Nazis get little advantage from their slaving, but the countries they occupy suffer.

A couple of days ago the Kommandantur issued the declaration that six lawyers of high professional standing, known to be blameless but friendly neither to Fascism nor to Nazism, had been arrested. They are to be kept as hostages and shot at the first attack on any individual Germans or after any act of sabotage.

Yesterday as I was walking in the grounds I was hailed back to the house because the Germans were at hand, slave-driving and carrying away cattle, horses, asses, edibles, anything they could lay hands on. As I approached the house, groups of young and youngish people were sheltering under its shadow.

Then it turned out that the alarm was caused by two German soldiers, tired out—deserters perhaps—hungry and thirsty, who humbly asked for bread.

July 11th

FOR HOURS before and after midnight, one kept not only hearing the muffled boom of the cannon but seeing in quick succession flashes of light. This forenoon, continuous sound of explosions. The Germans are blowing up and destroying what they cannot carry away, that might be of use to the Allies. They do not spare hospital furniture and fittings. Even the dear Florentines—accustomed to regard characters and events as being mere Tweedledum and Tweedledee, one people as good and one government as bad as another and all of us, as Holy Church teaches, miserable sinners and nothing to choose between us—after the experiences of the last ten months, on coming in contact with the Allies may be moved to consider whether a better humanity, with more decent ways of keeping law and order, may not be attainable. For centuries they have stewed in political atheism and the conviction that the struggle "naught availeth."

I am saying this from my more than fifty years' acquaintance with them, and their history. I know this history not as they write it with frothy magniloquence. Diaries, letters, memoirs, the humbler storytellers are more informing. These recount what life is like in Tuscany, what their preoccupations, what their politics. How free from humbug, from so-called idealism, how close to the existence of higher animals—as indeed is the lived life of most of us everywhere!

July 12th

THE TWO Italian regions which in early years I explored most minutely are the Marches and the Sienese. Alone or with my wife, I returned to them again and again, and few were the towns and villages, monasteries and churches I did not study. It was an enchanting adventure, the joy of being the first to recognize the authorship of countless altarpieces that had not been correctly attributed before.

Little did I think then that some fifty years later American troops, our Sammies, would be fighting around and in these same towns and villages, furlong almost by furlong, against German hosts. Even when Mussolini had the puerile impudence to declare war against us, I had no idea that my happy hunting grounds would soon be battlefields for our soldiers.

I wonder how many among them realize that they are treading holy ground—ground, I mean, that has been tended and cherished for three thousand years and more. Are they aware of what lives have been lived in these thirty centuries, and what traces and records they have left behind? Has any one of my fighting countrymen my *Italian Painters* and my *Italian Pictures* with him, to tell him what places he is occupying, and what to see in them?

The Germans whose business it is to interrogate American prisoners say that the great majority have no idea or ideals and no notion where they are, and why. Europe does not exist for them, Japan does, and Japan they hate.

July 13th

PERFECT SUMMER WEATHER. Fresh mornings. Throughout the forenoon, even when one stands in the sun, the air is cool and invigorating. A caressing breeze flatters one's senses. Toward evening a golden light glimmers and flashes from all objects, trees, towers, palaces, churches. Attavanti, at the end of the fifteenth century, tried to produce the effect with touches of gold. On the scale of an inset on an illuminated page, it is merely gaudy. Even in panel paintings, as in the earliest Peruginos, it is more quaint than successful. The great Flemings used more sober means.

*   *   *

The *carabinieri*, that is to say the Italian gendarmerie, have been ordered to Germany or at least to Northern Italy, as I have noted already. Many have taken to the woods or joined the bands.

The instant we are abandoned by the Nazis they are ready to return to help establish and maintain order in the interval between the two regimes.

The police are doing the same. Thus, the well-known subchief of the Florence police, to avoid leaving with the Nazis and specter Fascists, has gone into hiding but is ready to return the moment the enemy has cleared out.

I purposely say the "enemy." In Florence certainly, and I am told the same holds for the rest of Italy, the police has always been anti-Fascist, and particularly so since the German occupation. I need scarcely add that so have been most of the newspaper people obliged to write the stuff that filled their papers.

It must be clear now to thoughtful Germans in the army that they have lost the war. Why do they go on?

In the first place, Hitler and his gang command them and they are "conditioned" for obedience. Hitler and Co.—many thousands —know that the moment fighting has ceased there will be no place for them in the land of the living. Naturally, they will defend themselves to the end. Every day is to the good. And *après nous le déluge*—what care they for what their criminal resistance may entail upon their country!

As for the rank and file of officers in the present German forces, they have little to go back to. The majority are neither capitalists nor landowners. If they had houses they are in ruins, their belongings scattered to the winds. In the army they still eat their bellyful, more than civilians at home. They still enjoy a sense of power. What awaits them when peace comes? Why, then, should they not wish to go on even though the war is lost?

July 15th

FRIENDS OF MINE have seen the German who represents Himmler in the whole of Italy. He is a certain Dollmann, good-looking, in the early forties, cultivated, affable, a man of the world, and claiming to have spent sixteen years in Rome. In just what capacity remains uncertain. Not in diplomacy, nor in the consular service. Neither in finance nor in trade. He speaks of the smartest society ladies as intimates, calling them by their Christian or pet names.

He has no high esteem of them and of the way they threw themselves into the arms of Ciano, whom they spoiled. The first time the latter dined as Minister of Foreign Affairs at the German Embassy, he started making love to the Ambassadress, Frau von Mackensen, in a way so disgusting to this lady that she loathed him ever after.

Dollmann regretted that the frivolous, venal, ultrasmart world had so much influence in politics. Many important matters, internal and international, were decided by Ciano offhand, at the golf course, in the midst of his houris and their gigolos.

I fear it is not only in Rome that the smart world has its finger in the political pie but in Paris and perhaps in Washington as well. Otherwise how account for our accepting a mayor of Versailles as French Ambassador at our seat of government? How account after the last war for our harshness to statesmen and refugees like Count Karolyi, and our favoring titled "White Russians"?

To return to Dollmann. He is here to wind up affairs before removal. He does not disguise his contempt for the specter-Fascist gang and regrets that his people countenanced and aided them. Although the Swiss Consul considers the Fascist prefect here an angel compared to those of Pistoia and Grosseto, Dollmann puts him down as a blackguard and holds him responsible for many of the brutalities and massacres committed by Major Carità and others. As for this Major, of whom I have written again and again, Dollmann has induced him to leave, not by ordering as he could have but by assuring him that he could not protect him against enemies who were hotfoot after him.

How can a civilian of such culture, sense, and judgment be the lieutenant of Himmler?

About the war he said little or nothing, but made this interesting remark: Both sides were handicapped by having to conduct it in the halls and corridors of an art museum.

The Nazis are carrying off all the printing presses and for some days we shall be without a daily paper. A more serious privation will be the drainage carts, which also are being seized. Entire families of peasants are being driven northward, leaving farms unattended and deserted.

Italy has suffered nothing resembling this invasion since the Lombards came, nearly fourteen hundred years ago. Those barbarians did not have the possibilities their remote cousins, the Nazis, own of asserting their will and power over a prostrate people. Present events help us to understand what a Lombard and even a milder Gothic invasion meant. Indeed, it was the German way of carrying on war in the first world conflict—so humane, so gentlemanly compared with their present behavior—that drew my attention to the history of our third to seventh century. It has absorbed me ever since.

July 17th

THOSE ITALIANS who will not and cannot purge themselves of the ill will against Britain injected into their veins by Mussolini on the occasion of the sanctions decreed against him for his felonious attack on Abyssinia keep sneering that the Allies never take a place until the Germans, the invincible, unshakable, steadfastly unmovable, have chosen to leave it. Why have they left it? Because it amused them, or because when the war was planned to the minutest detail by all-foreseeing German intelligence, such and such a position or stronghold, defended obstinately, bitterly, for months even, was to be abandoned for the adversary to occupy on the prescribed day? What they will not admit is that the Germans were compelled to leave if they were to escape the alternative of death or surrender.

It is to be feared that, as after the last war, many of the incurably German-minded, allying themselves with other politically and socially dissatisfied elements, will conspire against any government that tries to restore administrative, economic, and cultural order in this much-tried land.

I hear already of cells left behind by escaping specter Fascists, cells consisting of individuals intelligent enough to whisper persuasively, armed enough to use violence in order to hinder and if possible to prevent the settling down of the people to tolerably promising conditions. These individuals will take advantage only of every mistake made by the Allied occupation, as well as by anti-Fascists. They look forward to profiting by the relative freedom of a liberal regime. They are no negligible gang, and it will not be easy to deal with them!

July 18th

THE DULL THUD of cannonading all the time. Through the dark hours of the night, flashes of light in continuous succession, from beyond the hills.

A journalist who claims to have been present through the condemnation and execution of Ciano insists that the latter behaved like a man throughout and died heroically.

I would gladly believe it, but there is an insistent other version that he broke down and had to be dragged to execution.

Which version is exact? A mile below us all sorts of things have been happening during the last ten months. When I try to learn just what, just where, just how, I get nothing but mutually contradicting reports. Something has happened, no doubt. Just what, few if any get to know. The rest of us have to be satisfied with the "fable agreed upon" called "history."

July 19th

HAVING CARRIED AWAY or destroyed everything that might serve the Allies or allow life to continue in tolerable conditions, the Germans are now blowing up the roads they no longer mean to use, and mining the others.

Mining roads, discharging flying death-carriers, is legitimate, clean, chivalrous war, think the unconvertible Italian nationalists; but Allied air warfare remains cowardly and contemptible. These same nationalists are in despair over the vanished dream. It was a dream of empire, of reacquiring all that Rome once had, even if it begins modestly, with the conquest and control of all Mediterranean shores. Their good right, derived from the fact that they inhabit the same land as the ancient Romans, and are therefore their heirs.

Their mourning is sincere enough. If they knew German they might find alleviation in murmuring with Goethe: "*Weh, weh, sie ist zerstört die schöne Welt*"—"the beautiful world is in ruins"; or if they knew English, with Shelley: "Out of the day and the night/A joy has taken flight."

But these same nationalists know only golf and jazz English and no German whatever, nor have they any idea of the resources, the character, the traditions, the history, and the literature of these peoples.

Heading such dreamers of glory and world conquest, Mussolini, when he declared war first against England and eighteen months later against America, reminded me of the Tsar Paul of Russia. This intermittently mad monarch one day expressed his intention of tearing India away from the British. When his advisers ventured to suggest that the enterprise offered difficulties, he answered: "*Man schickt die Kosacken voraus und das Übrige findet sich*"—"We send the Cossacks ahead, and the rest will follow."

Two days ago the radio spoke of German lads of eighteen taken prisoner, and behaving arrogantly, insolently, declaring it did not matter if they lost this war, they would win the next one some twenty years hence.

These boys have been fed with Nazi propaganda and conditioned to act as "human bullets." Many, the majority, will survive and not only work but wait for *den Tag*, the day when they will conquer the earth and be the lords thereof.

Some five years ago there was staying with us the sixteen-year-old son of an American mother and an Austrian father. He horrified us with his utterances, his deep conviction that while Germany might lose the war he expected to break out soon, it would not matter, for they would make another, and another. Nothing would stop them from ruling the earth.

July 20th

THE FASCIST RADIO and press are hard driven to invent atrocities in the Italy occupied by the Allies. The latest is that these have requisitioned all the radios so as to oblige people to purchase American ones. Obviously, the U. S. A. has gone into the war, which before it is over will have cost it a good hundred milliards at least, for the profit of selling a few thousand radio sets.

As we were sitting out on the terrace after dinner yesterday evening, servants and peasants dashed up in a panic. Germans were in a farm below, and there was no telling what they might not want to take or do. Would the *padrone* come and see. He went and when he returned told us that the Germans were two n.c.o.'s, one toward thirty perhaps, the other barely twenty, and that they were shouting Prussian-wise, as if addressing deaf malefactors. The younger spoke some Italian. A handsome lad he seemed, but rather insolent and probably capable of any cruelty. They disappeared when it turned out that what they were really after, a pig and a good fat one, was not to be had on the farm.

One of the most arduous afterwar problems will be to re-educate and humanize the Hitler youth of Germany, conditioned as they have been to Nazi cannibalism.

July 21st

WHEREIN DO I DIFFER from a good Catholic? Only in this: he believes that his Church knows, and believes what, having unquestionable authority, his Church has told him. I have long ago concluded that my mind has not been made for coping with these problems. I go so far as to question whether any human mind can deal with them. Yet I too have my faith.

My faith consists in the certainty that life is worth living, life on its own terms. I know it is limited, a tiny speck as even the earth in the infinite. But there is the infinitesimal, the infinitely little, and reality pervades it as completely and is a reality I can live by. What is that but faith? Confidence in life as worth while, confidence in humanity despite all its devilish propensities, zest for suitable exercise of function, enjoyment of the individual human being as a work of art.

July 22d

ALL DAY YESTERDAY there was louder cannonading, and more continuous, than I had ever heard before, even at Eastertide of 1918 in Paris. In my bedroom it sounded as if heavy rollers were rumbling over my head. In the evening a great river of flame was flaring in the near distance, and reminded one of descriptions of burning lakes of naphtha. It was a Neronian spectacle. Nobody knew what it meant, nor do we know yet. It looked as if the Germans had drenched with benzine the sleepers of the railway toward Pisa, and set fire to them so as to stop the train service as soon as possible.

What would I not give for a copy of the *Neue Zürcher Zeitung*, to read what it, the best-informed and most impartial daily known to me, has to say about events within Germany! That something like a serious menace to Hitlerism is cooking up is clear. But how organized, how widespread, with what forces, what leaders?

Read *Egmont*. It leaves the impression that Goethe must have conceived it in his youth, when he was lyrically creative, but composed most of it when he had lost this vein and was already on the way to become a verbal Canova or Thorvaldsen in his plays, and elsewhere a great gnomic poet, and even greater man of letters. As a man of letters he was probably the greatest that ever lived. As a creative artist of the highest order, he counted less and less after his early thirties.

There is a wild west wind blowing from the sea. It invigorates me despite the heat, and I enjoy it as much as reading Shelley's "Ode" written at the end of the Cascine, the public park that I see from afar even as I write.

July 23d

THE RUMBLING more and more continuous, and even nearer. I can understand that one gets used to it, and if it lasts long enough one misses it as one does the rolling of a vessel on which one has crossed the stormy seas.

July 24th

LESS BOMBARDMENT but no fewer explosions. The Germans blow up the roads, not only the highways but the byways as well, and burn what they do not blow up. They can have no dearth of petrol and dynamite, seeing the way they employ the one and the other.

And things go on in the most exquisite summer weather, fresh, bracing, breezy, sparklingly radiant, with incense hanging on every bough. This morning at six by solar time, the thermometer marked only 65 Fahrenheit, and although the sun in the afternoon yesterday was glowing, the west wind made it agreeable.

It seems that the German commander in chief, Kesselring, has assured the Cardinal that he would not touch either the water or light. Yesterday the supplies of both were being mined, and when the German authorities were appealed to, they declared they had had orders to destroy them, and that these orders had not been countermanded. Meanwhile, Kesselring himself is said to have disappeared. Every time the light goes out, one asks whether it is for good. Italian engineers declare that once destroyed it will take two years to restore. We should be in a fix, for petrol and oil lamps have vanished, and neither petrol nor oil is to be had.

The *Wehrmacht*—the German army—must be reduced indeed if obliged to seize the few cabs that still circulated in Florence. They not only took the vehicles and the horses but forced the drivers to deliver their reserves of fodder.

I am told their privates now make a miserable show, haggard, dust-bitten, ragged, and discouraged. The spirit of the lively and gay war has disappeared from their faces. Those that reach their homes will bring as sorry a sight as they will find.

July 25th

REREAD Schiller's *Don Carlos,* a fascinating dramatic poem rather than stage play, except for the last act, which has theatrical possibilities.

Never before Schiller or after him in any other country, any other language, have there been such eloquent appeals for personal freedom and humanity. His plays are the operative, spiritual heritage of every German; for not only does he learn them at school but he hears them on the stage. Every educated German knows their tirades by heart.

How, then, account for the German's abject submission to authority, even of a Hitler, a Göring, or worse still a Himmler?

In the first place, there is the good historical reason that the authority of the state—of Prussia, let us say—saved the German from the insecurity, the caprice, the violence of the feudal classes. This was followed more and ever more by the Potsdam spirit, which was ripening to perfection just as Schiller was composing his youthful plays and, with the enactment of universal conscription, was destined to reduce the German to the automatized, mechanized biped he becomes, the moment he is called upon to form part of the ARMY. Be it remembered that in the enlarged Prussia which is the Germany of our day, it is the army that disposes of a nation to feed, clothe, lodge, and amuse it, not a nation that has an army to defend it.

The same German who as private individual is sentimental, tender, romantic, literary, artistic, will, like a Jesuit with his *perinde ac cadaver,* carry out any and every order of his military superiors without turning a hair—without a moment's hesitation derived from personal feeling.

The trouble with the German is that he cannot break the logical thread which he follows through the labyrinth of war, no more than in any other of his activities. Where these activities, the exact sciences, for instance, can profit by the logical chain, the German is wonderful. Everywhere else he ends as the monster he is in war, and the cuttlefish he is in philosophy. It takes intellect, intelligence, and judgment to know when to snap a dialectical process short.

July 27th

THE ESTATE known as Torre Galli happens to lie near several roads, and the Germans have occupied it. They do not remain more than some days at a time, and are relatively decent, although they take as their own whatever suits them. The agent and his wife try to remain on good terms with them, and the individual German, being as human as the rest of us, chatters and even talks. Now that the Allies are imminent the Germans are saying that people have nothing to fear, that English and Americans are kindly, but beware of Moroccans!

Despite the fact that the Germans are so reduced for transport that they have seized every motorized vehicle, every draft animal, and nearly every bicycle and wheelbarrow, they have just sent a train of some eighty lorries to carry away the works of art stored in Florence.

What can be their object? To prevent their falling into the hands of the Allies? Can the Germans really believe that the Allies would claim them as Italy's share of reparations; or are the Germans carrying them away to use them—if indeed they reach their destination—as things to bargain with, threatening to destroy them if the Allies insist on hard terms?

Or is it possible that German leaders still believe they will win the war with the help of the specter Fascists, and restitute the works of art to a covictorious Mussolinian Italy?

July 30th

NOT WRITTEN for several days, the situation being too confused, uncertain, unintelligible—as much as Waterloo was to Fabrice del Dongo in Stendhal's *Chartreuse de Parme*. Continuous explosions have been going on of factories, mills, bridges, roads. From beyond the cosmic apse of the southwestern sky flashes, huge columns of smoke and growling, rumbling booming of artillery, aerial and terrestrial.

But yesterday evening as we were peacefully sitting out on a terrace as romantic as any in Tuscany, a man came up with the order just given out by the Kommandantur. It was something like this: Seeing that the Allies have vouchsafed no answer to the German request to treat Florence as an open city, the *Wehrmacht* would have to do everything in its power to prevent the Allies from attacking and damaging it and destroying the bridges. Therefore a rhomboid of territory both sides the Arno in the heart of the city must be evacuated by noon today.

Of course, now it will be said that the stupidity of the Allies is as destructive as the criminality of the others and that they have but one notion, which is to push forward like a steam roller pushing the Germans before them by brute force alone.

Did not Napoleon and Clausewitz teach that war consists of the effort to bring superior force to bear on the enemy?

I would feel like saying: "Yes, the English and Americans are neither military-minded nor war-minded. When you make war on them you cannot crush and conquer them by surprise as the Germans have the Poles, the Dutch, the Belgians, the French even. They will take time to get ready, and when at long last they feel ready they will be cautious, make sure of their rear, and advance inch by inch, at snail's pace—not a bit like the Russian armies you admire so much. Moral: do not go to war with the slow, stupid Anglo-Saxons, unless you feel materially and morally ready to have it long and devastating."

My own house is occupied by Germans. Luckily, they are decent people. They have taken the first and second floors, obliging my wife, bedridden as she is, to occupy an apartment under the roof, where, at this season, it is boiling hot. They have been urging her to leave, as they believe it likely that I Tatti will be under heavy fire and may suffer destruction or at least serious damage. They went so far as to offer transport to take her down to the best hotel in town.

I fervently hope this has not been carried out, for the same hotel has to be evacuated, by noon today, along with every other building in that region.

Much genuine distress here over the destruction going on: the Germans deliberately make a desert of every bit of country they leave; the countryside will never be the same, the towns will be rubbish heaps. True. As for the towns, I fear the worst from re-building. When I think what in the last fifty years the Genoese have made of their superb city, and what under Fascist rule has been done to every considerable town in Italy, I cherish no hope that rebuilding will not be in the worst taste attainable.

For the countryside the prospect is not so dark. It has been fash-ioned by three thousand years of culture. Impenetrable forests, dreary marshes, bare hillsides have been turned into the great park which Italy now is. True that visually it has lost a great deal, owing to immense increase of population and the accompanying decline of taste—a decline amounting to indifference to every-thing but the showy, the smart, and the new. How unlike us in America, who build houses to look "weather-beaten"!

Happily, the Italian countryside is, like humanized nature everywhere, indestructible; and the damage done through ma-terial violence or aesthetic vulgarity will be licked into shape, assimilated, and absorbed.

I almost forgot to add that since yesterday, just before mid-night, we have been without light. It means that the supply of electric power has been cut off, and nobody need be told what that means nowadays when so much depends on it. No more laid-on water, no mills going, no hygienic services, no more trams, no more radio. The telephone was cut off days ago. At last we are completely isolated. We can look over the battle that is raging, but without the interpretation of the radio or even the newspaper we can make little sense of what we see.

July 31st

THE TERRACE of this villa, facing the heights, hills, and mountains that environ the vale of Florence southward and westward,
is like the dress circle of a theater, Florence itself being the orchestra and the hills beyond the stage.

From this dress circle, by moonlight yesterday we enjoyed—
not in a physiological but in the aesthetic sense of the verb—a
marvelous spectacle accompanied with appropriate music. The
music consisted of the growl, the rumble, the roll of cannon that
sounded antiphonal. Visually it was more impressive still. A distant mountain flamed up like Vesuvius. From beyond the hills
came flashes of light, fan- or pyramid-shaped. This spectacle, this
music, went on for hours. Just what it meant was beyond me, although my fellow spectators interpreted it to their satisfaction.

I could not help being frivolous, and wondering what people
would not pay for a seat in our dress circle: to see the same performance, if it were merely theatrical, and not fraught with tragic
possibilities.

Tragic-minded must have been many of the hundred thousand
who, before noon yesterday, had to evacuate their homes from
both sides of the Arno.

People of all classes were seen waiting for their turn to lap up
water in any kind of vessel, no matter how humble, from ground
taps. Others carrying what they could with them, to provide for
the most rudimentary necessities. Still others taking away the sick
on wheelbarrows.

Why? I cannot believe that the Germans mean to defend Florence house by house. It does look, however, as if their plan is to
blow up the bridges, including the Ponte Vecchio and the Ponte
della Trinita. For my part, as I already have written, I could more
easily forgive the destruction of any other building.

Besides learning what war nowadays really means, people under fifty are offered free of charge the experience of a world where

electric power was not everything, where steam was still the ruling omnipotence, where the telephone, the wireless, and air traffic
did not exist.

So far so good and a salutary lesson for those who take these
facilities and comforts for granted, with no thought of what they
cost. They cost the passionate effort of genius on the part of inventors, improvers, and perfectionists. And they may cost us our
freedom.

Now that power is so overwhelmingly electrical and this power
so concentrated, what is to prevent a gang from seizing it and
thereby reducing us to mercy? A brilliant Italian journalist, a political atheist, Curzio Malaparte, some fifteen years ago wrote
his *Technique d'un Coup d'État*—Technique for Seizing Power—
and asserted that the Bolshevik revolution was brought about
that way. Despite Trotsky's sneers, we should take Malaparte's
warning seriously.

People under fifty must not, however, jump to the conclusion
that we were as badly off as they are now. We had kerosene lamps
and gas to light us. We had water that did not depend on electrical pumping. We had trams and other horse-drawn vehicles, for
long and short distances. We had all sorts of contrivances for comfort that have disappeared and are not easily replaced.

Should our present condition continue, even if it got no worse,
we soon should be transported not to the life after the Napoleonic Wars but to the time of the barbarian invasions. One thing
after another is missing without which trades cannot be carried
on. Most medicines not to be had; doctors disappear for fear of
being carried off to German slavery; barbers likewise; hospitals,
clinics, and nursing homes taken over by the Germans, often at
only a few hours' notice, with no pity for the patients. A savage
and embittered "ally" of the Italian is the German who answers
every protest with "Go and see what it is like in the Fatherland,
you who still are wallowing in luxury"; for what they find here
seems luxury to them, and they take a malignant pleasure in spoiling or making way with it. Here in Italy as widespread and

thorough a decline of material civilization and standard of life has not been known since the Lombard invasion fourteen hundred years ago.

August 1st

A MOONLIT EVENING like yesterday's, enjoyed on the terrace of this villa with its fronded arbors framing oblong landscapes, with its cypresses exhaling incense as they dip upward into the limpid ether, could be worded only by a Shakespeare. It was not spectacular like the previous evening and was almost silent. Far away lights and rumblings. This quiet went on through the night, and is continuing.

Rumor has it that the Allies instead of advancing have retreated. How stupid and cruel of them to leave the population of Florence in the fix they are in at present! Even vegetable gardens have been irrigated with electrically laid-on water. Now all will be dried up and perish. *C'est la faute de l'Angleterre!*

By the way, with a true instinct that in the long run language makes "race," the people here refuse to speak of us Americans as separate or distinct from the English.

It reminds me of hearing years ago an Italian lady speak of her brother-in-law as having married an English person in New York. I ventured to ask how it happened that he had to go to America to find an Englishwoman. "No, no," she protested, "I mean an English-speaking American."

German privates say that they are retiring from Florence but will remain in the mountains some five and twenty miles away till September, when the new weapon is ready that will give them back all they seemingly have lost. They say that the King of England has brought his Life Guards with him. They are to be clean-shaved, their gorgeous uniforms in apple-pie order, with drum majors swaggering and privates parading, all to impress the Florentines and to point a contrast with the ragged, dusty, tired Germans.

Among German subalterns, admiration of Nazi rule is not yet

extinct. They say it has been marvelous and it will be a great pity if it fails.

August 2d

YESTERDAY, relative quiet. The evening as silent as the moon, which seemed to be rounding out before our eyes. Only toward midnight cannonading and the churning of aircraft began and went on for hours. Again it sounded as if stone rollers were hurtling over my head. It has gone on this forenoon.

I have already settled down to short commons in the way of baths and to the light of one candle or oil lamp. I still miss the radio. We are cut off from news. Even the local daily papers do not appear. We are reduced to bits of gossip.

If true, the most important rumor is that Turkey has declared war against Germany. It would facilitate the advance of the Allies through the Balkans, where the overwhelming majority of the populations must be in sympathy with them, in Bulgaria no less than in Yugoslavia, and perhaps even in Rumania.

The Bulgars are a strange people, and the passionate propaganda of a Bourchier in their favor at the beginning of the last war blinded English policy to the fact that while the nation was Russophile, the government was Russophobe. Nor has the situation changed. It is the same today. Ever since the Greek campaign, if not earlier, the head of the Bulgarian government has been a mere Quisling, an excellent archaeologist known to be wholeheartedly German-minded but with no trace of political sense or experience.

The battle is fast approaching and we may soon be in the firing line. The villa of Quarto, where most of my valuable books as well as my collection of photographs are stored, seems to be there already.

August 3d

THE VILLA I mentioned yesterday was occupied in the afternoon by the Germans. It is a palatial house with magnificently furnished apartments. The owners were busy putting my books in safety when the Germans arrived and unceremoniously stalked from room to room to pick out what best suited their fancy.

The officers were civil in a way. Nicky, whose mother tongue is German, spoke them fair and they responded. They said they expected to stay only two or three days, and would be followed soon by Allied troops. They, the Germans, would leave everything as they had found it, spoiling nothing and taking nothing away. When the others came it would be another story! They had been at Montegufoni, where they had enjoyed the company of beautiful pictures—particularly a portrait by Rubens. Unfortunately, they could not save them from the rapacity of the Americans, who would carry them off and sell them at fabulous prices.

As a matter of fact, Montegufoni is a medieval castle built, if memory does not fail me, by the Acciauoli. In the seventeenth century it was humanized and made inhabitable as a country house. In the last century it became a rabbit warren for riffraff, and the present owners had no little difficulties in getting rid of them and asserting their proprietory rights.

These owners now are the well-known triad of Sitwells. To my knowledge they had no old masters that I would have given a hundred dollars for.

So much for Montegufoni.* To return to the German officers, the chief of whom was a first lieutenant, they spoke with the greatest contempt of Italians, of their indolence, of the way they lounged about the streets instead of being at the front, and above all of the bad reception they, the Germans, had met with everywhere. Not even in Russia had the civil population behaved so ill.

It takes the dense conceit of Germans to blind them to the fact that from the beginning of their occupation they treated people and things in a way to confirm the stories of massacres, devastations, and terrorism rumored but scarcely believed.

---

* I was not aware while referring to Montegufoni that many of the Florentine Gallery masterpieces had been stored there to be out of the way of air raids (October, 1944).

What is the result? The very name of "German" fills the inhabitants of this land with fear. It is as if the devil incarnate was coming with his bull's-eye stare, his horns, his fangs, and his claws. They run and hide. The most humble and harmless privates make them blench. As a rule all these want is drink and food.

Last night from the porter's lodge, a fifth of a mile down, came the telephone message that they were there. It turned out that they were two poor devils perishing with thirst, who said there was no water to be had in the neighborhood, and could they have some wine to drink.

Returning again to the villa of Quarto, and the German officers, a comic episode was the following.

The villa has been sheltering many hiding from the Nazi-Fascist terror, or from possible bombardment. Among them five Jews, a mother with a son, a daughter-in-law, and two grandchildren, one of these a baby boy of some eight months, looking like an infant Buddha. A German youthful sergeant took it, dandled it, fell into raptures over it while his comrades were laughing at him and asking whether, when he got married, he would not like to have just such a baby. And he, the German, never guessed that he was caressing an offspring of the calamitous, infectious, subhuman, verminous Jewish race.

Before going further let me add that these Jews had been among the most respected, most public-spirited, and wealthiest of their "race" in Italy. At the appearance of the Nazis they hastened to leave the villa where they had been hiding since autumn. Nicky last saw these people, accustomed to every luxury, walking toward the town, pushing before them the baby carriage and a hand cart laden with all it could hold.

Yesterday evening the moon was nearly full and it was more romantically lovely than ever—an Arcadia. Until after eleven almost complete silence. Since then even till noon today continuous growling, grumbling, bombarding, and exploding. While in my bath this morning, it sounded as if the house were going to tumble on my head.

The battle is approaching, and closing us in. Yet we can find out no details of what and where. At any moment we may have to leave. From this morning's aerial incursions shell splinters have been picked up on the terrace, just outside where I am writing.

In a house below this, the Germans arrived toward midnight, Prussian-wise ordered everybody out of their beds, occupied the place, and ate and drank up everything they could find.

They accuse the Italians of having betrayed them not only in Africa, in Sicily, and here, but everywhere. All German defeats are the fault of the Italians—even Stalingrad!

August 4th

DESPITE THE PROMISE that they would leave the place as they had found it, breaking nothing and taking nothing, the orderlies and privates, if not the officers themselves, smashed the huge terra-cotta vases containing lemon trees at Quarto, threw down an over-life-size statue, carried away provisions of every sort and all else they fancied, typewriters, footgear, traveling bags, kodaks, etc., etc. They decamped in the late afternoon of the next day, because the armored cars and ammunitions they brought along were immediately discovered by our aircraft and blown to bits.

The last twenty-four hours have been eventful and no inmate has slept in the interval. The evening passed in relative quiet. From this outlook, we enjoyed the Neronian spectacle of a huge fire which flared up like an immense column of thick, glowing flame, thinner in the middle than at the ends. At the same time a great explosion seemed to burst from the heart of Florence. It threw up a serpentine jet of smoke that reached the sky, and then bent to the right as if to meet the flames of the conflagration. We fear the sound was of a bridge dynamited by the Germans. Flashes and many-colored rockets kept lighting up the horizon.

I was undressing toward midnight when I was told to keep doors and windows wide open.

About a quarter of a mile below this hill runs a lane which

narrows into a bottleneck. At the narrowest point are a number of houses grouped around a grocery. The occupiers of this hamlet had just been given orders to evacuate within two hours. It was to be dynamited in order to clutter up the way with enough debris to provide an obstacle to the pursuing Allies.

The same lane debouches in a road that leads to the great highway to Bologna. It is the Germans' principal line of retreat, and they do what they can to delay pursuit. They are reported to have used the same technique in every village, road, or lane passed through. If so, it would go some way to explain the slow progress of the Allies in this Italian campaign.

*　　*　　*

While we were waiting for this explosion, sleep was not easy. It had scarcely come when I heard the voices of fellow inmates talking together. I lay quietly and after some time Nicky came to tell me that the Belvedere, a small villa with peasant house annexed, on this same estate, was being occupied by the Germans. First they asked for food and drink, and then told the tidings that they had come to plant a battery to defend the hillside against the oncoming "Tommy." Protests were unavailing, and the terrified peasants, as well as the refugees in hiding, implored the landlord to come to the rescue. Nicky, who went with him, could not get anything out of the troops except that they were obeying orders. Finally they offered to take her to their superior officer, who might be appealed to.

I must not forget to say that straggling, footsore, weary troopers came up again and again through the night, some asking where they could find their squad, others for a bit of food, others for shelter. One solemn, almost sepulchral cry I shall not easily forget: "Let me lie down somewhere, and please be quick, for morning will be here soon, when we must start out again—*bald wird es Morgen sein und da müssen wir weiter gehen*. Despite myself, I could not help recalling the refrain in the Provençal aubade: *l'alba, l'alba tan tost va*—dawn is coming so soon.

While Nicky was being taken to the officer, other troops to the number of forty, at least, invaded our own terraces and declared that they had come to occupy the house, that it was to be the foremost spot of their new line of defense, and that we must get out at once.

Happily, I did not know of this before Nicky returned from her first mission. I saw in a flash my works of art, priceless paintings and rare sculptures, either destroyed by explosion and fire or, at best, carried off to Naziland. Moreover, I might be captive not only as an alien enemy but as a "non-Aryan" and sent to Lublin if not killed first. Until the situation improved, as it did after several hours, I remained as in a nightmare, saying: "No, no, it cannot be, it is only a horrid dream."

Where could one go if one was allowed to go? Florence we could not get to. Where else? Nor could I trudge far on foot, carrying with me some few bits of apparel. Then there were the manuscripts of four years' scribbling, and the books I brought here for my work, publications of an expensive kind, for many years to come irreplaceable. Without them my present task could not be continued, as many of these volumes would not be found in the libraries of Florence even if I could afford the time and energy it would use up in getting to them and returning to the villa.

Again Nicky appealed to the Germans, individually not bad fellows, although parachutists. They too answered that they were obliged to carry out orders, but that she might apply to their superiors, who were to be found some three miles away, under Cercina. A corporal offered to guide her.

As Nicky can speak Germans fair in their own Ladeen and, as it were, sing the songs of the Fatherland to these hard-visaged but not always hardhearted and nearly always homesick lads, she succeeds in softening them and gaining their confidence.

The corporal was bitter against the English. He grimly enjoyed telling her that in France they were being massacred by tens of thousands and their armored cars smashed. The flying bombs were reducing London to a heap of ruins. Other towns suffered little less. Germany had still more formidable arms to launch. Besides, he knew for a fact that the British were so war-weary that their falling out of the fight was a matter of days.

They were good fighters, no mistake, and clean fighters. The Americans were redskins destroying everything as they came along.

The officers Nicky had to see spoke in the same strain and insisted that the Russians would never touch an inch of the sacred soil of the Fatherland, and that this time the Anglo-Saxons would learn the lesson not to fall on Germany when fighting for her life.

At last Nicky reached the commander of the squad camping on our terrace. With his men he was occupying the rooms adjoining a wayside wineshop. This camp, as indeed the one she visited earlier, was a picture of filth, confusion, and squalor. Dirty dishes, chunks of meat, opened tins, broken crockery, some soldiers fast asleep in uncomfortable positions, some shaving, and others washing. Complete comradeship between officers and men. No trace of the Styx that used to separate them. The commander, a captain, received Nicky with an icy blue look and no little hardness, but he too softened as she talked and when, at one moment, she said: "Can't you be a little human?" he laughed heartily and said it was asking too much after five years of war. Nicky explained that our house is just above the hospital city, which they should not expose to being bombarded, and besides that our place was the official residence of a functioning neutral Minister, and therefore enjoyed extraterritorial rights. Moreover, if they respected its neutrality we could expect the Allies to do the same. It might be more advantageous as neutral than as occupied ground.

He would not listen, said he knew nothing about extraterritoriality and that he had not studied law, and that it was out of the question that the line of defense as it had been decided upon could be changed; yet he gave in, and in Nicky's presence had himself put in telephonic communication with his direct superior, an *Oberstleutnant,* to whom he reported the case. Evidently the answer was not unfavorable, for he told Nicky that he would have to go himself to re-examine the positions, then to speak to his superior, and that in the afternoon he would let us know. He offered to send her back in a car which was to take one of his colleagues, a lieutenant, to our place. There was much cursing and swearing before the car could be got ready. Finally it started and to our great relief Nicky reappeared feeling rather hopeful about the result of her mission.

Meanwhile, the lieutenant commanding the unit that should have been quartered here had had a look at the house and had shown some disappointment over its having no cellars and no bomb shelters. Waiting for the reply from his superiors, he did not take possession, but remained sitting on the terrace with his noncoms, while the privates spread themselves out all over the grounds near the house, some sleeping, others shaving, others preparing their midday meal, hanging about the kitchen door and clamoring for all sorts of things. A squad of pioneers was digging holes for the machine guns to be placed along the terrace and pergola. About two o'clock the *Hauptmann* appeared, inspected the grounds, and reported by telephone to the *Oberstleutnant* that he would suggest respecting the house itself but keeping the excellent position on the terraces. Evidently the reply was favorable to us, for, shortly after this conversation, he had Nicky called out and told her that they were leaving the place but that the Minister was to put up the flag of his legation on the towers of the villa.

This was done at once and the squad began to pack and retire.

They did not go far, some two or three hundred feet higher up on the hill above our grounds. As a matter of fact, they use these freely for going up and down, and their battteries are placed just above us. We are not occupied. The owner's magnificent collection of incunabula and rare books as well as my own works of art, and perhaps even my own life, are safe.

All recognize that we owe our relative safety to Nicky.

August 7th

THREE NIGHTMARISH DAYS, and the end is not yet. I doubt whether at any time one has been more cut off than we are here now. We look over Florence and, with a glass, can identify churches and palaces in every detail not only in the town itself but on the semicircle of hills beyond. Yet we know nothing of what goes on. Even rumors do not reach us. We see smoke going up from fires across the Arno, but we cannot make out what is burning.

The bombing has been more and more deafening, more and more frightening. Left to myself, I should not have thought of shelter, but my host, feeling his responsibility, insists on my keeping indoors and sleeping in the safer part of the house. The two first nights we slept in a room to the back. It is under an overhanging rock of the hillside, is built of concrete, and has over it a room of the same dimension and same materials. There we lay, some ten persons, including a baby of fourteen months. Yesterday this did not seem safe enough to the head of the house. He insisted on establishing us in the vaulted corridor running along the back wall.

We passed these nights listening to the whirling of shells, the rattle of machine guns, and the crackling of grenades. At times I seemed to hear hoarse German voices and their heavy tread just outside.

At last, toward five, on the first two mornings, the firing stopped and with a full feeling for St. Ambrose and his flock greeting the dawn after watching through a night of terror, we could retire to real beds.

Our hillside happens to lie between the principal line of German retreat along the Via Bolognese and a side road reaching the same Via Bolognese after a few kilometers. The Allies are bombarding both these roads and the hill above us as well, for it creeps with parachutists hiding in dugouts in the wood and keeping their batteries going at the top. We are at the heart of the German rear-guard action, and seriously exposed.

"Pleasant or unpleasant, it is always an experience," as I heard a Californian patrician say after visiting nocturnal haunts in Arab Cairo.

No news of what is happening in my own place and to my bedridden wife, although they are not two miles away as the crow flies.

On the other hand, from Quarto reports come through, all bad.

It seems that since the departure of the first unit, other isolated groups of parachutists have been tramping through the house, bursting open doors and safes, opening cabinets and drawers, scattering on the floor everything they found, and picking out, as from a rag fair, whatever they could carry away.

It is a sign that even the iron discipline of the Germans is giving way, and that officers no longer can or dare keep the troops from turning into marauders.

The bulletin of August 2d distributed to the German troops has fallen into my hands. It is supposed to keep them informed of what is going on. It is propaganda of the grossest kind. Successful *Abwehr*—defense, repulse of enemy—everywhere. Two Lithuanian villages only, with names never heard of before, lost. In Normandy, the Allies have been using their terroristic aircraft. In the same breath they are told that German aviation has successfully attacked North African ports and that German flying bombs were creating havoc in England. They have been tenderly respectful of works of art, and for that reason have treated Florence as an open city. The Allies, on the contrary, would not consent to do likewise, and did not care what happened to the noble mother of the arts and her marvelous monuments, if they, the Germans, were driven to defend it.

While this inferno has been going on, we have been reading Goethe's *Iphigenie*. What a contrast between the noble humanity of this beautiful drama and the bestiality of Hitlerism, both products of the same soil, same air, same fundamental living conditions. How is it possible that the same people should produce such opposites? The answer perhaps is that the great majority of Germans were alien to the traditions, the training, the culture— the *Bildung*, in short—of the classes that could beget a Goethe and his readers. What this *Bildung* meant to the ruling class in Germany not more than fifty years ago may be read in Harry Kessler's autobiography.

August 9th

THE NIGHT from the 7th to the 8th was infernal. Booming, banging, crashing, whistling, hissing, and the house creaking and shaking, threatening to crack open. Early yesterday it was decided that the women should migrate to Quarto. Sacked and gutted as they might find the house, it had roomy dry cellars where they could feel safe.

Yesterday repeatedly they came saying that after all they must place machine guns on our terrace. Nicky rushed to their camps to mollify them. They promised they would do their best to put the guns not on our own grounds, which they would try to respect as neutral territory, but to right and left just outside. More than that they could not do, because they must defend the hillside, as it commands an important line of retreat.

How long will they defend it? They themselves told us that the Allies were already bivouacking near the Piazza Beccaria, well on this side of the Arno, and that they had heard the shouts of joy with which these were received.

Nor are there many Germans remaining. So it is not even to save the shedding of sacred Nordic blood that their rear is so obstinately defended. Whatever their reason, we still run great risks until they receive orders to withdraw.

As individuals, the subaltern speak fair. Here, when they come, they are treated to coffee and cigarettes. They know no Italian, almost no French, and only a trifle more English. Nicky interprets, and one tries to keep them in a good disposition of mind.

Meanwhile, nothing can surpass the visual beauty of these days, and the delightfulness of the weather. It is fresh yet radiant, and a pleasure to remain in the sun even at noon. Except when bombardment is going on, or an airplane is buzzing in the sky, it is the silence of an abandoned city. Not a sound comes up from Florence, nor of traffic on the roads.

As a great concession by the Germans, women at certain limited hours are allowed to leave their houses to fetch water and to do their marketing and hasten home. Males must keep indoors.

Never have I been so cut off, so isolated from the rest of the world. It is like being on a whaler of the good old days, which did not touch port for many months together. Only that here I am not two miles from the heart of a populous town and not farther away, as the crow flies, from my own home.

Whether my wife is there and still alive, whether it has not been sacked, gutted, bombed or burnt—I have had for ten days no means of knowing. Nor of what is going on in Florence. We hear explosions and see smoke going up; but just what they mean, what, where, we keep guessing and disputing, with no conclusive results.

And the rest of the world? Has Turkey really joined up? Or does she at least allow us airports and passages for troops? And what have the Russians done these days? Have they penetrated the "holy ground" of the Prussians? And in Normandy, just where are our friends?

August 11th

A RELATIVELY QUIET NIGHT following a day of nearly uninterrupted bombardment. For a whole hour in the afternoon the shells seemed to burst over our heads after emitting a whistling sigh as of the "dying pig." We hid in the most out-of-the-way and massive parts of the house, crouching like Maeterlinck personages in the dark, for we are reduced to small oil lamps which serve merely to make the darkness visible. Oil itself—olive oil, usually so abundant in Tuscany—has been turned by Nazi-Fascist exactions into a rare and expensive liqueur. Only toward evening do we venture out to enjoy the colors in the clouds, deep rose, rich amber, pale purple, glowing with the gold of the setting sun. This morning as I reached my bedroom after a night spent in a Piranesian corridor, I heard a tremendous explosion and saw a vast volume of smoke shoot up as from an Indonesian volcano. The rising sun lit it up, and made it look like the basaltic Staffa in the Western Islands of Scotland and similar formations I recall seeing in southern Auvergne. It remained bulky and compact for quite a while before it began to dissipate.

Explosion has been following explosion. Destructive as these must be, and no doubt of irreplaceable buildings, we cannot help greeting each as a promise of the German retreat.

From Quarto comes authentic news confirming and detailing the pillage, the sacking, the wanton destruction committed by the German troops. An appeal to their chief brought a higher officer to inspect, and he declared what he found *eine Schweinerei*. He left a couple of military police, presumably to see that no further jollification of the kind occurred.

The lady of the place and her two granddaughters lost no time in beginning to wipe up. They are leaving one or two of the worst mishandled rooms as they found them, till they have been photographed.

My books and photographs at Quarto seem to have escaped intact.

Three days ago a fashionable Florentine couple were turned out at midnight from their fine villa close by and, after passing the greater part of the night in a ditch, found their way here. They turn out to be two very dear human beings and a most welcome addition to our little group.

*   *   *

Read Ben Jonson's *Volpone*. It had no little success in Paris some years ago. It must have been so modernized that of the original only the subject matter remained.

Heavy, dull, pedantic, uncouth even in language; archaic in plot, and with no idea of creating character. The personages remain mere functions as much as in a Punch and Judy show.

To the child in us, such a show appeals when presented to the eyes; and to an Elizabethan public *Volpone* as a spectacle may have seemed great fun. Today some who prefer Stravinsky's *Petrouchka* to other music may work themselves up to believe that they enjoy the performance of this puerile play.

There is a smart saying here and there which still works; and there are sideswipes against Marston, against Shakespeare and his discovery of Montaigne, which may have tickled contemporaries.

What contemporaries were they who could stand this automaton, with its creaking mechanism, after any play of Shakespeare even the least good? Did his contemporaries realize the impassable gulf between Shakespeare and Ben Jonson? Probably not, and the most influential preferred Ben's verbose pomp and donnish pedantry to Will's "wood notes wild."

Tieck has written a story about the young Shakespeare and the already famous Marlowe, and how the latter recognized the measureless superiority of the former on reading his first play. It takes genius to recognize genius. The public in general, even an Elizabethan, even an Athenian public, does not encourage it, but exudes it as the oyster does the pearl with as little recognition of its beauty. It wins through only if it is strong enough to survive and to educate a fresh and unspoiled audience.

Surely the same circumstances that produce the genius produce his inferiors. Who could remember them, who would recall them but for the interest we take in him? We hope to understand him better by seeing what they were like; how near they came to him and how much he to them. Were it not for this curiosity, who but professors of literature would turn their pages? In the case of the Elizabethans most would be more satisfied with Lamb's extracts.

It is Shakespeare who makes us read the Elizabethans, as Dante the poets of his circle. As to what made Dante, what made Shakespeare, that remains a mystery of mysteries, the mystery of genius.

I recall reading in Renan that there might have been no Greeks, that there might have been no white race at all. So there might have been no Shakespeare and Marlowe, there might have been no Schiller and Goethe, there might have been no Mozart and Beethoven. And then?

Is there just a chance—may we hope—that from our mold will flower a race more universally human than we are, and geniuses in great numbers at all times and not so rare and infrequent as up till now?

August 14th

THE DAYS GO BY, serenely radiant midsummer days. We see and we hear only as if we were looking at hieroglyphs. We understand nothing. Only vague and contradictory rumors reach us. We know less of what is going on two miles away from us in the heart of Florence than do the citizens of San Francisco or Melbourne, so many thousand of leagues away. They are informed hour by hour. We are shut out, cooped in. No civilian may come or go across the forbidden line.

The noise last night was so continuous, and the shelling seemingly so near, that sleep was unattainable. One could only pray for dawn.

Just now comes word from the neighboring convent, the home of sixty nuns, that the Germans insist on placing machine guns right in front of their infirmary. Nicky has gone over to see how this can be averted. We here are protected by our extraterritoriality, which they make great show of respecting—they, who did not hesitate to invade Holland and Belgium, Norway and Denmark. The *Oberstleutnant* wrote to my host to that effect, assuring him, at the same time, of his eagerness to spare every building of artistic interest, and every work of art.

One thing is certain. It is that the fighting is coming nearer and nearer to our hillside. The obstinate delaying action of the Germans can be due only to their wish to keep the Allies busy here until their Maginot line on the Futa pass is completed. It was to take eight weeks, and these were over yesterday.

I conclude that fear takes hold chiefly of the people who have few if any interests outside their own bodies and the extension of their own bodies, namely, family and tangible belongings. So little else exists for the peasant woman and the domestic! And how possessive they are! They will talk to you for as long as you

will listen about a glass, a cup, a towel, of what not that Germans
have broken or carried off. Catch them being Communists! They
would seize on their allotted share of the property of those rich
but, once acquired, wild horses could not part them.

❉ ❉ ❉

Read Goethe's *Clavigo* and *Stella*. They have the nimbleness,
the alacrity, the vivacity of the early chapters of *Wilhelm Meister*.
What goes on in woman toward the man she loves has seldom
been rendered as well. The interest of these plays lies in the conflict between love and ambition, and between love and love—the
impossibility of giving up one love for another.

No doubt when Goethe composed these plays, he was tor-
mented by such conflicts, and they can be used as documents in
the biography of the author.

The contrary is not true. The knowledge of what was happening to an author while creating a masterpiece can inspire zestful
curiosity to read, to hear it, to see it. It cannot make it more com-
municative, more convincing, more life-enhancing.

These few remarks might serve as text for discussing the way
literature is being treated by critics, and taught in schools. It
amounts to little more than prying into the private recesses of
authors, exploring the paths of their wayward hearts, investigat-
ing their conjugal troubles or money difficulties, not neglecting
quarrels with other authors, publishers, newspapermen, etc., etc.

Seldom have I come across an interpretation that illuminates
like Yoshio Markino's two or three T'ang poems in his *When I
Was a Child*.

August 15th

THIS IS THE FEAST of the Madonna, the most popular holiday
of the year. It is the seventeenth or eighteenth day since we have
been without electric power, and in consequence without light,
without city water, with alarmingly diminishing provisions, and,
worst of all, without the radio and the news. The first bit of comfort has just reached us with the sound of church bells that can-

not be far away, yet already under Allied occupation; for since the "state of emergency," some ten days ago, the Germans have not allowed them to be rung.

Strange how quickly one settles down to getting on with the least of everything! As oil for lamps is strictly limited and candles even more, one thinks twice before using them. One shrinks from using more than the smallest quantity of cistern water for washing, and of spring water for drinking. Although we are reduced in number by half, while the menservants seem to be increased, things begin to have a neglected, dust-bitten, run-down look.

We are not free yet. At the end of the terrace yesterday evening I heard the German soldiers just above us singing to the accompaniment of a concertina, and manifestly enjoying life, saying "yes" to it.

Why not! For them war is a picnic, a rather perilous one, but as jolly as if it were in the Forest of Arden and perhaps, to some few sensitive ones, as idyllic as Arcady. Here they are, sheltered under pine, cypress, and ilex, food seemingly abundant—and besides who dares to refuse them the supplements they ask for, as they do here for wine, milk, coffee, and cigarettes?

A far from Vergilian spectacle was offered to our fellow refugees who strayed over to their house on the Via Bolognese. It had been occupied by the Germans, and what they had not smashed or spoiled they carried away.

There were seven bathrooms, each with W.C., but the Germans did their business into the baths.

I heard from Belgian refugees, during the last war, that in princely country houses the Germans would squat on the most sumptuous beds, when nature called.

How account for this? It would look almost as if the lowest classes in Central Europe, and no doubt more so farther east, instinctively resent being pulled up from the neolithic slum ways of life where they feel at home, and revenge themselves not only by destroying but by befouling whatever reminds them of a standard of life that their flesh resents and abhors. I wonder at times whether today's conflicts are not mainly over standards of life. In that case the Anglo-Saxon missionaries who, wherever they go, endeavor with evangelical zeal to impose their own standards, are laboring not so much in the vineyard of the Lord as in the garden of a graded capitalistic society. Unconsciously, of course. Capitalistic society has no less interest in lifting humanity out of proletarianism than Bolshevism, Fascism, and Nazism have in keeping it there or pushing it still lower down. Thus far the country in Europe where the nearest approach to complete proletarization has been made is Russia, where the standard of life was lowest and hardest. In Asia it is probably the Chinese proletariat that has the greatest difficulties in life. If the American missionary can raise its standards, he may save it from Bolshevism.

Be that as it may, let me tell of the neighboring convent with its sixty nuns, mostly of good family. Their buildings are far more exposed than we are, so that all of their windows are broken. Shells, shrapnel, and splinters have peppered their walls. A missile penetrated a room where they were sitting together, and but for a miracle would have struck down one or more.

They have with them just now the head of a religious order on his way to Rome from Northern Italy. Unable to go farther, he has taken refuge with them. A fine-looking man who but for his black gown, with the red cross reaching from chest to knees, might easily pass for an intellectual lawyer or administrator. He came a day or two ago to consult my host. I asked him whether the nuns were frightened. He said no, that every evening before they retired he gave them absolution and that comforted and calmed them.

The non-Catholic must be informed that to die unabsolved is the greatest evil that can befall a person. What confidence faith still gives!

August 16th

LAST NIGHT the pocket electric lamp that was lighting me upstairs gave out. The only one left over will follow. We are nearly at the end of matches. If this goes on, we shall be reduced not to flint, for we do not possess any, but to the most primitive of all methods of making fire, twirling a pointed stick on dry leaves till they begin to burn. It is a tedious process.

Rumor has it that the Allies, to avoid the horror of street fighting and the destruction of buildings, are trying to encircle the town, so that the Germans must leave it or surrender.

These same Germans do not seem to have the slightest regard for Florence. If they have blown up the bridge of Santa Trinita we shall never see the like of it again. Its moldings were too subtly delicate to be copied; and besides, the whole fabric has been caressed by centuries of sun and shadow and given a patina, a color, between ivory and honey that restoration cannot supply.

We are told as well that the huge castlelike palace opposite has been dynamited. It was built toward the end of the fourteenth century for Niccolò Acciaiuoli, as enterprising and successful a European as ever lived.

This huge building in my time has served various ends, including apartments for strangers. I had one there some hundred steps up, and it faced the bridge. My desk was in the embrasure of the wall. As I looked out from work, I could see the crowd streaming across the pea-colored river, and San Miniato lit up by the sunset glow. I spent my first three Florentine years there, and there I wrote my earliest articles for the *New York Nation*, the *Essay on Connoisseurship*, the *Venetian Painters*, and the monograph on *Lorenzo Lotto*. I never could pass this building without recalling one or more of a thousand memories.

I will not put down the stories that reach us of brutality of every kind committed by the German soldiery, and of their rapes of very young girls. They are too abominable to be believed. No worse in ancient chronicles.

As we were finishing luncheon yesterday, a missile came through the window, passed between me and my hostess, and hit the wall opposite. It was the splinter of a shell which had burst near the kitchen door. Another bursting near the chapel smashed several windows, damaged the ilexes, and did other damage. We are being more and more exposed as the battle approaches this hill, which commands the German line of retreat and is occupied by them.

August 17th

LAST NIGHT, from nine in the evening till this morning, the cannonading louder, more insistent, more menacing, more continuous than ever. Sleep was scarcely possible. One could but doze and wake, wake and doze. On returning to my room I found not only the window sills but my bed powdered with plaster that the blast of artillery fire had shaken down from ceiling and cornices.

Yesterday began well. A Red Cross doctor living a mile or so below, and seeing how much of a target our hillside had been the day before, came early to see whether we were dead or alive. He had various bits of good news to tell us.

The Allies seem as yet not to be in full force this side of the Arno, but Florence is already in the hands of their vanguards and of Italian *partigiani*. A new mayor has been appointed in the person of Dr. Pieraccini, a Socialist deputy before Fascism, a saintly physician and great scholar, whose life at Mussolini's order, to use Mussolini's own words, had been made "difficult for him."

An Allied general and his a.d.c. are said to have been shot at and killed from a house they were passing. It was immediately surrounded and turned out to be an arsenal filled with arms and explosives. Eight hundred Fascists were lurking there to receive the Allies. I noted weeks ago that the Fascists and Nazis in combination were organizing groups for mischief in every Italian town; but that they would attack openly, desperately, and in numbers passed expectation.

So much for local news. From the outside the following: The Russians seem to be still knocking at the gates of Warsaw. Strange, by the way, that these lightning warriors should be even slower in taking the Polish capital than the Anglo-Saxons the Tuscan one. Then, that the Allies have made another landing in France, this time between Fréjus and Marseilles, and that in Normandy they are doing well and advancing toward Paris.

Incidentally, I got the comforting news that my house is occupied by Germans who are behaving correctly and that my wife is still there and the Anreps are with her.

The Anreps are the sister, the brother-in-law, and the nephew of Nicky, and took up residence in my villa the moment I left it. Thanks to their knowledge of German, and German ways, they have done through an entire year for my wife and my place what Nicky has done here the last three weeks.

All to the good, and we were comforted. Our host is convinced that such a feeling is invariably followed by the opposite. This time it certainly was.

At the end of the terrace where you enjoy one of the loveliest views in Mediterranean lands, there is a turn to the right, like a long L. It is occupied by a chicken coop and hen roost, a rabbit hutch and some turkeys. Toward noon all was there. By 6 P.M. they had disappeared.

What happened was clear enough. The Teuton lads picnicking just outside the fence either tired of canned goods and, lusting for fresh meat, or just out of sheer fun, broke through the wire netting and carried them off. Not only could traces of their hobnailed boots be followed but later on the fowls could be heard in their camp. This livestock was, for as long as this situation lasts, our only reserve of food, supplying us with eggs and meat. Their loss casts a gloom on my hosts, which had not lifted when we parted for the night.

August 18th

THE WORST night yet! Every species of cannonading from the Germans above us and from the Allies seemingly not far below on our left. This was followed by a series of explosions each louder and more terrific than the last. The Germans have dynamited viaducts, bridges, roads leading here, have made houses to fall on the roadway, all to delay the pursuing Allies. The group of dwellings just below, belonging to very humble people, has been blown up. The least poor of them, the grocer, gave a bribe of forty thousand lire to be spared. No avail. This destruction, this misery on the pretext of delaying the enemy! If only it teaches that war is not an affair of rhethoric, drums, and trumpets but of blood and iron!

According to rumors reaching us yesterday, the Allies are surrounding Florence on every side, and the only part of the ring still incomplete would be the wedging mass of our hill. These rumors seemed substantiated by the fact that the Allies could almost be seen to our right at Calenzano—a few miles away—and that to the left the Germans were blowing up the highway to Bologna. Their only remaining retreat would be, therefore, on both sides of our hill by rather tortuous byroads leading northwards to join the Via Bolognese at some distance. All this encourages me to expect our liberation in a day or two.

Complaints that domestics and peasants have had a hand in the stealing that has been going on these last three weeks. I hope it is true. If domestics and peasants saw the Germans using up and carrying away everything they could lay hold of, they surely were right in taking it for themselves and using it up before the same Germans snatched it from them. Successfully hidden valuables remain in the country as parts of its wealth; and, besides, domestics and peasants may return them to their owners.

*   *   *

Goethe's *Bürgergeneral* and his *Aufgeregten* treat of the effervescence occasioned in Germany by the French Revolution. People of all classes, from highest to lowest, have their say, each according to his station, interests, and character. In the person of the Baron, in the first of these plays, Goethe tells how he would treat the situation: not with measures inspired by herd panic but with understanding, with calm, with humanity, with good will, with readiness to meet fair claims, with persuasion—with reason, in short.

Surprised to discover in Goethe a prose flowing so swiftly, rippling so gaily, and as crystal-clear as in these plays written after 1790. By that time he is apt to write in a somewhat embarrassed, rather dragging way, as in his later *Wahrheit und Dichtung* as well as in the *Wahlverwandschaften.*

Strange how little mankind learns. The fight toward 1100 for the freedom of the municipalities, "the communes," inspired the same crazed horror in the feudal classes that "Communism" alias "Bolshevism" inspires in the upper and middle classes today, and "democracy" during the French revolutionary period.

The reactionary ferocities of the Restoration in France, and to a milder degree of the Biedermeier decades in Germany, have been paralleled and "more than paralleled" by our conduct toward Bolshevism. What did the revulsion after Napoleon produce comparable to Fascism and Nazism, which were "to save the world from Bolshevism"! Every kind of oppression, humiliation, assassination, as of Matteotti and the Rosselli brothers, shootings, massacres of tens of thousands of innocent Abyssinians, hundreds and thousands of Spaniards, millions of Poles and Jews; and a war now of five years' duration which, before it is over, will have cost tens of millions of lives and the savings of generations. I trust the shades of the bankers who boosted Mussolini with a huge loan are satisfied.

August 19th

THE BATTLE FRONT is pressing more closely and narrowing like a belt around our hill. This morning the denizens of this strip of ground have been ordered to keep indoors except from seven to eight in the morning, and seven to eight in the evening. Anyone who is seen out at other hours will be fired at.

Yesterday passed in relative calm. Much skirmishing and cannonading and dynamiting: sounds and sights with no meaning.

In the course of the day a German trooper appeared, surly, harsh-voiced, asking for food and saying they had none. He was offered all that could be spared, potatoes and peas. He refused them disdainfully. So they were not so famished as all that. He hoped, no doubt, to get dainties.

I daresay this same youngster if I met him in his civilian clothes and character, and asked him the way, would answer politely and even kindly.

I have often been struck by the abyss in Germans between their manners in society and their official manners. The first are almost embarrassingly polite. I recall a very great gentleman, a reigning prince, in fact, who had preserved and carried over into my time, until the last war even, the high breeding and exquisite courtesy of the Maria Theresa period. His politeness called out my nostalgic admiration, although at the same time it made me feel like a clod-hopper. One day when I happened to be in his office I heard him talk to a subordinate of no mean rank in a way that horrified me. No doubt our great businessmen can be gruff enough and curse when something dissatisfies them, but they would not treat a person with such insulting and humiliating contempt.

August 20th

WHEN I CAME DOWN yesterday toward noon, I was no little surprised to find our friends not cowering in the shelters withindoors but sitting on the terrace. Fear had left them. It returned soon enough when cannonading, machine-gunning, and dynamiting drove us back into the house. With longer or shorter intervals these have continued; the dynamiting grows closer and louder and all the time making one more and more jumpy. The Germans are blowing up houses along the roads, in the hope of delaying the pursuer.

Indeed, it is in preventing, or at least delaying, pursuit that the originality of German tactics is revealing itself in this war. One of their subalterns, haunting this hill, confessed that they did not dream of giving battle but meant to hold positions as long as they could, and then retire.

Just now some of them clamored for chickens and eggs at the lodge gate, as if every fowl had not been stolen days ago.

Toward evening the Germans bombarded the suburbs of Florence to this side but not far from the center.

❋   ❋   ❋

Goethe's *Epimenides* followed by his *Pandora*. There is little in either that could not have found place in the second part of the *Faust*. They are parallel passages, side paths, tentative efforts which he discarded from the great work but used as building material for more modest compositions.

What reservoirs of ink there must have been in Goethe to be overflowing so copiously and pouring down so continuously! It would be interesting to calculate from what remains how much he wrote every day from his twentieth to his eighty-third year. Most probably this has been done already, for "Goethe research" has been a favorite pursuit of German scholars.

August 21st

NIGHT-LONG artillery fire and dynamiting. The Germans have already destroyed everything that might serve the enemy or permit a return to normal life. Now they are busy smashing and ruining the dwellings of the poor and lowly in the industrial suburb below, with the sole object of delaying pursuit by a day or two, perhaps only by hours. The fact is that the chivalrous, clean-fighting German *Wehrmacht*, from the pious Catholic Field-Marshal Kesselring, their commander in chief in Italy, down to the common soldier, are still raging because they had to leave Rome before they could deal with it as they had with Naples. The colonel of the parachutists commanding the troops in Florence is reported to have declared that since Smolensk had been completely destroyed before it was abandoned there was no reason why Florence should be spared.

Yesterday Allied troops had approached the hospital quarter at our feet. The German artillery shot into it at once, ruining buildings and wounding and killing patients. To spare further innocent lives, they withdrew.

Strange how little indignation German behavior rouses among my Italian friends. True, they are not given to indignation. Yet they had it in abundance against the Allied bombardments of Naples, Milan, Turin, Genoa, and still more against "terroristic at-

tacks" on German towns. The Germans must be granted every
advantage, for God has given them a chivalrous, exquisitely dis-
ciplined, invincible army. As for the Allies, did not Mussolini describe their troops as "men without jobs pushed into uniforms to
consume five meals a day"!

After being cut off for some time from the rest of the world,
people around me are getting bored and confess that they can
turn to no activity.

That is not my case, because my dominant interests are unac-
tual. Theirs depend on the events and contrasts of the day. Mine
do not. Mine go on despite alarms and excursions. I can read and
be read to by the hour. I can write and I can meditate. My occupations can continue absorbingly so long as I retain my mind,
so long as my eyes do not give out, so long as I have access to
books, pen, and paper. Even if deprived of everything but one's
mind one could still carry on for a good while, and bridge over an
interlude like this.

I have often thought that there is no guarantee against listless-
ness and boredom like historical pursuits of any kind: history not
only of events but of ideas, of literature, of the fine arts, of the
sciences. Nor do I mean to exclude interest in anthropology, in
travel, and in the descriptive sciences; far from it.

Individuals armed with these hobbies never come to the end
of their tether, as I have known mathematicians to do—or get fed
up with their job, as friends of mine who have philosophized for
many years. True that days come when I feel saturated with what
I have been doing. Almost unconsciously I veer over to another
curve of my horizon, and before long I can come back to the first
with renewed zest, and even excitement.

August 22d

NOTHING NEW. The German rear guard, consisting of young parachutists in their vestments of protective coloring, seem to be digging in all around as if expecting a trench war indefinitely drawn
out.

The only pleasure I had yesterday outside of the working of my own mind was in the sunset. It was like a Turner of the most extravagant kind, of the kind described by jeering critics as a "lobster-salad slapp't upon a pallet." It was fuliginously golden and azure and green and yet rosy withal. The sunsets of previous days were scarcely less romantic—a compensation for the great heat, which at last is troubling us. Heat that means dripping with sweat while doing nothing.

Yesterday three German officers came for a friendly call, were polite, and talked. From them and from privates one could gather the following.

Between Florence and us here, there are many partisans, as many as thirteen thousand, the privates say, troublesome and frightening.

It seems that the Germans take these partisans—that is to say anti-Fascist volunteers—much more seriously than do many Italians, who, as I wrote again and again earlier, said they were mere shirkers who ran away because they would not fight.

The German officers added that they themselves were not many but that the Allies were scarcely more numerous and consisted chiefly of Moroccans and New Zealanders. On being asked if there were any real French in the Allied armies, they replied that there were any number, and good fighters too. How many bitterly anti-French Italians would have been disappointed to hear that the North African Corps did not consist only of Jews forcing Moroccans and Senegalese to fight for them!

If it be a fact that there are so few Allied troops in the neighborhood, what has become of the rest of their forces, the 5th and 8th Armies—what are they doing? Even Allied aviation has seldom appeared the last days, except an observer or two. Yesterday for the first time there were as many as twelve churning over us.

What would I not give to know what our forces are doing here and what is happening in other sectors! Our armies cannot be doing nothing.

The Germans say their own morale both at the front and behind the lines is high. Their seeming retreat on all fronts is but a taking position for the final spring. It will crush all enemies, and procure a lasting German peace. Not their numbers, their discipline, their courage, their steadfastness, their endurance will bring about this glorious result, but a new weapon: that is to say a mechanical invention, a Jules Verne discovery. How far we are from the armor and plumes of chivalry with which the friends of Germany decked the *Wehrmacht!*

People are half inclined to believe in this new arm, and prepare to be circumspect in the interval between the complete German withdrawal and their possible return.

August 23d

THE CANNONADING which had been continuous through the night sounded at six this morning like the rush and swish of a gale, while above my head a stone colossus danced a hornpipe. Gradually it quieted down, and just now I heard the cathedral bell as one seldom does normally when the manifold noises of a city absorb the sound.

Yesterday passed with frequent calls for Nicky to see this German, to talk to the other, and to try to mollify a third. They were taking away a door from the porter's lodge at the convent and the nuns thought it was to be used for firewood. Not at all: it was to construct an observatory on what the Germans had recognized to be neutral ground that they were bound to respect. It turns out to be an admirably camouflaged affair that perchance a veteran might suspect, but he alone.

Toward evening a German subaltern turned up and talked a little more freely, said that he for his part was not so sure that the Allies were not close at hand in great force. He feared a terrible attack tomorrow or the day after. Nor did he believe that they would resist long on the Futa—their *ligne Maginot*. What were they doing here, anyhow, when the Russians were already less than a hundred miles from his home in Silesia!

We had been indoors all day, owing to the great heat, and after dinner were taking the air on the terrace when the dragging shuffle of German boots was heard. We stepped to the railing and Nicky asked, "*Wer da?*" No answer, but the sound of retreating steps, and muttered curses of the most obscene kind.

Probably the same man who had successfully stolen chickens and rabbits the other day now hoped to take a calf. The cattle belonging to this place are gathered in the *limonaia*—the shed for the lemons in winter—under the terrace. It was decided to make them come up to the upper terrace and tie them to the colonnade before the house. There, marauding Germans would not venture to approach, and besides peasants would remain on watch. Followed a clatter, a kicking, a lowing, a bellowing which lasted a good while before these cows and calves and oxen were shepherded up steps not meant for quadrupeds, to their quarters for the night. All this by the light of the stars, as no lamp or lantern could be lit.

Provisions seem inexhaustible, although it is more than three weeks since they have been replenished. The housewife laid in abundantly for an emergency. Only fresh meat is at an end. Who cares in this season when one has all the homemade *pasta* and home-baked bread one wants, plenty of green vegetables, luscious pears, huge succulent plums, and honey-sweet figs!

What a paradise this Italy, and how kind to its children if only inky-tongued agitators with their belching rhetoric did not whip them up to run amok at Abyssinia, at Spain, at Albania, at Greece, against England, Russia, and America!

August 24th

"FOR THE SKINNY JADE the Lord provides horseflies," says a Neapolitan proverb. On top of our hallucinated, cooped-up, unventilated way of life for now almost a month, scarcely daring to put our noses out of doors for fear of stray shots or splinters, full of worries for the poor and the peasants as well as for relations and ourselves; tired of the Germans even when they bring gifts as a sort of peace offering for the marauding of some among them —on top of all we are macerated by the great heat. Every door and window is shut to keep as cool as possible inside; yet in my spacious bedroom the thermometer neared 90. It was warmer still when I took a step or two on the terrace after sunset.

Artillery fire the night through, but no appreciable result. In the hospital city below, not only patients but many who took refuge there are starving. Their own provisions are coming to an end, and the Germans have nothing to give them.

One of the officers whom Nicky went to see when the Germans wanted to take this house has been killed—in a motor accident, they say. But their rage against the partisans, whom they still go on calling "rebels" and "brigands," the fact that they are searching every house and hut, that they allow no male to show his head out of doors, incline one to suspect that he was shot dead by one of them.

❁   ❁   ❁

Yesterday read Shelley. Something subconscious in me made me want to reread Leopardi's poem about the Oriental shepherd and the moon. I was amazed to find how much it had in common with Shelley's various poems and references to the moon; how many similar images and even epithets, not to speak of the identity of mood. The form is different enough, Leopardi's being more severe, more marmoreal, while Shelley is more rhythmic, more fluent, and more wavelike, more aerial even. The difference in attitude is significant. Though they feel so similarly about things as they are, the Englishman is buoyed up with hope, dances with excitement over the conviction that all will come right, and the Italian does not even wish to look for a remedy.

I have no books here to satisfy my curiosity, but I wonder whether Shelley did not know Leopardi's poem. He was a great reader of Italian while in this country. If he did not know it or any other of Leopardi's writings, then the singular likeness would be an unusual instance of the time-spirit inspiring in the same way an Italian and an Englishman. Let me add that by time-spirit I do not mean anything mythical or mystical as many do when they talk of *Zeitgeist*. I mean the advance in feeling, thought, and expression that manifests itself almost simultaneously in the creations of gifted artists in our world. Artists are autonomous in the sense that they owe nothing to each other, or at least are not so ready to receive the same revelation that the merest hint suffices.

August 25th

A FAINT BREEZE sprang up yesterday after sunset, and clouds appeared. One hoped for a change in the weather, but this morning the sky was like a gem of purest ray serene.

I no longer mind the deafening, crashing, spluttering noise of the cannonading. It seems to signify no more than the serving of tennis balls.

For days the Allies have made no appreciable progress, while the Germans, who, when they blew up viaducts, bridges, and roadways, were expecting to retreat immediately, now seem to be digging in as if for trench warfare. They must regret their own demolitions and destructions. It leaves them almost no way open for counterattack except through the hospital city at our feet.

The Germans claim that they have respected the neutrality of the hospital city: by which they seem to mean that they have used it as a thoroughfare and in every other way that suited their convenience, but did not fortify it or place batteries there.

They must be itching to do so now, and it is not impossible that this explains the visit of two captains which delayed our luncheon yesterday by a full hour.

One of them seemed a quiet, tolerably human individual; the other talked in the clipped jargon and with the arrogant sneer of Potsdam.

They came, they said, on a purely humanitarian errand. In the hospital there were twenty-five hundred sick and fifteen hundred refugees. They had no water; and while the Germans did all they could to feed them, supplies were not sure, seeing how much their only remaining connection with their depots were under constant fire. Would the Minister of a neutral government not take a step toward alleviating the situation? The patients and refugees were clamoring to be taken into town, where, if not better fed, they would be free from the fear of bombs and shells, and having so frequently to run for shelter.

Would not the Minister write to the Allied authorities already in Florence, to the Cardinal-Archbishop, to the Swiss Consul, to the Director-General of the Hospitals urging them to evacuate the hospital city of the sick and the refugees? Of course they would have to supply the transport, as the Germans no longer had any.

My impression would be that one of these officers meant what he said; but as for the other, he may have had it in his mind that, once evacuated of sick and silly, the hospital could be occupied and turned into a fortified camp.

The letters have been written and are to be taken under the white flag by the chief doctor of the hospitals. I await the result with curiosity.

The Potsdamish officer asked with a sneer whether we had not been bombarded. "Not so far." He gave a malignant grin. "You'll be lucky if you fare no worse." No doubt he thought that we should be.

August 28th

THE DAY BEFORE YESTERDAY, after a pretty noisy night, artillery sounding ever nearer, it was decided not to lunch in the dining room but to picnic in the library. This is a large room backing against the rock and lit by clerestory windows. The meal passed off cheerfully and we retired to shelter for the siesta. Soon after four, Nicky and I thought of returning to the library to go on with the reading of Shelley's "Prometheus." We had scarcely settled down when an ominous rattle, clatter, and swish made us start up. As I reached the drawing room, I saw gliding along the shut window blinds what I should have taken for hissing snakes if I had not recognized that they were splinters of shell. We ran to the shelter, which our friends had not abandoned, and at four-thirty a systematic shelling of this house began and lasted a full half hour.

It was done with smallish missiles not more than two or three inches in diameter. They did no serious damage to the fabric but left few windowpanes unbroken, few doors, shutters, and wire nettings unshattered, untattered, or unperforated. Indoors the splinters behaved in the erratic way that projectiles have. The drawing room, after the bombardment, looked like an antiquity shop that was hastily being demolished. Thick layers of plaster over every object and dust rising from them in a mist. The furniture damaged: here a leg gone, there a desk torn asunder, a chair punched through, books lying about, bitten off at the edges, while frail glass flower vases remained untouched. In the library not only had the glass of the clerestory gone but chairs, tables, rugs, folio volumes thrown here and there as by a hurricane.

In my bedroom, besides broken windows, little damage. A bit of shrapnel not an inch long pierced the door of the clothespress, went through a silk jacket, and lodged in the trousers that were folded over the same hanger.

This morning at seven, all as quiet as this countryside can be between bombardments, silent to the farthest horizons, not a bird chirping or stirring, no voice from the valley below with its million of human bipeds, I stole out and walked up and down the full length of the terrace and could take account of the damage done out of doors.

The house itself untouched except in the most superficial way. The staff of the legation flag on a tower had its neck broken. On the terraces marble tables and balustrades were in fragments, the ground pitted with shells, and the ilexes with broken branches tattered and despoiled.

I spoke of "stealing out." Ever since the bombarding grew serious, my hosts have been increasingly nervous if any guest attempted to put his nose out of doors. I was particularly unruly and would not obey. They assured me that every time I went out they had their hearts in their mouths.

After the shelling of the house we were kept indoors more tightly than ever. Not only indoors but in the dark, for every opening was closed up with temporary contrivances. No reading, no writing.

It is curious whom fear takes and whom it leaves. The servants turned out to be much more resistant than I expected, the house maids particularly, but bravest of all a young man who had interrupted his training as a *carabiniere* to go into hiding from the Germans; he seems not only untouched by fear but goes on serving meals and carrying knives, forks, plates, and dishes, as if he had done nothing else for many years. The example given to them by our perfectly fearless hostess has a great deal to do with it, I imagine.

In the face of every difficulty, meals are as well cooked, as varied, and sufficient as at any time since our siege began—for siege it is that we have been submitted to, for a full month.

It is curious how Mediterranean people take fear. It is for them a disease, a disturbance as physiological as, say, toothache to which you give in as unresistingly. They feel no more shame in confessing to it than to any other physical fact—and I need not add that they discuss our animal nature with a frankness that I, after fifty years of living with them, have not yet got used to.

✿   ✿   ✿

THE EVENINGS are tedious. Our hosts have been assured that no matter what you contrive to leave no fissure open, the light, even of the tiniest pocket lamp, traverses not only barred and sealed opening but stone walls, and hovers around the house like a halo which artillery observers can perceive ten or more miles away, inviting them to bombard us.

So we pass the evenings like Maeterlinck's *Aveugles,* and after having been cooped up together for a month, talk is apt to run stale and dry up altogether. The favorite subject is speculation as to what the Allies are doing, how near they are approaching, and when they will relieve us. Our host, the Minister of a neutral power, is not a little indignant that this house, with the legation flag flying over it conspicuously, should have been subjected to deliberate shelling by the Allies. Nor could I take their defense or offer an explanation. Most likely armored-car people not far off have inferred that this house was occupied by the German staff commanding this sector. If that is so, I can scarcely wonder, seeing how free the Germans have made with these grounds, respecting only the house and its own terrace. Not even that much, for hardly a day has passed without one or two or even more appearing to ask for something. As they come in helmeted and fully armed, artillery observers could easily have noticed them.

I hope the error has been recognized. Yesterday there was no repetition of the bombardment.

Speaking of the damage done in and outside this building, I forgot to mention that a cow and calf, stalled under this terrace, were killed. And unfortunately a peasant who went about his work early yesterday morning, lower down in our grounds, stepped on an unexploded shell and was blown up. These unexploded shells are a symbol of the unspent rage that will go on festering when the war with arms is over.

This experience not only of a close siege but also, as it were, of an unlit prison will remain to feed imagination for the rest of my days.

I must not forget a word about that *mulier fortis*, that "woman of price," our hostess. Not only her housekeeping under serious difficulties and danger but her spirit, her cheerfulness, her gaiety, are beyond praise. Let us allow that it is just the least bit put on to buck up the rest of us; that is only more laudable.

August 29th

YESTERDAY FORENOON one could write and read by daylight. At lunchtime, keen bombardment began again and we had our meal in the refuge. Yet merrily enough! Somewhat later, the bombardment grew more and more deafening, and suddenly came a sound of something falling indoors, and the patter of plaster reached our ears. Before long, the bravest of the servants came screaming and shouting that a bomb had flown into our hostess' dressing room, turned into the bedroom, where it leaped and bounded from wall to wall, from one piece of furniture to another, doing damage as it went, before it came to rest in the middle of the floor—unexploded.

Our hosts were exemplary. Instead of wailing, they said they were grateful that the bomb, which might have blown up the house, had not exploded. Yet what to do with it? A letter was written by Nicky to the lieutenant of the parachutists to our left (with whom we have had good relations from the start) begging him to send a specialist to deal with this affair. None of the privates at the observation post near us would take it yesterday, but this morning some were willing, and soon two boys appeared, one being the mine expert and the other an ambulance driver. The expert examined the bomb and declared that it was not spent and could still explode. In a touching way he said to his comrade: "Must I risk picking it up?" The other answered: "You must." Then he sent all of us away to the other wing of the house, and after a few minutes he reappeared beaming, having carried the bomb to the rocks behind the house.

I hope our hosts and their guests will recall this when inclined to condemn Germans in the lump. It is a painful part of our mental machinery that we tend so to abstract and simplify, and to forget that a nation is made up of all sorts, more good than evil perhaps, and different as individuals from what they are as part of a collectivity. The nearer we come to a collectivity, let us say a nation, the less human it is apt to be. But to condemn all the individuals constituting a group for the crimes of the collectivity is to rival Caligula when he wished the Roman people had but one throat for him to cut.

This night it seemed as if the German artillery above us had placed their guns closer to get a better aim at the English below, for the noise was deafening. Even under the vaults of our corridor one felt shaken. Mosquitoes, with their buzz and sting, kept me awake more than the noise outside.

Living like moles in the dark is depressing, stupefying, and hypnotizing. The mind gets lazier, emptier, and almost ceases to function, leaving one in a kind of hallucination. Then there is the lack of exercise, which I feel particularly. I do Swedish gymnastics twice a day but it does not replace my daily walks.

What a part these daily walks have played in my life from earliest boyhood till now! They have been not only among my best hours but among the most formative. I owe to them in great part my love of "nature," my feeling for poetry, even my love of beauty. When I am deprived of my walk, a day is not a day.

August 30th

No change for the better. Yesterday was stuffy, sticky, muggy, tepid, oozing, and produced restlessness, bad temper, and impatience. The artillery practice went on with such violence that at times the house shook to its foundations.

If our incarceration lasts much longer, the resources of our provident hostess will be exhausted and we shall be reduced to feeding on bread and water—if we can procure them. Water for washing is running short, and we are not like the Arabs of the desert who can cleanse themselves with sand. We shall have to scrape our bodies with the gravel from the shell-pitted terrace. My silvery beard will get so large before I can see a barber that it may wave as a white flag!

And the Germans on this hillside are taking it easy as if they never would move. One drops in for a smoke and another to cook a turkey in our kitchen. To the amazement of the servants he stuffed it with grapes and any other fruit he could find.

It reminds me of the disgust with which an Italian friend turned away when, in a Munich restaurant, he was handed stewed fruit with his venison and exclaimed, "*Come, il dolce col manzo!*"— What, sweet with meat!

August 30th

Finished a third or fourth rereading of Shelley's "Prometheus." As after previous perusals, I leave it saying "never again." It is, as Pierre Mille of the Paris *Temps* used to say, an *ennui auguste*—a solemn bore. Critics seem to accept it as the poet's masterpiece. Naturally, it has touches of beauty, but the whole reminds me of the vaguest, least vital, least evocative parts of Goethe's second *Faust*.

How often Shelley recalls the aging and aged Goethe! Similar airy rhythms, curling like faint mists and dissolving before they take shape and substance in my mind. I have often asked what may have been the connection between the two poets. I cannot recall that the German ever mentions the Englishman, who undoubtedly knew him. But how much? The likeness is strongest in his versification, and this he surely had perfected before he read Goethe.

After going over the greater part of Shelley's verse I conclude that the best has been skimmed by anthologies like the *Golden Treasury,* the *Oxford Book of Verse,* and one or two others. I go so far as to approve the way Tennyson and Palgrave have lopped and pruned the "Lines Written among the Euganean Hills," giving them a continuity and concentration of feeling and thought that, as left by Shelley, the poem lacks.

No doubt this is a drastic proceeding but more than justifiable, if our first interest is poetry and not the poet. If, as seems to be the case with most of our professors, students, and critics of literature, interest is focused on the author, no jot or tittle can be omitted, for an iota subscript may give the key to this or that minute point in the hero's career still awaiting elucidation. And if the author is as fascinating a person as Shelley or Byron, and his writings are regarded as so much autobiography, every syllable counts. Only do not let us believe that by doing so we are studying poetry, and devoting our best energies to getting its full meaning.

Which leads me to wonder whether perchance antiquity, while still itself, did not select for us what was best in Greek lyrical poetry, as well as in the drama. The fragments that the sands of Egypt have preserved for us, even of Sappho and Pindar, are disappointing enough, and Bacchylides, so much admired by the Greeks, turns out to be a sort of Tupper, a versifier ordinary in feeling and obvious in expression.

But to return to the "never again"—how often I have said it to places that disappointed me, to music, to books, to sculptures, to pictures, or to people—yes, to people. Then accident, and at times a bad conscience or curiosity, led me to experience the object again, and often the result was a complete change. What I previously was too unreceptive, too lacking in a state of grace to perceive, to penetrate, and to admire, now revealed itself at last, and added so much to my House of Life.

My conclusion is that what has been admired by generations, let alone centuries and millennia, contains something worthy of sympathetic attention; and that, failing to give it and refusing the proffered gifts, we take our punishment into our own hands. One must try again and again. Only now in advanced age have I got to enjoy Dickens, although I have not yet become an ardent admirer.

August 31st

YESTERDAY was the worst day yet. The cannonading grew more and more terrifying and seemed to be ever nearer, obliging us to spend most of the long day and even longer night in the oval shelter supposed to be the safest on the premises. The house trembled, shook, and rattled. It was not easy to keep one's heart from quaking.

Early morning brought the rumor that the Germans had withdrawn from our hill to a position five miles higher up, and that the English were already masters of the hospital city at our feet.

This was confirmed later by a man who came up from Florence. He reported that there all was well, that half a pound of good white bread was being distributed to every person, that the troops, English and American, were behaving nicely, that there were no black savages among them as had been feared, etc., etc.

As for news from abroad, it seems that almost the whole of France is already liberated and that Soviet troops are on German territory.

The tension here has been too great to allow one to enjoy the imminence of complete freedom from fear of Fascists, of Germans, and of bombs. The last affected me little, so little that but for my protectors, who felt responsible for me, I scarcely should have taken to shelter. But human malevolence makes a coward of me and I blench at the approach of any person whom I suspect of coming to annoy me, especially when it is to ask what they know I ought not to do for them.

September 1st

EVENTS HAVE BEEN LEAPING and outracing each other the last thirty hours. It is hard to select what to write down in these notes.

The cousin of my host, a young officer who had been taken prisoner in Crete after the armistice a year ago and sent by the Germans to a concentration camp in Poland and, on his return to Italy in the spring, spent some time here as fellow refugee—this same young officer appeared in the door of my bedroom like a full-length portrait in a frame, and I had a momentary hesitation in placing him as I have at times in attributing a picture.

He was the first visitor to appear and bring news from the outer world. He confirmed the worst rumors that had reached us about the deliberate German destructions in Florence. All the bridges down except the Ponte Vecchio, and their approaches blown up. After evacuating the town the Germans shelled it without the least care for the monuments and hit the cathedral, Giotto's tower, the baptistery, and San Lorenzo—luckily, without serious damage. He told us that the Fascist radio and press, and no doubt the Nazis likewise, hurled indignation at the Allies for blowing up the bridges over the Arno and their approaches, as well as for the deliberate bombardment of the cathedral, campanile, and baptistery—a fine transmutation of fact to fiction.

Here we were not yet quite rid of the Germans. A bunch of ten continued to camp close by and several of them insisted on cooking in our kitchen. Nicky warned them that it was no longer safe to linger. They did, and presently a troop of partisans appeared on the terrace, made two of them prisoners, and shot a third trying to escape.

Our friends were terrified lest the comrades of these Germans would return to take reprisals.

So much for yesterday. This forenoon began with a visit from young Contini in partisan outfit with two companions, followed by a partisan fighter with a note from my friend Colacicchi, who appeared in person later in the day. Then came Captain Cagiati, followed by Major Sampson (the head of the Allied Office for D.P.s), the last with offers of assistance. He will take me over tomorrow afternoon to see Mary and arrange to move me toward the end of next week, bag and baggage, that is to say with the pictures and other works of art, as well as the books I have had here.

Furthermore, he brought the news that he had been to my house, which had been left unharmed by the German occupants, and seen my wife, who seems to be no worse for all we have gone through this past year.

Of intimates, the first to appear this morning was Igor Markevitch, who occupies a *villino* on our place and besides being one of the most gifted composers and a remarkable conductor is one of the most stimulating and entertaining of young men. He also brought encouraging news of my wife's health and of the state of repair in which my house remains. The garden seems to be in a sorry way, as the population of Ponte a Mensola would crowd in for safety from air attack and other alarms.

Strange how instinctive it is for the "lower orders" to seek safety in huddling close to some building bigger and stronger than their own. Originally it may have been a stronghold of sorts that drew them. Much later the feeling of security was transferred to the man who occupied this structure. Thus as gods first took shape long after man had begun to grope for the numinous, so authority, lordship, and finally sovereignty may have proceeded from faith in the impersonal protection of the stockade, the tower, and finally the castle.

In the afternoon Colacicchi, Arturo Loria, and other friends trooped in, among them also Carlo Steinhaüslin, the Swiss Consul, and his wife. I was told that the head of the Committee of Liberation, the body which is to represent civil government in Tuscany, is a youngish art historian with whom all, including the Allied Command, are well satisfied.

So this thirty-year-old art critic may turn out one of the rulers of reviving Italy. How often during the last war teachers from schools, colleges, and universities at home, who in ordinary times might have passed obscure and perhaps tedious lives, revealed talents which turned them into important government functionaries! Needless to say, they never returned to their posts as teachers.

The only time I met Woodrow Wilson, he was still professor at Bryn Mawr. I no more suspected that he would live to be, first, the astute and powerful party chief, and then the messianic statesman, than that Monsignor Ratti, who some fifty or more years ago, as underlibrarian of the Ambrosiana, used to fetch and carry manuscripts for me, would end as Pius XI, the Pope who first hailed Mussolini as the "man sent by Providence," and later came little short of stigmatizing him as anti-Christ. Nor when I was charmed by a youngish couple named Franklin Roosevelt that I met during the Peace Conference in Paris did I foresee that he would become the most remarkable President we have had since Lincoln, and she a helpmate such as no former chief of our state had had.

September 3d

YESTERDAY AFTERNOON a car sent by Major Sampson came to take me for a visit to my home.

An errand obliged us first to go to the Piazza dei Giudici on the Arno, close behind the Uffizi. Driving there, I could get an impression of what had happened. On both sides of the Mugnone nearly all the houses were empty shells, like buildings I remember seeing at Rheims after the first German retreat during the last war. Driving by the outer avenues toward the Arno, the destruction showed up less and less till we came to our destination. There I got out of the car and walked to the Ponte Vecchio. In the course of these few steps I saw nothing but piles of ruins heaped high as in eighteenth-century drawings of the Roman campagna. Only the early medieval towers remained erect. Of the S. Trinita bridge no more than parts of the pillars remained standing. Between the two bridges the so picturesque and continuous façade of houses was pounded to dust. I doubt whether deliberate havoc like this has been perpetrated before in the course of history. Attila the Hun and Genseric the Vandal may have had the will but lacked the machinery. It has taken science, at the service of the dehumanized spirit of militarism, to bring about what my eyes have seen.

What I heard was worse still. I cannot begin to recount it, but one fine Nazi act I must note. I am assured that, before leaving, the Germans put mines in the rubbish coating of the ruins so as to blow up the first who rummaged in them.

These monstrosities were ordered by a commander who is a fervent Roman Catholic. But of what avail is Roman Catholicism pitted against Potsdam militarism?

If they had been fighting hard to take a town, there might be some faint excuse. This sadistic destruction of one of the most beautiful, as well as most historic, spots on earth for no more useful purpose than to hold up their enemy's advance for a couple of days at most.

They continue to bomb Florence. Already they have killed some three hundred and fifty, mostly civilians, for there are few Allied soldiers as yet in the town. So, at least, I am told. If I was to judge by the numberless tanks, armored cars, caterpillars, etc., we saw lining the roads as we dashed along, I should say there were a great many. All the way to my own house, the drive, the farm, and the orchard grounds opposite were crowded with vehicles and swarming with troops. These looked anything but military and like nothing else than factory hands in their overalls, like laborers in steel and other heavy industries. We have touched the fundamental fact, at last. War, no matter what its origin and our attitude towards it, turns out to be an outlet for overproduction and unemployment; or, if you like to mythicize it, war now unites in one person Mime the forger of the sword and Siegfried who wields it.

I found my wife no better for the year, less one week, that has separated us. She was suffering spasms of acute pain, and her speech was clogged. I carried away a sad and painful impression.

Nicky's sister, brother-in-law, and nephew, the Anreps, I saw next. They cared for my house and my wife while I was away. Thanks to their devotion and their tact, the Germans who in successive hundreds occupied the place did not sack it or damage it. The only mischief these did was to soak in full bathtubs, carelessly letting the taps open so that both our copious reservoirs have been emptied and are now without water. I may add that in times of drought all the houses surrounding us profited by our supply, and are now suffering from a water famine.

It is not the only calamity that afflicts the peasants and small people in our neighborhood. They are starving. Even the Anreps are living chiefly on rationed bread and tomatoes. The German soldiery have plucked every fruit tree bare, have left no vegetable on the ground, have even picked the olives, although they do not begin to be ripe before January. They have seized what wheat they could lay hands on and dragged the cattle with them when they left. Needless to add that they left no fowl or rabbit alive.

To return a moment to the Anreps. In 1918 they had to run for their lives from the Bolsheviks invading Estonia. Their country mansion was burnt to the ground with its contents, accumulated by generation after generation. Later the entire estate was confiscated. All they could bring away were jewels, trinkets, a few miniatures, and other souvenirs.

At last they succeeded in making a new home for themselves in a house between the two bridges in Florence. There the Baroness received company as few others in Florence—men of letters, artists, musicians, and interesting people of every kind, residing or passing through.

Now this is gone like their Baltic home. I trust it is a rare case that the same family should suffer in the same way, and for the same reasons, in the course of one lifetime.

My house has had the honor of a visit from Marshal Kesselring, the so pious and so humane commander in chief of the Nazi forces in Italy. Perhaps it was at his orders that artillery was placed in the garden not a hundred feet away from my wife's bedroom. It is a miracle that the place has not been more damaged.

Most of the glass has gone—a serious matter, as it cannot easily be replaced and rain followed by cold will soon be here. Part of the *fattore's* house was smashed, with all his furniture. The garage bore marks of shelling. The garden looked unkempt and shaggy, not so much through damage as through lack of care. With the approach of the Allies, and the consequent intensification of bombardment, two of the gardeners deserted, as did half of the domestics. When I proposed that the cook should be ordered to return, I was answered that there was no need to hurry for there was nothing to cook.

The disastrous impression I carried away was due most of all to the squalor, the filth, the disorder conspicuous on the farmland and in the orchard opposite—a combination of city refuse heaps, automobile cemetery, and gypsy camp. Unfortunately, narrow and winding as the road is which, after passing through my estate, climbs up the hill, it happens to be at the moment the only one available for our armies to reach the Via Bolognese in pursuit of the Boches. Every kind of mastodontic ponderous vehicle goes up and down all the time, raising clouds of dust unbreathable, bumping into and smashing park walls and gates.

I went away discouraged. I could not face returning home until at least this traffic stopped and the fields were cleared of squalor. Indoors we can manage—somehow. The problem is how to feed the household and how to light it now that days are getting short and then, in the near future, how to heat the few rooms into which we must huddle.

September 5th

I FORGOT TO SAY that a couple of days ago there came here a nut-brown giant of a Cossack speaking English with an unmistakable Russian accent. He had been sent to find out how I was, how I was faring, and if possible to see me.

He saw me and I asked him whether he was a Soviet officer detached to our troops. Not at all: though born in Russia, he was a good American and a captain in our army. He had left the corn-

fields and steppes in 1917. Had he been back? Yes, with a detach-
ment of the Air Force some little time ago. At Ekaterinoslav, at
Elisavetgrad, at Kharkov, and other Ukrainian towns he saw
with his own eyes the huge trenches which the Jews in their thousands had been made to dig before they were stripped almost
naked and machine-gunned. Then he told us that ever since the
taking of Rome, American troops were yawning their heads off
doing nothing. They were not allowed to stir. And what were the
English up to? He knew the Germans here all together were
about only some hundreds, and millions upon millions were being
wasted on firing at them with almost no results, while if permitted
he could wipe up in a jiffy all that was left here of Nazi squads.

✿   ✿   ✿

The *fattore* of I Tatti has come and reports that an American
unit has placed heavy guns in our fields and given warning that
windows and doors must be left open; for if they began to fire the
blasts might smash them. Our farms are trodden to powder and
will take time and hard work to recondition.

It appears that the behavior of the Allied soldiers gives great
satisfaction. The bobbies controlling traffic are the wonder of the
Florentines. They have never imagined so much kindness and
such good manners in police. Wherever quartered, they amaze
people by their cheeriness, their jolliness, their happy-go-lucky
carefreeness. A lady who had Germans quartered on her told us
yesterday that they always were taking precautions about light
and constantly running to shelter. The English replacing them
keep lights going, play the piano, sing and pass the time gaily.

I hear that among the Fascist desperadoes remaining in the
town there is a fair percentage of women. For instance: the street
where the Etruscan Museum is placed was made unsafe by firing
from a window. It took some time to locate the exact spot, when
out came the perpetrator, an old hag.

There can be no question about the sincerity of most of these
desperadoes. They run imminent and certain risks for a most uncertain reward. Yet we do not hesitate to shoot them when we
catch them. But when an individual of the upper crust incites to

murder and massacre of radicals, or Jews, or Rooseveltites, we are all forgiveness and smiles because he is so "sincere."

More and more accounts from eyewitnesses come in of the conduct of the Germans: how much they rejoiced in every species of iniquity and obscenity, not to speak of deliberate rapine and vandalism.

Individually many were decent enough. One of these was asked by a countrywoman of their own, here resident, why they, including chaps like himself, behaved as they did. He assured her that but for some few who got out of hand and went on their own, the others did only what they were ordered to do.

The individual German trooper, like the individual Fascist, has nothing to do but what he is told by his superiors. Not for him to act as in ordinary life, not for him to reason why—*perinde ac cadaver.*

September 6th

ONE FRIEND AFTER ANOTHER comes to recount what happened to him and his during the month that the Nazis were trying to hold on to Florence, or merely to delay the Allies. It is the same story of inhumanity, brutality, and sadism.

Toward evening yesterday loomed up over the terrace a tall, well-made, rather Socratic-faced youngster. It was my cousin Robert Berenson, who had been looking for me for some time. He told me that having been active in shipping he wanted to join the navy but was refused a commission. The army likewise. He then volunteered as a private.

The refusal was based on the ground that his wife was the daughter of the most fashionable dressmaker in Paris, the Italian Schiaparelli. Our sea and land forces evidently were told that she was a militant Fascist and the conclusion was drawn that her son-in-law could not be trusted to serve his country as an officer.

As a matter of fact, Madame Schiaparelli was a pronounced anti-Fascist and must have become a French subject, for she was turned back at the frontier when, just before the war, she wanted to revisit her Italian home.

I was interested in what Robert told me about the American-born Japs in our army. Despite dissatisfaction with the way their immigrant parents were being treated, they are among the best fighters in the army. Is it patriotism? Is it eagerness to prove that they are as American-minded as any others? Or is it that racially they have more fight in them than most? By "racially" I mean, of course, a body of men who for a matter of fifteen hundred years at least have been welded into one community originally composed of Ainus, Mongols, and Malays.

Baroness Ritter de Záhony, née de Fénelon-Salignac, the mother-in-law of my hostess, the Marchesa Filippo Serlupi Crescenzi—I now feel free to give names—returned yesterday from the neighboring great villa of Quarto and related her adventures during the siege she stood while we were having ours.*

September 7th

IT DISTRESSED ME to hear somebody say in my presence that the young anti-Fascists are no better than their opponents. They are accused of having the same tendencies to violence, to self-assertion, to repaying private grudges. Little to be hoped from them. . . .

September 17th

AT THIS POINT the pen fell from my hands because I felt too sick to go on. For several days I, who have never got over infantile disgust with the eliminating functions of the body, had my body turned into a drain, a sewer. It was accompanied by acute stomatitis, from which I am still suffering. Both left me exhausted and, as it were, hollowed out. The little energy that bubbled up had to be given to correspondence; for at last, after two years, I could write home as well as to England.

I doubt whether I shall be able to continue these notes. Cor-

---

* I have just read the diary she kept those days. It is as interesting as delightfully told, and will no doubt appear before long in some French review. Nicky has written hers, swift and vivid. (January, 1945.)

respondence and professional writing will consume the little ink
I produce daily. I should, however, like to wind it up with my
home-returning, which I expect to take place in a few days, and a
few words about prospects for Germany and Italy.

It will not be easy to pacify Germany. The Nazi desperadoes
have nothing to lose by continuing as long as they can get the
Wehrmacht to drag it on as a "legal war" or by themselves afterwards as partisans. They will not be easy to get rid of, and will
hold out long enough to embitter further a situation already
bitter.

When law and order—*our* kind of law and order—reign at last,
Germany should be treated as a patient broken down by the ill-
treatment she suffered at the hands of the madmen who broke
loose and ran her, as in Poe's story of "Drs. Tarr and Fether."

An American officer, returning yesterday from the front, deplored the death of such fine-looking fellows as the German youth
we were mowing down. They are as gifted a stock as the world
has ever seen. In the past they contributed to invigorate and enrich the blood of European lands all the way to the Crimea, all
the way to Portugal. Today I discover an unusual percentage of
German names among prominent Americans in military as well as
civil positions. In France the Alsatian contribution to every nobler
activity has been remarkable, and in 1919 thoughtful Frenchmen
told me that their eagerness to get Alsace back was not a question
of territory but of a sturdy stock to set off the more volatile elements in their country.

We must convince the Germans of the moral necessity we were
under to fight the Nazis as well as the *Wehrmacht*. We must reconcile them by treating them not vindictively or with short-
sighted selfishness but with reason and even humanity. We must
not leave them thinking that they have the right to pity themselves as victims of brute force. It will be no easy task to re-educate a generation brought up in the schools described by Georg
Ziegler in his *Education for Death.*

This account of how a whole people was being trained to live
and die for one individual and his dream of world dominion

makes one thank the stars that the present war came so soon, when only the youngest recruits had enjoyed this training. They are the most cruel, the most savage, the most fanatical. If all the German forces had been like them, we should be having greater difficulties in beating them.

One word about frontiers, even at the risk of repetition. I hope they will be the same as those left by the Treaty of Versailles, with one exception, the Polish Corridor and East Prussia. I would abolish the first and give the second to Poland on condition that, despite history and propaganda, it ceded Poznan to Germany.

Poznan is a deep intrusion into the very heart of Prussia, and its belonging to a possibly hostile state might be justly resented. Moreover, it has been German off and on for more than a hundred years, much Germanized in that time and—to speak politically— in these war years, cleared of Polish subjects. It should not therefore be too difficult to transfer to Poznan the population of East Prussia when it is taken over by Poland.

As for economic considerations, they are out of bounds for me and I must leave them to the competent, among whom I should take the advice of the experienced rather than of the theologians of finance and the students of that geometrical abortion, the so-called "economic man."

"Vengeance is mine," saith the Lord, and I should not be punitive to the German community as a whole, nor overmuch to individuals. I should be severe with Hitler, Himmler, Ribbentrop, Göring, Goebbels, and their spawn of underlings. I should not be opposed to using the surviving Gestapo, S.S. men, and parachutists to slave in restoring the countries they did so much to ruin, if their labor can be profitably employed.

I should make the Germans restore loot of every kind when it can still be traced, and when it cannot they should furnish its equivalent, whether in works of art, furniture, or household goods, linen, wool, leather, etc., etc.

I should oppose any attempt at money payments.

I should encourage them to return to the federal system of largely autonomous states that they enjoyed before 1918. Only

I should allow Prussia no foot of Brunswick, Hanover, Schleswig-Holstein, Westphalia, or the Rhineland. I should restore the ancient landmarks of these regions and erect them into autonomous communities.

In short, I should not try to put five quarts into a gallon measure. You can no more squeeze a given quantity of human beings than a given quantity of water. As the latter will burst through its recipient so will the first through frontiers unless indeed you allow them to build skyward in order to replace what you have taken from them on earth. We cannot hope for peace or prosperity for ourselves with a Germany self-pitying, self-justified, and resentful.

* * *

I am too well acquainted with Italy to sum up in a few words what I hope for her in the immediate future.

We must recollect that she has only just started out of a nightmare that has lasted for over twenty years, and that she is not yet quite sure that it is over. She is confused, wavering, and distrustful of us as well as of herself. I hope we shall be easy with her and do nothing to offend her pride as a nation. If only Italians had as much political sense as they have humanity they would be in the forefront of great powers. But as I must have said again and again in these pages, their leading classes are in their hearts political atheists. They do not believe in the possibility of good government and therefore "why bother"? If by "government" they mean the highly centralized French type of rule which Piedmont imposed and Fascism screwed down on them, this opinion is not ill-founded. In the course of the fifty-six years that I have followed Italian affairs I often have wondered whether its central government's chief function was not to put its people at loggerheads with those of other governments.

I believe that there would be no lack of civic sense in Italy if government began with the municipality. Everybody would be interested in it because he could see and feel how it affected him immediately. The most intelligent would recognize the identity of municipal interests with those of the region—say, Tuscany,

Lombardy, Latium, Campania, Sicily, Piedmont, etc., etc.—and they would end by believing in the identity of national with regional interests.

We should use our influence discreetly, inaudibly, and invisibly, to promote decentralization in Italy; to encourage regional autonomies; to reduce the functions of the central government to interregional and international business only. And I should try to insinuate that government is business and not theology.

Thus, the form of the regime is perhaps less important than most of my Italian friends seem to think. If my ideal of a confederation, of a United States of Italy, could be made compatible with it I should have no objection to a monarchy, provided—provided it was demilitarized; provided the sovereign and his heirs were not brought up as soldiers having soldiers for governors, tutors, and teachers, their minds filled with military matters and canalized towards them. A soldier's training fits him to obey and command. A sovereign of today, a constitutional sovereign, cannot command, he can only persuade; and to prepare him for that he should be brought up as a civilian and given a civilian education.

"Education"—it is that which our world, friend as well as foe, most needs. What I, who am not an educator, could say on this subject would take a stout volume. Here I can allow myself but a few words.

They are to this effect: Let us, if we can do so tactfully, urge Italians to stop training their young to be rhetoricians, forensic orators, makers of phrases, forgers of catchwords, and rapt admirers of verbal performances as such, regardless of their sense. Where else could the manipulator of a gorgeous vocabulary and orchestral phrases have infected a people's taste, morals, and, worst of all, politics as D'Annunzio did! Even as a demagogue, he prepared the Italian public to enjoy by contrast Mussolini's stinging whiplash pronouncements. As in the schools of all other countries, I should propose a strict control of history teaching, and revision of textbooks to see that they are unpartisan and do not unduly exalt national merits or instill contempt of other peoples and even hatred of them—like the hatred of England taught by the Fascist schoolbooks after the aggression on Abyssinia.

Economically, we can do a great deal for Italy by loans, by helping to restore shipbuilding and the construction of motor vehicles—the only heavy industries for which there is possibility and aptitude here—by encouraging her carrying trade, by buying the products of her soil and the handiworks of her arts and crafts, and by reconciling her with her Yugoslav neighbors. For these have the wood, the livestock, the grain, and many of the raw materials which Italy needs; she could pay for them with her industries, while the expense of transport would be low, seeing how relatively short are the distances to be traversed. Surely if there are two peoples on earth whose interests are reciprocal it is the Italian and the Yugoslav.

We should insist on the restoration of government by discussion and persuasion, of parliamentary government, in short, not only in Italy but, to the extent of our authority and influence, in all lands where these have been silenced by tyrannies, in panic, fear of free speech and a free press. I say deliberately in all lands, so as to include Spain, now ruled by police, priests, and absentee landlords, who for selfish ends perpetuate Baroque seventeenth-century ideas, ideals, and methods. Let me add that by "absentee landlord" I mean any considerable landowner who for the greater part of the year does not live on his estates and does not take an active part in their management.

In these notes I have spoken of the Danubian Confederation. My ideas are not essentially different from those that—as I happened to discover a few days ago—Kossuth entertained seventy years ago and many another Danubian since. If this confederation on a Swiss model could embrace the Balkanic Slavs as well, it would go far toward stable conditions in Europe. They have been the springboards for most wars in the last hundred years and more, originating in hereditary class hatreds of the most primitive type, kept alive in our day by internal folly and external fraud. The lasting reconciliation of Bulgars, Serbs, Macedonians, Slovenes, and Croats would dry up the springs whose waters filibustering foreign statesmen kept troubling so as to fish in them.

Likewise in the north I would encourage every effort to con-
federate Norway, Sweden, Denmark, and Finland so that they
might enjoy more respect from both Germany and Russia than
they have in recent years.

I have already gone beyond my billet and yet feel an urge to
jot down a dream I have dreamt again and again since my earliest
maturity. It is of putting language groups, that is to say nationhood, out of politics; to stop identifying language groups with
states; to allow different language groups to flourish within the
state. Great Britain has done it with Welsh and Gaelic; in good
sooth, because for two whole centuries these, for their part, did
not act eruptively, and did not claim, like the various language
groups in the late, ever-to-be-lamented Austrian Empire, each to
form a separate state.

If that depoliticizing of nationalities could be achieved, we
could encourage each language group to cherish its own individuality, its own peculiarities, its own traditions, its own myths
and legends, its own folk songs, thereby enriching the rest of us
with all that this language has to contribute to our common culture, instead of suppressing it, as Russia did under the last Tsars,
and Germany under its last Kaiser, and Italy under Fascism.
Smaller communities, on their side, would not fear being dena-
tionalized if they learned the language of their powerful neighbors, as was lately the case with Czechs toward German and of
Greeks toward Italian. If this dream could come true, we might
have everywhere examples like the one given in Carl Burckhardt's
Ariel-like account of a visit to a bookseller in Paris. He and Rilke
meet there Lucien Heer, whom many years ago I knew as the
staunchest of Frenchmen although an Alsatian by birth. With
Carl Burckhardt, he comes out as a thoroughbred Alleman, who
ranks Hebbel with La Fontaine and declaims him with rapture, to
the confusion of Rilke, who cannot catch the beauty of the dialect.

I can recall reading in Matthew Arnold, when I was still an un-
dergraduate, of all the nations of Europe—or was it of all nations?
—being so many strings to a harp, none of which could be spared,

for each contributed its timbre to enrich and harmonize the music the instrument was playing. That no doubt was the source of my dream.

September 24th

FIRST MORNING at I Tatti. Less than three months ago Serlupi talked of not letting me return till it was again in apple-pie order exactly as I left it.

Meanwhile I Tatti has been through the wars, has been at the forefront of battle; and the glimpses I had three weeks ago of its squalid bareness gave me an attack of acute xenodochiophobia.

I daresay the polysyllabic word just employed will not be found in dictionaries. I invented it long ago to designate the sinking feeling that in my travels often overcame me: of fear lest the inn or hotel at which we were to lodge would be sordid, would not let me have the promised apartment; that my bedroom would have the wrong proportions, mulling or flattening me out of my normal shape and squeezing me out of my own way of breathing; that the lights would be glaring and no reading lamp by my bed; that there would be sharp or clattering sounds outside, or bad smells without or within. Motoring in the Vendée or Poitou, in Spain or Greece as evening darkened, tired or even exhausted, I would wish the destination farther and farther away, for fear of what I should find when I reached it.

In such cowardly fashion I could have delayed returning to I Tatti. As in the twilight of yesterday evening I came in sight of the broken-down garden walls and scorched fields, I sank into a pool of despair.

It ebbed quickly when I found the dear Anreps and domestics at the door to receive and lead me into the ground-floor corridors, where everything was in place. Upstairs my study, my bedroom, the adjacent passages, in a most unexpected magical fashion, looked exactly as I left them, September 10th, 1943—looked in fact more peopled with dear and half-forgotten *objets d'art*, chiefly Chinese, that had been stored out of view for several years.

Mary, too, seemed in a less painful state of health than I feared.

Even the dinner, although it consisted of a thin vegetable soup, boiled potatoes, a salad, and fruit, was appetizing. The only depressing sensation came from the smoky kerosene lamps, with their uncertain light and foul smell. How we shall revive when we have odorless electric light again! I wonder whether the oil and kerosene lamps of years ago were less offensive when servants were trained to attend to them and kerosene was of the best quality; or was it simply that we were so used to them from the cradle that they did not offend us?

After dinner in the small sitting room, everything in place, bookshelves, writing desk, chairs, tables, sofas, each saying: "You need lean over only so much to reach me, to move me." And then later stretching out in one's own bed, with just the right pillows to support head and neck and shoulders, and the crisp cool sheets —"all as before, love, only sleep."

September 26th

HAVING NO CAR at my disposal, the *Wehrmacht* having ripped off the tires from the one I might have used, and another set not to be had under fifteen hundred dollars, I engaged the ragged, rickety village cab with its apocalyptic horse to take me to the dentist's in the Piazza Santa Maria Novella.

The driver took me a way I never took before, not avoiding the narrow, more crowded streets, but straight along through the populous quarter leading from the shoddy, grandiose Piazza Beccaria to the cathedral. Before reaching the Piazza I passed along houses shattered in pieces, houses pock-marked with shot, and houses untouched. Nothing more seemingly capricious than the behavior of missiles, unless it be the conduct of the High Command which orders them to be fired off.

From Piazza Beccaria the streets and squares showed up more Allied troops than Florentine civilians. I take it that they were British for the most part, but knew too little of their uniforms, signs, and signals to distinguish a Canadian from a New Zealander. They went about not as if they owned the place but yet as if at home. All looked like workmen, like proletarian workmen.

As I drove along Borgo alla Croce I suddenly came to a squalid void which made on me a far more painful impression than the ruins produced wantonly by the "so humane *Wehrmacht*." There was something tragic and romantic about those, while this desert was sordid and disheartening. It was, I am told, created by the Fascist regime on the pretext of improvement, of clearing out slums and giving breathing place to the town. The result is hideous to the eye. In the summer the glare and heat, in the winter the skinning cold of the bitter north wind, and at all times choking dust will haunt this bareness.

Years ago at Genoa I was taken by the town architect to visit some of the oldest houses near the port. He told me that, properly cleaned and drained, these tall houses in narrow streets were far healthier than the up-to-date palaces on wide avenues in the modern quarters of the city. His explanation was that the narrow streets were shelters against the wind, and the houses, sharing side walls, helped to keep each other warm; whereas in the new parts of the town the winds raged and the dust filled nostrils and throat. Ever so many more cases of pneumonia there than in the old, narrow lanes.

October 15th

BACK HOME three weeks now and not yet settled in. It takes time to find my bearings after having been away so long. Besides, I cannot settle down satisfactorily, for I shall not be able to remain in my usual apartment. We shall have to shut off those two rooms, the corridor leading to them, the libraries, all the rest of the house, in short, and huddle into the three guest rooms small enough to be warmed. I am to keep my study as well. Stoves are being put in, hideous terra-cotta monstrosities in themselves, and ruinous to space-relations and color-harmony. Nor are we sure as yet of procuring enough fuel for the coming six months. Wood is to be had at no place nearer than over thirty miles by road. It will take twenty-five hundred dollars to fetch it, apart from its cost on the spot. Then there is the difficulty of lighting. With the miserable lamplets available and the foul kerosene, reading is nearly excluded.

I never thought before of how little is printed for eyes as old as mine. What fervor and determination, what ingenuity are devoted to producing publications for the wholly blind! Nothing to my knowledge for the aged. Perhaps the Bible, the Prayerbook, and the Hymnal exist in type large enough for our ease of reading. Shakespeare and other classics can be had no doubt in pages suited to our sight, but only in *éditions de luxe*, cumbrous to handle and ruinous in price.

As money can procure scarcely any of the customary necessities, one is reduced to begging. Scarcely one of our Allied friends comes without being asked for anything and everything he can spare: food, medicines, cigarettes, candles, matches. I hold open my hand for print, no matter what, in English, of which we have been deprived for four years and more; for from the moment that Hitler began his war, Mussolini's censorship prevented the delivery of any book or review of a thoughtful nature, no matter how unpolitical. All respond with comforting promises, and some few are not called elsewhere before fulfilling them.

The Anglo-Saxons who come to see me are of three kinds: sons or close relations of friends at home and in England, as a rule attractive youngsters, good-looking, cultivated, and free as well as liberal-minded; others, older as a rule, brought by Italian friends on whom they are billeted, more official than the first, but affable, eager to understand, and ready to help. The third category, chiefly American, consists, as I might have expected, of accredited journalists who, before they joined up, had taken "art courses" or had been teaching the what and the why of art in various colleges. A surprising percentage of these are of Jewish Lithuanian origin, good, sound, even distinguished-looking. All no doubt come with the intention of seeing and substantiating what was behind a name with which their studies had made them familiar. One, a Jew—but not Lithuanian—was frank enough to say that I was a sight one had to see. They bring or send reading matter, and I spend most of my time perusing it. I am devoured with curiosity to learn what people who enjoy a free press think, and what they plan for the future not only at home but abroad. It is as well that I had no access to them earlier. I should have lacked the courage to write my own reflections. I find most of these anticipated, or better put. My meditations may have more sweep, but they have less immediacy.

The pine-clad, cypress-studded hills above me, cobwebbed over with innumerable paths, my favorite haunts for nearly half a century, must now be untrodden ground. They have been sown by the Germans with mines, and wayfarers have lost their lives. Walks must be limited to the highroad winding steeply past Vincigliata to the hilltop above—a little arduous for my eighty years.

Little by little I discover that my art possessions have not come out so well as at first flush I was led to believe. Of the thirty-two pictures buried under the ruins of Borgo San Jacopo—in the quarter of Florence dynamited by Field-Marshal Kesselring—two have not yet been found, several are severely damaged, and the rest require repairs before they can be placed on walls again.

I cannot resist the temptation to recount the efforts made to save my treasures. It illustrates how little planning and plotting mattered; how much it was touch and go. The same is true of personal safety. Many a one would still be alive if he had trusted luck or fatality instead of leaving home and house for some remote refuge.

When I first left, September 10th, 1943, I expected to return soon, but before long German as well as Italian authorities warned me that I had better hide my possessions. So in a great hurry the paintings and sculptures we valued most were removed and brought to the Fontanelle, where I was myself. Likewise all the photographs and some twenty thousand volumes less easy to replace, if lost, were secreted at Quarto. Both places seemed so safe that the art superintendent, as well as the German Institute, wanted to follow our examples and store books, documents, and pictures either at Quarto itself or in a house some few minutes away from ours, known as the Belvedere. To prevent Göring's

beaters, should they come to I Tatti, from seeing how much had
gone, remaining books and pictures were redistributed so as to
look as if nothing were missing. Moreover, the photographs of the
hidden-away pictures were removed from the collection of the
art office and of the German Institute, and the sequestrator's in-
ventory of the Tatti was retyped so as to leave them out. Had the
Nazis insisted on coming to the Tatti they would have missed
nothing of which they had seen the photographs. Sometime in
June Ludwig Heydenreich (the successor of Kriegbaum as director of the German Institute), on receiving official orders to have
my pictures and other works of art packed up and sent north,
managed to create so many difficulties by insisting on the agreement of the Italian Sequestration office, that finally there was no
time left to do anything about it.

My house was occupied by successive waves of the *Wehrmacht*, and as the Allies approached, German officers, as I must
have recounted already, warned the Anreps that it was likely to
suffer from severe bombardment and that works of art and other
valuables had better be carried elsewhere. No place seemed less
likely to suffer than the heart of Florence, where the Anreps had
their home. This was totally ruined when Kesselring dynamited
the bridges between which it stood, while no object left at I Tatti
suffered damage.

At the Fontanelle we were in the hands of the parachutists and
were constantly shelled in consequence. A miracle saved from
destruction the house and its contents, among them my most precious possessions. A like miracle turned away the attention of the
German marauders who were pillaging Quarto, from the books
and photographs stored there.

In war as now fought there is no shelter, no safety, whether for
persons or property. Men and women, take heed!

November 12th

YESTERDAY a Florentine friend in position to know what is going
on said he was sorry the Allies were favoring the continuation of

the monarchy. If retained, many would be driven to Communism.

He went on to say that the Communists were by far the strongest party here. In Florence alone they had between twenty and twenty-five thousand enrolled members, while his party, that of action, equivalent to the ultraradical in England before this was absorbed in Labor, had only fifteen hundred.

I asked what he supposed "Communism" meant to most of its adherents. He thought it was composed of many threads, newness and otherness being the most attractive.

If elections were held now, the Communists almost certainly would have the majority and begin to impose all sorts of hasty experiments, and of course the dictatorship of the proletariat.

The supporters of Mussolini, here and abroad, in France, in England, and America, would rejoice in having upheld Fascism as the one and only effective opponent of Communism and shout: "We told you so." To be sure, they did, but Fascism was doomed to fail. If Communism is an experiment we cannot avoid making, or only a catchword hypnotizing ever greater numbers of the variously discontented, it is not by violence that we can suppress it but by persuasion, and in the last resort by trial and error.

Epilogue

September 1945

I HAVE NOT *continued this diary. For one thing I had too many calls on my leisure to enjoy the serenity required for composition. Then, if I had gone on, I should have got involved in jotting down the misunderstandings, the mistakes, the disappointments, the unpleasant, upsetting surprises, rumor or even knowledge of which came to my ears daily; besides tales of hunger, cold, and disease, suffered by the middle and lowest classes.*

No less distressed was I to hear so much carping criticism of one section of the Anglo-Saxon community by the other. American against English, and vice versa. *One felt how true it was that we could be one people if the same language did not separate us.*

Using the same language makes us oversensitive to differences we should not as much as notice in speakers of other tongues. As I recall saying here before, we are almost indignant to discover differences where we expected identity. Once started on ferreting out differences, we go far and every divergence from our own folkways, our own standards, our own valuations and our own aspirations is counted as an inferiority in those who differ from us.

So much for our fellows whose mother tongue is some kind of English.

It would have distressed me no less to put down in black and white the invincible misconceptions of Italians on the part of our officers, and the know-nothing, care-nothing humor on the part of the men. Among the first, a few, more English than American, felt drawn to Italian landscape, Italian street life, Italian easygoing ways.

As, however, I look back on the past year and the "contacts" made therein, I can recall but few Anglo-Saxons who seemed to want to find out what Italians were like in themselves, what they cared for, what they wanted out of life; how we could try to give them what they thought they desired as distinct from what we thought they should want.

One may say we were not here for that purpose; that we were here to drive out the Germans, and that the presence of the Italians in the peninsula did not concern us. Yet our propaganda before our landings insisted we were coming as liberators. Liberators of what? The earth is indifferent and cares not who tramples over it, and shows no preference to Anglo-Saxons over Germans. It was the Italian then we came to liberate from what? From the person of the German, from his mere presence? No, of course not. It was to free him from restrictions, moral as well as material, from arbitrariness, from tyranny, from terror, but also from starvation.

True, we have freed the Italians from the terror entirely, from such tyranny and arbitrariness as, under the existing conditions, human nature allows. Promises fulfilled are soon forgotten; the unfulfilled rankle, particularly when they were of food, light, heat and raiment.

It was vain to say that we were doing our best. Unhappily our propaganda had succeeded in convincing the Italian public that we were a Christmas tree from which one might pluck whatever one needed and wished for, without diminishing its abundance. Nothing would convince them that in relation to the demand made on us, we, the "world's dear papa," were poor. If we did not, then we would not. And I confess our behavior again and again, behavior dictated by red tape more binding than the iron clamps that held Prometheus fast against the cruel crags of Caucasus, went some way to justify their suspicions. True we were here not as fair-minded, good-hearted individuals but as a machine to fight and defeat the Germans. We had to achieve our ends, but Italians cannot be blamed for feeling that the cost was appalling.

To go into details would lead too far, and besides the time is not yet when one can say all one could wish.

As for myself, I am glad I withstood persuasion and pressure to return home, and that I stuck it through in Italy.

The six years of the war went a good way to complete and perfect my acquaintance with Italian mankind. It has been worth while: for, when their material interests, their personal dignity, and their national vanity are not put in question, they are the most understanding, the most easygoing, the least censorious, the least "I-am-holier-than-thou" of peoples. Their sympathies for suffering, whether physical or moral, are wide and warm. No other society is so indulgent to the frailties flesh is heir to, or expects less by way of heroics. (That, by the way, may be the reason why they so inordinately admire stunts, moral and spiritual, no less than physical and material.) Nowhere else have I encountered like generosity and self-sacrifice.

Marchese and Marchesa Serlupi Crescenzi were little more than acquaintances when they offered me shelter at serious risk to their peace of mind, and even to their personal safety. They took me in, and treated me not as a refugee whom one has to be nice with, but as if it made them happy to have me, to serve me, to see to my every comfort, to study the wants of a man of my advanced age. It was caritas *in the most human and Christian sense of the word.*

Unforgettable proofs of friendship were given me by the German Consul, Gerhard Wolf, and by the assistant chief, now chief of police, Virgilio Soldani Benzi. Both of them not only knew where I was, but spread the semi-official declaration that I had gone to Portugal. Hundreds of persons could have known and some did know my macchia—*my hiding place. Despite alarms and excursions, nobody in any situation gave me away. I learned afterwards that some friends deliberately avoided finding out where I was, not to run the risk of betraying it under torture.*

I have already spoken of what the two directors of the German Institute, the late Friedrich Kriegbaum and Ludwig Heydenreich have done to defend my property.

Other friends made when Europe if not yet Italy was already at war, and who afterwards came forward with efficient help although I had no claim on them whatever, were ex-Prime Minister Orlando and his family, his daughter Carlotta Garabelli in particular, Countess Marina Volpi, Count Vittorio Cini, Count Alfonso Gaetani, for years Prefect of Florence, the Swiss Consul, Carlo Steinhäuslin, and Achille Malavasi, chief of the press bureau of the prefecture and close friend of Count Gaetani.

Thanks to the Serlupis, this year of sequestration seemed already, while I was living it, and seems more and more in retrospect, one of the most satisfactory of a lifetime. For many a day I had been longing for leisure, for freedom from workaday matters, and from over-much society. All this and more was granted me at the Serlupis. I was cut off from company except of the fewest. I could not write letters or be written to. I could not worry or vex myself over big or little, because literally I was not in a position to do anything about it. Luckily I was free from fear. Goethe in his Märchen, which I read as a youth, says that small annoyances distress and even exasperate one, while tragic possibilities have wings and carry us beyond ourselves. That certainly was my case during darkest prospects.

Then I feel justified in having stayed here, because I thereby saved my art treasures as well as my books and photographs. They would have been carried off perhaps to Germany, and recovery would have been incomplete if not problematic.

The library has only some forty thousand items but scarcely one that, in the course of sixty years, has not been acquired for the quality of its contents whether literary or scholarly. Few masterpieces of our world's great authors are missing, the European in the originals, the others in translations. Criticism likewise, whether of the written word or of the visual arts. And histories of events, of ideas, of religion, of science, of the arts again. Books for use only, for most part indispensable to the student and, given the destructions suffered in the last six years, a fair number of them irreplaceable.

The greatest loss of all might have been the photographs. They comprise a fair showing of the world's art in every phase, and reproductions of Italian paintings down to the seventeenth century, more complete possibly than elsewhere, and a certain number perhaps unique.

It would not have been anybody's business to save them if I had been away. I could put them in presumable safety, thanks not only to the Serlupis and the Baroness Ritter de Záhony who took them, but to the assistance of the art superintendent Giovanni Poggi, and to the personal attendance during packing and transport of a dear friend, the delicate restorer and picture expert, Giannino Marchig.

Elsewhere in these pages I have spoken of my deep gratefulness to Baron Egbert and Baroness Alda Anrep as well as to their son Cecil, for their devotion to my interests and the care taken of my wife during my absence. In the same connection I take pleasure in mentioning my agent, Geremia Gioffredi, whose loyal service during all the past difficult years has been invaluable. Indeed not one of the servants attached to the house, or of the peasants, has taken advantage of the political situation to behave in a disloyal way.

INDEX

A

abstractions, dread of, 239
  power of, 190
Abyssinia, 42, 154, 183, 222
Adams, Henry, 214
adults, deference to, 94
adventure, craving for, 213
Aesthetik des Tragischen, by
  Volkelt, 73, 74
after-life. *See* immortality
age-consciousness, 27
aged, the. *See* old
air transport, future, 108
air war. *See* World War II
Allenby, Lord, 219
Alliance Israélite Universelle.
  See Jews
Ambrose of Milan, 289, 312
America and Americans. *See*
  United States
Amiel, Henri Frédéric, 65
amusement, search for, 214
"androplasm," Russian, 78
Anglo-Saxons. *See* Great Britain;
  United States
Annunzio, Gabriele d'. *See* D'An-
  nunzio

Anreps (family), 399, 422, 433,
  445
antecedent probability, 304, 308
anthologies, 86
anthropology, 297
anti-Semitism. *See* Jews; *also*
  names of countries
Aosta, Duchess of, 247
archaeology, 92
architecture, Gothic, 167
  rebuilding, 250
  "restoration," 250
aristocracy, 97
Aristophanes, 344
art
  "abstract," 166, 220; and sur-
    realist, 207
  ancient, 92
  exchange of, 170
  German, preservation of, in
    wartime, 292
  identification of a painting,
    304
  interpreters, 220
  Mediterranean, 220
  of a people, 54
  painters, 340
  talents for, 216

447

About the Author

BERNARD BERENSON *was born in Lithuania in 1865 and was taken to Boston at the age of ten. There he remained until he was graduated from Harvard University in 1887. During these twelve years in the States he became a devoted Bostonian, New Englander, and American. Sixty years of living abroad have not diminished, but rather enhanced, his love for the land and the people who were so kind to him during his formative years.*

After frequenting many schools and universities, artists, and authors all over Europe (west of Berlin, Dresden, and Budapest), he settled down in Florence. By that time his interests had taken definite shape. He determined to learn all he could about Italian art from Giotto and Duccio to Bronzino and Tintoretto. He concentrated not only on Italy itself, but on all the lands bordering on the Mediterranean and its inlets.

He has published a number of books on Italian art, treating of subjects only where he believed nobody knew more than he did. At the same time he was scarcely less interested in the art of the rest of the world, from the Paleolithic age down to the drying up of creative genius which in his view occurred with the passing of Renoir, Degas, Cézanne, and Rodin.

For the last thirty years he has been more and more concerned with the problem of the decline of the visual arts. A book he has begun on that subject was interrupted by the last war. He has recently published a study of Aesthetics and History, a sketch for a self-portrait, and a work on the Arch of Constantine. He is now revising a book on Lorenzo Lotto which he originally wrote more than fifty-seven years ago. He is a member of the American Academy of Arts and Letters, and of the Royal Academies of Norway and Belgium, and is an Honorary Citizen of Florence. Since his first work, Venetian Painters of the Renaissance, *published in 1894, he has written twenty-eight books.*